Praise for
We All Fall Down: The Dissolution of America

Similar to Dr. Johnston's recent earlier work, *34 Days & Holding*, *We All Fall Down* begins with a factual, chronological recounting of the first 100 days of the new administration. This sets the stage and establishes a strong foundation to lead you into the subsequent sections of the book which provide unique, logical, and insightful perspective of what this all means to us Americans now, and more importantly into the future. Johnston's direct and honest approach allows us to take a step back, thoughtfully evaluate what really happened, and what is really happening, and to re-form a perspective based on truth and the values that make America great. I highly recommend this book to help regain the perspective that our country desperately needs!

—Jeff Milton
Business Executive

An honest and well documented presentation of what is taking place in our country is an extremely difficult task to perform! In *We All Fall Down*, Dr. Johnston has been able to do so with clarity. I thank him for having the courage and relentlessness to complete such a task. Regardless of your political persuasion, I would encourage all to read this! It will be well worth your effort.

—Glenn Jones
Retired Navy and Commercial Airline Pilot

A must-read! Roy Johnston explains the dangers of a misinformed and ignorant citizenry as Americans confront the disaster of the "Biden Train Wreck". His detailed insights reveal how Democrat and globalist policies got us into this mess and offer common sense solutions to get the country back on track.

—Julie Hayden
The Chuck and Julie Show

WE ALL FALL DOWN

The Dissolution of America

The Last 1st 100 Days

Second Edition
Updated through June 2022

ROY A. JOHNSTON

We All Fall Down
The Dissolution of America: The Last 1st 100 Days
Second Edition
Copyright 2022 by Roy A. Johnston

ISBN: 978-1-7374738-2-4

Published by:
Johnstini Enterprises
Denver, Colorado

The author can be reached at:
heydrj94@aol.com

All rights reserved. Without limiting the rights under copyright reserved above, no part of this publication may be reproduced, stored in or introduced into a retrieval system, or transmitted, in any form, or by any means (electronic, mechanical, photocopying, recording, or otherwise) without the prior written permission of both the copyright owner and the above publisher of this book.

Previous Books by
Roy A. Johnston

Two Things

*34 Days & Holding:
America in the Balance*

Dedication

*This book is dedicated to my grandkids:
Norah, Rozzie, Charlie, Brooks, Brady & Elise.*

They are the light in my life.

Contents

PART 1 THE LAST 1st 100 DAYS 1

   Preface to Second Edition 3
   Preface 5
   Introduction *Squirrels in the Attic* 9
   Chapter 1: *Ethereal Truth* 21
   Chapter 2: *Alternative Universe* 29
   Chapter 3: *Trust Me!* 59
   Chapter 4: *The Urge to Splurge* 81
   Chapter 5: *Kumbaya* 123
   Chapter 6: *There's Nothing Like a Good Purge* 137
   Chapter 7: *Don't Mess with Mother Nature* 157
   Chapter 8: *Halftime Update* 165
   Chapter 9: *The Canine Idiom* 187
   Chapter 10: *It's Circus Time* 191
   Chapter 11: *Nine Zeros* 213
   Chapter 12: *Beyond Parody* 229
   Chapter 13: *The Biden Train Wreck –*
        A Damage Assessment of the 1st 16 months 243
   Prelude to Part 2 317

PART 2 IMAGINING THE FUTURE 321

   Chapter 14: *Re-Imagining America* 323
   Chapter 15: *Re-Imagining the World* 347
   Chapter 16: *Antidisestablishmentarianism* 375
   Postscript 389

References 401
Acknowledgements 457
About the Author 459

PART 1

THE LAST 1ˢᵗ 100 DAYS

Preface to Second Edition

It has now been one year since the first edition of *We All Fall Down: The Dissolution of America* was published, and 16 months since Joe Biden became president. I did not plan on writing a second edition but the damage this president and the Democratic party have done in 16 months is unprecedented in American history. America is on the precipice. If the mid-term elections of November 2022 do not go strongly Republican in the House and Senate, we can kiss the America we have known goodbye.

The progressive left is on a fast track to dismantle everything society has been built upon since the inception of the country. As I described in my first book, *34 Days & Counting: America in the Balance*, the 'Towers of Power' are pulling out all the stops to 're-imagine' the future and societal structure. The towers of power (progressive government & bureaucracy, all levels of education, the mainstream news media, social media, sports, and entertainment) are all dominated by left wing ideologues. 'Wokeism' is their mantra and nothing is sacred.

Almost half of the country is living off the government dole, the other 50+% is the hard-working middle-class. I wrote these books for you, my children, and grandchildren. America has two enemies: the progressive Democrats and conservative complacency. The middle class is working to make ends meet, driving their kids around to kiddie sports, and trying to catch a few hours of down time or friend time. They don't read books. Many in my generation have given up, so they don't read books either. So, writing this second edition may be an exercise in futility, but I cannot stand by and watch my country destroyed and my grandchildren's future sacrificed.

The second edition retains the integrity of the original text since it was a history in real time. The factual support remains and is easily verified. The 2022 updates come in two forms: updated data or outcomes embedded within the original text and a totally new Chapter 13.

The forecasts from the first edition (i.e., the prediction of the war in Ukraine and fearmongering regarding a new virus threat) are also updated. The utopian goal of the progressives has not changed. The aggression of the World Economic Forum (Klaus Schwab, Bill Gates and others) remains. The wild cards, as predicted in the 1st edition, are China and the global health consortium (i.e., the CDC, WHO and the major pharma companies. They are not our friends).

My only agenda is the truth, hence, the meticulous documentation of fact in my books. The facts I present are irrefutable. Since we live in a 'sound bite' world, no one can remember the history that has transpired. The value of this book is this history has been assembled in time sequence and concise, easy to read prose. This is your toolbox to win the debate with the uninformed.

When asked, "What can we do?" My answer is "stand up and don't be silent".

The 'Silent Majority' elected President Ronald Reagan and gave America a 'reset' that held until the election of Obama. May God grant us a reprieve once again. So, what can you do? My answer: Don't be silent.

Roy Johnston
June 2022

Preface

Perspective is everything. We, as people of the modern world, have allowed our lives to be ruled by the tyranny of the urgent. We allow the external influences to dictate how we spend our time, and too often, the things that scream the loudest are least important.

In such a world, the first thing sacrificed is perspective. Perspective gives us understanding but it requires the investment of personal time. When we move to a new place, most take the time to find the neighborhoods with the best schools, services, and amenities nearby and, that are safe. We will drive 45 minutes to work to be able to live in such a place. The rest of our lives, however, are not much more that a sequence of reactions to stimuli. We don't have to answer the cell phone every time it rings. We don't have to stop and read the text every time our phone beeps.

We convince ourselves that a few sound bites of news each day keeps us informed. Even though that 'news' influences how we vote and what we 'believe.' We are too easily swayed by comments from friends and associates. I know many intelligent people who, in frustration, have disengaged altogether. I understand, but we are all in this boat and it's headed for the rocks.

The pressure to be accepted in social circles requires acquiescence to group think. It requires trusting without verifying. P.T. Barnum understood this human tendency and made millions. There are consequences from misplaced trust and not wanting to 'make waves.' Going along to get along is the easy road. There was a time in the not so distant past that these words were accepted by many but difficult to prove. Now, people are losing their jobs for voicing their opinion or openly stating inconvenient facts. The Towers of Power (see *34 Days & Holding*) extol the virtues of diversity every day but are intolerant of a diverse point of view. Perspective is not allowed. So, we self-censor ourselves to avoid being cancelled by others.

This is why I wrote *34 Days & Holding: America in the Balance* and why I have written this book. You don't have the time, but I do, and have dedicated it to giving you a single trustworthy source that provides perspective.

The United States, and the world, are on the precipice of dangerous and possibly irreversible change. There are very few people alive today that were in World War II, or that went through the Great Depression. We no long have that perspective. When you go into the desert or the mountains for the first time, you are vulnerable. You don't know what you don't know. How can you? You've never been there before.

We All Fall Down: The Dissolution of America was written in 'real-time' beginning January 20th and ending April 30, 2021, the first 100 days of the Biden administration. Part One is the history of the first 100 days [this second edition has extended this history to the first sixteen months]. It is different and more valuable than a traditional history because it not only records and thoroughly documents the period, but also provides perspective shortly after the period has ended. My goal has been to capture the critical events and issues of these volatile times and to give you a reference from which you can gain perspective and make your own 'informed' conclusions.

Part Two focuses on the future, thus is subtitled: 'Imagining the Future.' It succinctly explains how we got here. It pieces together, via open-source, incontrovertible evidence, a roadmap which will surprise many. You will gain perspective on how society and culture, has, and continues to be, changed and why. The foundation for an elitist, globalist, multi-cultural world has been laid. It will be a world that bears more similarities to the society described by Orwell in *1984* and *Animal Farm* than any in history. Many will try to pass this off as 'conspiracy theory' but this is no clandestine, behind closed door conspiracy. This is not my 'opinion', hence the exhaustive reference section of open-sourced references.

I encourage you to reject the lie that one person cannot make a difference. History is replete with examples to the contrary, although not all made a difference for good.

Truth and mankind's God given need to be free always win in the end, but freedom is never free nor easy. If we have ever needed this perspective, it is now.

God bless you,
Roy A. Johnston
May 25, 2022

Introduction
Squirrels in the Attic

> *"Left unchecked, these real-life pests can poke holes in your siding, damage insulation, and even chew through electrical wiring."*[1]
> —Amy Lynch & Bob Vila

In 1980, Philip Crosby made popular, a new paradigm regarding the 'quality of work.' It was capsulized in the acronym DIRTFT and stands for 'Do it right the first time.'[2] The concept could not be any simpler. Take the time to do the job right the first time and you won't have to do it again. From a business perspective, it is a win for everyone. It should result in products that work as advertised, they are lower cost because the cost of rework is significantly reduced, and the company is more profitable. This is business nirvana: a great product, a low cost and improved profit.

Government, however, never got the memo. Our elected officials, who promise everything and deliver very little, could care less about you. If they cared, why are they pushing the country to insolvency? Almost 10 years ago (2011), Jeanne Shahadi asked the question, "Is $14.6 trillion too much to handle? The real problem is not that the country owes $14.6 trillion today. It's that the number could grow to $23 trillion by 2021 and keep rising thereafter."[3] Shahadi's article begins accurately with baseline numbers then sadly slips into Keynesian economics and progressive political bias. (Figure 3.)

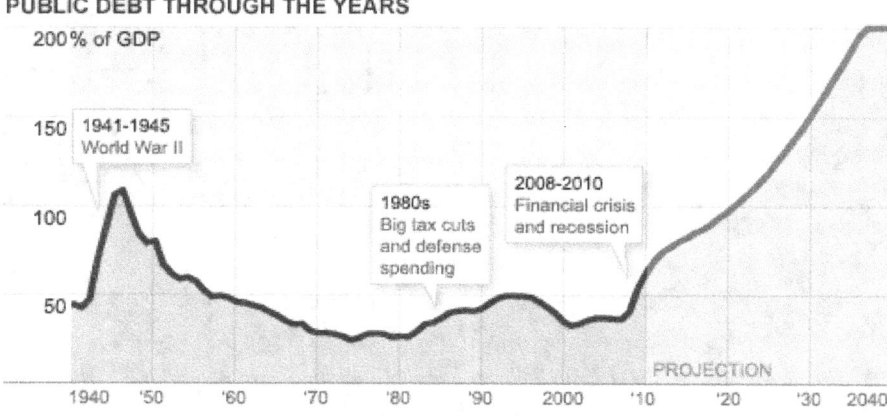

Figure 1. U.S. National Debt as a % of GDP
From money.cnn.com[3]

Stephen Moore writes, "The United States has been gradually transformed from a nation with almost no government presence in the marketplace to one in which the government is now the predominant actor in the domestic economy."[4]

Moore wrote this article in 1993 and makes three key points:

- "In the past 25 years the federal government has spent $2.5 trillion on welfare and aid to cities. This is enough money to purchase all of the assets of the Fortune 500 companies plus all of the farmland in the United States."

- "In 1987 U.S. farmers received more money in government subsidies than they did in selling their crops in the marketplace. In short, farmers now produce for the government, not for U.S. consumers."

- "In three states today—California, Maine, and New York—almost half of all middle-income family wages are captured by government through income, payroll, property, and sales taxes, and other levies."

Scott Grannis wrote on the financial website seekingalpha.com in June 2020 (note: this section is being written in Jan. 2021, only 6 months later), "A simple virus, potentiated by aggressive shutdown mandates, has caused government spending to explode and revenues to crater. Measured on a rolling 12-month basis, the federal deficit in the past two months has more than doubled, reaching the obscene level of $2.126 trillion, and it will be higher still when the June numbers are tallied (Figure 2). Our national debt now stands at $20.1 trillion, and as a percent of GDP, the national debt is about as high as it was during the height of World War II - about 110%."[5] Note the $20.1 trillion national debt is within shouting distance of the Shahadi forecast back in 2011.[6]

His phrase, 'a simple virus' is quite avant-garde. Our national media does not consider Covid-19 as 'simple.' Nor does Dr. Anthony Fauci, one of the only holdovers from the Trump administration and the new Chief Medical Advisor to President Joe Biden. The recommendations from the Center for Disease Control and Food and Drug Administration continue to be inconsistent and often not supported by scientific data. They are de facto arms of Big Pharma and thus unreliable. This inconsistency and extreme 'err on the side of caution' decision-making and messaging, have left much of the populace in a state of fear. This state of fear and confusion gave the Democratic party the White House. Now over a year after it first hit the United States, we still have tele-learning, tele-medicine, TV-only sports events and so on. A 'simple virus' he says!

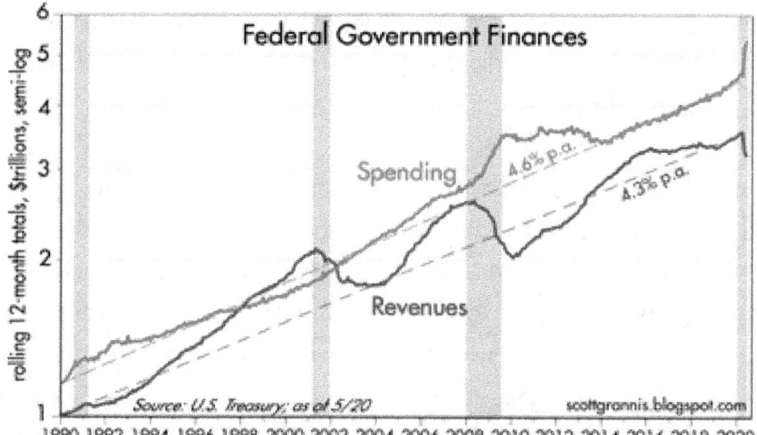
Figure 2. 12 month moving averages of U.S. Federal spending and revenue. from: seekingalpha.com[5]

In the Epilogue of the book, *34 Days & Holding: American in the Balance*, the author provides medical research data that confirms Covid-19 is a virus with 'flu-like' lethality.[7] It 'accidentally' escaped from a Chinese Bio-Level 4 virology lab just in time to alter the course of the U.S. presidential election and essentially shut the world down. How could a 'simple' virus have this kind of impact? The virus per se, did not cause the economic calamity, corrupt medical 'experts', compliant government leaders and the billionaires that pull their strings did.

Covid-19 is a deadly virus for the elderly and people with co-morbidities, diabetes, and obesity. People younger than 65, without the aforementioned health issues will get sick and recover, like the flu, like pneumonia, and other bronchial, upper respiratory diseases. Therapeutics are available for treatment and vaccines began to become available in November 2020.

Trusting Science vs the Experts

We live in an extraordinarily complex world. Everywhere you look, there is technology, pharmacology, physics, computer programing, engineering, etc that we do not understand yet use every day. It is impossible to be an 'expert' on everything. Our only choice is to trust that the 'experts' know their stuff, are not cutting corners, and are committed to delivering extremely high quality, low risk products. Trusting the 'experts' is critical and herein lies our dilemma. What if they are not trustworthy? What if their honor and integrity is for sale? Or even more sinister, what if they are hostage to some coercion scheme. For example: Our new President had foreknowledge about his son's and brother's shady deals with foreign governments, including Russia and China. Is Biden hostage to a Chinese coercion scheme?

Newt Gingrich wrote in January 2019, "Consider the FBI's multi-layered attack on Trump compared to its treatment of Senator Feinstein after officials discovered that her driver and San Francisco office director of 20 years had been spying for the Chinese government. In 2013, when Feinstein led the Senate Intelligence Committee, FBI officials politely approached her to inform her that her staffer had been covertly sharing information with the San Francisco Chinese consulate – which Feinstein helped open when she was mayor – for roughly a decade. Feinstein was briefed. She apparently allowed the man to retire. No charges of espionage or acting as an unregistered foreign agent were ever brought against him."[8]

Our elected officials, like senior executives in corporations, rely heavily on 'experts.' It is essential, but dangerous when the person in leadership will only listen to one side or does not allow free and open debate. Congress has rules and protocols that require debate in a setting where it can be recorded for future reference, but the outcomes are rarely based on a bi-partisan decision relying on facts.

Keeping our focus on the President and his cabinet, we must remember they (the cabinet) are employed at the will of their boss (which is not the people). He can fire them anytime for any reason. Each cabinet member has their own huge department with thousands of employees. They also hire 3rd party experts. All of these people want to remain employed. They have families, mortgages and probably a working spouse contributing to family income. Losing their job can be a significant personal crisis. The average person does not want a job that is up for grabs every four to eight years. Thus, the inclination to not to rock the boat and support the party that will provide job security. The Washington bureaucracy is little more than an organizational parasite, deriving its life from the hard work of the taxpayer and politicians who milk them. This is reality and the optimistic scenario.

The actual structural and decision-making complexity in government today, has been warped and convoluted by special interest groups, lobbyists, and foreign governments who work in the shadows rewarding their 'contacts' to influence information flow (i.e. the FBI illegally withheld documents during the Russia-Gate hoax in 2017-18), to make things disappear (i.e., Hillary Clinton's cell phones and laptops), to plant disinformation (the fake Dossier paid for by the Democratic National Party) and even promote falsehoods (i.e., The National Oceanic & Atmospheric Administration promotes climate alarmism, the CDC, FDA and NIH promote Covid-19 testing that give false positives 90% of the time, the teachers unions refuse to go back to the schools on the false premise that it is a danger to them (even the CDC & the WHO say schools should open). Fauci famously said everyone should wear two masks! The list goes on and on.

President Trump tried to clean out the attic, but it proved an impossible task. He wanted to make government accountable so the American people could see and feel the benefits of their tax dollars. He made great strides by 'doing it right the first time,' but the bureaucracy didn't like it. The Swamp of lobbyists and special interest groups hated it. So, they took their money to those who could be manipulated for selfish, personal gain.

People without principle will do what they are rewarded to do, collateral damage be-damned. Truth and the common good are sacrificed on the altar of personal gain. This single pillar of truth undergirds the entire lobby industry and all criminal enterprise. Is it good for America? They don't care, it's good for them. This corruption has always haunted government but never to the extent to which it does today thanks to the growth of the billionaire class, as explained in the book, *34 Days & Counting: America in the Balance*.[9]

We have heard *ad nauseum* the promise that they will 'follow the science.' It is just another 'trust me', statement. If you randomly asked 100 people how they stay informed on the 'science' of a particular issue, Covid-19 for example, what would be their answer? Do you think anyone would say they look up the scientific literature? Most people are passive on science because it is complicated. So, they 'trust' the 'expert,' and obediently follow government regulations. An acquaintance recently told me she 'loved' Dr. Fauci. What she means is that his style puts her in a comfort zone. She trusts him because he makes her 'feel' good, not because he is telling the truth. She has no educational basis to assess his veracity. Fauci has had more flip flops on the 'science' of Covid-19 than Carter has liver pills. Yet, he presents himself confidently in interviews and press conferences and always has that grandfatherly smile. This book is not challenging Fauci's intelligence, but it is challenging his integrity on his Covid-19 messaging and leadership.

What about other areas of science that are impacting our lives today? There is no science that supports children being given sex hormones or considering gender identity change. This is the most grotesque form of child abuse in modern times, yet where are the 'experts' and how do they fare in open debate? Why is this being allowed? The same goes for climate alarmism issues. Open debate is not allowed and those who voice disagreement with the dogma are labeled, defamed, and ostracized, while the mice ignorantly follow along.

Insight into Science

There is nothing worse than a person who knows the truth but intentionally, and for personal gain, misleads those who trust him. Most people don't know the science of anything.

There are two critical points everyone needs to understand.

1. *Science is not static.* We are always learning, investigating, adjusting our understanding, and remaining open to challenge. When science becomes static (i.e., fixed and unchallengeable) it is either an established Law of Science (i.e., the Law of Gravity, the 2nd law of thermodynamics) or religious dogma (i.e., Galileo was confined to his home because he provided evidence that the sun was the center of our universe. In other words, he challenged the dogma of the church.) Untold thousands of lives have been sacrificed on the altar of 'fill in the blank.' Much of the 'science' regarding Covid-19 is fabrication. The effectiveness of lockdowns, the inefficacy of hydroxychloroquine, the effectiveness of masks, the effectiveness of remdesivir, the threat to those under age 70 and without co-morbidities to state a few. Due to these falsehoods people have died, businesses were lost, and a selected few enriched (i.e., Big Pharma). Executive orders have been issued to ensure the dogma is followed; real science be damned. Notice that the loudest voices are those of leftist politicians (Biden, Democrat Governors, etc.) and globalists (i.e., Bill Gates).

    Anyone who claims the science is settled and refuses to have open debate should be dismissed.

2. *Experts or Scientists are human, thus fallible, corruptible, and coercible.* The entire philosophical basis of science is testing hypotheses, failing, adjusting and testing again. Failure, mistakes and learning from mistakes is inherent in the process. Scientists should say, 'Here is what we know today based on this and that.'

It used to be like that, but no longer. Science today is all about money. Stephen Moore wrote in 2018, "Federal funding for climate change research, technology, international assistance, and adaptation has increased from $2.4 billion in 1993 to $11.6 billion in 2014, with an additional $26.1 billion for climate change programs and activities provided by the American Recovery and Reinvestment Act in 2009."[10]

"The 2018 GAO report found that, while the Office of Management and Budget has reported that the federal government spent more than $154 billion on climate-change-related activities since 1993, much of that number is likely not being used to directly address climate change or its risks. Many of the projects reported as "climate-change-related activities" are only secondarily about climate change."[11]

In December 2020, Congress passed, and the President signed a massive $1.4 trillion spending bill purported to provide economic stimulus and assist those who have suffered economically from Covid-19 restrictions.

Science Magazine, referencing the bill said, "the modest hikes for 2021 have left the research community wanting more."[12]

"The final budget package includes increases of 3% for the National Institutes of Health (NIH), 2.5% for the National Science Foundation (NSF), 2.3% for NASA science, and 0.4% for the Department of Energy (DOE's) science office. Those numbers (see details below) put the cherry on top of 4 years of robust growth under Trump despite his persistent attempts to eviscerate federal science budgets."[13]

"NIH's budget now stands at $42.9 billion, a 33% rise over its 2016 level of $32.3 billion. Similarly, spending by DOE science tops $7 billion, compared with $5.4 billion in 2017, a boost of 30%. NASA science programs rose by 8% and 11% in 2018 and 2019, respectively, before slowing in 2020 and 2021. NSF's budget, now nearly $8.5 billion, has grown the least among the four biggest federal science agencies. But even so, a 14% rise since 2017 compares favorably with an overall increase of only 4% during the second term of former President Barack Obama."[14]

These references hopefully make clear how dependent academic and government research agencies are on the U.S. taxpayer and how it is never enough. President Trump tried to reign-in the outflow of billions of dollars with no strings attached. What did the American people get in return for just the climate related research? The answer is zilch. The Federal government has created a monster called the 'climate industrial complex'. Its hunger is insatiable. It has penetrated virtually every aspect of our lives and its basic tenets are taught to our children like a catechism. They are to be 'believed in' and non-believers must be punished. If I were to title this book 'Climate Alarmism is a Lie', it would probably not pass approval to get published. Always remember:

> *"When you see one voice silenced, while another is promoted, question the veracity of the one being promoted."*
> —Roy Johnston

Americans must ask themselves, 'Who is now really in charge of our country?' A 78-year-old man with 50 years in politics and no accomplishments, just won an election over a sitting President who had more positive accomplishments in 4 years than any President in history. To help connect those dots, I wrote: *34 Days & Holding: America in the Balance*. [15]

Now we enter a new era. Former Obama CIA Director John Brennan, in a January 20 interview on MSNBC said, "I know, looking forward, that the members of the Biden team who have been nominated or have been appointed are now moving in laser-like fashion to try to uncover as much as they can about what looks very similar to insurgency movements that we've seen overseas, where they germinate in different parts of the country and they gain strength, and it brings together an unholy alliance frequently of religious extremists – so authoritarians, fascists, bigots, racists, nativists, and even libertarians,"[16]

He goes on, "Unfortunately, I think there has been this momentum that has been generated as a result of unfortunately the demagogue of rhetoric of people that just departed government, but also those who continue in the halls of Congress," Brennan continued. "And so, I really do think that the law enforcement, Homeland Security Intelligence, and even the defense officials are doing everything possible to root out what seems to be a very, very serious and insidious threat to our democracy and our republic."[16]

This is perhaps the most outrageous and dangerous public statement made by a former senior level government leader in modern times. His party won the election and is now going to begin an inquisition of the losing party. The target is "an unholy alliance frequently of religious extremists – so authoritarians, fascists, bigots, racists, nativists, and even libertarians."[18] Each of these terms have meaning that most people understand, but in the new world order, the intelligentsia practice 'negative projection' when describing their opposition. They project their own negative traits and behaviors onto Republicans or anyone who opposes them. For example, consider how the Democrat Governors have ruled their states during the pandemic. They have no problem stripping away Constitutional freedoms (i.e., to gather, to worship, to protest) and mandating certain behaviors (mask wearing, banning of certain words). These actions are authoritarian and fascist. They are usually guilty of the very things they accuse their opponents. So, they are also being duplicitous (pretending to have feelings that his actions contradict.)

People with principle who take a stand for honest debate and inquiry may be labeled 'libertarian'. A fundamental Bible believing Christian may be considered a bigot. Those who insist we follow the Constitution might be called 'nativists.'

Most people can quickly be reduced to Maslow's lowest state of need by coercion. Brennan has signaled that will soon begin.

Donald Trump was elected in 2016 to clean the squirrels out of the Washington attic. Over 74 million people wanted him to continue. But, the Dealer has thrown us a Joker.

So, if you think bigger government is better for America, please think again. All it does is put more squirrels in the attic.

Chapter 1
Ethereal Truth

"Beware of false prophets, who come to you in sheep's clothing, but inwardly they are ravenous wolves. You will know them by their fruits."
—Matthew 7:15-16 NKJV

Just Another Inauguration Day

Joseph R. Biden was sworn in as the 46th President of the United States on January 20, 2021. But instead of pomp and circumstance and huge crowds, there were 25,000 National Guard troops. Susan B. Glasser, was there and wrote about her experience in *The New Yorker*.

"Words matter. Just two weeks ago, Donald Trump's words—his lies—were powerful enough to send a crazed mob into the Capitol, seeking to overturn the democratic will of the American electorate. Shortly before noon on Wednesday, when Joseph Robinette Biden, Jr., was sworn in as the forty-sixth President of the United States, he offered a very different vision of the power of language to remake political reality. His bet was that, if words can divide us, they can bring us together, too. Biden spoke of unity, of national reconciliation, and also—and perhaps most important of all—of the need for leaders "to defend the truth and defeat the lies."

"Only after four years of the Trump Presidency would the mention of "truth" in an Inaugural Address become an applause line. But we are where we are. The country has had so much lying.

Much will be made of Biden's plea to "end this uncivil war," and of his stirring language about democracy prevailing. But it was his love letter to the role of truth in a free society that rang loudest to me during his twenty-minute speech, which took place under a sunny Washington sky, amid a crisis like no other in our modern history."[1]

What beautiful and eloquent prose. What a giant crock of horse doodoo. Since her focus is on 'words' and 'truth', let us take a moment to do a little 'thought exercise.'

She said, "Words matter." Who could disagree with that? If they didn't matter, humans would not have developed verbal and then written ways to communicate. Of course, 'words matter.' However, in her first two paragraphs, she explains what she means. When words are uttered by Democrats or socialist sympathizers, they matter, should be listened to, and considered. If the words, however, are Trump's, and by extension anyone who voted for him, they are lies and should not be considered. So, to say 'words matter' is really stupid and takes us nowhere.

What does matter, however, is truth. She first mentions the word 'truth' by quoting Biden: "to defend the truth and defeat the lies." Once again, who would disagree? But "In 2019, the former vice president told reporters: "I have never discussed with my son or my brother or anyone else anything having to do with their businesses. Period."[2] Our now President was referring to all the shady deals his brother Jim and son Hunter had going on with foreign governments and companies. Hunter Biden introduced business partner, Tony Bobulinski, to his father at the Beverly Hilton Hotel. Bobulinski said, "Biden's denial of knowing about his son's business affairs with the Chinese energy firm was a "blatant lie."[3] Glasser would have us believe that Bobulinski is the fibber, but there's more.

Figure 3. NY Post photo composite, October 14, 2020[4]

"Hunter Biden introduced his father, then-Vice President Joe Biden, to a top executive at a Ukrainian energy firm less than a year before the elder Biden pressured government officials in Ukraine into firing a prosecutor who was investigating the company, according to emails obtained by The Post. The never-before-revealed meeting is mentioned in a message of appreciation that Vadym Pozharskyi, an adviser to the board of Burisma, allegedly sent Hunter Biden on April 17, 2015, about a year after Hunter joined the Burisma board at a reported salary of up to $50,000 a month," wrote Emma Jo Morris and Gabrielle Fonrouge of the New York Post.[5]

The email from Pozharskyi is reported to say:

> "Dear Hunter, thank you for inviting me to DC and giving an opportunity to meet your father and spent[sic] some time together. It's realty[sic] an honor and pleasure."[6] How many other 'Dear Hunter' emails are floating around in cyber-space?

So, where were we? Ah yes, Joe Biden and the truth. On September 23, 2020, the Senate Committee on Homeland Security and Governmental Affairs released a memo summarizing its investigations into Biden conflicts of interest. It began by saying, "U.S. Senators Ron Johnson (R-Wis.), chairman of the Senate Homeland Security and Governmental Affairs Committee, and Chuck Grassley (R-Iowa), chairman of the Senate Finance Committee, released a report that revealed millions of dollars in questionable financial transactions between Hunter Biden and his associates and foreign individuals, including the wife of the former mayor of Moscow and individuals with ties to the Chinese Communist Party."[7]

The initial of many findings were:

- "In early 2015 former Deputy Chief of Mission at the U.S. Embassy in Kyiv, Ukraine, George Kent raised concerns to officials in Vice President Joe Biden's office about the perception of a conflict of interest with respect to Hunter Biden's role on Burisma's board. Kent's concerns went unaddressed and in September 2016, he emphasized in an email to his colleagues, "Furthermore, the presence of Hunter Biden on the Burisma board was very awkward for all U.S. officials pushing an anticorruption agenda in Ukraine."[8]

- "In October 2015, senior State Department official Amos Hochstein raised concerns with Vice President Biden, as well as with Hunter Biden, that Hunter Biden's position on Burisma's board enabled Russian disinformation efforts and risked undermining U.S. policy in Ukraine."[9]

Now President Biden is our 'defender of truth!' PS: The FBI has been investigating Hunter Biden for over a year.[10]

Ms. Glasser titled her New Yorker article: *'Joe Biden's Love Letter to the Truth'*.

Democrats and the Truth

While Ms. Glasser swoons over 'Honest' Joe's speech, let's walk down memory lane with previous Democrat leaders:

- Bill Clinton said, "It depends on what the meaning of the word 'is' is.[11]

- Bill Clinton: "I did not have sex with that woman!"[12]

- Barack Obama promised, June 6, 2009: "If you like the plan you have, you can keep it. If you like the doctor you have, you can keep your doctor, too. The only change you'll see are falling costs as our reforms take hold."[13] Politifact lists 36 other variations on the same quote by Obama or his administration.

- Jonathan Gruber, Obama administration economic consultant on the Affordable Care Act, said during a panel session at the Annual Health Economics Conference in 2013, the "stupidity of the American voter" was a factor in passing Obamacare in 2010.[14]

- Eric Holder, Obama Attorney General was held in contempt of Congress in 2012 for lying about the Obama 'Fast & Furious' scandal. The vote to hold him in contempt was 255 to 67.[15]

- Eric Holder, lied so many times to Congress, that Investor's Business Daily wrote an entire editorial on it in 2013.[16]

- National Public Radio lied to its followers regarding the Contempt of Congress decision when it said the vote was 'along party lines.'[17] The final vote included 17 Democrats and Nancy Pelosi, Steny Hoyer and the Black Caucus staged a 'walk-out.'[18]

- Amy Berman Jackson, Federal Judge in D.C. did not hold Attorney General Eric Holder, 'In Contempt of Court' in October 2012 for withholding documents from Congress.[19] She was also the judge that presided over the Roger Stone conviction that was a set up by the FBI.

- Hillary Clinton: "Clinton lied to the American people about Benghazi. At 10:08 p.m. the night of the attack, she issued a statement that blamed the attack on "inflammatory material posted on the Internet" with no mention of terrorism or al-Qaeda. But an hour later, at 11:12 p.m. she emailed her daughter, Chelsea: "Two of our officers were killed in Benghazi by an Al Queda-like[sic] group." The next day in a phone call with the Egyptian prime minister, Clinton said: "We know the attack in Libya had nothing to do with the film. It was a planned attack, not a protest." Yet two days later, as she welcomed the caskets of the fallen in Dover, Del., she blamed that attack on "an awful Internet video that we had nothing to do with."[20] Marc Thiessen goes on in this piece to enumerate several other Clinton lies.

- James Comey, fired Director of the FBI, lied to Congress during the Mueller investigation.[21]

- Andrew McCabe, Deputy Director of the FBI, lied to Congress during the Mueller investigation.[22]

- Adam Schiff repeatedly lied to the American people regarding the Trump-Russia collusion hoax according to the Boston Herald.[23]

This is just a sampling of the most egregious Democrat lies since Bill Clinton. When Hillary Clinton destroys her cell phones and wipes her memory discs with bleach bit, the FBI does nothing and the media ignores it or provides cover. The entire Mueller investigation was a lie based on a 'Dossier' the Democrat National Committee paid mercenaries to create.[24] The trashing of Judge Kavanaugh in his confirmation hearings were based on Democrat lies.[25] The impeachment was based on Democrat lies.[26]

The Democrats and the media are making chumps out of the American people. Susan Glasser and her media cohorts are propagandists. The irony is extraordinary. They claim they are the arbiters of truth when they are exactly the opposite. Half of America has gone to sleep.

Chapter 2
Alternative Universe

> *"You're traveling through another dimension, a dimension not only of sight and sound but of mind. A journey into a wondrous land whose boundaries are that of imagination. That's the signpost up ahead—your next stop, the Twilight Zone!"*
> —Rod Serling, introduction,
> The Twilight Zone
> (Season 2, 1960)[1]

Impeachment – Part Deux

As former President Trump wraps up his first week as a private citizen in Mar-a-Lago, the House Democrats introduced articles of impeachment for the ex-President! Never in history has a congressional body decided to impeach a private citizen. This is the new unhinged Democratic Party.

"The House on Monday formally delivered an article of impeachment charging former president Donald Trump with inciting the deadly insurrection at the Capitol, as Democrats prepared to use his own words as evidence against him in his Senate trial next month," writes Seung Min Kim, of the Washington Post.[2]

They are going to use his 'own words as evidence.' Sounds bad. Here is the incriminating verbatim quote from Mr. Trump as he closed his Jan. 6, 2020 speech in D.C.:

Donald Trump: (01:12:43) "So we're going to, we're going to walk down Pennsylvania Avenue, I love Pennsylvania Avenue, and we're going to the Capital, and we're going to try and give... The Democrats are hopeless. They're never voting for anything, not even one vote. But we're going to try and give our Republicans, the weak ones, because the strong ones don't need any of our help, we're going to try and give them the kind of pride and boldness that they need to take back our country."

"Donald Trump: (01:13:19), "So let's walk down Pennsylvania Avenue. I want to thank you all. God bless you and God bless America. Thank you all for being here, this is incredible. Thank you very much. Thank you."[3]

Charlie Savage of the New York Times, reported on Jan. 10, "The speech that President Trump delivered to his supporters just before they attacked the Capitol last week is a central focus as House Democrats prepare an article of impeachment against him for inciting the deadly riot."

"Mr. Trump had urged supporters to come to Washington for a "Save America March" on Wednesday, when Congress would ceremonially count President-elect Joseph R. Biden Jr.'s win, telling them to "be there, will be wild!" At a rally just before the violence, he repeated many of his falsehoods about how the election was stolen, then dispatched the marchers to the Capitol as those proceedings were about to start."[2]

If there is anything 'inciting', it is false reporting like the above quote. I have given you the President's speech in the references to read for yourself. There is *nothing* inciting unlawful behavior in the speech. The mainstream media is lying to its readers. Savage says the Trump supporters 'attacked the capital.'

Consider the following:

1. "A National Park Service spokesman told NBC News that organizers expect as many as 30,000 people at the event near the White House. The

permit originally was submitted for a crowd size of 10,000, but the group has tripled its estimate based on responses and people already in the D.C. area as of Tuesday, according to the official."[3]

2. The President tweeted on Jan. 5, "I will be speaking at the SAVE AMERICA RALLY tomorrow on the Ellipse at 11AM Eastern. Arrive early – doors open at 7AM Eastern. BIG CROWDS!" pic.twitter.com/– Donald J. Trump (@realDonaldTrump) January 5, 2021[4]

3. The author of this book spoke with a person today (Jan. 26) who attended the rally. He said there were at least 1 million people there. "There were 30,000 lined up for the porta-potties." He said, when the speech ended, they walked down Pennsylvania Avenue with the crowd and upon coming in sight of the Capital, they could see a relatively small group climbing through windows. The vast majority of the crowd went the other way.

4. Even though the mainstream 'Newspeak' media 'fact checkers' say there were no BLM or Antifa people involved in the Capital breach, the facts indicate otherwise. John Sullivan, confirmed Antifa member, said after being arrested, he was "just there to "document" it." Earlier, he was quoted as saying, "We gotta ... rip Trump right out of that office right there,"[5]

5. Congressman Mo Brooks, Republican from Missouri said, "he actually got intel from a Capitol Police officer that "ANTIFA was going to try to

infiltrate the Trump rally by dressing like Trump supporters."[6]

6. "According to a former FBI agent on the ground at the US Capitol, at least one bus load of Antifa goons infiltrated the Trump rally as part of a false flag operation."[7]

7. Tayler Hansen posted a series of tweets indicating Antifa played a key role in the Capital breach. He identified, BLM activist and Insurgency USA head, John Sullivan, posing as media at the Save America rally and wearing a "gas mask." Hansen tweeted, "I have video evidence confirming Antifa's presence within the Trump Supporters today. I will post later once I am safely out of DC."[8]

8. D.C. mayor Muriel Bowser, downplayed Capital security on the day of the rally, making it easy for a breach of the building.[9]

9. The National Guard was put on alert but not utilized on the day of the rally (Jan. 6). Why? "Simply put, the National Guard only shows up to D.C. when they've been invited, and the Capitol Police did not extend that invitation until after the breach, according to a source with knowledge of the process, who was not authorized to speak about it on the record."[10]

10. "Data on unrest-related arrests from Washington D.C. Metropolitan police highlight the stark differences between authorities cracking down on racial justice protests last summer and an

underwhelming law enforcement response to Wednesday's insurrection on Capitol Hill, after commentators drew comparisons between police response," writes Robert Hall of Forbes.[11]

11. Ever since George Floyd died, many of the nation's cities have had riots, buildings burned, people murdered, people injured, hateful graffiti painted on government buildings and businesses. How much of this death and destruction was caused by conservative groups? **None**, except the Capital building breach.

12. We have had 9 months of mayhem, destruction, vandalism, and murder at the hands of Antifa and BLM.

13. Here are the facts:

   a. "Between May 30 and June 2, 2020, the height of the racial justice protests, 427 "unrest-related" arrests were made in D.C., including 24 juveniles, the police department says."[12] This is just D.C. folks.

   b. "On June 1 alone, more than five times the number of people were arrested than on the day the Capitol was stormed, with 289 people booked."[13]

   c. "14,000. That's the estimated number of arrests made across 49 U.S. cities during anti-racism protests last summer, according to the Washington Post."[14]

d. By June 8, 2020, **17 people had died** as a result of the protests following George Floyds death.

The average American is busy with their life. They work five days a week, take care of their kids in the covid world created by Democrats and don't have time to follow the news. I use the term 'news' loosely. Today, we have Newspeak, not honest reporting.

Author's Truth Meter: The tragic irony is that George Floyd was on death's door when the police picked him up (autopsy revealed it was a 5x fentanyl overdose). The video clearly shows the officer kept his knee on Floyd's neck for over 8 minutes, thus he was convicted of second-degree unintentional murder, third-degree murder and second-degree manslaughter.

The media also lied about the cause of death for Capital Police officer Brian Sicknick.

Politifact writes on Feb. 22, 2021, "An early report from the New York Times said Sicknick was struck during the riot with a fire extinguisher." politifact.com/article/2021/feb/22/what-we-know-about-capitol-police-officer-brian-si

Andrew McCarthy writes in the 'National Review' on Feb. 15, 2021, that the title of the NY Times, Jan. 8, 2021 article was, "Capitol Police Officer Dies from Injuries in Pro-Trump Rampage." In the same issue, they published another article titled, "He Dreamed of Being a Police Officer, Then Was Killed by a Pro-Trump Mob."

In fact, officer Sicknick texted his brother after returning to police headquarters saying, "he had been "pepper sprayed twice," but was "in good shape." He died on the evening of Jan. 8 from a stroke. The NY Times quietly corrected its story a month later. nationalreview.com/2021/02/the-times-corrects-the-record-on-officer-sicknicks-death-sort-of

Impeachment – 'Dead on Arrival'

"The Senate just voted on my constitutional point of order. 45 Senators agreed that this sham of a "trial" is unconstitutional. That is more than will be needed to acquit and to eventually end this partisan impeachment process. This "trial" is dead on arrival in the Senate," wrote Republican Senator Rand Paul.[15]

The Senator said in his speech to the Senate, "This impeachment is nothing more than a partisan exercise designed to further divide the country. Democrats claim to want to unify the country, but impeaching a former president, a private citizen, is the antithesis of unity."[16]

The Constitution requires that the Chief Justice of the Supreme Court preside over all presidential impeachment trials, but John Roberts refuses. So, the Senate president pro tempore, Patrick Leahy, Democrat from Vermont will preside. Hours after being tapped for this duty, however, Leahy was admitted to the hospital with un-reported issues.[17] Another Shakespearean tragedy.

> *"The world is a stage, and all the men and women are just actors. Each successive plays different roles in a drama in seven ages."*
> William Shakespeare
> *The Seven Ages of Human Experience*

Author's Update: The impeachment fiasco ended Feb. 13, 2021 with a final vote of 57 against – 43 for.

Biden the anti-Trump

"Mr Biden in his launch video seems to be defining himself as much by who he isn't - Donald Trump," wrote Anthony Zurcher, for the BBC leadoff article about the Biden campaign, titled, 'Democrats 2020: What their key issues are.'[18]

Executive orders fly as Congressional Democrats forget about the American people and obsess over a second Trump impeachment.

The inauguration was January 20th and before the 21st had arrived, Biden had signed 19 new orders[18] that will make America worse again. He became President just after 12pm eastern time, then he gave his speech, walked a military review, went to Arlington cemetery, and got back to the oval office approximately 5:15pm. He took the next 30 minutes to sign 10 executive orders and nine memoranda. Then, approximately 5:45pm he performed a ceremonial swearing in of appointees.[19]

Executive orders (E.O.s) and memoranda are short documents, they are not legislation, but have the power of legislation until or unless the Judicial branch decides otherwise, or they are formally challenged in court.

The first three executive orders signed (on camera), mandated social distancing be practiced, and masks be worn on all federal property; the second focused 'support for underserved communities'... because we need "bedrock equity/equality as it relates to how we treat people in health care and other things", and the third ordered rejoining the Paris Climate Accords.[20] Of course, he was wearing a mask while signing, even though there was no one within 20 feet and they all had to get screened before they could enter the room. It was Kabuki theatre at its finest.

A good leader will work from a list of priorities. The most important and impactful will get the most effort and attention. The first three signatures represent, presumably his highest priorities were:

1. Social distancing & wearing masks on Federal property.

2. Support for 'underserved' communities

3. Rejoining the Paris Climate Accords (not an E.O.)

We will consider these first three in more detail, but it is important to note that his first 30 minutes of official actions as President eliminated several thousand jobs. When the 11,000 people working on the Keystone pipeline woke up on January 21st, they had no job. The many thousand who have been building the border wall suffered the same experience. Biden's first tangible acts cost hard working Americans their jobs. They now have no income. He took his commemorative pens and signed their livelihood to the dustbin. Poof!

Before we review his top three priorities, a quick glance at Table 1 reveals that not one of the E.O.s will make America better. Some will make it a lot worse. Table 1 provides only the E.O.s through January 22, his first three days.[21] It does not list the Proclamations, Directives or Memoranda. Let's look at a few in detail:

Executive Order 13991: *Protecting the Federal Workforce and Requiring Mask-Wearing.*

> Section 1. Policy. 'It is the policy of my Administration to halt the spread of coronavirus disease 2019 (COVID-19) by relying on the best available data and science-based public health measures. Such measures include wearing masks when around others, physical distancing, and other related precautions recommended by the Centers for Disease Control and Prevention (CDC). Put simply, masks and other public health measures reduce the spread of the disease, particularly when communities

make widespread use of such measures, and thus save lives.'[22]

We will now place the comments in this opening statement next to the scientific facts:

1. The order is effective only on Federal property. Someone could be asymptomatic or even have very mild symptoms and go to work on Federal property, as long as they put their mask on when they get out of their car. They can rub their nose, shake hands, yawn with their hand over their mouth, then go about touching stuff and transmitting the disease.

2. As Fauci said on '60 Minutes', "Right now in the United States, people should not be walking around with masks. Interviewer says, "You're sure of it, cause people are listening really closely?" Fauci responds, "No, people should not be worried, there is no reason for people to be walking around with a mask. When you're in the middle of an outbreak, wearing a mask might make people feel a little bit better, and it might even block a droplet, but it's not providing the perfect protection that people think that it is, and often there are unintended consequences, people keep fiddling with the masks and they keep touching their face." Interviewer, "And can you get some smutch staying inside there?" Fauci, "of course, of course, but when you think masks, you should think of health care providers needing them people who are ill. You see people in other countries walking around and they are all wearing masks and that's fine. I'm not against

it, if you want to do it, that's fine. Interviewer, "But, it can lead to a shortage of masks?", Fauci, "Exactly, that's the point, it could lead to a shortage of masks for the people who really need it." END OF 60 MINUTE INTERVIEW[23]

3. "Novel coronavirus is believed to be tiny enough (0.08-0.14 μm) to penetrate through face mask, thus protection offered by cloth mask may be too low."[24]

4. A recent 2021 study by A.K. Daoud et.al., concluded "cloth mask use was associated with significantly higher viral infections than the exclusive use of medical masks."[25]

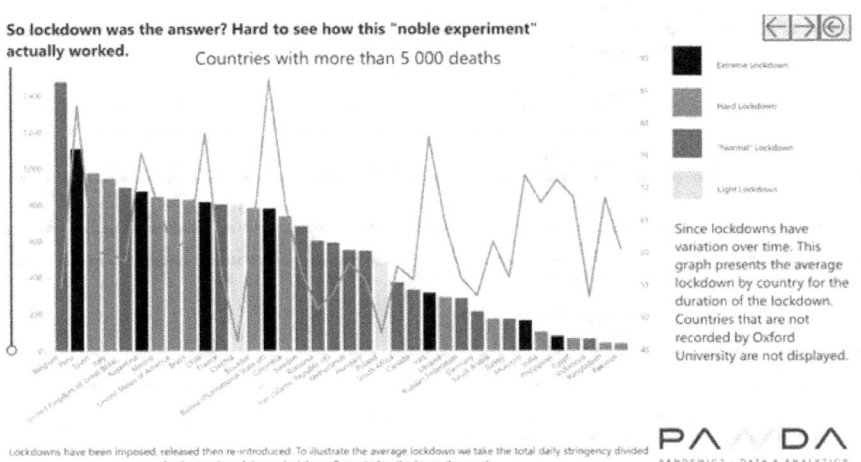

Figure 4. Lockdowns & Masks had no effect on death rate.
Source: mises.org/wire/theres-still-no-evidence-either-lockdowns-or-masks-are-game-changers[26]

Table 1. Biden Executive Orders - First Three Days in Office (January 20-22)

Order	Date	E.O. #	Executive Order Title*	Good for America	Why?
1	20-Jan-21	13985	Advancing Racial Equity & Support for Underserved Communities	No	Divisive, enforces racial preferences
2	20-Jan-21	13986	Ensure Lawful & Accurate Enumeration and Apportionment Pursuant to Decennial Census	No	Counts non-citizens, dilutes representative government
3	20-Jan-21	13987	Provide Unified Response To Combat COVID-19	No	Deny's state's rights
4	20-Jan-21	13988	Preventing and Combating Discrimination on the Basis of Gender Identity or Sexual Orientation	No	Allows biological males to participate in women's sports
5	20-Jan-21	13989	Ethics Commitments by Executive Branch Personnel	Yes	If followed, it is a good pledge & similar to Trump's
6	20-Jan-21	13990	Protecting Public Health and the Environment and Restoring Science To Tackle the Climate Crisis	No	This E.O. will do great damage to the country
7	20-Jan-21	13991	Protecting Fed Workforce & Requiring Mask-Wearing	No	Creates more, unneeded bureaucracy, adds costs and have no effect on virus spread
8	20-Jan-21	13992	Revoc Certain Exec Orders Regarding Fed Regulation	No	Revokes important Trump E.O.s
9	20-Jan-21	13993	Revise Immigration Enforcement Policies & Priorities	No	Prioritizes non-citizens & illegal over Americans
10	21-Jan-21	13994	Ensuring a Data-Driven Response to COVID-19 and Future High-Consequence Public Health Threats	No	Government data is not trustworthy, fosters authoritarianism
11	21-Jan-21	13995	Ensuring Equitable Pandemic Response & Recovery	No	Forces discrimination based on skin color
12	21-Jan-21	13996	Establish COVID-19 Pandemic Testing Board & Ensure Sustainable Public Health Workforce for COVID-19 & Other Biological Threats	No	PCR tests are grossly innacurate, enforces authoritarianism
13	21-Jan-21	13997	Improving and Expanding Access to Care & Treatments for COVID-19	Unnecessary	A total joke. Covd-19 has been in decline, mortality rate is like seasonal flu
14	21-Jan-21	13998	PromoteCOVID-19 Safety in Domestic and Int'l Travel	Unnecessary	Violates state's rights, these practices already in place
15	21-Jan-21	13999	Protecting Worker Health and Safety	Unnecessary	Already being done by Trump Admir
16	21-Jan-21	14000	Supporting the Reopening and Continuing Operation of Schools and Early Childhood Education Providers	No	Violates states rights, does not help education system, adds cost, schools are open in Republican run states
17	21-Jan-21	14001	A Sustainable Public Health Supply Chain	Unecessary	Already being done by Trump Admir
18	22-Jan-21	14002	Economic Relief Related to the COVID-19 Pandemic	No	Subsidizes states that managed virus response poorly, ie New York
19	22-Jan-21	14003	Protecting the Federal Workforce	No	Revoked Trump E.O.s making hiring & firing more efficient & less costly

* Some E.O. titles were shortened to fit the chart. Remember: titles do not always accurately reflect E.O. contents.
Source: https://www.federalregister.gov/presidential-documents/executive-orders/joe-biden/2021

Executive Order 13985: *Advancing Racial Equity and Support for Underserved Communities Through the Federal Government. Section 1: Policy.*

"Equal opportunity is the bedrock of American democracy, and our diversity is one of our country's greatest strengths. But for too many, the American Dream remains out of reach. Entrenched disparities in our laws and public policies, and in our public and private institutions, have often denied that equal opportunity to individuals and communities. Our country faces converging economic, health, and climate crises that have exposed and exacerbated inequities, while a historic movement for justice has highlighted the unbearable human costs of systemic racism. Our Nation deserves an ambitious whole-of-government equity agenda that matches the scale of the opportunities and challenges that we face."[27]

How does this opening statement compare to the facts?

1. Diversity is a strength. This is a factually false statement. When Democrats speak of diversity, they only look a skin color, gender, and sexual orientation. They require uniformity and conformity when it comes to thought and ideology.

2. In an unguarded moment of candor, German Chancellor Angela Merkel claimed the country's attempts to create a multicultural society have "utterly failed". The Guardian reported that while "speaking to a meeting of young members of her Christian Democratic Union party, Merkel said the idea of people from different cultural backgrounds living happily "side by side" did not work." "This [multicultural] approach has failed, utterly failed," Merkel told the meeting in Potsdam, west of Berlin, yesterday.[28]

3. "We conclude that multicultural policies appear to have some modest positive effects on sociopolitical integration for first-generation immigrants and likely little direct effect, positive or negative, on those in the second generation." This quote, from a Berkley study titled, '"Utter Failure" or Unity out of Diversity? Debating and Evaluating Policies of Multiculturalism', demonstrates 'utter failure' of the Academy to produce anything of value.[29]

Now let's dabble in some 'common sense.' Why are basketball teams today over 80% black?[30] The answer is because the most talented players make the team. It is not racist, and no one is complaining. Yet, Biden's destructive E.O. 13985 will force quotas and put people in positions they have not earned nor are qualified for. This is counterproductive and everyone loses. It's affirmative action on steroids.

Rejoining the Paris Climate Accords

"I, Joseph R. Biden Jr., President of the United States of America, having seen and considered the Paris Agreement, done at Paris on December 12, 2015, do hereby accept the said Agreement and every article and clause thereof on behalf of the United States of America."[31]

In the signing order, Biden said, he had "seen and considered the Paris Agreement, and "do hereby accept the said Agreement and every article and clause thereof on behalf of the United States of America."[31]

Well, the author of this book actually read the agreement[32] and any president of a western country who would sign and commit his country to it, does his people a huge disservice. Presidents of underdeveloped, 3rd world countries will benefit, because all it does is transfer wealth from the developed (especially America) to the underdeveloped.

American taxpayer money will be handed over to the United Nations for redistribution to underdeveloped countries. Here is how the United Nations summarized it:

> "The Paris Agreement provides a framework for financial, technical and capacity building support to those countries who need it."[33]
>
> "The Paris Agreement reaffirms that developed countries should take the lead in providing financial assistance to countries that are less endowed and more vulnerable, while for the first time also encouraging voluntary contributions by other Parties."[34]

James Hansen, former NASA scientist who is credited as the father of impending climate catastrophe, said in 2018, "All we've done is agree there's a problem," Hansen told the Guardian. "We agreed that in 1992, at the Earth summit in Rio, and re-agreed it again in Paris [at the 2015 climate accord]. We haven't acknowledged what is required to solve it. Promises like Paris don't mean much, it's wishful thinking. It's a hoax that governments have played on us since the 1990s."[35]

If the guys who started 'climate alarmism' say the Paris Agreement is 'wishful thinking' and a 'hoax', why did Biden sign it?

What do other 'Experts' say?

Roy Spencer, Ph.D: "You see, when it comes to global warming, modern environmentalism depends upon feelings over facts. Even if all CO_2 emissions in the U.S. were to end, the impact on global temperatures by 2100 would be small. This is because the U.S. now produces less than 15% of the global total greenhouse gas emissions. The same is true if all countries abide by their commitments under the Paris Climate Agreement, which makes Biden's rejoining that Agreement rather pointless. The effect of 'Paris' is calculated to be a 0.2 deg. C reduction in warming by 2100, which is too small to measure over the next 80 years with temperature monitoring technologies currently in place."[36]

Who is Dr. Spencer? He has been a Principal Climate Research Scientist for 20 years at a major university. Prior to that he was a Senior Scientist for Climate Studies at NASA's Marshall Space Flight Center and received NASA's Exceptional Scientific Achievement Medal for their global temperature monitoring work with satellites. Dr. Spencer's continues as U.S. Science Team leader for the Advanced Microwave Scanning Radiometer flying on NASA's Aqua satellite. He has provided congressional testimony several times on the subject of global warming and has never received funding from the fossil fuel industry.[37]

Cost of Paris Agreement for Americans.

"The weakness of the Paris Agreement was that it was lopsided, requiring little from China and a great deal from the U.S. President Obama committed the United States to reducing carbon emissions in 2025 by 26 to 28 percent, which would have meant a substantial jump in electricity costs.," wrote Liz Peek in The Hill.com.[39]

Why would the United Nations give China a better deal than the United States? "China is the biggest emitter at 26% of global greenhouse gas emissions, followed by the United States at 13%, the European Union at 7.8% and India at 6.7%.[40] Even more puzzling, why would a U.S. President sign an agreement that gives China, the world's worst polluter, an advantage over America?

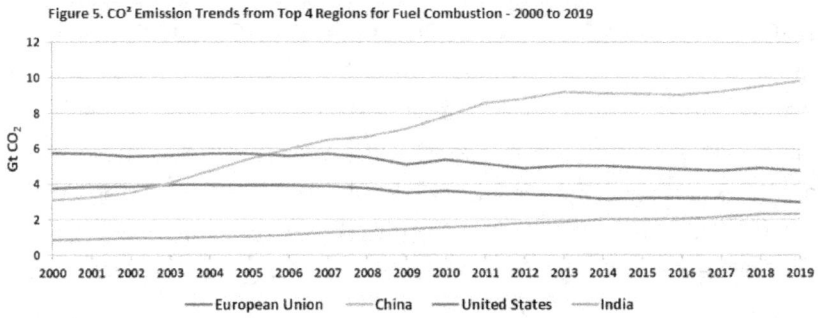

Figure 5. CO_2 Emission Trends from Top 4 Regions for Fuel Combustion - 2000 to 2019

Source: IEA, 2020, CO2 Emission Trends from for Fuel Combustion [40]

No one really knows what it will cost because the domino effects that will occur throughout society are so complicated it is impossible. So, we are left with statistical models that are based on assumptions that are not or cannot be verified. Sound like a good plan to you?

The BBC reported in 2017, after President Trump said he was pulling the U.S. out of the Paris Agreement, "As Mr Trump noted in his speech, one goal of the Paris Agreement was to raise $100bn (£77.7bn) a year by 2020 to support climate action in developing countries, first discussed as a target in 2010. The money would be used to help poorer countries invest in green energy and renewable technology. The Green Climate Fund is one mechanism set up to raise money to reach that annual target."[41]

The top 5 pledges to the Green Climate Fund as of June 2017 were: US - $3bn (£2.3bn); Japan - $1.5bn (£1.2bn); UK - $1.2bn (£931m); France - $1bn (£776m); Germany - $1bn (£776m). The BBC noted, "President Obama submitted the second half of that amount only three days before Mr Trump's inauguration. It came from the State Department's Economic Support Fund."[42]

Three days before Obama left office, he sent $500 million to the Green Climate Fund, bringing the total U.S. contribution to $1 billion of taxpayer money. *This money was not approved by Congress, nor did it benefit U.S. taxpayers.* Obama released 5 Guantanamo terrorists and secretly sent $1.8 billion in cash to Iran as partial payment for release of the traitor Bowe Bergdahl.[43, 44, 45] Obama also released approximately $150 billion in Iranian frozen assets so he could secure the impotent nuclear non-proliferation deal negotiated by John Kerry. Obama admitted there was no guarantee the terrorists released would not start up where they left off. The Brookings Institute said without a doubt much of the money given or released to Iran will be used to fund terrorism to kill Americans. Why bring these Obama fiascos up in this context? To demonstrate that the Democrats put Americans last when setting their priorities. They would not agree to fund a border wall that offered clear benefits and safety to Americans, but happily send money for Iran to use for terrorism and for the United Nations to redistribute in the name of 'climate change.'

Stated Goal of the Paris Agreement.

Article 2

1. *This Agreement, in enhancing the implementation of the Convention, including its objective, aims to strengthen the global response to the threat of climate change, in the context of sustainable development and efforts to eradicate poverty, including by:*

    (a) Holding the increase in the global average temperature to well below 2°C above pre-industrial levels and pursuing efforts to limit the temperature increase to 1.5°C above pre-industrial levels, recognizing that this would significantly reduce the risks and impacts of climate change;

> (b) *Increasing the ability to adapt to the adverse impacts of climate change and foster climate resilience and low greenhouse gas emissions development, in a manner that does not threaten food production; and*
>
> (c) *Making finance flows consistent with a pathway towards low greenhouse gas emissions and climate-resilient development.*
>
> 2. *This Agreement will be implemented to reflect equity and the principle of common but differentiated responsibilities and respective capabilities, in the light of different national circumstances.*[46]

Science vs Empty Promises & Lies

The optimistic impact on global warming is a reduction of 0.2-0.3C.[47] Joe Biden is going to give billions of dollars to the United Nations Green Climate Fund yet a measurable reduction in global temperatures will not be achieved!

Read the stated Paris goals again:

> Goal 1 "aims to strengthen the global response to the threat of climate change, in the context of sustainable development and efforts to *eradicate poverty.*" Have you ever been to India? How long have we been sending money to Africa? Think about how you have benefitted. It is your money down a rat hole.

These utopians think they are going to eradicate poverty. It's an idea almost as absurd as the arrogance of thinking reducing CO_2 emissions will lower global temperature.

Goal 2 "will be implemented to reflect equity and the principle of common but differentiated responsibilities and respective capabilities, in the light of different national circumstances." What the hell does that mean?

This was President Biden's number 3 priority and may actually be unconstitutional because Congress must approve all treaties.

Benefit of the Paris Agreement to America

American taxpayers will fund infrastructure and development projects in third world countries. The rich will get richer and the rest of us, will just have to make do. That's what John Kerry told the 11,000 people who lost their Keystone pipeline jobs. Kenneth Rapoza of Forbes writes, "President Biden's new "climate czar" John Kerry says laid off workers in the fossil fuels industry should be able to easily transfer their skill set into solar. He specifically said they can "make solar panels." The only problem with the Czar's suggestion is that of the 10 solar panel manufacturing sites in the world, eight are in China.[48]

This is what they call a zero-sum game. They win, we lose.

Biden will renew Obama's pledge to reduce U.S. output of greenhouse gasses by 26-28% versus a 2005 baseline. But, as already reviewed, science tells us the Paris agreement will not reduce global temperatures.

Biden has already 'paused' offering new energy exploration leases on government land.[49] This will morph into a ban by increasing the cost of leasing and adding burdensome regulations that make exploration and production untenable. Obama did the same thing to the coal industry.

Under President Trump's leadership, the United States achieved emission reductions that were 16% under the 2005 baseline.[50] This trend started when fracking hit full stride and natural gas production drove down energy prices and reduced emissions by trading gas for coal. Trump gave it support by approving Keystone and creating more access for fossil fuel exploration and production. America became energy independent for the first time, yet Biden is now moving to reverse these gains.

Nicolas Loris of the Heritage Foundation provides us with some closing thoughts on the benefits of re-joining the Paris agreement:

> "Following through with the Obama administration's commitments would impose clear economic harm on the U.S. by driving energy prices higher—and that's just a small part of the overall cost. Americans would pay more for food, health care, education, clothes, and every other good and service that requires energy.
>
> "These higher costs would be spread across the entire economy and would shrink overall economic growth and employment. Heritage Foundation analysts estimated that the regulations required to meet the Obama administration's commitments would impose the following costs by 2035:
>
> "An overall loss of nearly 400,000 jobs, half of which would be in manufacturing.
>
> "An average total income loss of more than $20,000 for a family of four.
>
> "An aggregate GDP loss of over $2.5 trillion.
>
> "Other countries would continue getting a free pass under the agreement, but if the U.S. signed back on, one can be sure that environmental activist lawsuits would make sure the U.S. kept its obligations."[51]

Other Orders that Will Irreparably Harm America

Executive Order 13988. *Preventing and Combating Discrimination on the Basis of Gender Identity or Sexual Orientation*

Section 1. Policy. "Every person should be treated with respect and dignity and should be able to live without fear, no matter who they are or whom they love. Children should be able to learn without worrying about whether they will be denied access to the restroom, the locker room, or school sports. Adults should be able to earn a living and pursue a vocation knowing that they will not be fired, demoted, or mistreated because of whom they go home to or because how they dress does not conform to sex-based stereotypes. People should be able to access healthcare and secure a roof over their heads without being subjected to sex discrimination. All persons should receive equal treatment under the law, no matter their gender identity or sexual orientation." [52]

It remains to be seen if the courts will suspend this disgusting order. If they do not, women's sports will be forever dominated by biological men who 'self-identify' as women. This is insanity and it is coming from the Democrat party. Biology is binary, male and female.

Secondly, equal treatment is already the law of the land and has been since Lincoln. It has not always been practiced because humanity is flawed. Look how those who supported President Trump are being treated today. Look how Christians and Jews are treated today. All are ridiculed, slandered and discriminated against.

If you have a penis, you go to the men's room and play on the boys/men's teams. If you don't, you go to the women's room and play women's sports. This is child abuse dressed up in progressive lingo.

Executive Order 13988. *Protecting Public Health and the Environment and Restoring Science to Tackle the Climate Crisis*

Section 1. Policy. "Our Nation has an abiding commitment to empower our workers and communities; promote and protect our public health and the environment; and conserve our national treasures and monuments, places that secure our national memory. Where the Federal Government has failed to meet that commitment in the past, it must advance environmental justice. In carrying out this charge, the Federal Government must be guided by the best science and be protected by processes that ensure the integrity of Federal decision-making. It is, therefore, the policy of my Administration to listen to the science; to improve public health and protect our environment; to ensure access to clean air and water; to limit exposure to dangerous chemicals and pesticides; to hold polluters accountable, including those who disproportionately harm communities of color and low-income communities; to reduce greenhouse gas emissions; to bolster resilience to the impacts of climate change; to restore and expand our national treasures and monuments; and to prioritize both environmental justice and the creation of the well-paying union jobs necessary to deliver on these goals."[53]

First of all, there is no 'climate crisis'. Here are the indisputable scientific facts:

1. Earth's temperature has risen 1.5°F over the last 150 years (1870-2020).

2. The Little Ice Age ended around 1860.

3. The primary sources of atmospheric CO_2 are decaying organic matter, the oceans, volcanoes and wildfires.

4. The rise of earth's temperature is not correlated with the rise in CO_2. Oceans 'out-gas' CO_2 due to ocean warming.

5. Life could not exist without CO_2. Plants consume CO_2 from the atmosphere and through a process called photosynthesis that combines the carbon with oxygen and hydrogen to form the organic molecules of life.

6. Humans could not exist without green plants because photosynthesis is our oxygen source.

7. Earth is heated (irradiated) by the sun during the day.

8. The greenhouse gases keep the earth from freezing. They are our protective blanket giving us an atmosphere that allows life to flourish.

9. Earth's atmosphere is 78% nitrogen, 21% oxygen, and 0.9% argon. That's 99.9%.

10. The remaining 0.1% is made of all the greenhouse gases.

11. Water vapor is approximately 96% of the total greenhouse gases or 0.0955% of the atmosphere. Today there is 410 ppm of CO_2, or 0.0041%, and methane (CH_4) 1.8ppm is not worth mentioning.

>   (see globalchange.mit.edu/news-media/in-the-news/greenhouse-gases-water-vapor-and-you)
>
> 12. 70% of the world's surface is ocean. The oceans regulate our global temperature and regional weather.
>
> 13. CO_2 has been increasing faster since 1950 due to population growth, proliferation of combustion engine transportation, increasing demands for electricity due to population growth and industrial growth and the expansion of coal fired plants in China. In 1950 CO_2 was 280 ppm, it is now about 410 ppm. As a result, the planet has become greener due to more CO_2. Crops are more productive. That's good.

The only crisis is the willingness of 'experts', 'scientists' and others to lie about it so their funding won't go away. They will not debate the honest scientists.

So, the premise upon which E.O. 13988 is based is a lie. It is easily proven, as I have just done, but they've been telling the lie so long and teaching it so long, it has become accepted dogma. It is a religious belief and nothing more.

Michael Mann, Biden's Climate Czar has been caught forcing data that leads to erroneous conclusions. His famous hockey stick is one example, and the Climate-gate emails is another. But, since he is one of the high priests, he is untouchable. Thus, when the order says it will 'listen to the science' it means it will listen to the guy who has a history of making data fit the outcome he is promoting. That is not science.

So, we are in trouble. This order is so expansive, government can go anywhere and regulate anything. Costs of everything will increase. With the unrealistic push for solar or wind, we will have more brownouts or blackouts. Government may force you to shut off your air conditioner if electrical capacity is over-burdened due to insufficient fossil fuel back-up. This E.O. will or could reduce individual freedoms and increase the cost of living, which hits the lower class the hardest.

The E.O. introduces the term 'environmental justice', which like racial justice is in the eye of the beholder. The Democrats are essentially creating a social conformance police force that I'm afraid will come very close to Big Brother intrusions never before experienced in America. To help them enforce these rules, they 'will listen to the science.' The problem is their 'science' is what they decide it is without open debate. It cannot be challenged. At this point, E.O. 13988 is a can of worms.

Executive Order 13993. *Revision of Civil Immigration Enforcement Policies and Priorities.*

> Section 1. Policy. "Immigrants have helped strengthen America's families, communities, businesses and workforce, and economy, infusing the United States with creativity, energy, and ingenuity. The task of enforcing the immigration laws is complex and requires setting priorities to best serve the national interest. The policy of my Administration is to protect national and border security, address the humanitarian challenges at the southern border, and ensure public health and safety. We must also adhere to due process of law as we safeguard the dignity and well-being of all families and communities. My Administration will reset the policies and practices for enforcing civil immigration laws to align enforcement with these values and priorities."[55]

Once again, if we eliminate the flowery, feel good, politically correct dogma from the order, there is not much left. But what they are doing is revoking Trump order 13768, which directed the enforcement of all immigration laws in place today and to eliminate sanctuary cities. "Sanctuary jurisdictions across the United States willfully violate Federal law in an attempt to shield aliens from removal from the United States. These jurisdictions have caused immeasurable harm to the American people and to the very fabric of our Republic."[56]

E.O. 13933 weakens our immigration law and will take us back to the days of Obama when trains of people were caravanning to the border. There is zero benefit to American citizens. The burden of the cost of new, unskilled immigrants that do not speak English will be paid for by American citizens who had no voice in this decision. This is bad for our country and did not give the people a voice.

Executive Order 14003. *Protecting the Federal Workforce.*

> Section 1. Policy. "Career civil servants are the backbone of the Federal workforce, providing the expertise and experience necessary for the critical functioning of the Federal Government. It is the policy of the United States to protect, empower, and rebuild the career Federal workforce. It is also the policy of the United States to encourage union organizing and collective bargaining. The Federal Government should serve as a model employer."[55]

This is a bad order. It revokes the Trump E.O. 13957 that required advancement based on merit and consistent positive job performance and made it easier for senior management to fire employees that broke confidentialities, that were disobedient, non-productive and negligent.[56] These are all standard employee expectations for most working Americans, but Biden's E.O. revokes 13957 and thereby destroys the merit system and fosters bureaucratic bloat and ineffectiveness. It re-institutionalizes the 'job-for-life' nature of government employment.

Summary of First Eleven Days

Executive Orders. President Biden signed 28 Executive Orders in his first eleven days. The Ethics Pledge, E.O. 13989, is good. All Presidents have done this, but Biden does not address the 'revolving door' (people cycling from government to lobbying and back again) problem in a small way. The restrictions on the revolving door should be 5 years, but two is better than nothing. There should be a provision that prevents family and relatives from profiting from the employee's tenure in the administration, but I don't think Republicans or Democrats have the honor to close that door.

The 27 other orders will not make America better, those reviewed in detail earlier, will make it worse. Many are neutral, like the eleven that deal with Covid-19 actions. Most are redundant to the Trump administration or slightly nuanced.

Presidential Memoranda.[57] The President signed 8 memoranda, six of which were racial or identity preference directives:

1. Preserving and Fortifying Deferred Action for Childhood Arrivals (DACA). Trump tried to pass legislation in favor of the 'childhood arrivals' but was blocked by the Democrats every time.

2. Reinstating Deferred Enforced Departure for Liberians

3. Condemning and Combating Racism, Xenophobia, and Intolerance Against Asian Americans and Pacific Islanders in the United States

4. Redressing Our Nation's and the Federal Government's History of Discriminatory Housing Practices and Policies

5. Tribal Consultation and Strengthening Nation-to-Nation Relationships

6. Protecting Women's Health at Home and Abroad

Except for the DACA memoranda, the others will not make America better. They may provide some small advantage to a small segment of society, but even that is questionable. The other two dealt with Covid-19 and Federal regulatory review process, both of which will just add bureaucracy and cost.

What Foundational Bricks were Cracked or Removed?

- **The Constitution.** The principle of the Federal government acting within the parameters of The Constitution. (Biden will look the other way regarding immigration law).

- **America First.** The principle of putting law abiding, tax paying Americans first (non-citizens will be given most of the benefits of citizenship at the taxpayer's expense and climate/energy policies will favor other countries and export American jobs).

- **Ideological Debate.** The principle of open dialogue and debate (Biden's people will determine 'the best science' without debate, transparency, or accountability).

- **Equality**. The Founders considered equality as the principle that no person is better than another. We are equally human, with each life being of equal value. Since the human experience began, man's selfishness incessantly seeks personal gain at the expense of others. Cain killed his brother. Jussie Smollett faked a hate crime in the attempt for personal exaltation. Those who use the word 'equality' as an arbiter of 'fairness', do so to divide not unify. In the eyes of God, we are all 'equal.' But man does not see with the eyes of God. One man's equal right to believe in God has no impact on another's right to believe there is no God. This is the meaning of 'equality' as used by Jefferson in the Declaration of Independence. (Biden, however, uses it as a cudgel for identity politics and skin color in almost everything).

- **Self-Determination**. The principle of individualism and self-determination. (Biden provides preference and advantage to people based on their skin color and identity preference. Merit will be replaced by quotas).

- **Trust**. The principle that a man's word is his bond, that the media's word is true and verifiable, that government will follow the Constitution and execute our laws consistently and without bias. (The only thing one can depend on today is that these principles will be consistently violated.)

Chapter 3
Trust Me!

"I'd rather entrust the government of the United States to the first 400 people listed in the Boston telephone directory than to the faculty of Harvard University."[1]
—William F. Buckley, Jr., early 1960s

Susan Walsh, photographer for the Associated Press maneuvered herself up the Capital Building steps to gain an elevated view of the Swearing-in ceremony of Joe Biden.[2] "As President-elect Biden was introduced at his inauguration ceremony at 11:15 a.m. Wednesday, he was greeted by swirling snow flurries amid partly sunny skies," reported Jason Samenow of the Washington Post.[3] Other photos of the first couple showed the sunlight on their faces; sometimes wearing masks, sometimes not.

Walsh's photo shows the audience almost perfectly socially distanced and wearing masks even though the risk of Covid-19 was virtually zero. "What's that?", you say?

All attendees were required to test negative prior to attending. In fact, U.S. Rep. Raul Ruiz, from southern California tested positive just before his scheduled flight, so had to stay home in self-quarantine. "In preparation for attending the inauguration of President-elect Biden and Vice President-elect Harris, I have taken multiple COVID-19 tests over the last 72 hours," Ruiz said. "After receiving an initial negative result over the weekend, this morning I tested positive for COVID- 19. While I do have mild symptoms, over all I am feeling well and will self-isolate for the recommended time," stated Mr. Ruiz.[4] No one was reported to have contracted it at the ceremony. I know that is not proof, but these things are usually reported. Other than Mr. Ortiz, there were no reports of others having to forego the trip due to a positive test. Yet we are told that the audience was restricted due to the threat of Covid-19. James Poniewozik of the NY Times wrote, "Because of the pandemic, the inaugural's organizers asked the crowds to stay away…"[5] Yet, two weeks earlier, on January 6, President Trump held a rally in D.C. with well over 30,000 people crammed together. There were no reports of Covid-19 infections from that event either. Again, that is not proof, but given the rabid hatred the media has for Donald Trump, it would have been reported. There were reports a couple of days later of some National Guard troops testing positive but no follow up to confirm if the tests were false positives, which happens 90% of the time.

Figure 6. Biden Swearing-in Ceremony, Washington, D.C., January 20, 2021
Photo by Susan Walsh, Associated Press[2]

And then there is the science question that the media never asks. Why are people wearing masks outside when they are distanced? First of all, it is proven that sunlight ultra-violet light kills airborne and surface Covid-19 quickly.

April 27, 2020, Dr. Deborah Birx, reviewed the data in Figure 5 in a televised coronavirus task force update.[6] This was **before** the initial 'shelter-in-place' directive from President Trump. This is critically important information. Outdoor activities and businesses were shut down unnecessarily. People engaging in sports could've done so freely, with no masks with little risk. She only made the announcement nine days after it was leaked on April 18.

Increased temperature, humidity, and sunlight are detrimental to SARS-CoV-2 in saliva droplets on surfaces and in the air

CONDITION	Temp	Humidity	Solar	HALF LIFE
Surface	70-75°F	20%	None	18 hours
Surface	70-75°F	80%	None	6 hours
Surface	95°F	80%	None	1 hour
Surface	70-75°F	80%	Summer	2 minutes
Aerosol	70-75°F	20%	None	~60 minutes
Aerosol	70-75°F	20%	Summer	~1.5 minutes

Figure 7. Covid-19 Airborne & Surface Survival Rates Dept. Homeland Security Science & Technology lab study. April 2020.[6]

STOP! Look at Figure 7 more closely:

Covid-19 Half-life on surfaces

1. High humidity, ½ life declines 300%, 18 to 6 hours
2. As temp & humidity rise, ½ life declines 18 to 1 hour
3. Sunlight at high humidity, ½ life declines 18hrs to 2 mins

Covid-19 Half-life in the Air

1. No sunlight: ½ life is < 1 hour
2. With sunlight: ½ life is < 1½ minutes

Colby Hall reported on April 18, "A *recently leaked* and unclassified government study shows promising data on the direct effect of sunlight on the deadly COVID-19 contagion. The study was conducted by the U.S. Department of Homeland Security's (DHS) Science and Technology Department and is titled "S&T's Research, Development, Testing and Evaluation (RDTE) Efforts on COVID-19." The Department of Homeland Security has declined to comment on the leaked report that indicates that sunlight destroys the coronavirus in about three minutes."[7]

On April 17, a few other on-line news agencies reported the leak, but my on-line searching finds no major media reported it in the United States. Mr. Hall said the DHS declined comment. Why? With extremely bad timing, an inept reporter for a Galveston paper ran an April 14 headline, 'Sunlight cannot kill the coronavirus.'[8] Thirteen days later, April 27th, Dr. Birx finally came clean and admitted sunlight did kill the virus!

Check out this quote from the Journal of Virology, "Sunlight or, more specifically, solar UV radiation (UV) acts as the principal natural virucide in the environment. UV radiation kills viruses by chemically modifying their genetic material, DNA and RNA."[9] That's pretty definitive.

Dr. Fauci, who is a Director at the NIH and is considering recommending we now wear two masks, must not have read this conclusion from a study posted on the NIH website: "Cloth face masks have limited efficacy in combating viral infection transmission. However, it may be used in closed, crowded indoor, and outdoor public spaces involving physical proximity to prevent spread of SARS-CoV-2 infection."[10]

Alas, sunlight kills Covid-19 and masks are ineffective. So, why is everyone at the swearing-in ceremony wearing masks and social distancing? Hint: it's not because of a virus threat. Trust me.

The CDC track record of failure on Covid

1. They botched the Covid-19 test kit, which delayed the ability to test about 8 weeks. Trump gave the task to industry and we soon had several tests.

2. Director Redfield was 2nd only to Fauci on flip-flops

3. They could not even confidently develop a system to quantify cases, hospitalizations, and deaths, so Trump had to pull that into the White House.

4. They were against hydroxychloroquine, which research has now proven is an effective therapeutic.

5. They recommended the lockdowns, which have been proven ineffective.

6. They still recommend Remdesivir, which research has proven ineffective.

The Occupation of Washington D.C.

The Set Up. Late December, "The New York Police Department sends a packet of material to the U.S. Capitol Police and the Washington Field Office of the FBI. This raw intelligence… indicates that there will likely be violence when lawmakers certify the presidential election." NPR continues, "But the **DHS and the FBI**

do not create an intelligence report focused specifically on the upcoming pro-Trump rally."[11]

Muriel Bowser, mayor of Washington, D.C. said, on January 4, the National Guard will be activated to support the Metropolitan Police Department (MPD) to assure safety during President Trump's rally on January 6.[12]

Also, on January 4, NPR reports, "The Metropolitan Police Department arrests Enrique Tarrio, leader of the far-right Proud Boys group. He is charged with destruction of property and possession of high-capacity firearm magazines. He's released the next day and told to leave Washington."

The NPR report continued, "U.S. Capitol Police Chief Steven Sund asks permission from House and Senate security officials to request that the D.C. National Guard be placed on standby in case the protest gets out of control. The Washington Post reports: "House Sergeant at Arms Paul Irving said ***he wasn't comfortable with the 'optics'*** of formally declaring an emergency ahead of the demonstration." Sund said.

"The FBI Field Office in Norfolk, Va., issues an explicit warning that extremists have plans for violence, so they share what they have discovered with counterparts in D.C., the Post reports. The head of the FBI's Washington Field Office, Steven D'Antuono, later says that information is shared with the FBI's "law enforcement partners" through the bureau's Joint Terrorism Task Force. That includes the U.S. Capitol Police, U.S. Park Police, D.C.'s Metropolitan Police Department (MPD) and other agencies."[13] They decide to do nothing!

Then the mayor issued the following statement, "To be clear, the District of Columbia ***is not*** requesting other federal law enforcement personnel and discourages any additional deployment without immediate notification to, and consultation with, MPD if such plans are underway."[14]

Reporter Jordan Davidson further explains Bowser said, "D.C.'s Metropolitan Police Department in coordination with the U.S. Park

Police, Capitol Police, and Secret Service **were well-equipped to handle whatever problems could come up** during the Trump rallies planned for Wednesday."[15]

"The District of Columbia Government has not requested personnel from any other federal law enforcement agencies," she continued. "To avoid confusion, we ask that any request for additional assistance be coordinated using the same process and procedures." Bowser also explained that the presence of "unidentifiable" federal law enforcement agents in D.C. could "cause confusion" and "become a national security threat" because of the lack of distinction between them and "armed groups."[16]

So, to review:

1. In late December NY Police have good intel indicating violence on January 6, but the FBI & DHS do not create an intelligence report!

2. January 4th: new intel arrives from Virginia FBI office and is reviewed by all D.C. law enforcement. They decide to do nothing because it might not look good!

3. The mayor of D.C. calls up the National Guard on the 4th.

4. On the 5th, she tells other law enforcement agencies she has it covered, and they are to stand down to avoid confusion. She did request and received a limited force (340) from the D.C. National Guard to help with traffic flow — not law enforcement — which is to be handled by D.C. police.

5. Now the law enforcement left hand doesn't know what the law enforcement right hand is doing.

> *The Captain said,*
> *"What we got here is failure to*
> *communicate."*
> —from the 1967 movie *Cool Hand Luke*

Still on the 5th, "A law enforcement official tells ABC News that there are no known threats over the next few days, **but** a separate law enforcement source said that the police presence is "all hands-on deck." Reporter Luke Barr writes, "As law enforcement in Washington, D.C., braced for protests at the Capitol and around the nation's capital Wednesday when Congress meets to ratify Joe Biden as winner of the presidential election, the leader of the alt-right group, the Proud Boys, urged members to show up in support of President Donald Trump."[17]

At 8:15 pm on the evening of the 5th, a street video cam captures a medium build man, fully covered, carrying one of the bombs planted at the party headquarters. The video was released by the FBI on January 29th.[18] The man has not been identified nor tracked down.

The following compares January 6 timelines produced by the Washington Post (W)[19], National Public Radio (N)[20] and the Epoch Times (E).[21] If all three sources are very close in agreement or redundant, I will use the notation (A). The publish dates were: (W - Jan. 9th), (N - Jan. 15th) and (E - Jan. 13th). Each source also includes videos and photos:

11:00 am - Rally attendees gather at White House ellipse (W)

Noon - President Trump begins to speak (W, E)

12:30 pm – People begin to gather outside the Capital building behind the barriers (W). *Author Note:* Trump is still speaking, no gas masks in the audience.

12:37 pm – "A stream of people leaving Trump's speech early slowly make their way down Constitution Avenue toward the Capitol." (E)

1:00 pm – "We see this huge crush of people coming down Pennsylvania Ave. toward the Capitol," reports NPR's Hannah Allam. "We follow the crowd as it goes up to the Hill, toward the Capitol. There's scaffolding set up for the inauguration already," she adds. *"But as far as protection, all we really saw were some mesh barriers, some metal fencing and only a small contingent of Capitol Police.* And we watched them being quickly overwhelmed. (N)

A 26 second video shows people wearing gas masks charge the weak barriers and attack the few police standing the line (W, E). *Author Note:* There are no National Guard but some Capital Police in view. Trump is still speaking. So, logic would dictate the people attacking the barriers were not there to listen to the President.

1:03 pm – Another police line forms at the Capitol's double staircase. Riot police arrive. (E)

1:12 pm – President Trump ends his speech and says let's walk down Pennsylvania to the Capital. (W, E)

1:20 pm - A temporary fencing perimeter is reestablished in the Inauguration platform area at the bottom of the double staircase. (E)

1:30 pm - The Post says, "supporters begin marching toward the U.S. Capitol." (W)

> **Author's note:** The Post must be referring to the main body of ~30,000 people.

> **Author's note:** Google maps shows the walk from The President's Park down Pennsylvania Avenue to the Capital is 1.6 miles and would take 33 minutes. But this is a massive crowd, so it will take much longer, making the earliest arrival time after 2:00 pm. This is an hour after the Capital attack began. The 30,000+ attendees had no knowledge of what was happening.

1:30 pm - The Post says, "The crowd outside the building grows larger, eventually overtaking Capitol Police and making their way up the steps." (W)

> **Author's note:** This was obviously not the crowd that listened to the President, the Post timeline proves that is impossible. So, there were over 30,000 people listening to the President 1.6 miles from the Capital while another smaller group began the breach. The Post video reportedly taken at 1:30 pm clearly shows the many of the men fighting with the police were wearing gas masks. When you do a Google search on people involved in the breach wearing gas masks you get stories reporting on gas masks being passed out

to Congressional people, nothing regarding the people breaking into the Capital.

> The Lone Ranger: *"Who were those masked men, Tonto?"*
> Tonto: *"Me don't know, Kemo Sabe. Maybe they were Antifa terrorists disguised as Trump supporters."*

1:34 pm - Mayor Bowser asks Army Secretary Ryan McCarthy for additional Guard forces, according to a Pentagon timeline. (N)

1:35 pm - "Police fire irritants into the crowd, likely from the upper level of the Capitol, above the double staircase." (E)

1:49 pm - "Capitol Police Chief Sund speaks with the commanding general of the D.C. National Guard Maj. Gen. William Walker by phone and requests immediate assistance." (N)

2:02 to 2:07 pm - "The temporary fencing and police line set up about 250 feet from the central east Capitol entrance is breached. The temporary fencing and police line set up at the steps of the central east Capitol entrance is breached. The crowd climbs the stairs and spreads through the upper level." (E)

2:10 to 2:11 pm - "A crowd breaks through temporary fencing at the top of the northern staircase. Several officers guarding it retreat. The central east Capitol entrance door is opened. It's unclear how. (E)

2:15 pm – "The pro-Trump mob breaches the Capitol, breaking windows and climbing inside the building, then opening doors for others to follow." (A).

> **Author's note:** The photo (W) that accompanies the article, credited to Win McNamee, shows some who were breaking in wearing gas masks. The photo was taken from **inside looking out**. How did the photographer get inside before the intruders?

2:16 pm – "Another crowd reaches the entrance to the northern wing, which houses the Senate chamber." (E)

2:22 pm – "On a conference call with Pentagon officials, D.C. Mayor Bowser requests National Guard support and Capitol Police Chief Sund pleads for backup. "I am making an urgent, urgent immediate request for National Guard assistance," Sund told The Washington Post he said on the call. "I have got to get boots on the ground." (N)

"D.C. officials on the call told the Post they heard director of the Army Staff Lt. Gen. Walter Piatt say that he could not recommend that his boss, Army Secretary McCarthy, approve the request and that *he did not like "the visual"* of a line of National Guard soldiers in front of the Capitol.

2:24 pm – Trump tweets criticism of V.P. Pence (A)

2:30 pm – "Acting Defense Secretary Miller, Chairman of the Joint Chiefs of Staff Gen. Mark Milley and Army

Secretary McCarthy meet to discuss the requests from Capitol Police Chief Sund and Mayor Bowser. (N)

2:31 pm – Mayor Bowser announces a 6 pm curfew.

2:38 pm – President Trump tweets, "Please support our Capitol Police and Law Enforcement. They are truly on the side of our Country. Stay peaceful!" (E)

2:44 pm – **Ashli Babbitt is murdered by Capital Police**

> **Author's note:** The Capital Police officer who shot and killed Ms. Babbitt was exonerated from any wrongdoing by the D.C. Attorney General and the U.S. Justice Department on April 14th. His identity remains hidden. (2022 update: it was Lt. Michael Byrd).
>
> You can read the official statement from our corrupt 'justice' system at justice.gov/usao-dc/pr/department-justice-closes-investigation-death-ashli-babbitt.

2:59 pm – "The group had rushed the steps after a handful of protesters called on others to "storm the Capitol!" (W)

> **Author's note:** This is reported elsewhere but seems out of time sequence.

3:00 pm – "Acting Defense Secretary Miller determines that all available forces of the D.C. National Guard are required to reestablish security of the Capitol complex." (N)

3:13 pm - The President tweeted, "I am asking for everyone at the U.S. Capitol to remain peaceful. Remember, WE are the Party of Law & Order - respect the Law and our great men and women in Blue. Thank you!" (W)

3:35 pm - V.P. Pence tweets, "The violence and destruction taking place at the US Capitol Must Stop and it Must Stop Now. Anyone involved must respect Law Enforcement officers and immediately leave the building. Peaceful protest is the right of every American but this attack on our Capitol will not be tolerated and those involved will be prosecuted to the fullest extent of the law." (E)

3:35 pm - "The Department of Homeland Security says it's sending in agents to aid Capitol Police." (E)

3:35 pm - "White House press secretary Kayleigh McEnany tweets that the National Guard and federal forces are on their way to the U.S. Capitol." (N,W) Epoch Times gives the full tweet, "At President [Donald Trump]'s direction, the National Guard is on the way along with other federal protective services. We reiterate President Trump's call against violence and to remain peaceful." (E)

3:36 pm - "White House press secretary Kayleigh McEnany tweets that the National Guard and federal forces are on their way to the U.S. Capitol." (N,W) Epoch Times gives the full tweet, "At President [Donald Trump]'s direction, the National Guard is on the way along with other federal protective services. We reiterate President Trump's call against violence and to remain peaceful." (E)

> **Author's note**: The initial error was the FBI and DHS deciding to ignore early warnings. The mission of these two agencies is to protect the American people. Given the corruption among FBI leadership over the past four years, one cannot help but wonder if their lack of preparation was willful.
>
> It is clear that were it not for the incompetence of mayor Bowser, Chief of the Capital Police - Steven Sund, the Metropolitan Police, Lt General Piatt and others, this breach would not have happened.

4:00 pm - "The National Guard mobilizes 1,100 troops. As per KSTP News, Pentagon officials say the D.C. request for troops wasn't rejected earlier in the day, but troops can't be used in a law enforcement role. They need to be deployed to replace police in different roles. The freed-up officers can then join the law enforcement action." (E)

> **Author's note:** Had mayor Bowser requested their presence before the rally began, none of this would have happened.

4:17 pm - "Trump posts a video on Twitter reiterating to his supporters that the election was stolen, but that there must be peace and they "have to go home now." Shortly after, Twitter deletes the video." (E)

5:40 pm – "National Guard troops arrive at the Capitol." (E)

6:00 pm – "D.C. curfew takes effect. Most of the 69 people arrested Wednesday afternoon through early Thursday were on curfew and unlawful entry charges." (W)

6:01 pm – The President tweeted, "These are the things and events that happen when a sacred landslide election victory is so unceremoniously & viciously stripped away from great patriots who have been badly & unfairly treated for so long. Go home with love & in peace. Remember this day forever!" (E)

I have captured all the pertinent timeline events of January 6th published by two progressive (W & N) and one conservative (E) news organization. As noted in the following *'Author's note'*, the NPR timeline was listed first and Washington Post was second. The next 20 were other progressive sources, then came The Epoch Times.

> *"The American people should be made aware of the trend toward monopolization of the great public information vehicles and the concentration of more and more power over public opinion in fewer and fewer hands."*
> —Spiro T. Agnew, Vice President of the United States ~ 1973

Author's note: When using Google search with the words: 'Timeline of Jan 6 DC rally' on Feb. 4, 2021, the rank order on page one was: 1. NPR, 2. Wash Post, 3. Wikipedia, 4. Bill Moyers, 5. ABC News, 6. Politifact, 7. USA Today, 8. The Wire, 9. Bloomberg, and 10. NY Times. The Epoch Times was 23rd. I clicked through **33 pages** and found no other conservative voice; not Fox News (#1 in cable news or NY Post, 4th largest newspaper in the U.S.) I did confirm they both had timeline stories.

The Epoch Times is much more detailed and provides a fuller perspective. The fact that Epoch includes the President's 6:01 tweet, is indicative of unbiased reporting. The Washington Post, however, chose to embellish its timeline with inflammatory, biased and false rhetoric. Here are some examples:

1. "During his speech, Trump reiterated multiple falsehoods, claiming the election was rigged and that Democrats had committed voter fraud."

    Fact Check: False. *The book 34 Days & Holding: America in the Balance*, proves there was fraud in multiple states. The book also makes a strong and documented case on the Democrat's gaming the system.[22]

2. "Pro-Trump mob breaches Capitol"

    Fact Check: Mostly False. The Post's own timeline disproves this. They reported that the violence at the Capital began at 1:00 pm, but the President's speech did not end until 1:10 pm. The 30,000+ people listening to the President were 1.6 miles away when the violence began. They had no knowledge of it. So, the 'mob' was a much smaller group who obviously were not there to listen to the President. It is also true that not all of those who started the violence were Trump supporters, yet the media paints all Trump supporters with the same brush.

3. "Trump refuses to condemn violence as conflict intensifies."

Fact Check: Absolutely False. The Post's own timeline quotes the President's tweet that said, "No violence!"

Was it All a 'Pro-Trump Mob'?

No. As we just proved, the 30,000+ attendees of the 'Save America Rally' were peaceful and 1.6 miles away from the violence at the Capital when it began. So, who were the people at the Capital causing trouble while the President was still speaking? I believe most of them were Trump supporters. But it is lying to claim there were no Antifa or BLM members posing as Trump supporters.

Three days later, January 9, we learned there were BLM and Antifa anarchists participating. Look up this reference and you can look at the mug shot of one of them.[23] Yet, if you ask a search engine about 'antifa and BLM involvement in the Capital breach' the first several pages are articles that start: "No, Antifa and BLM were not...". It is so over the top and uniform across dozens of media that one cannot avoid the idea of 'The Ministry of Truth.' Yet, if you know how to look, there is stuff out there. Here's some examples:

- "Capital Police wave Trump supporters through barricades." So, the truth is, early on, a small fringe group forced their way through the barricades, but as the 'true' rally attendees arrive, the cops wave them through. No wonder there were so many people inside the Capital building."[24]

- "In one video, an officer can be seen posing for selfies with members of the mob and interacting with them in a congenial manner."[25]

- "Some people are worried today that some police were complicit with the protesters," Cooper said. "It's one thing to be friendly and to de-escalate the violence. But it's one thing to take selfies with them (rioters) and let them go through the lines."[26]

- Donnie O'Sullivan, 29, reporter, CNN: "We got to the barrier at the base of the Capitol as they broke through. It was a dramatic moment, but also surprisingly undramatic in that, you know, *there were obviously not sufficient numbers of police or barricades.*"[27]

- Marcus DiPaola, freelance journalist said, "I take my first video – like six cops against 600 protesters."[28]

- J. Scott Applewhite, A.P. said, "By 2:54 p.m. the mob has retreated."[29]

- Zoeann Murphy, Washington Post: "One of the Trump supporters who's been participating in the screaming at police pulls out her cellphone and says: "Oh, my God, guys, listen up. The president tweeted. He says we're a country of law and order, and, um, I think we should go." She read the tweet out loud maybe 15 times. It was so clear that, even if the president wasn't intentionally giving direction, people were receiving it as direction. And then that area dispersed quite a bit."[30]

- Video shows Trump supporters trying to stop the Capitol breach. The video posted by TownHall shows Trump supporters trying to stop a guy from breaking a window and you can hear the crowd booing and a woman shouting "No Antifa, no Antifa." Another yells, "Don't break that window," a person yells.[31]

- Andy Ngo, independent journalist tweeted "#Antifa are continuing to put out the call for riots throughout the U.S. on 20 Jan. These are some of their flyers for Seattle, northern California & Denver." The park in Denver mentioned in this BLM-Antifa poster is one block from the author's apartment.[32]

The media ignores Antifa and BLM, even though they have rioted in America's major cities since May 2020. They have burned city blocks, destroyed innocent people's businesses, committed murder and injured many. Downtown Seattle and Portland are danger zones due to the anarchist groups.

Throughout that entire period there were several Trump rallies with zero property damage or injuries. Yet, the Democrat Congress is illegally trying to impeach Mr. Trump for holding a final rally in D.C.

The Biden swearing-in ceremony went smoothly. There were very few people attending but there were 25,000 National Guard troops. The Antifa-BLM poster calling for protests in Denver is only one of many. That is why the police and Guard were out in force, not because of Trump supporters. The late December warnings from the New York police and Virginia FBI were based on intel they had from anarchist groups like Antifa and BLM.

There were early intel advisories warning of trouble on January 6 and authorities did not prepare. There were early warning intel advisories warning of trouble on January 20 and authorities brought in 25,000 troops! The incompetence in leadership is a given but this type of disparity in preparedness, one wonders if it was intentional.

Were far-right nationalist groups heavily involved in the Capital breach? Yes. Were Antifa and BLM anarchists right there with them? Yes. Yet, the Democrats, media and Washington bureaucracy (i.e., the FBI) are saying it was all Trump and expect us to trust them.

Author's 'D.C. Occupation' Update: The last public report I could find was March 12 when Defense Secretary Austin approved a reduction in force to 2,300.[33]

Chapter 4
The Urge to Splurge

"Throwing money on the fire is normally not the solution to every problem. You put the fire out by listening to the people who are smarter than you are."
—Shahid Khan, owner of Jacksonville Jaguars

"Executive actions are far more ephemeral and easily discarded than legislation, which can set up a whipsaw effect, as each president scrambles to undo the work of his predecessor. Just as Mr. Trump set about reversing as many of President Barack Obama's directives as possible, Mr. Biden is now working to reverse many of Mr. Trump's reversals. With executive orders, there is always another presidential election just a few years off, threatening to upend everything," wrote the NY Times editorial board on January 27th.[1] They are exactly right.

Biden has been in office for 16 days and issued 48 actions (executive orders, proclamations, and memoranda). Ashlyn Still and Adrian Blanco of the Washington Post itemized these actions today, February 5.[2] They note:

- "16 of these actions reversed one or more Trump policies' more than a third have to do with health policy" *(Author's note: Covid related),*

- "14 actions revoke Trump immigration policy,"

- Some "revoked or put up for revision 15 of the energy and environmental actions taken by the Trump administration and reinstated two of President Barack Obama's previously revoked actions."

- "Other actions signed by Biden cover issues of gender and racial equality, the economy, trade, national security and ethics in government."[3]

The Post reporters calculated that, "Biden has signed three times the number of executive orders his recent predecessors had at this point in their presidencies."[4]

No one has yet tried to tabulate the cost burden these actions will place on the American taxpayer, but it will be in the hundreds of billions in 'new' spending, if not more. This is not good for America.

If the editors of the New York Times are alarmed at the pace of Biden executive orders and actions, that should tell you something.

A table of E.O.s from Biden's first three days was provided in Chapter 2. Aside from the Ethics statement, none of these orders will make America better or stronger. Most are bureaucracy building and money wasting. Others will benefit only a few.

Now, after 16 days in office, we have 48 orders, that will not benefit the average American. Even the Times is alarmed! We have 1,424 days left in Biden's presidency. Will American be recognizable by then?

Taxpayers Will have to Splurge for Biden's Surge

A comprehensive report by the Federation for Immigration Reform (FAIR) breaks down the cost of illegal immigration to U.S. taxpayers: $115.9 *billion* annually.[5]

If you don't mind, I'm just going to round it up to $116 billion/year. "Illegal aliens are net consumers of taxpayer-funded services and the limited taxes paid by some segments of the illegal alien population are, in no way, significant enough to offset the growing financial burdens [they] impose on U.S. taxpayers," the report states. The annual bill of $135 billion equates to more than $8,000 per illegal immigrant and dependent, per year. While some illegal immigrants do pay certain taxes, the report states, many employers pay them lower wages, or in cash, and do not deduct their wages from payroll taxes, with most of their income unlikely being reported to the Internal Revenue Service (IRS), FAIR states. Due to these varying factors, FAIR argues the federal, state and local governments are not collecting enough taxes from illegal immigrants to cover the costs of federal benefits they receive."[5]

In spite of the fact that crossing illegally is ILLEGAL, some of Biden's initial actions seek to make it easier for aliens to enter based on 'asylum' claims or just sneak over. Rebecca Beitsch reports for The Hill, "President Biden on his first day in office suspended construction of the border wall pending a review of its legality. The next day the Department of Homeland Security (DHS) suspended Trump's "remain in Mexico" (we address the MPP later in the chapter) policy, which blocked migrants from crossing the border to apply for asylum." The Supreme Court, however, "canceled upcoming hearings challenging President Trump's border wall and asylum policies...," her report continues.[6] Stop and ask yourself why. The Wall and the tougher asylum policies make America safer. They also make the lives of the would-be migrants safer by providing a disincentive. The parents who pay the traffickers to take their children or take the whole family, place their trust in people who will likely rape their daughters and wives on the way and force their sons to join the gang or become mules for illicit drug smuggling. The winners under Biden's plan are the drug gangs and the Democrat Party. The migrants are nothing more than pawns easily sacrificed in a game they do not understand.

U.S. immigration policies have always provided a pathway for people to immigrate. A country that has no secure border is NOT secure. Isn't security a good thing? We live in an age of terrorism, drugs and human (primarily young females) trafficking. Immigration policy should help fight these crimes against humanity. Yet, Biden and the Democrats are against the stronger policies President Trump implemented. The question is why? I have a hard time believing that it is just to gain votes. But no Democrat will stand up and defend these measures that make America safer, in fact, it is quite the opposite.

"President Biden on Tuesday signed an executive order revoking former President Donald Trump's ending of the controversial practice — which allows undocumented migrants to remain in the US while awaiting immigration proceedings," writes Lia Eustachewich of the New York Post on February 5th.[7] This was Obama's 'catch and release' program. The Border Patrol would catch people entering illegally, but Obama required them to be released into the U.S. on the promise they would return for a court hearing. Most then just melt into the population, protected by relatives, join gangs like MS-13 or are sold into prostitution.

The U.S. media does not report the tragic, ugly side of illegal immigration but instead spin the 'catch and release' as humanitarian. I used to help care for an elderly woman in our building. I had a new TV installed for her with voice command remote and all the bells and whistles. She wanted to watch the news one evening and I said let's watch Fox News for a change. She had never watched it. They just happen to air a story about the ugly side of the illegal border crossing, and she got up and ran out of the room saying it is lies, that not what she was told in her Episcopal church. She had been fed the false Democrat narrative for so long, she refused to watch the truth.

"President Biden will raise the cap on refugee admissions to 125,000," reads the New York Post headline on February 4th.[8] Under Obama it was 110,000 then Trump reduced it to 15,000. Biden's plan is over an 800% increase! Biden described it this way, "I'm approving an executive order to begin the hard work of restoring our refugee admissions program to help meet the unprecedented global need," the president said in a speech at the State Department. "It's going to take time to rebuild what has been so badly damaged."[9]

First of all, these people are not refugees. They paid coyotes to bring them to the border. They were not forced out of their country. Yes, there are drug gang problems in Honduras, El Salvador and Nicaragua but why should that be the problem of the United States? Where are the United Nations? Where are the Bill Gates of the world? Are we to import people from every country that has internal law and order problems? This is insanity. Yet, Biden says his motivation is to 'meet the unprecedented global need." He is triggering a domino effect that is going to severely and irreparably, harm every citizen of this country. An extra 110,000 people, who don't speak English, have few transferable work skills, no money, and no place to live are going to come in every year. Biden calls this 'hard work!" No, all he did was write his name, it is you and I who will do the hard work to fork over $880 million more in taxes next year and it will go up every year by the same amount until the 'hard work' is done. How many Americans working entry level jobs today will lose those jobs due to Biden's 'hard work?" What will happen to the competitive wage market? Why do you think it is that today that you never see a Caucasian American with a lawn care business, or a house painting business, ad nauseum?

Killing the Golden Goose

Biden, the Democrats, and their media lackies are killing the Golden Goose with their splurging. The money they spend does not grow on trees, it grows on the backs of every working American, and the actions Biden is taking is going to kill that goose. You have voted, you are now expendable. By the time the next election rolls around in 2024, he will have let in 500,000 people (4 x 125,000). They are going to need jobs, where are those jobs going to come from?

[**Update May 2022** – Customs & Border Patrol encountered a record 234,088 trying to enter the U.S. illegally during the month of April 2022. usatoday.com/story/news/politics/2022/05/18/immigration-border-encounters-april-biden/9813204002/?gnt-cfr=1]

One More Giant Splurge for Mankind

The House Democrats just passed a $1.9 Trillion stimulus plan. "The House gave final approval on Friday to a budget blueprint that included President Biden's $1.9 trillion stimulus plan, advancing it over unanimous Republican opposition," wrote Jim Tankersley and associates of the New York Times.[9]

Biden justified this unnecessary spending this way, "I know some in Congress think we've already done enough to deal with the crisis in the country. That's not what I see. I see enormous pain in this country. A lot of folks out of work. A lot of folks going hungry." Well, Mr. Biden should get some new glasses. Here are the facts:

- Democrat Governors have kept their states locked down unnecessarily for almost a full year. Over 200,000 small businesses will never come back, and the over one million plus jobs they supported evaporated due to these lockdowns.

- The mortality rate of Covid-19 is like that of the seasonal flu, about 0.2 percent. It is selectively hard on those over 70 or with comorbidities. The survival rate for everyone else is 99.8%

- A shut down was never needed. The economy was decimated unnecessarily and maybe intentionally.

- Unemployment prior to the lockdowns was 3.6%, it moved to a peak of 14.7% in April and is now 6.7%[10]

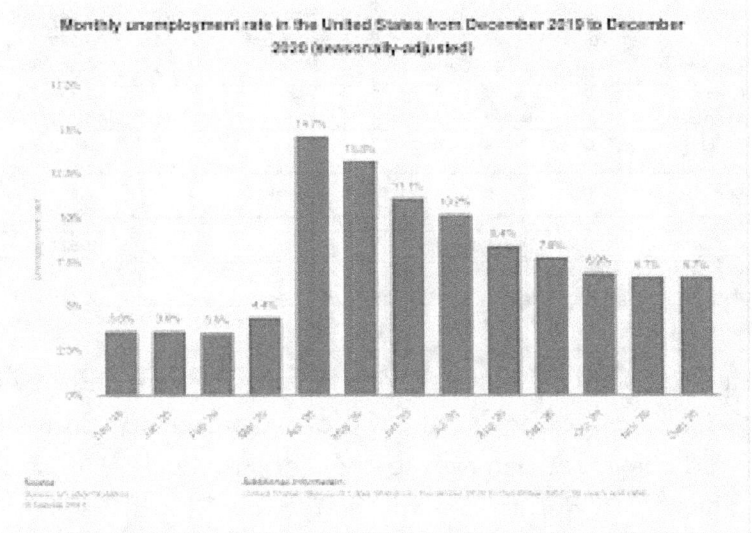

Figure 8. U.S. Unemployment Trends Source: Statista[10]
Dec 2019 is the 1st bar (unemployment was 3.6%),
Apr 2020 is 5th bar (UE 14.7%), last bar is Dec 2020 (UE 6.7%).

State leadership is everything. The states with the highest unemployment, as of December 2020, are all Democrat run states. The top 10 states with lowest unemployment are all Republican run states (Table 2).

Author's Comment: Earth to Democrats – Einstein is misquoted as saying, "Insanity is doing the same thing over and over but expecting different results." I will not debate whether it is 'insane' or just 'stupid.' No one with neurons still firing will pour boiling water on their bare skin twice. But Democrats continue to elect politicians who 'burn' them time and again!

Table 2. Worst 10 & Best 10 States: Unemployment Rate (as of December 2020)

Rank	Worst States	% Un-employed	C-19 Deaths*	Govenor's Party	Rank	Best States	% Un-employed	C-19 Deaths*	Govenor's Party
50	Hawaii	9.3	418	Democrat	1	S. Dakota	3.0	1,809	Republican
49	Nevada	9.2	4,556	Democrat	2	Nebraska	3.0	1,968	Republican
48	California	9.0	44,148	Democrat	3	Vermont	3.1	183	Republican
47	Colorado	8.4	5,731	Democrat	4	Iowa	3.1	5,108	Republican
46	N. Mexico	8.2	3,399	Democrat	5	Utah	3.6	1,736	Republican
45	New York	8.2	44,979	Democrat	6	Kansas	3.8	4,111	Republican
44	Rhode Isl.	8.1	2,212	Democrat	7	Alabama	3.9	8,515	Republican
43	Connecticut	8.0	7,214	Democrat	8	N Hampshire	4.0	1,104	Republican
42	N Jersey	7.6	21,989	Democrat	9	N. Dakota	4.1	1,428	Republican
41	Illinois	7.6	21,738	Democrat	10	Arkansas	4.2	5,076	Republican
Total U.S. Deaths >>		474,933	156,384	33%				21,621	5%

Data Source: Stastista [11], Table created by author.
*C-19 Deaths from Worldometer.com Feb. 7, 2021; https://www.worldometers.info/coronavirus/country/us/

Not surprisingly, the states with the most severe shutdowns, as denoted at the bottom of the Oxford Coronavirus containment index, did the most damage to their economy. The most severe restrictions for a Republican run state was Ohio (it is 3 notches below New Jersey).

Most states implemented moderately strong restrictions in April (Figure 8), because little was known about the virus, at that point. The poorly managed Democrat run states, however, maintained the restrictions through November. Why? It was clear that people over 70 and/or with comorbidities were the 'at risk' population. Republican states recognized this, took steps to protect the 'at risk' segment and opened back up. The Democrat states chose to retain severe restrictions (see Figure 8 for results).

Today, (Feb. 7, 2021) New York has 9.4% (44,979) of all the deaths in the country due to Covid-19! The Governor forced people who had not fully recovered from Covid-19 into nursing homes, thus transmitting the virus to innocent residents. The Javits Center had beds. President Trump had sent the Navy Hospital ship USNS Comfort to New York harbor. New York was never in jeopardy of running out of medical care capacity. But Governor Cuomo sent these people into nursing homes, many more died and Hollywood gave him an Emmy!

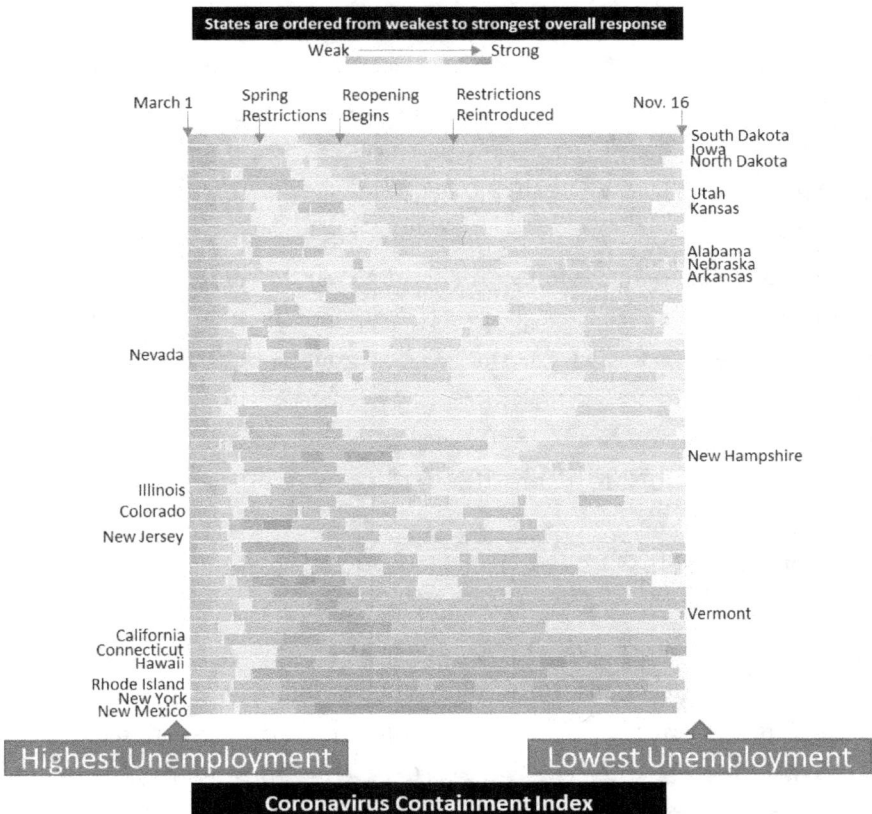

Figure 9. Economic Impact of Lockdowns. The highest unemployment is in Democrat run states with severe shutdown restrictions. Lowest unemployment is in Republican run states with less draconian restrictions.
(Employment data from Statista[11] and Coronavirus containment index was developed by University of Oxford – the 'Oxford Covid-19 Government Response Tracker' and was published in the *New York Times*, November 18, 2020.[12])

California is right behind New York with 44,148 deaths. In fact, when deaths are totaled for the Democrat states with the highest unemployment, we find they collectively accounted for 33% of all Covid-19 deaths (Table 2). The Republican states with the lowest unemployment accounted for only 5%. The headline of the NY Times Nov. 18 article was, 'States That Imposed Few Restrictions Now Have the Worst Outbreaks.' What is the Times selling here?

The article begins, "Coronavirus cases are rising in almost every U.S. state. But the surge is worst now in places where leaders neglected to keep up forceful virus containment efforts or failed to implement basic measures like mask mandates in the first place, according to a New York Times analysis of data from the University of Oxford."[13] They are talking about 'cases', as determined by a positive PCR test. The way these PCR tests are run, with 45 cycles of amplification, they give false positives 90% of the time. So, the case numbers are grossly inflated. The New York Times knows this because they reported on the inaccuracy of PCR testing back in August.[14]

Trust Me Update – Jan. 20, 2021

World Health Org issues notice on PCR test accuracy.

"WHO reminds IVD (In Vitro Diagnostic Medical Device) users that disease prevalence alters the predictive value of test results; as disease prevalence decreases, the risk of false positive increases (2). This means that the probability that a person who has a positive result (SARS-CoV-2 detected) is truly infected with SARS-CoV-2 decreases as prevalence decreases, irrespective of the claimed specificity."

"WHO guidance Diagnostic testing for SARS-CoV-2 states that careful interpretation of weak positive results is needed (1). The cycle threshold (Ct) needed to detect virus is inversely proportional to the patient's viral load. Where test results do not correspond with the clinical presentation, a new specimen should be taken and retested using the same or different NAT technology." WHO Information Notice for IVD Users 2020/05, Jan. 20, 2021who.int/news/item/20-01-2021-who-information-no tice-for-ivd-users-2020-05

The progressive media, medical intelligentsia and Democrats have been peddling 'case' numbers as if they mean something. The human tragedy suffered because of this canard is immeasurable. The economic tragedy is terrible, but the human tragedy is beyond the pale of all morality.

"President Biden pledged to act aggressively to get the coronavirus pandemic under control, and he used his first two days in office to issue some limited mask mandates that his predecessor had long resisted. Yet it remains largely up to state and local officials to determine what restrictions, if any, to impose to slow new infections," begins the NY Times February 5, 2021, article titled, 'See Coronavirus Restrictions and Mask Mandates for All 50 States'.[15] When you check this article, you will find it provides a nice visual status on state-by-state restrictions and mask mandates. It is well done. It also provides the case load curves for each state, which is also informative. Their explanations and comments leave a lot to be desired, the introductory sentence above is an example. The most important take away, however, are the 'case' curves. These are PCR cases, thus not a real reflection of 'sick' people. But note: these are typical curves for the flu. Every state is very similar, but state restrictions are not similar. So, the take-away, is the restrictions are not making an impact. Zero, zilch, nada!

[**2022 Update**: Research has now proven that the lockdowns did not stop virus spreads nor protect people from becoming infected. washingtonpolicy.org/publications/detail/comprehensive-research-finds-that-lockdowns-dont-work]

Trust Me Update – Feb. 11, 2021

New York Governor, Andrew Cuomo covered up the nursing home death toll because the Dept. of Justice had advised the state of a possible investigation, admits Secretary to the Governor Melissa DeRosa.

State Health Commissioner, Howard Zucker, said on Jan. 27 nursing home deaths were 8,711, The next day, NY Attorney General, Letitia James, said it could be 50% higher. Zucker responded that the real number was 12,743.

Cuomo responded in a press conference on Jan. 29, "Who cares [if they] died in the hospital, died in a nursing home? They died."

In a letter to state lawmakers, on Feb. 10, Zucker revised the total nursing home deaths again to 13,297, but when assisted living/adult care facilities are added the total jumps to 15,049.

DeRosa told fellow Democrats they were sorry for the political inconvenience it caused them. "So, we do apologize," she said. "I do understand the position that you were put in. I know that it is not fair. It was not our intention to put you in that political position with the Republicans."

NY Post, Feb. 11, 2021 nypost.com/2021/02/11/cuomo-aide-admits-they-hid-nursing-home-data-from-feds

[**2022 Update**: Andrew Cuomo was forced to resign as Governor on August 10, 2021, due to numerous charges of sexual harassment. It seems sexual harassment is a worse crime than sending 15,000 seniors to the deaths. nytimes.com/2021/08/10/nyregion/andrew-cuomo-resigns.html. He nor his state health director has been charged with the deaths of over 15,000 nursing home residents.]

Follow the Science

"Novel coronavirus is believed to be tiny enough (0.08–0.14 μm) to penetrate through face mask, thus protection offered by cloth mask may be too low. However, the use of cloth face mask in community has been recommended by the United States Centre for Disease Control and Prevention and regulatory bodies of other countries. There is paucity of literature on efficacy of cloth face mask in preventing SARS-CoV-2 infection transmission; thus, this review aims to update the available most recent evidence on efficacy of cloth face masks in prevention of viral infection transmission", writes Suresh K. Sharma in the July 2020 peer reviewed article titled, *'Efficacy of cloth face mask in prevention of novel coronavirus infection transmission: A systematic review and meta-analysis.* [16]

Please note the first sentence. "Novel coronavirus is believed to be tiny enough (0.08–0.14 μm or micrometers or microns) to penetrate through face mask." There are 1,000 μm in a millimeter (mm). Look at your ruler. In the case of Covid-19, we are talking 8/100ths of a micrometer or 80-140 nanometers (nm). That's pretty small. Anyway, the diameter of a human cell is 25 μm, or 178 to 312 times larger than Covid-19.

The meta-study concluded, "Cloth face masks have limited efficacy in combating viral infection transmission. However, it may be used in closed, crowded indoor, and outdoor public spaces involving physical proximity to prevent spread of SARS-CoV-2 infection."[17] Whoops. This article is posted on the NIH website. Dr. Fauci is a Director at the NIH.

But, there's more!

The Center for Infectious Disease and Research Policy (CIDRAP) published a commentary by two experts titled, 'Masks-for-all for COVID-19 not based on sound data', on April 1, 2020. It was not an April Fool's joke these two ladies are serious.[18]

Drs. Brosseau and Sietsema, added an update on July 16, 2020 saying, "The authors and CIDRAP have **received requests in recent weeks to remove this article from the CIDRAP website**. Reasons have included: (1) we don't truly know that cloth masks (face coverings) are not effective, since the data are so limited, (2) wearing a cloth mask or face covering is better than doing nothing, (3) the article is being used by individuals and groups to support non-mask wearing where mandated and (4) there are now many modeling studies suggesting that cloth masks or face coverings could be effective at flattening the curve and preventing many cases of infection."[19] They don't say who was asking them to stand-down, but they stood their ground. This is uncommon valor these days, so I am going to quote them extensively, because you need to hear what they have to say.

"We agree that the data supporting the effectiveness of a cloth mask or face covering are very limited. We do, however, have data from laboratory studies that indicate -cloth masks or face coverings offer very low filter collection efficiency for the smaller inhalable particles we believe are largely responsible for transmission, particularly from pre- or asymptomatic individuals who are not coughing or sneezing. At the time we wrote this article, we were unable to locate any well-performed studies of cloth mask leakage when worn on the face—either inward or outward leakage. As far as we know, these data are still lacking."[20] You go girls!

"The guidelines from *the Centers for Disease Control and Prevention (CDC) for face coverings initially did not have any citations for studies of cloth material efficiency or fit*, but some references have been added since the guidelines were first posted.

We reviewed these and found that many employ very crude, non-standardized methods (Anfinrud 2020, Davies 2013, Konda 2020, Aydin 2020, Ma 2020) or are not relevant to cloth face coverings because they evaluate respirators or surgical masks (Leung 2020, Johnson 2009, Green 2012)."[21]

"*The CDC failed to reference* the National Academies of Sciences Rapid Expert Consultation on the Effectiveness of Fabric Masks for the COVID-19 Pandemic (NAS 2020), which concludes, "The evidence from…laboratory filtration studies suggests that such fabric masks may reduce the transmission of larger respiratory droplets. There is little evidence regarding the transmission of small, aerosolized particulates of the size potentially exhaled by asymptomatic or pre-symptomatic individuals with COVID-19." As well, the CDC neglected to mention a well-done study of cloth material filter performance by Rengasamy et al (2014), which we reviewed in our article."[22] The italics are mine, for emphasis.

"Wearing a cloth mask or face covering could be better than doing nothing, but we simply don't know at this point."[23] Honesty is so refreshing, isn't it?

"We are concerned that many people do not understand the very limited degree of protection a cloth mask or face covering likely offers as source control for people located nearby."[24]

"In summary, though we support mask wearing by the general public, we continue to conclude that cloth masks and face coverings are likely to have limited impact on lowering COVID-19 transmission, because they have minimal ability to prevent the emission of small particles, offer limited personal protection with respect to small particle inhalation, and should not be recommended as a replacement for physical distancing or reducing time in enclosed spaces with many potentially infectious people. We are very concerned about messaging that suggests cloth masks or face coverings can replace physical distancing. We also worry that the public doesn't understand the limitations of cloth masks and face coverings when we observe how many people wear their mask under their nose or even under their mouth, remove their masks when talking to someone nearby, or fail to practice physical distancing when wearing a mask."[25]

> **[2022 Update:** A Federal judge in Florida stuck down the CDC requirement to wear face masks on airplanes on April 18, 2022. statnews.com/2022/04/18/federal-judge-voids-us-mask-mandate-for-planes-other-travel.
> The CDC, however, on May 3rd issued a statement "recommending" people continue to wear masks. They provided no scientific study or evidence to support this recommendation. reuters.com/world/us/us-cdc-says-travelers-should-still-wear-masks-airplanes-2022-05-03]

Can We Get an Amen?

"The protective capabilities offered by N95 masks are largely attributed to the masks' removal of more than 95% of all particles with an average diameter that is 300 nm or less. It has been estimated that N95 masks can filter approximately 99.8% of particles with an average diameter of 100 nm. In this aspect, the size of a virus particle largely determines how individuals can protect themselves and those around them from acquiring SARS-CoV-2", writes Benedette Cuffari of Medical and Life Science News.[26]

Conclusion: If you are not around people who are coughing, sneezing, yelling in your face and you are not in an elevator, a mask will not help, unless it is an N95.

Weren't we Talking About Splurging?

Sorry for all the Science, but we really should 'follow' 'it', and you can't follow 'it' if you don't' know what 'it' is! Sadly, we are not going to get 'it' from Fauci, Biden, the CDC, the FDA or, in most cases, your personal physician.

We began this chapter addressing the 'Splurge' of wasteful spending Biden is going to unleash in the name of 'Science', helping others and social justice. The country would be better off, if they just took our money, put it in a big pile and burned it. At least that would generate some heat and give us a fire on which we could roast hot dogs. Instead, they will create new bureaucracies that will reduce our freedoms and require annual feeding at ever increasing rates.

The Buckets of Splurge

Covid-19 Relief. The country does not need another trillion-dollar stimulus. But the authoritarian Democrat run states do need it. The rest of the country, the states and citizens that managed the pandemic in the right way, will now have to pick up the tab for the idiots that did not. It's nothing more than welfare for certain states earned through incompetence. Cuomo should get an Oscar for his incompetence.

> **Trust Me Update – Feb. 26, 2021**
>
> Democrats propose $1.9 billion Covid Stimulus.
>
> Joe Biden's bold, aggressive leadership is on display, as, after his afternoon nap, the House Democrats proposed a $1.9 billion Covid Stimulus bill (called 'The American Rescue Plan'). They vote on it today, Feb. 26.
>
> The genius of the plan is that only 9% is Covid related!
>
> See Chapter 12 for the details.

Paris Agreement and Climate Protection Money

The lie of climate alarmism has become an entrenched dogma of the progressive religion. This is why the Priestly Order of Climatism will not debate the topic. "The Science is settled," they proclaim. My formal education resulted in a professorship at a major university but not in physics or climatology. Yet, I can destroy climate alarmism in 5 minutes to anyone who is not yet totally brainwashed.

The driver here is globalism. The sponsors of globalism are:

1. Many in the billionaire class and their NGOs (non-government organizations, ie the World Wildlife Fund, the Environmental Defense Fund, the Nature Conservancy, Greenpeace, Center for Environmental Research and Conservation and the Sierra Club, just to name a few.)

2. Global corporations (their motivation is the cheapest labor possible)

3. Neo-Malthusians (ie those who believe the earth cannot continue to support a growing population),

4. The 'suckling' class (anyone or any institution that derives is livelihood from the climate alarmism lie – for example, academia is attached to the government underbelly like a sucker fish.)

5. Walking-dead media who have become automatons and can no longer think for themselves.

6. Teacher unions (may be the most dangerous because they dictate what our children are taught).

Social Justice & Equity

This component of the progressive belief system has no basis in fact at all. A more accurate description of it is 'Class Warfare'. The haves versus the have-nots. The 'Fairness Doctrine'. The Robinhood protocol. Whatever you want to call it, it is taking assets from a group that worked hard for them and giving them to a group who sat on their ass. This has nothing to do with race, skin color or ethnicity, if it did, the black community would have benefitted by now from Lyndon Johnson's 1965 civil rights act.

The Welfare State we have in place is there to ensure the recipients continue to vote for the people who send them money for doing nothing. What has been the result? Unwed mother births have skyrocketed to the point where it has become a major sub-culture. Black women, in some cases, are told by their Mommas to have more children to bring in more money. To say this is a highly inflammatory issue would be an understatement. Yet, it is the elephant in the room. There are many strong and honest leaders in the black community working to restore the nuclear family culture, but they are not funded by the billionaire class. They are on their own and thus losing ground.

The cost of social justice

Personally, this category is the most disgusting because it is dishonest, coercive, (vote for me and I'll cancel your student debt) and unjust (soothsayers entice the vulnerable with empty promises). The progressives are the new plantation owners.

The left always has a label and a slogan to divide people. Conservatives didn't invent political correctness, nor derogatory labels (white supremacist, people of color, gender neutral, Islamophobe, xenophobe, etc.), it was the progressive academy. Human-centric special interest groups were all created by progressives (women, LGBTQ, people of color, first nation people, etc). It is all 'doublespeak', Orwell's term to indicate the true meaning is exactly the opposite of the term used. Progressives are regressive, democrats are authoritarians, justice means injustice, fairness means unfairness, science means non-science, *ad nauseam*.

The Democrats need the votes and their charlatan, pied pipers ensure they are delivered by playing the people for fools. They get rich and the people get the shaft, as usual. Democrats create a governing system that fosters dependency and thus enslaves the people. Get out of line and we'll cut you off. To enslave another person through deception is worse than the slavery of the old south, which was forced. The programs launched by progressives always have strings attached. These strings (requirements that must be met to stay in good graces) are the new 'chains' that ensure the cycle is perpetuated. Everyone is offered a choice in America:

- Freedom – to be their own person, make their own way, enjoy the self-satisfaction that comes from work and accomplishment by merit, to raise a family and achieve the classical American dream. Or …

- Slavery – the sacrifice of self-determination for the promise of eternal care from the government.

So, the real cost of 'social justice' is self-respect, honor, trust, equality, the future generations, and even life itself. These attributes are among the many foundational principles and values upon which America was built.

When Democrats speak against immigration restrictions, deportation, etc, they flout the rule of law. They trade American safety, job security, quality of life to gain votes. The lives lost by the innocents kidnapped by drug lords, girls sold as sex slaves, lives lost in America from illicit drugs are nothing but collateral damage. Trump's wall would reduce that carnage and save lives on both sides of the border; a point that is lost in the progressive greed for votes.

Illegal Immigration

We have already reviewed the monetary cost of Biden's recent actions, about $880 million a year in new spending just to support the 110,000 new refugees per year. But the human toll is worse. Look at the website: immigrationshumancost.org. This organization catalogues the human tragedy with one sickening story after another. Innocent people sacrificed by the left on the altar of vote-getting.

Christopher Giles, BBC, updated the world on the status of President Trump's border wall, "... 452 miles (727 km) in total, according to the latest US Customs and Border Protection (CBP) information (4 January 2021). However, only 80 miles of new barriers have been built where there were none before—that includes 47 miles of primary wall, and 33 miles of secondary wall built to reinforce the initial barrier. The vast majority of the 452 miles is replacing existing structures at the border that had been built by previous US administrations."[27] The fact that the 'existing structures' were porous is lost on Giles. He does give us a nice chart showing how few illegals were detained by Obama, which was bad for America. But it seems to have started in the Bush years. Let's take a look.

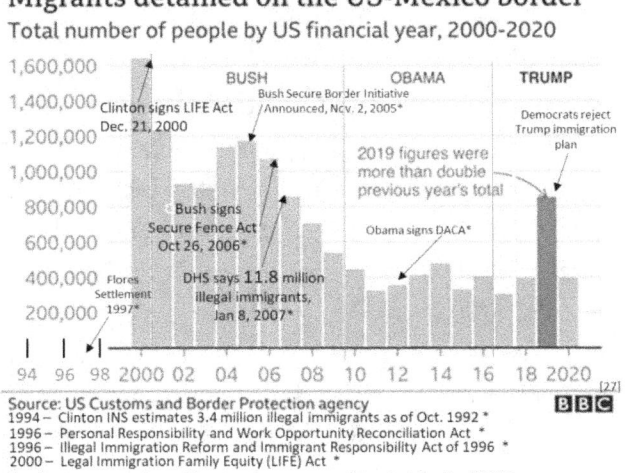

Figure 10. Annual migrants stopped from entering the U.S. illegally

In 1994, the Immigration and Naturalization Service (now a part of the Dept of Homeland Security), gave the first ever estimate of illegal immigrants living in the United States. It was 3.4 million.[28] In 1996, with the leadership of Newt Gingrich, Speaker of the House, Congress passed, and President Clinton signed two important laws:

- Personal Responsibility and Work Opportunity Reconciliation Act of 1996. Signed August 1996. The law was a cornerstone of the Newt Gingrich Republican Party's "Contract with America," and also fulfilled Clinton's campaign promise to "end welfare as we know it."[29] The new law required work in exchange for time-limited, welfare assistance. It also included provisions that would deny most forms of public assistance to most legal immigrants for five years or until they attain citizenship.[30]

- Illegal Immigration Reform and Immigrant Responsibility Act of 1996. Signed September 1996. President Clinton said this law would strengthen "the rule of law by cracking down on illegal immigration at the border, in the workplace, and in the criminal justice system – without punishing those living in the United States legally."[31] It passed overwhelmingly in both the House and the Senate.

- These were two of the most important laws Clinton would sign, but he did so under duress, the election was only two months away. His first two years in office were so scandalous, that the Republicans took the majority in both the Senate and the House in 1994. These laws were part of the Republican 'Contract with America' and were good for Americans.

Clinton was reelected in November 1996, thanks to an extraordinarily stupid Republican party that nominated the robotic Bob Dole. It didn't help that successful billionaire businessman Ross Perot decided to run as a third-party candidate. Ralph Nader also peeled off some votes, but Perot used the debate over the North American Free Trade Agreement to slam both Clinton and Dole. Perot was right but being right rarely matters until the history books are written. Too many people are swayed by charisma and Dole did not get the charisma gene. Clinton, on the other hand, could sell ice cream to Eskimos. Even without Perot, Dole was so weak, Clinton would have won anyway, barely. If you add Perot's vote count to Dole, he would have gained 99 electoral votes for a total of 258, Clinton would have had 280. The popular vote would have been close to a virtual tie.[32]

The Republicans held majorities in both houses of Congress, but lost seats in the House. Speaker Gingrich was weakened, and Clinton gained confidence and the media began to attack Gingrich.

In February of 2000, the AFL-CIO executive council came out for amnesty for illegal immigrants.[33] Clinton was a lame-duck, and his V.P. Al Gore was making a strong run for the presidency. The strategy to raise an issue to curry favor with Latino Americans was obvious. Amnesty was a step too far and George W. Bush prevailed by the narrowest of margins and a decision by the Supreme Court. But Clinton and the Democrats would set the stage for the mass illegal immigration and weak border control George Bush inherited. On December 21, 2000, the 2000 Legal Immigration Family Equity (LIFE) Act by narrow margins. Section 245(i) of the act, allowed persons with immigrant visas to apply for adjustment of status. Section 245(i) allowed those who had entered illegally or violated a previous status forgiveness. It also created a new 'non-immigrant' status for spouses and minor children of lawful permanent residents (ie legal visa holders) to be admitted to work in the United States while they are waiting for a visa number.[34]

This mistake built off the mistakes of the Lyndon B. Johnson 1965 Immigration and Nationality Act and the George H.W. Bush 1990 Immigration Act. There is a need for legal immigration, obviously. The 1965 and 1990 Acts, I believe, were mostly well intentioned and, to a great extent, intended to retard illegal immigration. The well-worn maxim, 'give them an inch and they'll take a mile' is appropriate. When people violate the law in mass numbers and are then forgiven out of human compassion and advocation by those who have something to gain, it only incentivizes further violations. So, the pump was primed before George W. Bush took office and the steady decrease in apprehensions at the border decreased and illegal entry increased. It also tremendously expands legal 'chain migration'.

One final comment. Note on the graph that 3.4 million illegals were estimated in 1994, which grew to 11.8 million by beginning of 2007. Biden and the Democrats continue to claim the 11.8 million number is accurate, 14 years later. "C'mon man, trust me!"

Most parents teach their children is it wrong to cheat, to lie, to steal, to lay false blame and to harm another person.

This book has already given you several examples of the Biden administration, the Democrats and their media surrogates violating what their parents tried to teach them. Let's see how their words and actions line up with facts regarding immigration.

Route of barrier between US and Mexico

Figure 11. Man-made barriers on U.S. – Mexican border as of January 20, 2021.[35]

Trump Action: Between May 31 and October 28, 2019, the Trump administration had signed 11 agreements with Honduras, Guatemala, and El Salvador with the stated purpose:

> "...to develop an economically vibrant region. Together, DHS and its partners are developing a safer and more prosperous region so that Central Americans can feel confident in creating futures in their home countries, rather than putting their lives in the hands of smugglers and criminal organizations to make the dangerous journey across the U.S. border."[36]

Biden's response: On February 6, 2021, "Secretary of State Tony Blinken announced the Biden administration has terminated agreements between the United States and northern triangle countries that significantly cut down on asylum fraud, which caused previous illegal immigration crises on the U.S. southern border with

Mexico."[37] Note he says the signed agreements with the 3 countries 'caused' the immigration crisis. It is another blatant lie, easily disproven.

A Few Facts

- The 2019 fiscal year (Oct. 1, 2018-Sep. 30, 2019): 457,871 migrant family units were apprehended, up 406% from 2018.[38] (Note: a family unit is at least one adult/one child.)

- Family units from Guatemala, Honduras and El Salvador accounted for almost 92%.[39]

- Unaccompanied minors apprehended spiked in 2019, to 72,873 after 11 months, a 60% jump from 2018. The previous full year record was 68,631 (2014). The suspected cause of the surge was belief that the lax enforcement over the last 8 years would be ended by Trump. Vicki Gass, Oxfam expert said, "I've heard people saying that these smugglers are seeing a closing window and are offering deals because that window is closing. So, 'If you take your 5-year-old daughter, I will give you a 30% discount.'"[40]

- Historically, 90% of illegal immigrants came from Mexico. They were single adult men, typically seeking work. They paid smugglers (coyotes) to guide them.[41]

- In 1985, liberal groups sued the federal government for alleged mistreatment of alien minors in detention facilities (notably a 15-year-old Salvadoran girl named Jenny Flores). This led to a consent decree, aka 'the Flores settlement' with the Clinton administration, in 1997.[42]

- The litigant groups (plaintiffs) were: The Center for Human Rights and Constitutional Law (Los Angeles, CA) and National Center for Youth Law (San Francisco, CA). Assisting the plaintiffs: ACLU of Southern California and Streich Lang (Tucson, AZ). The Defendant (the United States) agreed to pay plaintiff attorney fees totaling $374,110.09 (from the certified settlement agreement).[43]

- Clinton officials indicated they were partially motivated by a desire to cooperate with the activist plaintiffs to loosen asylum rules.[44]

- The Flores settlement resulted in detention standards for unaccompanied alien children (UACs).[45]

- The Central District Court of California, presiding judge Dolly Gee, gradually loosened the definition of UACs to include all minors, accompanied by their parents or not, and limited detention to no more than 20 days.[46]

- In recent years, illegal immigrants, aided by progressives, learned to game the system by claiming a credible fear at home (the initial step in an asylum request). 2018 asylum requests jumped 67% versus 2017 (Trump's first year). They are up 10-fold from George Bush's last year (2008).[47]

A few weeks ago, Mario Durate, former head of Guatemalan intelligence, told investigative journalist Sara Carter, "the people using the migrants and pulling the strings, "are the real criminals, because you're talking about kids, children, women, young women, being exposed to all these pedophiles, these heartless cartel members. You just have to look at Homeland Security statistics on their websites. How many of those Latino girls that reached the border were raped multiple times with STDs (sexually transmitted diseases), some of them even pregnant? That's what these kids are exposed to. And then you're talking about the elderly, most of them don't make it all the way over there."[48]

From 2009 to the signing of the agreements with El Salvador, Guatemala and Honduras, the inhumanity against the trusting migrants was horrendous. The trafficking and drug organizations were the only winners.

Trust Me Update - February 17, 2021

Protectors of the children. Results of Democrat policies:

1. "Women and girls, some as young as 14, were coerced or abducted and then smuggled across the southern border to perform sex acts for willing buyers. Some victims were forced into sex as many as 45 times daily. These women and girls did not voluntarily enter into prostitution; their captors sold them into the sex trade through beatings, sexual assaults, and threats to their families and children at home."[49]

2. "CHICAGO - A small but growing number of teens and even younger children who think they were born the wrong sex are getting support from parents and from doctors who give them

sex-changing treatments, according to reports in the medical journal Pediatrics."[50]

3. Nearly 9 in 10 parents are worried about their children falling behind academically due to coronavirus-related school closures, ranking higher than any other financial or socioemotional concern. 8 in 10 parents say their child(ren) are experiencing heightened stress levels and about half (51%) of parents reported challenges with distance learning."[51]

Trump Action: Implemented the Migrant Protection Protocol. "The Migrant Protection Protocols (MPP) are a U.S. Government action whereby certain foreign individuals entering or seeking admission to the U.S. from Mexico – illegally or without proper documentation – may be returned to Mexico and wait outside of the U.S. for the duration of their immigration proceedings, where Mexico will provide them with all appropriate humanitarian protections for the duration of their stay."[52]

"Misguided court decisions and outdated laws have made it easier for illegal aliens to enter and remain in the U.S. if they are adults who arrive with children, unaccompanied alien children, or individuals who fraudulently claim asylum."[53]

"Historically, illegal aliens to the U.S. were predominantly single adult males from Mexico who were generally removed within 48 hours if they had no legal right to stay; currently over 60% are family units and unaccompanied children and 60% are non-Mexican. In FY17, U.S. Customs and Border Protection (CBP) officers apprehended 94,285 family units from Honduras, Guatemala, and El Salvador (Northern Triangle) at the Southern border."[54]

Biden's Response: On inauguration day, Biden suspended new enrollments in the MPP.[55] On February 12, the Dept. of Homeland Security (DHS) announced they would begin process the approximately 25,000 migrants waiting in Mexico for asylum hearings. Alejandro Mayorkas, secretary of the DHS said they will start processing approximately 300 people per day at three ports of entry.[56]

A Few Facts

- Assuming that means 100 people/day/port of entry, it will take 83 days for a new 25,000 people to enter the country.

- Kingsville, Texas has 25,605 people, so in 83 days, Biden will create a new city the size of Kingsville. The only thing is everyone in Kingsville today speaks English.

- Unemployment in Kingsville back in February 2020 was 4.4%. The Trump economy was at full steam. Then Covid hit and it went to 13.5%. Today it is down to 8.4%.[57]

- This is the situation throughout the country.

Biden's action indicates he believes it is a good idea to bring in 25,000 non-English speakers with few skills. How is that good for America? The Constitution says the Presidential priorities should be the safety, health and welfare of Americans. His actions are clearly counter with Constitutional directives.

Here are quotes from the Biden Whitehouse on February 2, 2021:

QUOTE 1. "Today's actions build on executive actions the President took his first day in office, including steps to preserve and fortify protections for Dreamers, end the Muslim and Africa ban, halt border wall construction and protect Liberian nationals living and working in our country."[58] Four things are mentioned: 'Dreamer protection', Muslim/African ban, the border wall and protecting Liberian nationals. Let's review the facts:

Perspective on Dreamers & DACA

Fact #1 - The Development, Relief, and Education for Immigrant Minors Act (DREAM) was a bi-partisan bill introduced in the Senate on April 1, 2001 but did not pass.[59]

Fact #2 - Since 2001, bipartisan attempts have come close to passage but fallen short. The text of the bill has been placed in other immigration bills (i.e., Comprehensive Immigration Reform Act of 2006 & Comprehensive Immigration Reform Act of 2007) without success.[60]

Fact #3 - President Obama signed the Deferred Action for Childhood Arrivals (DACA) Executive Order June 15, 2012. The primary purpose of both DREAM & DACA was to protect young people who were brought into the United States illegally. "74% of Americans favor a law that would provide permanent legal status to immigrants who came to the U.S. illegally **as children**."[61]

Fact #4 - DACA recipients Sep. 4, 2017 were 689,800. DACA recipients Mar. 31, 2020 were 643,560.[62, 63] Work permits granted is approximately 800,000. Not all signed up for DACA.

Fact #5 - September 5, 2017, Attorney General Jeff Sessions announced the DACA Executive Order would be allowed to expire in 2018.[64] "Trump has urged Congress to pass legislation by March

2018 that would give legal status to unauthorized immigrants enrolled in DACA."[65]

The Trump administration thought that the 5th Circuit's ruling against 'Deferred Action for Parents of U.S. Citizens and Lawful Permanent Residents' (DAPA) and the Supreme Court's non-decision (4-4 tie) on DAPA, indicated how SCOTUS would rule on DACA (also an executive order).[66] DAPA would have allowed up to 5 million adults, who had entered illegally, to become permanent residents (amnesty). To qualify they had to have lived here continuously since 2010 (impossible to disprove) and have had a child in the U.S. It took advantage of the 'anchor baby' loophole.

The country should not be ruled by Executive Orders. If Congress will not act, then we might as well abolish them and have the Executive and the Courts. This is a Republican and Democrat problem. There are really great people in Congress but there are too many 'my-way-or-the-highway' ideologues and swamp creatures. Trump was not a politician. He would not play the game and thus had to be aggressive. This turned many people off because of style. It also gave the media lots of ammo. He thought he had a winning hand in the immigration question and could force Congress to do their jobs. It was the right thing to do. But, in this case, the Democrats would not play.

Fact #6 – Pew Research reported in June 2019, "About 3.9 million kindergarten through 12th-grade students in U.S. public and private schools in 2014 – or 7.3% of the total – were children of unauthorized immigrants, according to new Pew Research Center estimates based on government data."[67] This confirms the 'anchor baby' issue.

Fact #7 – "About 250,000 babies were born to unauthorized immigrant parents in the United States in 2016."[68] This is a new Buffalo, NY every year.

Fact #8 - On June 18, 2020, the US. Supreme Court issued a 5-4 decision against the Trump administration's expiration of the DACA executive order. Chief Justice Roberts sides with liberal colleagues.[69]

Fact #9 - In January 2018, Trump compromised with the Democrats, agreeing to essentially grant amnesty to 1.8 million illegal immigrants. He also allowed 'chain migration to continue for a while, with an eventual termination. The Democrats would compromise by ending the 'draft lottery', which allows 50,000 immigrants per year and agree to funding for a border wall. The Democrats would not budge[70]

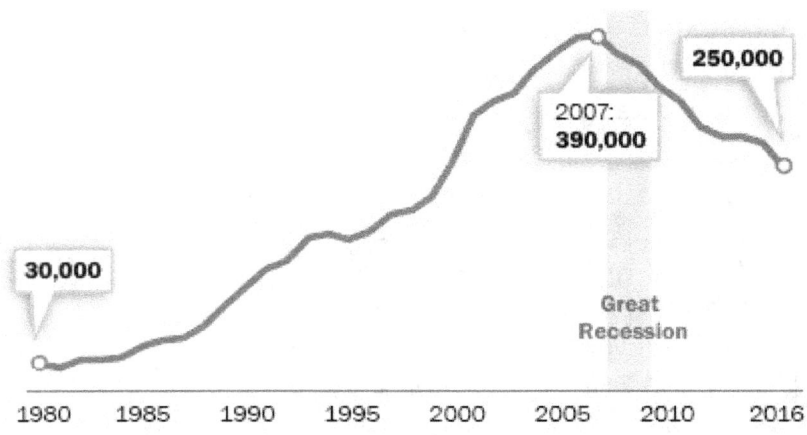

Figure 12. Trends in births to illegal aliens.

Americans lose, people who cheat the system win.

Author's note: Illegal immigration has not always been a polarizing topic. Every country in the world has immigration laws and protects its borders. Yet, Democrats conflate illegal with legal immigration to make it a wedge issue (i.e., one that divides) and the media, with few exceptions, serves up only the progressive narrative (the 'Newspeak' of Orwell).

A country that does not protect its borders and at the same time provides incentives (i.e., free schools, medical etc.) for illegal entry will eventually cease to exist. This is the road we are now on.

The research for this short section on the 'Dreamers & DACA' was challenging because the search engine algorithms push the progressive message. In some cases, I had to go 14 to 20 pages deep to find articles or reports that provided a perspective different from the approved narrative.

Biden's Plan Creating Border Nightmare

Forty-three days into the Joe Biden/Democrat train wreck, the southern border is a nightmare. Migrants show up wearing Biden T-shirts and holding professionally created signs at the Tijuana border crossing. Audrey Conklin writes, "Biden has promised to accept more refugees into the country during his time in office and implement more "humane" policies, such as a proposal to pay for the transportation and health care costs of migrant families who were separated at the border under the Trump administration. Congressional Democrats in February introduced Biden-backed immigration legislation that includes a path to citizenship for an estimated 11 million immigrants who are already residing in the U.S. illegally."[71]

It also includes expanded distribution of automatic green cards to immigrants with Temporary Protected Status as well as Deferred Action for Childhood Arrivals (DACA) recipients and a plan to give $4 billion to Central American countries in an effort to target the "root causes" for migration into the U.S.

Figure 13. Migrants at the San Ysidro crossing port in Tijuana, Baja California on March 2, 2021. (Photo:REUTERS/Jorge Duenes)[71]

The rank-and-file Democrats who voted for Biden, however, don't know about this because CNN, MSNBC, NPR etc. are not reporting it.

At least 108 illegal immigrants have tested Covid-19 positive in Brownsville, Texas and were then released! The Border Patrol spokesman said Brownsville does not have the authority to prevent those testing positive from traveling elsewhere in the U.S. But relax, the illegals promised to quarantine and follow the Centers for Disease Control and Prevention (CDC) guidelines and socially distance. Thirteen illegal died in Southern California when the SUV they were packed into crashed into a semi. The SUV apparently drove through one of the holes Biden decided to leave open.[72] It's sure nice to have a 'humanitarian' in the White House.

Author's Observation on Biden Humanitarianism: Unaccompanied illegal teen immigrants are held in metallic storage units with strangers and mainstream media says nothing. If Trump did this? C'mon man! nypost.com/2021/02/24/white-house-defends-kids-in-containers-as-aoc-cites-hypocrisy

Perspective on Muslim/African ban:

Fact #1 – There has never been a ban on Muslims or Africans.

Fact #2 – On January 27, 2017, President Trump signed an executive order denying entry for 90 days ... for individuals from Iraq, Iran, Syria, Yemen, Sudan, Libya, and Somalia.[73]

Fact #3 – Nigeria, Myanmar, Eritrea, Kyrgyzstan, Tanzania, and North Korea were added later. These countries have active terror cells and reliable background checks on people from these countries is impossible. To protect Americans, Trump acted. Democrats called it xenophobic.

Fact # 4 – "The seven Muslim-majority countries targeted in President Trump's executive order on immigration were initially identified as "countries of concern" under the Obama administration." Obama's order referenced, "the growing threat from foreign terrorist fighters."[74]

This kind of duplicity among progressives became common place when Trump won the election. Obama's actions were universally supported, yet when Trump extends or expands an Obama order, Democrats oppose it. A rational person must ask why. How was it in America's interest then, but not now? What is the logic that says a humanitarian benefit for a few non-citizens is more important than protecting American lives? Why aren't the

Democrat voters asking these questions? It is in their best interest too.

Perspective on The Border Wall

Fact #1 - Strong walls are the most effective, lowest cost means of protecting what is inside them. Israel's wall has protected them for decades. "As of May 2018, there were at least seventy-seven border walls or fences around the world."[75]

Fact #2 - "In 2006, the U.S. Senate voted in a bipartisan 80 to 19 majority to pass the Secure Fence Act, which authorized construction of physical infrastructure to secure the border."[76]

Fact #3 - Brandon Judd, president of the National Border Patrol Council told CNN, "It would be a huge mistake" for the Biden administration to cease construction midway.

> "If he (Biden) wants border security, then he should continue finishing the wall in the locations where the Trump administration has been building," he said, advocating for construction to continue in "strategic locations" that he says will help agents secure the border.[76]

Fact #4 - Ricky Garza, a staff attorney at the Texas Civil Rights Project, in the same CNN segment said, "What we saw, unfortunately, was almost all, if not all, the fence started under Bush *kept going under Obama*," referring to legislation signed under President George W. Bush that authorized 700 miles of double-layered fence on the border.[78] *Italicizing is the author's.*

Fact #5 – In fiscal year 2017, the U.S. spent $116 billion on illegal immigration.[79] This is a recurring (i.e., annual) expense that will only increase.

Fact #6 – On January 12, 2021, the Biden administration claimed they would save $2.6 billion by stopping the construction of the border wall.[80]

The estimated cost for 738 miles of wall was $15 billion. 453 miles were completed before Biden shut it down. The cost of cancelling the materials and construction contracts is not determined at this writing but could wipe out the purported cost savings.

> [**Update 2022:** Alec Shemmel of WCTI12 wrote on October 11, 2021, "A report released by Senate Homeland Security subcommittee ranking member James Lankford, R-Okla., indicated that between $1.837 billion and $2.087 billion of taxpayer dollars have been wasted since Biden took office and halted border construction contracts. This number is rising by $3 million every day too, according to records and data obtained by Republicans.
>
> "Lankford's report said the Biden administration has wasted roughly $2 billion on suspension and termination costs, which amounts to 20% of the original amount allocated by the Trump administration for border wall construction." wcti12.com/news/nation-world/biden-cancels-border-wall-contracts-in-laredo-and-rio-grande-valley-sectors
>
> "For perspective, Congress and the Biden administration has authorized sending Ukraine $14 billion as of May 5, 2022 and is asking for an additional $33 billion.

npr.org/2022/04/28/1095236237/biden-ukraine-33-billion-aid]

Fact #7 - There is now a seven-foot high, non-scalable fence around the Capital building.[81]

The fourth item mentioned was protecting Liberians who have been refugees in the U.S. for decades. It only affects a few thousand people.

QUOTE 2. "President Biden's strategy is centered on the basic premise that our country is safer, stronger, and more prosperous with a fair, safe and orderly immigration system that welcomes immigrants, keeps families together, and allows people—both newly arrived immigrants and people who have lived here for generations—to more fully contribute to our country. President Biden knows that new Americans fuel our economy, as innovators and job creators, working in every American industry, and contributing to our arts, culture, and government."[82]

This quote is fluff, motherhood, and apple pie. It contains zero substance, is weak marketing B.S. and insults the American taxpayer. Where are the benefits to the American citizens? Let's dispense with this sophomoric rhetoric quickly.

 Two very important but subtle points. First, the use of the word 'fair' in describing Biden's immigration system. Progressives use the word a lot, but it has no meaning. Fair is not a legal word. It is totally subjective and has no place in legal documents or policy guidance for any country. Fair to whom and based upon what measure? I have just spent several pages detailing how 'unfair' Biden's plan is to the American citizen. It would be more precise to say his immigration policy is abusive to the American citizen.

 The last sentence is complete Orwellian doublespeak. Illegal immigrants are a 'drain' on the economy not a boon. At least a

$116 billion a year drain, as earlier described. Strong, shall we say, 'Trumpian' immigration policy would have had a one-time cost for the wall which would have reduced annualized border patrol and enforcement costs, begun to cut the $116 billion societal cost, reduced illicit drug traffic, reduced human trafficking, reduced the influx of gangs and criminals, implemented a system that granted merit based visas, eliminated most of the human tragedy suffered by the migrants at the hands of the drug cartels while granting controlled legal immigration to law abiding people and those genuinely needing asylum.

What this book has reviewed is only the tip of the iceberg. I spent several hours reading more than eighty reports and documents (see references) on this topic and the nightmare keeps growing. The caravans are in full swing once again, citing Biden's lax policies as a justification.[83]

One of my wife's best friends (and mine too) is on the liberal side. I think she voted for Biden. She was over for much of the day yesterday and the three of us spent a couple of hours talking about the issues facing the country. After a while, I asked her if she had become a converted conservative.

My point is that our values, principles, and political differences are not that great. The key is dialogue (i.e., a two-way discussion). As a people, we have been sold a bill-of-goods by the media and allowed peer pressure to squelch honest dialogue. Our emotional triggers are too sensitive. It is too easy to shut someone down, call them names and walk away. We must all allow the facts to guide our decisions not our emotions.

We have reviewed a lot of facts in this chapter, that if known by all Americans prior to the election, likely would have led to a different outcome. Yet, over half of the country were not aware of these facts. Why? The answer, I believe, is they have grown comfortable with propaganda from CNN, MSNBC, PBS, NBC, New York Times, Washington Post, etc. It is the old 'you are what you eat' maxim. These 'news' organizations have been holding their 'daily sessions of Trump hate' for over 4 years. They are now the Ministry of Truth, which in doublespeak means, the Ministry of Lies.

I have had close friends (now former friends, I suppose) respond to my book *34 Days & Holding: America in the Balance*, with hate, disdain, and *ad hominem*. One did not even open the book and one read only two chapters. The book opens with a preface that emphasizes the importance of perspective. It is followed by a prelude that is mostly a thoroughly documented recitation of facts. Yet, these 'friends' attacked me. How can anyone believe this is the path toward a better world and unity?

When we allow emotion to overcome facts, we all lose. If you don't believe there is such a thing as truth, you may as well stop reading this book. If we can all have 'our own truth' then there is no truth and society will quickly self-destruct.

Chapter 5
Kumbaya

> "And now, a rise in political extremism, white supremacy, domestic terrorism that we must confront, and we will defeat. To overcome these challenges – to restore the soul and to secure the future of America – requires more than words. It requires that most elusive of things in a democracy: Unity, Unity."[1]
> —Joe Biden, Inaugural Speech, Jan. 20, 2021

We need to come together. Why can't we achieve unity? Haven't you had this thought and asked this question? Isn't this the exact sentiment expressed by President Biden in the quote opening this chapter? Isn't the desire real, heartfelt, and sincere? Yes, yes, and Yes. So, why doesn't it happen?'

The answer is progressive ideology and rhetoric is divisive. Biden opens by saying we have a rise in political extremism, white supremacy, and domestic terrorism. When saying this, he is pointing at conservatives, but the extremism is on the left, white supremacy is a lie, and the domestic terrorism is from far-left anarchists in ANTIFA and BLM. His opening plea is a complete fabrication and inflammatory. This is not how to begin a discussion designed to create unity.

When was the last time you had a serious dialogue with someone of an opposing view? It's been a while, right? I have tried to have two-way, respectful disscusions with liberals many times this past year and can remember maybe one or two times when they told me they agreed, even though there were many times I told them I agreed. I have labored to use facts only to be told they don't agree with my opinions. When I offer to show them the facts, to go to the sources, the conversation ends. They are not interested. They claim they have 'their own facts!' Can you imagine two engineers building a bridge having their 'own facts?' They try to flip the argument, saying 'it goes both ways.' It's a dishonest dodge because I just offered to review the facts and discuss their views, but it rarely gets that far. Biden begins his plea for unity by falsely accusing conservatives of things the Democrats are guilty of.

Here's the deal. To make progress we must communicate. No one disagrees. But effective communication requires listening. The Democrats have not listened since Obama became President. It's always a stalemate. If I were to insist to you that the only way we can have unity is for you to agree to a lie, you would tell me to shove it. In fact, it is worse than that. Biden is asking Republicans to accept the blame for destructive actions by radical Democrats. Try stealing a six pack of beer at the convenience store, and before the cops show up you hand it to the person next to you and tell them you'll be their friend if they take the rap. It is ludicrous.

Reasonable people will agree with this. Dialogue will only be productive when both parties agree on and build with foundational facts. Otherwise, it is a construct built on sand. Feelings, emotion, political correctness, and especially, selfish gain, have no place.

Conversations (i.e., negotiations) between groups (i.e., Congress) can progress as long as both parties first agree on foundational facts and justifiable goals. Facts are not debatable, they are truth. They can be substantiated. If there is ambiguity, then they are not facts, they are opinions. They accused President Trump using accusations cloaked as facts. When the accusations were finally exposed to scrutiny, they were proven false. The Nation suffered.

In honest conversation, the parties respond to each other with acknowledgement, disagreement, or requests for clarification.

People speaking past each other is not conversation. This is why TV talk shows today no longer have right versus left debate. They might have both sides present but they just spout talking points and never engage. The unwillingness to acknowledge points of agreement so the process can advance is the classic modern dance of our time. People are talking but no one is listening. In congress today, our representatives give their speeches to almost empty chambers. It is a farce.

Neither side wants to listen. They just want their way., which means their primary concern is 'what's in it for them?' Greed and self-interest, the inherent flaw of mankind always wins. This is the reason a true Democracy (i.e., majority rule) is a poor form of government; it has no checks and balances. It does not have safeguards to protect the will of the people. What are those safeguards? State government autonomy, a small federal government with limited power, bicameral legislatures (local representation from congressmen and regional or state representation from senators), a strong executive and a separate, honest and independent judiciary.

The Unrealistic Optimistic View

Let's assume we all got in the same room at the same time, read the previous section and committed to truly listen and engage. Are we home free? No.

Consider, once again, the quote from President Biden. He says, "To overcome these challenges... requires more than words." I'm sure we all agree with him. The process always begins with 'words.' First there is conversation, but the words must have an agreed upon meaning. I say potāto you say potăto, let's call the whole thing off. Some words are nuanced, others carry completely different meanings, while others are used as 'code.' Consider the following few warm and fuzzy buzz words that have lost conversational value:

Unity

Biden's use of this word is disingenuous on its face. There are two huge problems:

- The requirements to achieve unity are fake. He begins his thought with the contrived issues of 'political extremism, white supremacy, and domestic terrorism.' Just because Biden says these are issues does not make them issues. Republicans do not agree, the average citizen does not agree. What is 'white supremacy' anyway? According to Democrats it is everywhere but only they can see it!

- How do we know when unity is achieved? If only one side can see the problem, and thus assess if it is being addressed, that is acquiescence by the other party, not unity. How can we have unity when we don't agree what it looks like or what is required to get there? To achieve it, we must defeat issues that, at best, are not defined, and more realistically, do not exist?

Is it possible to defeat an enemy you can't see or only see fleetingly? No. We've had troops in the Middle East for over 20 years. When was the last time you fixed a problem without clearly knowing what the problem was? How much absurdity must we endure before people wake up? Oh yea, this is the 'Woke' generation.

Can you imagine a hockey game without goals or a basketball game without hoops? This is the absurd world of today's progressives and Democrats. The President of the United States is suggesting we chase after ghosts only he and his administration can see. If you have ever wondered what collective insanity looked like, this is it.

Unity is different from conformity and compromise. Like equality, unity is a pipedream. If you were to ask 100 people if unity would be good for America, they would say yes, not considering that everybody has a different definition of what that means.

Equality

Another utopian illusion. The only time we will have equality is when there is only one person left. Equality is a math term expressed by the 'equal's sign. One = one, hence when only one person is left, we will have achieved it. Democrats claim this to be one of their primary goals!

The House of Representatives narrowly passed the Equality Act by a vote of 224-206 (Feb. 25, 2021), *"with Republicans almost uniformly opposed."*[2] True to form, Democrat doublespeak is in play. The result of the act will be inequality. It "seeks to amend the Civil Rights Act of 1964 to add explicit bans on discrimination against lesbian, gay, bisexual and transgender people in both public and private spaces," writes Catie Edmondson.

The Supreme Court confirmed last June that the 1964 Act protected gay and transgender people.[3] "Representative Jim Jordan, Republican of Ohio, approvingly shared on Twitter, a Wall Street Journal op-ed that asserted that the measure would "threaten the existence of women's prisons, public-school girls' locker rooms, and women's and girls' sports teams."

The Equality Act abolishes biological gender. Men and women are finally EQUAL! Once again, the Democrats, in one great egalitarian flash of stupidity have declared that X = Y!

The headline should read, 'Breaking News: Democrats throw baby out with the bathwater.' Folks, sex is binary. It's what makes the world go round. It's the birds and the bees.

The existence of transgender people does not violate the biological truth that sex is binary. It validates the complexity and dynamism of human genetics. Transgenderism is more complex than the mere presence or absence of a Y chromosome, but it does not create new biologically stable types of humans. Science can sometimes be cruel, and the words used to describe genetic aberrations are clinical and cold. Democrats want to throw out the 'science' to appease 0.42% of the population.[4]

This act would create legislative license for child abuse and rampant discrimination. It would destroy foundational societal norms and abandon biological truth. It will never make it through the Senate but if it did, Biden would sign it.

Diversity

What does diversity mean to you? Is your definition the same definition of the progressives? Even if you are a progressive, you cannot answer that question with certainty, because 'it depends.' Right? You can't be so simplistic these days to just confer with a dictionary, that might be construed as 'racist' and 'insensitive.' If everyone can have 'their own truth', then they can have their own definitions. In fact, everything is up for grabs. With 'doublespeak' those with the power will determine the meaning based on expedience, preference and 'context'. So, just shut up or you'll be sent back for remedial 'sensitivity' training.

Stimulus

Stimulation is another one of those words that typically has a positive connotation. The effects of physical stimulation are usually a good thing: the heart beats faster, we burn more calories, endorphins are created, and we 'feel' better. We know when we've been stimulated, right? Can we have unity on that?

Just over one month into Biden's term, the Democrats have put forth a third stimulus bill. Its 'doublespeak' name is appropriately the American Rescue Plan.[5] The premise is that 14 months after

Covid-19 arrived on U.S. shores, the country needs another huge infusion of money. The White House description of the Act:

"Emergency Legislative Package to Fund Vaccinations, Provide Immediate, Direct Relief to Families Bearing the Brunt of the COVID-19 Crisis, and Support Struggling Communities."[6]

Let's break this down:

- **Emergency.** An emergency is a situation where if immediate and decisive action is not taken, the negative repercussions will be dramatic and possibly irreversible. So, do we have an emergency in February 2021? No, it's a lie. Unemployment in December 2019 was 3.6% with the Trump economy in full force. The Covid shutdowns forced it up to 14.7% by April 2020. That is an emergency. Congress passed and President Trump signed the $2 trillion CARES Act (March 17, 2020), a $484 billion aid program, including $320 billion for the Paycheck Protection Program and the $900 billion Consolidated Appropriations Act (December 21, 2020) 2020.[7] A total of $3.384 trillion in Covid-related relief in 12 months.
  $1 trillion or 29% of the 2020 stimulus has not been spent as of the end of February 2021.[8] Unemployment was 6.3% Jan. 2021. **There is NO emergency**.[9]

- **'Immediate, Direct Relief to Families.'** The Democrat American Rescue Plan (not passed as of this writing) proposes another direct payment to individuals of $1,400. If the bill is passed, this will be about the only thing that that goes directly to normal people. *But why send money to people who don't need it?* The Republican states have recovered (see Chapter 4), while unemployment remains high in many Democratic run states because the Governors kept the shutdowns in place much longer.

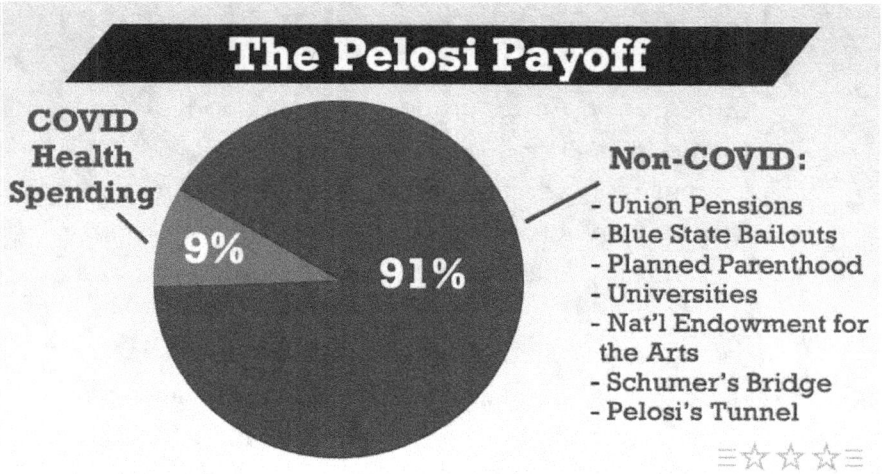

Figure 14. American Rescue Act apportionment.[10]

- Kevin McCarthy, tweeted the graphic of direct Covid relief versus Democrat pork with only nine percent ($171 billion) directly tied to Covid health spending. That leaves 91% ($1.73 trillion) for Non-Essential items: bailing out poorly run states (i.e., NY, CA, NJ, MI, PA), refunding union pensions, planned parenthood, universities, the arts, and a $15/hr minimum wage that would destroy 1.4 million jobs.[10]

The bill is not needed and is not good for America. So, why are the Democrats proposing it?

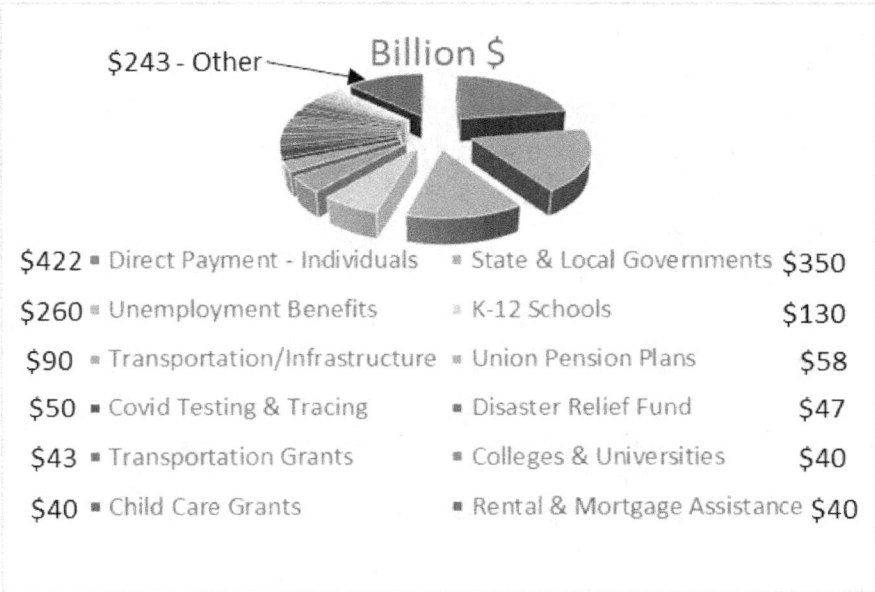

Figure 15. Democrat's American Rescue Plan Proposed Spending[11]

Democrat Doublespeak 101: Covid-19 Relief

Democrat Plan: 'American Rescue Plan' means 'lots of taxpayer money for New York, California, New Jersey, Michigan, Teacher unions, and a $15 national minimum wage that would destroy 1.4 million jobs. Only 9% of the $1.9 trillion would go to Covid-19 related needs. **Senate vote: 50-49**, *Signed into law March 11,* **2021** *(see Author's update at the end of this section).*

Republican Plan: 'Coronavirus Aid Relief & Economy Security Act' (CARES) means $2 trillion in assistance for individuals, small business, targeted large business (i.e., airlines). **Senate vote: 96-0**, *Signed into law March 17,* **2020**.

Notice a difference?

The $243 Billion for 'Other Emergencies'

Notice, there is $243 billion that I put in a bucket called 'other'. Remember, President Trump needed $15 billion for the southern border wall. Democrats were against it, even though it would make America safer.

Here are some of the minor critical expenditures the Democrats have lumped into this unneeded bill:[12,13]

$ 50 billion – FEMA
$35.5 billion – Increased Obama-care subsidies
$ 10s of billions – Government Oversight
$ 25 billion – Bars & Restaurants
$ 15 billion – Economic Injury Loans
$ 15 billion – Airlines
$ 8 billion – Airports
$ 7.6 billion – Improved Internet
$ 7.25 billion – Small Business Loans
$ 5.0 billion – Homeless Assistance
$ 1.5 billion – for Amtrak
$ 1.0 billion – for socially disadvantaged farmers
$880 million – extra funding SNAP (school lunch)
$270 million – Arts & Humanities
$200 million – Museums & Libraries
$ 19 million – National Institute for the Deaf
$ 1.5 million – Bridge from NY to Canada

Trust Me Update

None of this spending is needed. $1 trillion remains unspent from the December 2020 stimulus. The $15 minimum wage has already been removed. It would have cost 1.4 million jobs. A third economic stimulus will cause inflation. Your dollar will be worth less while a greater portion of the national budget will be dedicated to finance costs. Together with open borders, student loan forgiveness, and other wasteful spending, the Democrats are driving the country towards bankruptcy.

If, after reading this list of expenditures, you are thinking, "Well, these are all good causes." I encourage you to let that 'feeling' pass. The government has a money tree from which this funding comes, it's called the American taxpayer. If I suggested you take out a 2nd mortgage and give the money to me so I can spend as I like, you would laugh and call me crazy. But this is precisely what the Democrats are doing.

Psaki spins another yarn

Promoting this bill to the people on March 5th, Jen Psaki, Whitehouse Press Secretary said,

"Obviously, today is "Jobs Day." And with today's jobs report showing – show – while it shows some progress, it also shows the long road ahead. Right now, there are 9.5 million fewer jobs than at this time last year. This is a larger jobs hole than at any point in the Great Recession. At this month's pace, it will take us more than two years to get to pre-pandemic employment levels and will take even longer at the average pace over the last three months. This is unacceptable, and it's unacceptable when 4 million Americans have been unemployed for more than six months, or when unemployment is at 9.9 percent for African Americans and 8.5 percent for Hispanics. *Congress must pass the American Rescue Plan now so we can get Americans back to work, and so we can get relief to the millions of people who are struggling.*"[14]

What is unacceptable, is the continued lying to the American people by the Democrats. What is unacceptable, is that many states, as of this writing (March 26th) are still not completely open. The unemployment Psaki laments remains high because Democrat Governors have kept their states closed down unnecessarily (see Chapter 4). What is unacceptable is that over 100,000 small businesses have closed forever due to the lockdowns that did not help. What is unacceptable, is the teacher's unions refusing to go back to work. What is unacceptable, is that more young people have died from suicide than Covid-19. I could go on.

Author Update – March 11, 2021

The Democrats passed this bill as a part of budget reconciliation which only requires a simple versus a 2/3rd majority. It had no Republican support. "Since March 2020, Congress has passed five COVID-19 relief bills, all with overwhelming bipartisan support in the Senate and House, totaling roughly $4 trillion—by far the largest federal response to a crisis in American history. The most recent of these laws, passed in December of 2020, provided $900 billion in relief. There is still over $1 trillion from these bills that has yet to be spent." Senator Dan Sullivan, (R) Alaska.[15]

The Against the People Act

One of the most challenging exercises today is to uncover verifiable evidence of Democrats telling the whole truth and nothing but the truth. It does happen, but only with a double helping of B.S. to go. They use it like seasoning, just a dash of truth for eye appeal.

Consider the newly introduced, 'For the People Act', H.R. bill #1. It proposes to "To expand American's access to the ballot box, reduce the influence of big money in politics, strengthen ethics rules for public servants, and implement other anti-corruption measures for the purpose of fortifying our democracy, and for other purposes."[16]

This bill was initially introduced in 2019. Its goal is to enshrine vote fraud via mail-in balloting, ballot harvesting, internet voter registration, automatic voter registration, same day voter registration, registration of minors under age 18 and more. The only thing the Democrats left out is registering dogs and cats.

> [**Update 2022**: With the support of Democrat Senators Joe Manchin and Kyrsten Sinema, the Republicans were able to stop this dangerous bill. The key was the requirement of 60 Senate votes for passage. The Democrats tried to circumvent the 60-vote supermajority tradition with attempts to restrict the filibuster. "They then attempted to change Senate rules to exempt both bills from the filibuster, but Senators Manchin and Kyrsten Sinema joined Senate Republicans in voting against the change."] en.wikipedia.org/wiki/For_the_People_Act.

In the book, *34 Days & Holding: America in the Balance*, I meticulously document the Democrat actions to leverage the Covid-19 virus to relax voting law and protocols so fraud could proliferate.[17] The 'For the People Act', if passed, would formally legislate the weakening of voting integrity nationally. If this happens, the American experiment is over.

The next 18 months are critical because the Democrat House majority is narrow, and the Senate is 50:50 with V.P. Harris as the tie breaker. The American Rescue Plan, the Equality Act and the For the People Act will likely not pass due to this congressional gridlock. But the 'For the People Act' (relaxing voting laws) is the most critical. It was the relaxation of voting protocols (many instituted illegally) that ushered Biden into the Oval Office and flipped the two senate seats in Georgia.

The Democrat short game (next 2 years) is to open the southern border, grant amnesty, and dilute the conservative presence from Texas to Arizona. They will continue to use virus fear to control our freedom of movement and stall economic revitalization. Everything else is a distraction. Fauci and Bill Gates are already saying it will be 2022 until we can begin to get back to normal.

With the balance of power slightly in the Democrat's favor, the next step will be to freeze, isolate and purge anyone who opposes them. It's what all good authoritarian regimes do.

Democrat Doublespeak 101: Fair Elections

The 'For the People Act' aka HR bill #1 is classic Orwellian doublespeak. It can actually take several translations: Election Fraud R-Us Act, Let Us Cast Your Vote for You and Your Dead Relatives Act, Death to America Act, Make America Worse Again Act; are just a few more literal titles.

Chapter 6
There's Nothing Like a Good Purge

"How often and for how long one should engage in detox programs depends on how clean one is to begin with."
—Goop
(wellness brand founded by Gwyneth Paltrow)

The Night of the Long Knives

"If anyone reproaches me and asks why I did not resort to the regular courts of justice, then all I can say is this: In this hour I was responsible for the fate of the German people, and thereby I became the supreme judge of the German people!

"It was no secret that this time the revolution would have to be bloody; when we spoke of it we called it the 'Night of the Long Knives.' Everyone must know for all future time that if he raises his hand to strike the State, then certain death is his lot!"

–Adolph Hitler
to the Nazi Reichstag
July 13, 1934[1]

Authoritarians don't like opposition. Our founders, however, understood that freedom could only exist in a system that allowed dissent and put this right in its proper priority: the first Amendment to the Constitution.

In his speech at Columbia University on May 31, 1954, President Dwight D. Eisenhower said, "Here in America we are descended in blood and in spirit from revolutionaries and rebels—men and women who dared to dissent from accepted doctrine. As their heirs, may we never confuse honest dissent with disloyal subversion."[2]

Honest dissent or disloyal subversion? Why did Eisenhower's speech writer add the adjectives? Do you ever see dishonest dissent or loyal subversion? It's a trick question. The answer is yes. We saw dishonest dissent from the socialist Democrats throughout Trump's presidency, dishonest dissent is subversive. It is dissent founded in lies. In a *free country* dissent is allowed, if not, the country is not free. When a country is not free (i.e., China, Russia, Venezuela, Cuba), honest dissent is not allowed and even severely punished. In these cases, the people have a natural right to be free, thus subversion of the authoritarian regime is sometimes the only pathway to freedom, peace and the rule of law. I would posit, that subversion is always loyal to an ideology or cause. Eisenhower likely meant loyalty to a constitutional government that recognizes and defends freedom. Freedom without honesty and loyalty to the power that grants it (i.e., the Constitution) will not survive. Subversion of freedom, if it can be proven, is treason and treason and must be punished. Cowards subvert because they can't win with honest dissent and debate, thus they are disloyal to their countrymen, Constitution and the truth.

Today, the mainstream media is subversive. It undermines the truth. Here's an example using the topic of illegal immigration discussed in Chapter 4. We demonstrated illegal immigration is not good for America, nor for many of those who are trying to sneak in. The Editorial Board of The Washington Post, however, suggest 'Biden's bold immigration plan would really put America first.' They support this lie with comments like, "Mr. Biden's plan is in keeping with the United States' best traditions. It responds to the challenge of population stagnation," and '…the United States has returned to its roots as a beacon for refugees and a humanitarian role model among nations."[3]

Do you remember Biden, or anyone for that matter, saying one of our big problems was 'population stagnation?' Allowing 125,000 people per year, who cannot speak English and have few, if any marketable skills, is not putting America first. It is importing poverty. The people saying such things are one of two things: stupid or subversive. The Post writes this subversive B.S, but Biden is implementing the plan with the support of the Democrats. The elected officials now in power are implementing policies that are undermining the future of the United States and its people.

If Biden's anti-American immigration policies were going to make America better, why then is the rejoicing going on in Latin America? Kirk Semple reporting from Mexico City for the New York Times writes, "So, with President Biden now in the White House, migrants who had wept with joy and relief at his election hoped he would transform immigration policy and improve their chances of getting into the United States."[4] Do you think property values are going up in the Rio Grande Valley?

Americans have been subjected to overt high-level government subversive activity since 2016. The Democratic National Committee, the Hillary Clinton campaign, the FBI, DOJ and CIA all colluded in the development of a book of lies about Donald Trump for the sole purpose of subverting his presidency.[5, 6, 7, 8] They got away with it because the bureaucracy in Washington subverted the judicial process by withholding evidence, slow walking investigations, covering up and obfuscating the truth. The Obama administration teed all this up before leaving office.

"If you consider Russian election interference a crisis for our democracy, then you cannot read the Mueller report and conclude anything other than Barack Obama spectacularly failed America. Subsequent investigations of this matter should explore how and why Obama's White House failed, and whether they invented the collusion narrative to cover up those failures," concluded Scott

Jennings of CNN.[9] The active involvement of Obama administration officials in the Russia-Gate hoax was subversion and thus disloyal to the American people.

It was subversion, when the Internal Revenue Service selectively targeted conservative organizations in the run up to the 2012 elections. Obama allowed the IRS to silence a segment of society in an election year to gain unfair advantage. That was subversion of our electoral system, but Lois Lerner, then IRS Director of the Exempt Organizations unit, refused to cooperate and was held in contempt of Congress.[10] She left the government with full pension benefits. "After the IRS confession in 2013, its top echelons were quickly cleaned out."[11]

> [**Update 2022**: The John Durham has been investigating the subversive activities of the Hillary Clinton campaign, the Democratic National Committee and Obama's government bureaucracy and their actions designed to influence the 2016 presidential election. The first trial began in early May 2022 and involves Hillary Clinton's campaign attorney, Michael Sussmann, who is accused of lying to the FBI. The defense attorneys have allowed new information to be released in their efforts to convince the jury that Sussmann is innocent. Mark Moore of the New York Post writes, "In stunning testimony last week, Robby Mook, the campaign manager for Clinton, told jurors that she "agreed" to feed the since-debunked allegations connecting the Trump campaign to the Kremlin-linked Alfa Bank to the media." The Post records comments by Senator Ron Johnson (WI-R), "We've known for quite some time that the Hillary Clinton campaign paid for the Steele dossier. But now we are finding out that the whole Alfa Bank hoax ... was all made up," and "What is being revealed to the American public is the corruption at the highest levels of, A: the Hillary Clinton campaign, and B:

the FBI and the Department of Justice. The US government's law enforcement agencies knew the Clinton campaign was up to this, and yet they put America through this ... four-year political turmoil, which is all based on a lie developed by Hillary Clinton." nypost.com/2022/05/22/sen-johnson-says-sussmann-trial-reveals-clinton-corruption]

The challenge for the average middle-class American is knowledge. Many just don't know what is going on because their lives are full of work, family, friends, and leisure. There is not much personal time left for the individual to sort through the B.S. to get the truth. So, they don't know what they don't know. The 'Towers of Power' as described in the book, *34 Days & Holding: America in the Balance,* are all ruled by the progressive elites who regulate and control the message. The Towers of Power are government, education at all levels, news media, social media, sports, and entertainment.[12]

> *"There are laws to protect the freedom of the press's speech, but none that are worth anything, to protect the people from the press."*
> —Mark Twain

Once again, it comes down to trust. If those in whom we've placed our trust deceive us, we are unwittingly allied against our own self-interest. Think about it. Over time, because we are surrounded by others similarly deceived, we become invested in the deception (i.e., we vote for a candidate that supports open borders). We comfort ourselves with the thought that everyone else is doing it. How often did we hear the phrase throughout the Covid-19 information campaign, "we are in this together?" Personally, I take no comfort in the thought that I must unquestionably accept my fate and go down with a ship that could have been righted. Yet, those who question the status quo are branded as 'deniers' or 'heretics.' I will not sacrifice my grandchildren's futures to 'get along with' the 'believers.'

> *"The press is our chief ideological weapon"*
> —Nikita Khrushchev

When 'everyone else is doing it', a phenomenon called 'group-think' develops. Group think ironically is the absence of individual thought, it is sometimes called 'herd mentality.' We've all seen a flock of birds spin and pivot in flight in perfect unison. The group is 'hard-wired' to the lead bird, where he goes, they follow. Native American's often utilized this phenomenon to kill buffalo (American bison). They scare the herd then, from the edges, guide and move the herd leader in the direction of a cliff. The herd follows him to their death.

> *"Only two things are infinite, the universe and human stupidity, and I'm not sure about the former."*
> —Albert Einstein

We are now at this dangerous pivot point in history, not just in the United States, but the world.

No More Brown Shirts

Leading up to the 'Night of the Long Knives', the Brown Shirts, who were led by Hitler's Chief of Staff, Ernst Rhom, and viewed themselves as the 'people's army' began to yearn for more power and prestige. They had played a critical role in Hitler's rise to power in 1933, through street violence and intimidation. But these were mostly young, impressionable radicals, not unlike the Antifa and Black Lives Matters (BLM) of today. They were a tool, to be used and discarded. Hitler was the Reich's Fuhrer and needed to consolidate his power with the German army. He knew the people hated the Brownshirts and that decapitating them had no downside. Hence the Night of the Long Knives.[13] I predict this will eventually happen to Antifa and BLM in the U.S., but only after they help the progressive globalists (i.e., the Democrat Party) secure future elections. We have two more years.

Authoritarianism survives only if there is no competition. Thus, purges are necessary and must happen quickly. How will it play out?

> [**Update 2022**: Black Lives Matters is now being exposed as a fraud that has done little for the black community. Jamil Javani wrote for the National Post of Toronto in June 2021, "Last week, Patrisse Cullors, the executive director of the Black Lives Matter Global Network Foundation, stepped down, after weeks of scandal. She admitted to hoarding millions of dollars of real estate, despite claiming to be a Marxist. The head of BLM's New York chapter, Hawk Newsome, called for an investigation into Cullors' finances." nationalpost.com/opinion/jamil-jivani-judge-donald-mcleods-exoneration-has-exposed-the-feebleness-of-black-lives-matters-marxist-agenda

Tristan Justice, writing for The Federalist, reports in May 2022, "Public tax filings for the Black Lives Matter Global Network Foundation further exposed the racist organization built explicitly on Marxist values as a multimillion-dollar enterprise to enrich its leadership while cloaked in the self-righteousness of social justice. The document, published by the Associated Press on Tuesday, shows the organization that raised $90 million in the aftermath of George Floyd's death ended its fiscal year on June 30, 2021, with nearly $42 million in assets. According to the New York Post on

Tuesday, disgraced co-founder Patrisse Cullors, who stepped down last year amid scrutiny of a series of financial scandals, funneled major six-figure sums to family members from the network's donors. Paul Cullors, Patrisse's brother, raked in $840,000 from the nonprofit's charity funds. Damon Turner, who fathers a child with Patrisse, owns a company that was paid nearly $970,000 from the organization for "creative services" including "produc[ing] live events." thefederalist.com/2022/05/17/tax-documents-further-expose-black-lives-matter-organization-as-racist-multimillion-dollar-grifter-project]

Watch the Signs

> *"Tell us, when will these things be, and what will be the sign when all these things are about to be accomplished?"*
> —Mark 13:4

The disciples and others who followed Jesus always wanted a sign. They meant, give us some proof, something extraordinary, to give us confidence you are who you say you are. Their faith was weak.

I have just told you there will be a purge of those who oppose the globalist, socialistic message of today, yet people claim there is no proof. My response is "open your fucking eyes!"

I wrote *34 Days & Holding: America in the Balance* for one reason; to establish a permanent, digital record of what happened from October 1, 2020 to January 6, 2021.

Re-writing History

The first thing that gets purged or distorted is history. Here's some examples:

- American History – Boston University history professor, Howard Zinn, published *'A People's History of the United States*, in 1980. It was academia's most significant attack on America, at that point in time. It began the purging of American history.

- "Professors Michael Kazin and Michael Kammen condemn the book as a black-and-white story of elite villains and oppressed victims, a story that robs American history of its depth and intricacy and leaves nothing but an empty text simplified to the level of propaganda"[14]

- Zinn was fired from his first academic position for 'radicalizing' students, so Boston University hired him right away.[15] Wikipedia notes, "Biographer Martin Duberman noted that when he (Zinn) was asked directly if he was a Marxist, Zinn replied, "Yes, I'm something of a Marxist."[16] In 2008, the year before Obama became president, the Zinn Education Project was created to indoctrinate middle and high school students. Fifty years of lying to America's young people. What a legacy.

Shoot the Messengers
The second purge of the leading figures who are telling the truth.

- Bill O'Reilly – April 17, 2017, the Fox News network cancelled the Bill O'Reilly Show. The most watched cable news show in history. Why? O'Reilly was targeted by left-wing female commentators for sexual harassment. Was there proof? We will never know because O'Reilly chose to save his family from the public scrutiny and settled.[17,18]

- 'Lou Dobbs Tonight', early February 2012, the most watched show on the Fox business cable channel was abruptly cancelled on February 5, 2021.[19] It was rumored that it was due to a lawsuit from the election technology company, Smartmatic, which was implicated in alleged voting machine irregularities in the 2020 election.

- Conservative News. Late February 2021, two Democrats sent letters to content providers such as Apple, Amazon, Charter, AT&T, Roku, Comcast, DISH, Cox, Altice, Hulu, Verizon and Google's parent company, Alphabet asking they cancel Fox, OAN, and Newsmax. They claim these news outlets are "misinformation rumor mills and conspiracy theory hotbeds that produce content that leads to real harm."[20] For perspective, see Chapter 16, in *34 Days & Holding: America in the Balance*, that reviews the findings of Harvard University's Shorenstein Center on Media, Politics and Public Policy.

Purge literature

News flash from March 1, 2021: "Sale Of 6 Dr. Suess Books—including 'Mulberry Street'—To End Due to Racist Drawings."[21] It's about time, don't you think? These dangerous 'early reader' books for kids ages 4-8, have been poisoning children for over 70 years! They were published before I was born, maybe that's what's wrong with me? Anyway, if you hurry, there are a few copies left on Amazon for over $1,000 per copy. Here are some book banning highlights from the American Library Association.[22] I put an * by the ones I have read and highly recommend.

- Of Mice and Men – 2004 *
- The Color Purple – 2008
- The Catcher in the Rye – 2009
- Twilight – 2010
- Brave New World – 2011 *
- The Hunger Games – 2013
- The Kite Runner – 2014 *
- The Holy Bible – 2015 *
- To Kill a Mockingbird – 2017 *
- Harry Potter – 2019 *

Here are a few more that are no longer appropriate: Tom Sawyer*, Huckleberry Finn*, The Grapes of Wrath*.

Redefine words

For thousands of years, gay used to mean happy, now it refers to homosexual men. I think homosexual women are still called lesbians, hence the acronym LG, but I'm not going to look it up because I don't give a s***. That we are even talking about something like this is evidence of how nuts the left has become.

During the Senate hearing with Judge Amy Coney Barrett, the supremely stupid Democrat Senator from Hawaii, Mazie Hirono, told Judge Barrett, "Not once, but twice you used the term 'sexual preference' to describe those in the LGBTQ community."[23] *The next day*, "Merriam-Webster dictionary changed its definition of "sexual preference" to include the word "offensive".[24] This in the Ministry of Truth at work my friends. When Mazie speaks, Merriam-Webster listens!

Purge politically incorrect toys

I confess now, we gave our children Mr. & Mrs. Potato Head to play with. They loved the toy, but we had no idea the psychological damage it was doing. Now they are in committed heterosexual unions (formally called marriage) with three children each. We obviously failed as parents.

- Mr. Potato Head. "According to Hasbro Gaming, starting later this year, Mr. and Mrs. Potato Head will become the gender-neutral spud "Potato Head." "Culture has evolved," Kimberly Boyd, the senior vice president of global brands and general manager at Hasbro, told the Fast Company in an interview. "Kids want to be able to represent their own experiences. The way the brand currently exists, with the 'Mr.' and 'Mrs.', is limiting when it comes to both gender identity and family structure."[25]

- No Gender Please! Here's a mock question and answer in the typical Democrat family: "Mama, what am I? We don't know yet, Honey."
  August 2015, Target Stores: "Target's decision to eliminate "boys" and "girls" signs from its toys and bedding departments makes a bold statement: passé."[26]

- 'California wants to teach kindergartners about gender identity. Seriously', reads a Washington Post opinion piece, published May 2019.[27]

Hell, purge everything that offends anyone on the left!

- Disney+ purges animation classics: Peter Pan, Aristocats, The Lady and the Tramp, Dumbo, The

Jungle Book, and the live-action Swiss Family Robinson.[28]

- Purge all statues of Caucasian men. Antifa and BLM mostly completed this task for the Democrats in 2020.

- Food companies purge historic brand names[29]:
  » Aunt Jemima (130 yrs) – Quaker Oats
  » Eskimo Pie – Dreyer's Ice Cream
  » Mrs. Butterworth – ConAgra
  » Uncle Ben's – Mar's Foods
  » Cream of Wheat – B&G Foods

Attack the leadership

The third purge area is key leaders that oppose socialistic, autocratic globalism.

- President Trump. The collusion against President Trump began before he was elected and continued with a second impeachment after he had already left office. This is unprecedented in American history. Consider:

    1. Foreign agents collude with DNC to create fake dossier paid for by Hillary Clinton campaign. No one is charged with anything. [**Update 2022**: Clinton campaign attorney Michael Sussmann is the first person to be charged and his trial is underway]

2. FBI & DOJ use fake dossier to get wiretaps. No one is charged with lying to the FISA court.

3. General Flynn is entrapped by FBI, forced to resign, is threatened to plea to lying to the FBI to save his family, has to sell his house to pay for lawyers.

4. FBI Director Comey illegally leaks memo to press. Comey skates.

5. Deputy Attorney General Rod Rosenstein appointed former FBI Director Robert Mueller as special prosecutor

6. Special Prosecutor Mueller loads his team with Democrat attorneys

7. Two years and $32 million later, President Trump is vindicated.[30]

8. On September 24, 2019 Nancy Pelosi initiated an impeachment inquiry based on anonymous whistleblower opinions. Again, all charges proved to be bogus. [**Update 2022**: The whistleblower was Lt. Colonel Alexander Vindman]

9. Before the impeachment trial concluded, Covid-19 was already showing up in the country.

The important point is this: President Trump was innocent. He was exonerated every time. AND, he never backed down. He stood for the American people through the entire crap shoot.

- General Michael Flynn. Flynn was tapped by President Trump to be his security advisor. James Comey and the FBI, however, set up an entrapment based on illegal wiretapping. The result, this soldier, who had dedicated his life to his country was abandoned, falsely charged, his family threatened, bankrupted, etc. by the disgusting left-wing Democrats and the swamp.

- Other Trump officials and supporters who were targeted: George Papadapolous, Carter Page, Michael Caputo, Roger Stone and Paul Manafort. All except Manafort were unjustly targeted by the FBI and ultimately completely exonerated, but not until they had spent a fortune on defense attorneys. It was discovered during the expanded Mueller investigation that Manafort had illegal business dealings from years before, for which he was convicted. He was innocent of all charges related to the Mueller investigations. All of these men were targeted in an attempt to bring down Donald Trump. It gave notice to everyone else that Big Brother was watching.

- Rep. Mariannette Miller-Meeks (R-IA). Nancy Pelosi, (D) California has indicated for weeks that she would not recognize the duly elected congresswoman from Iowa, even though she won after a couple of recounts. Today (Mar. 31, 2021), her challenger, Rita Hart, withdrew her challenge to the official, state sanctioned tally. Miller-Meeks won by 6 votes, after leading by 282 votes, then 47, then 34 and finally, after recount, 6 votes.[31] Pelosi's attempted purge of a duly elected representative went down in flames.

University professors and high school teachers who strayed from the politically correct dogma (a *very* small sampling)

- John McAdams fired from Marquette University 2014 for suggesting that an honest debate on 'gay' marriage was appropriate. McAdams wrote, "was just using a tactic typical among liberals now. Opinions with which they disagree are not merely wrong, and are not to be argued against on their merits, but are deemed "offensive" and need to be shut up... In the politically correct world of academia, one is supposed to assume that all victim groups think the same way as leftist professors. Groups not favored by leftist professors, of course, can be freely attacked, and their views (or supposed views) ridiculed."[32]

- Michael Rectenwald, fired from New York University 2016. His comment, "I'm afraid my academic career is over, Academic freedom: It's great, as long as you don't use it."[33]

- Andrea Quenette, fired from the University of Kansas 2016. Robby Soave reported, "The movement to purge all offensive speech from American college campuses has claimed another scalp. Andrea Quenette, an assistant communications professor, was chased out of her own classroom—not because she was a bad teacher, but because her students said she wasn't agreeing with them quickly enough."[34]

- Bret Weinstein, biology prof at Evergreen State was "warned to stay off that campus by security officials after he questioned the logic of a student request that all white students and faculty members stay away during a day of protest."[35] Weinstein, a self-described progressive, won a settlement against Evergreen and is now at Princeton.[36]

- Justin Kucera, social studies teacher and coach, at Walled Lake High, Michigan, tweeted in July 2020, "Trump is our President" and was brought before school district leadership and offered two options: resign or be fired. He was fired.

  > "Other Walled Lake teachers have expressed their political views without any repercussions. Paulette Loe, a now-retired Walled Lake Western teacher, encouraged students to read an article from the Atlantic about "how to beat Trump" while still employed. Nicole Estes, a kindergarten teacher in the district, called Trump a "sociopath" and a "narcissist" on Facebook in 2016 and is still employed at Keith Elementary School. Neither Loe nor Estes responded to

requests for comment," writes Chrissy Clark of the Free Beacon.[37]

- Award winning Princeton University Physicist Dr. Will Happer, who served as the Director of Energy Research at the Department of Energy in 1993, says he was fired by Gore in 1993 for not going along with Gore's scientific views on ozone and climate issues. *"I was told that science was not going to intrude on policy,"* Happer explained in 1993. "I have spent a long research career studying physics that is closely related to the greenhouse effect, for example, absorption and emission of visible and infrared radiation, and fluid flow," Happer said this week. "Fears about man-made global warming are unwarranted and are not based on good science. The earth's climate is changing now, as it always has. There is no evidence that the changes differ in any qualitative way from those of the past," he added.[38]

Open Dissent Means No Grant Funding

Purging dissenters is usually not necessary because if/when they dissent, they know they will lose research funding and be shunned by their peers. Thus, the oft mentioned 'consensus' among scientists is bought and paid for.

Kenneth Haapala, president of the Science and Environmental Policy Project, concluded after examining government funding reports, and removing double counting, that funding of climate research from "Fiscal Year 1993 to FY 2014 total U.S. totaled more than $166 billion in 2012 dollars." [39]

Haapala notes, the entire Apollo space program (1962-1973) "cost $170 billion in 2005 dollars, which equals about $200 billion in

2012 dollars.[40] The difference is Apollo accomplished its mission. Funding climate research is pouring money down a rat hole.

> ***Author's Question:*** When some people are severely punished for speaking and other are not, what happens? Free speech dies.

Progressive Intolerance is Speech Control

- University Disinvitation of Speakers 2001 – 2014:
    » 2001 5 Bush is President
    » 2007 9 Bush
    » 2009 19 Obama
    » 2011 20 Obama
    » 2013 29 Obama
    See: thefire.org/disinvitation-season-report-2014

- The terms 'micro-aggression', trigger-warning and safe spaces begin to take hold in 2015. See: en.wikipedia.org/wiki/Safe_space

When does it end?

The purpose of this chapter is to give the reader sufficient evidence that a purge of anti-progressive, anti-socialist and anti-globalist thought has been underway for many years. It accelerated under Obama, and since Donald Trump's surprise victory in 2016, it has been moving at warp speed. The answer to the question, "When does it end?" is 'When the dissenters are silenced.'

Time to move on

I will leave you with a decision by Disney+, "children under 7 will be forbidden from watching *Dumbo*, *Peter Pan*, *Swiss Family Robinson*, and the *The Aristocats*."[40] Dumbo was made 80 years ago! Adults and children have enjoyed these animations for decades, yet now they are offensive.

This is what 'woke' means. It is what the Democrats stand for. The question remains will the majority of Americans adopt this idiotic crap. If the Democrats retain majorities in the House and Senate in the 2022 mid-terms, we will have the answer.

> **Author's note:** Changing the foundational morals, ethics and culture of a society is a long-term process. History, culture, literature, language can only be altered with precision and patience. Otherwise, people will notice. Put a frog in a kettle of cool water, then slowly keep turning up the heat. By the time he notices, it will be too late.

We are now in phase two. The younger generations have been indoctrinated. Thus, the process is more overt and accelerated. Hollywood, sports, music become more vocal. The media becomes more aggressive because they can. Coercion is used to pressure business to pay tribute or be attacked. The other purge areas are taken opportunistically, but are also constant, until overwhelming dominance is attained.

Chapter 7
Don't Mess with Mother Nature

> *"What we call Man's power over Nature turns out to be a power exercised by some men over other men with Nature as its instrument."*[1]
> —C. S. Lewis, *The Abolition of Man*, 1943

The Texas power grid is operated by a non-profit appropriately named, the Electric Reliability Council of Texas or ERCOT. The irony is so rich.

It turns out the ERCOT boys had a readiness meeting in November 2020 to assess the resiliency of the power grid for the approaching winter. They gave it a thumbs up, even under "extreme conditions." Mother Nature had other ideas. Winter storm Uri swept through the state in mid-February and, by the 16th, had knocked out 40% of the grid's generation capacity. Texas went dark and 23 people died. Such is the arrogance of man.

Notice the rapid increase of natural gas generated electricity beginning Feb. 8 and concurrent disappearance of solar and the almost disappearance of wind in Figure 10. Prior to February 8, the over-dependence on wind is obvious. How did this happen, especially in an energy rich Texas?

The answer: the arrogance and pliability of the statisticians and modelers and the stupidity of those in power (in this case, ERCOT, the Texas governor and legislature.) When I say, 'pliability', I mean the academics spin the message they are paid to spin. Consider the following analysis from Forbes in January 2020 by authors who state they are the 'thought leaders in energy from the University of Houston.'[3]

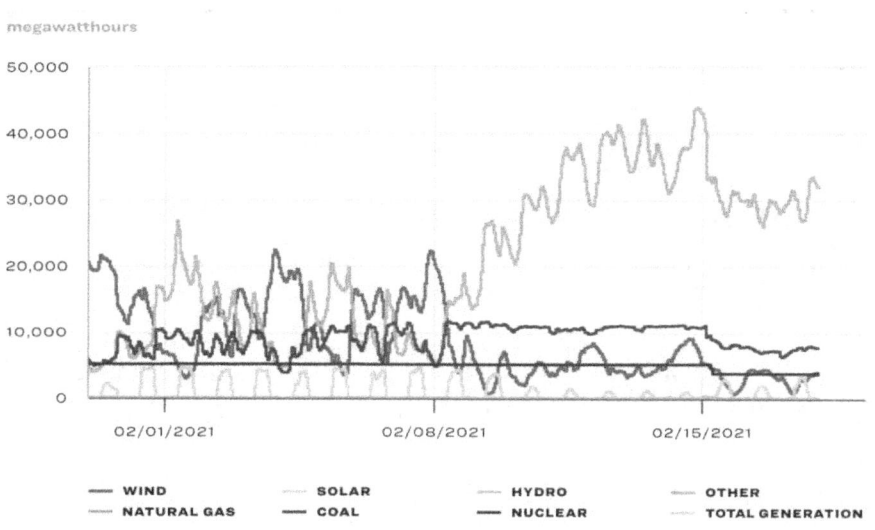

Figure 16. Texas Electricity Generation, Feb. 1-18, 2021
Source: U.S. Energy Information System (Texas Monthly)[2]

"The precipitous drop in coal-based power generation in Texas, from 32% of consumption in 2017 to 20% in 2019, has been hailed as the most significant step in decarbonizing electricity production in Texas," write Rananan Krishnamoorti and Ed Hirs, 'Energy fellows' at the University of Houston.[4]

OK, a 12% drop in 2 years, for the most strategic and essential energy resource in a society is HUGE! Let's dig a little deeper.

The authors state that, "The data suggest a more complex narrative. While wind has grown considerably, especially early in the last decade, the decline of coal has largely been due to a resurgent natural gas industry." [5] Their statement is 'it's complicated', we are 'energy fellows' at the University of Houston, you have to trust us. No, we do not. All we have to do is continue to read their article.

They continue, "The data for Texas' power production over the last three years indicates that coal has instead been replaced largely through the growth of natural gas and only to a small extent due to wind. Specifically, the growth of high efficiency combined cycle natural gas production has driven most of the surge to replace aging coal assets. Coal-based power generation is expected to continue to slide as more coal-fired power plants are retired in favor of renewables (wind and solar) and, more frequently, natural gas-based power generation."[6]

Notice, they begin saying the coal decline is due to cheap natural gas. Natural gas production from the expansion of fracking has driven costs down, this is a fact. But, to borrow their phrase, its more complicated. Electricity costs from coal have gone up due to environmental regulations initiated by Democrats, who under Biden's leadership, has voiced opposition to fracking. That means natural gas costs will go up as production declines. Government has created a false economy based on the bad science of CO_2 contribution to global warming. To prove this is a shell game, consider how the authors contradicted themselves in the same paragraph.

"Coal-based power generation is expected to continue to slide *as more coal-fired power plants are retired in favor of renewables (wind and solar)* and, more frequently, natural gas-based power generation."[7]

But they contradict themselves further by saying, "However, the growth of natural gas has not been smooth. And contrary to the recent trends, *growth of natural gas has not directly caused the shift in the energy mix of Texas.* A longer snapshot of consumed electricity over the last 12 years paints a more complicated picture. *Between 2007 and 2019, onshore wind has grown from making up 3% of power generated to 20%, or a 17% growth, while over the same period, coal-based power generation has fallen from 37% to*

20%, a 17% drop! Interestingly, over that same period, gas-based electricity generation has grown a meager 2%, while nuclear power has fallen by a similar value."[8] Finally, a clear, honest statement of facts. But the *cou de gras* finally arrives with a thud.

"Moreover, the sharp decrease in the cost of installed wind capacity, along with the on-again off-again *production tax credits (PTC) for wind, has been instrumental in the rise of wind power.* In Texas, the foresight to authorize and pay almost $7 billion for the Competitive Renewable Energy Zones (CREZ) by *state leaders and the Electric Reliability Council of Texas*, or ERCOT, has been unprecedented. (ERCOT operates the majority of the Texas grid). *Between 2006 and 2013, CREZ has enabled the construction of 2,400 miles of transmission lines to carry 18,500 megawatts of West Texas wind generation to major load centers in Dallas, San Antonio and Austin.*"[9]

The University of Houston energy thought leaders unwittingly confirm their duplicity in closing their article by shilling for electronic vehicles and then predicting the growth sector for Texas energy over the next 10 years will be solar. Solar, in 2020, accounted for 1% of the energy mix in Texas. The authors go way out on a limb to predict it will grow to 3%! Figure 8 shows energy from solar went to near zero from Feb. 8-18th, when the people needed it most. The only way solar will grow is with government subsidies, the same factor that has driven wind turbines.

The timing of their article could not have been better… almost exactly one year before the storm shut down the grid. It's not nice to mess with Mother Nature.

> **Author's Note:** The state of Texas spent $7 billion for wind generated energy transmission lines that will set idle when the wind is not blowing. It should've been invested in nuclear power, which is clean and reliable. Democrats in Texas fought the border wall which would be completed in one more year, with federally

approved funding. Biden stopped construction, leaving Texans the illegal immigrant costs of approximately $8,000/illegal/year. Biden has increased the quota for asylum seekers by 110,000/year. If Texas gets 27.5%, that is an annual cost of $242 million/year or about $1 billion during Biden's four- year term.

The Unreliable Electric Reliability Council

Jeffrey Ball writes, "...wind power generates 23 percent of Texas' electricity."[10] Once again, the legislature relying on 'expert' advice, has decided to risk 25% of the state's needs on intermittent wind and solar. This is insanity.

When a region is under a low-pressure cell, the sky is typically cloudy and the wind is minimal to non-existent. Figure 8 demonstrates this phenomenon. Wind and solar energy generation disappeared. This cost the experts nothing, it cost the legislature nothing, but 23 people died, water pipes burst, flooding homes in the midst of severe cold. Animal agriculture (poultry production and dairy) was devastated. This human and economic devastation was unnecessary. In fact, I would say it was criminal, because the entire enterprise is based on the false belief that CO_2 and methane emissions are a threat. This is categorically false.

Unfortunately, Mr. Ball places part of the blame on "Texans' thirst for cheap energy."[11] This statement is idiotic. The people of Texas have no voice in determining the energy production mix, system infrastructure, etc. Wind and solar generation add to the direct cost of energy but, also layers over a huge uncertainty cost (which is now being realized). Natural gas is currently the low-cost source, but the Biden administration commitment to continuing fracking is highly questionable. He has already banned fracking on government land.

Ball's Texas Monthly article rightly identifies the failure to winterize turbines and gas pipelines as significant failures. Both froze at the height of the cold snap. This 'cost saving' mistake rests on the shoulders of ERCOT, the Electric Reliability Council.[12]

Refer, once again to Figure 16, which appears in Mr. Ball's article. Wind generation declined significantly, yet he says, "As it happens, the performance of Texas's wind turbines over the past week wasn't all bad."[13] This is another example of media spin.

What are the Take-Aways?

The following conclusions should now be clear:

- Any energy source that is intermittent (wind, solar) should be capped at 10-15% of peak demand in a region.

- A surge capacity of 15-20% in excess of peak demand should be maintained at all times.

- We must consider the strategic value of coal. Once plants are closed, they never reopen.

- Burdensome regulations on coal that add costs but have little real environmental benefit should be repealed. (Author's note: remember, China is building coal plants as we speak).

- Government subsidies should be removed from all energy sources so we can have cost transparency for sound strategic planning.

- Nuclear power must be given top priority. It is clean, reliable, and cost effective over the long term. Burdensome regulations on nuclear that add significant cost and provide minimal real benefit should be repealed.

- The Yucca Mountain spent fuel repository must be opened in Nevada. The taxpayers paid for this repository and Democrat Senate Majority Leader Harry Reid ensured they remain unused. Think about the strategic implications of Reid's actions.

The above measures would secure long term energy independence along with supply reliability and optimized costs for the United States.

Biden and the Democrats presently stand in stark opposition to the entire list, while the press and academia, as demonstrated in the two references cited, serve to propagandize and spin.

Chapter 8
Halftime Update

*If "ifs" and "buts" were candy and nuts,
wouldn't it be a Merry Christmas?*
—Don Meredith
Quarterback of the Dallas Cowboys

After all, is football a game or a religion?
—Howard Cosell
ABC Sports Commentator

My generation is the only one left that remembers, and devotedly watched, Monday Night Football, as much for the banter between Howard Cosell and Don Meredith as for the game itself. The chemistry between these two pros, and straight man Frank Gifford were magical. From 1971-1973, 3 seasons, 50 years ago.

Now, everything.... EVERYTHING is different... and worse. Progressive politics has ruined professional sports. The players kneel at the National Anthem. They use their celebrity to preach 'BLM' and 'Racial Inequality', while they rake in millions a year. Yet, they are so stupid they don't see the irony. I can't remember the last NFL game I watched. The game used to be fun. The players were real people, and the little people loved them, and were entertained. Greed and politics made it all go away. A lot can change in 50 years, but they still have half-time.

Half-time for America

Today, it is half-time for America. Joe Biden's 50th day as President and still no press conference (a new record). He does have writer's cramp from signing a lot of Executive Orders to dismantle America, however. If the next 50 days are like the first, this country is going to be like the NFL.

It is important to clarify, at this point in time, when I refer to Joe Biden, I am talking about the guy, who on March 8th, while introducing two new female generals, could not remember the name of his Secretary of Defense.[1] It was inspiring. The President of the United States could not remember the name of "the guy who runs that outfit over there" as world news media videoed the event. The Federalist also attached a couple of other video quotes: "Barack and I think it's a right for people to have badakathcare," from October 31, 2020 and "I'll lead an effective strategy to mobilize trunalimunumaprzure," from October 30, 2020.[2] The White House has yet to clarify if Biden was speaking in tongues, in the last two quotes, or showing off a new language he invented.

Global Leadership. V.P. Kamala Harris spoke with the prime minister of Norway, Erna Solberg, today (March 9, 2021). While she "affirmed her commitment to deepening the strong alliance between Norway and the United States,"[3] President Joe Biden "visited a hardware store in the nation's capital."[4] Morgan Phillips, Fox News, reported, "Biden is to meet virtually with members of "the Quad," leaders from Australia, Japan and India. It will be his first multilateral conversation as president." She also added, Biden has already had a "flurry of phone calls" with other world leaders, "even some foes: He spoke with Chinese President Xi Jinping and Russia's Vladimir Putin."[5] Biden visits a hardware store and Harris spoke with the prime minister of Norway. It would be interesting to know how these priorities were determined.

Biden Press Conferences. Joe Biden has taken a bold, new approach to communicating with the American people. Tim Darnell, Atlanta Journal-Constitution, writes, "President Joe Biden has not held an open news conference since he took office Jan. 20, the longest stretch of any president over the past 100 years."[6] He notes that Obama was the weakest, breaking down and taking questions after only 20 days in office. "Biden appeared in a virtual event along with House Speaker Nancy Pelosi and the House Democratic Caucus. Biden was speaking to lawmakers on COVID relief and the ongoing vaccine rollout. He closed his remarks by saying he was happy to take questions from the lawmakers. The White House feed was then cut, with no explanation," writes Darnell.[7] Anonymous sources, who will remain unnamed, told me confidentially, on the condition that I would not disclose their identity that the FBI believes it was unidentified Q-Anons, using Harry Potter 'cloaks of invisibility.'

Las Vegas odds-makers are reported to be giving 2:1 odds Biden will breakdown by March 11 (his 50th day in office) and the long shot is 20:1 for April 1st, April Fool's Day. At least half of the country is just hoping they will wake up by then and discover this whole thing has just been a bad dream. President Trump held out for 27 days, in case you were wondering.

> **Real-time Update from Las Vegas! March 11, 2021:** Two hours ago, 8 pm eastern and well after the President's bedtime, Biden squinted at his teleprompter and addressed the nation. The response from insomniacs world-wide has been an overwhelming number of orders for the audio recording. It was not just a 'snoozer', it was 'catatonic', just what the country needed. If you put your bet on April 1, you are still in the game, because this was not a presser... he took no questions.

Down Mexico Way. Cinco de Mayo is two months away, but illegal aliens are lined up from the U.S. border to Guatemala. Please see Chapter 4 for a primer on the Democrat 'open border' policy. As of March 9, 2021, the situation is as follows:

- "The Department of Homeland Security (DHS) is seeking volunteers from among its agencies to assist in dealing with an "overwhelming" migrant surge at the U.S.-Mexico border, as the Biden administration continues to deny that there's a crisis," writes Isabel Van Brugen of the Epoch Times.[8]

- She continues, "The number of illegal crossings at the southern border has steadily risen since October 2020. The number of encounters at the southwest border between October 2020 and January was 296,259, an increase from 164,932 in the year-earlier period, according to data from the CBP, representing a 79.6 percent increase."[9]

- President Biden signed several executive orders his first week in office that dismantled the Trump border security measures.[10]

- Arizona and Texas attorneys general have sued Biden due to his order to freeze deportations for 100 days. A federal judge blocked the order January 26."[11]

One Citizen, One Vote. Once again, if you asked every U.S. citizen if one citizen, one should be the law of the land, they would overwhelmingly say yes. HR 1, however, would legalize vote fraud like we had in 2020. It would be good for Democrats but not for the country. The House of Representatives passed the 'For the People Act' by a vote of 220 to 210, on March 3, 2021. Not one Republican voted for it.[12]

- Unanimous Republican opposition will likely doom the bill, as Senate rules require a 60-vote majority to ensure passage. This is Senate Rule 22, the filibuster rule or cloture.

- Senate Rule 20, however, provides a loophole that has become known as the 'nuclear option.'

- This option was first employed by Senate Majority Leader Harry Reid (D) in 2013 for judicial appointees only. With this precedent, Mitch McConnell used it to allow simple majorities for approving Supreme Court Justices.

- Democrats could employ the 'nuclear option' to pass the 'For the People Act,' but, they would need unanimous support, which is not guaranteed. Thus far, the only Democrat Senator supporting retaining the filibuster rule in West Virginia moderate, Joe Manchin.

- On March 6, three days after the House vote, *Biden signed an Executive Order to implement much of the 'For the People Act.*[13] He did not even give the Senate a chance to schedule debate. Another first.

2nd Amendment. March 11, 2021, the House launched their initial salvos against the 2nd Amendment, the right to keep and bear arms. These were minor trial balloons.

- One proposed the extension of background check to private sales. Licensed sales (retail or on-line from an approved vendor) already require background check. So, they think the drug gangs are going to call the Feds and say, "Hey man, we want to sell some of our guns to friends."

- The other bill proposes to extend the deadline for completion of background checks from 3 days to 10. Little cracks are how dam breaks begin, but for now, it's a little crack.[14]

Military Strength & Readiness. "The guy who runs that outfit over there," meaning Lloyd J. Austin III, Secretary of Defense, announced his top 3 priorities on March 5: defending the nation, taking care of our people and succeeding through teamwork.[15] The following headers and italicized bullet points are verbatim from the Department of Defense (DOD) with my commentary after each. Quotation marks are used when exact wording is extracted from the DOD announcement.

Defend the Nation

- *Defeating COVID-19 is the greatest proximate challenge to our nation's security.*
  —Ridiculous on its face. The virus is real but not an existential threat requiring military intervention.

- *Prioritize China as the Pacing Challenge.*
  —This is so absurdly articulated, I have to quote it in full: "This is DOD's No. 1 pacing challenge, and it will develop operational concepts, capabilities and plans to bolster deterrence and maintain its

competitive advantage. The approach toward China will be coordinated and synchronized across the enterprise to advance DOD's priorities – integrated into domestic and foreign policy – in a whole-of- government strategy, strengthened by DOD's alliances and partnerships and supported on a bipartisan basis in Congress."

- *Address Advanced, Persistent Threats.*
  –It states we "remain ready to respond," yet "impose cost where necessary" and "right-size" its missions around the world in a transparent, principled manner." Right-size means reducing people numbers. I am starting to get nervous, how about you?

- *Innovate and Modernize DOD.*
  –It just keeps getting worse. "The department will be innovative at a speed and scale that matches a dynamic threat landscape, requiring advances in joint-warfighting concepts and a commitment to rapid experimentation and capabilities fielding. The DOD will divest itself of legacy systems and programs that don't meet its security needs any longer, while investing smartly for the future. The DOD will improve the efficiency of the force and guarantee freedom of action in contested, complex operating environments."

- *Tackle the Climate Crisis.*
  –And behind door #5, we have, the climate crisis! That's right Johnny, the U.S. military will begin deploying its troops in the 'war on climate.' China is hoping the Airforce will immediately ground all

greenhouse gas emitting jet aircraft, the Navy will transition from nuclear power to inflatable rafts and the Army, well, they will be 'right-sized.' God help us.

Take Care of our People

- *DOD will Grow its Talent.*
  —This is boilerplate HR blah, blah, until closes by saying, "and remove barriers that limit its people from realizing their full potential as partners in the department's work." I have provided examples in the insert at the end of this section. I encourage you to put the book down for a moment and go take a Xanax with a scotch chaser.

- *Build Resilience and Readiness.*
  —I'm only going to quote the 1st two sentences. I hope you took your Xanax. "The DOD maintains and enhances force readiness and develops capabilities to protect America when it fully embraces a diversity of backgrounds, experiences and thought. The DOD will lead with its values, building diversity, equity and inclusion into all aspects of its work."
  —Folks, I wish I was writing a script for 'Live, It's Saturday Night' but this is real shit. We are in deep doodoo.

- *Ensure Accountable Leadership.*
  —Once again, I must provide the full quote. This policy will destroy the military.

> "Some behaviors are antithetical to our values, undermine our readiness, and put our effectiveness at risk, but are alive within our workforce. Leaders at every level will be responsible for building a safe environment for DOD people and guaranteeing swift and clear accountability to anyone who does not act within the highest standards of the department. The DOD will not tolerate sexual assault and sexual harassment. Extremism also presents a complex and unique challenge to the DOD, which the department must meet head-on working to permanently stamp out extremism in the ranks. Both efforts and others will ensure that we provide every member of the department a safe and supportive place to serve their country - one free from discrimination, hate, harassment, and fear."

Do you understand why this will destroy the military? Because this is the 'Me Too' movement on steroids. Leadership, enlisted personnel, and civilians are now on notice that their careers and jobs are now at the mercy of the DOD Thought Police. What is the meaning of a 'safe environment', 'harassment' or 'extremism?' Don't worry, we'll tell you while on the way to the Tribunal.

DOD Dictionary of Military and Associated Terms[16]

The Military has its own 370-page dictionary. Words & acronyms must have fixed meaning for groups to function & communicate efficiently. But, like most things that are started from a logical, need-based foundation, the current version does go overboard. The danger we face now is 'redefinition' or 'expansion' due to our present hyper-sensitivity and push for 'inclusiveness'. It does not, however, provide definitions of 'safe environment', 'harassment' or 'extremism'. Can you imagine a field General calling the Pentagon to make sure his current dictionary can be used to interpret the words in his latest orders?

Succeed through Teamwork

- *Join Forces with our Allies and Partners*
  –"…the department's success will depend on how closely we work with our friends around the world to secure our common interests and promote our shared values."
  –Like so much coming out of the Biden administration these days, the wording is touchy-feely and does not take an 'America First' position. Under the most optimistic interpretation, this is the Obama apology tour redux. The worst-case interpretation is one world government.

- *Work in Partnership with Our Nation*
  –"The DOD will redouble its commitment to a cooperative, whole-of-nation approach to national security that builds consensus, drives creative solutions to crises, and guarantees that we lead from a position of strength, fielding a credible force, ready to back up the hard work of our diplomats around the world and our national partners."
  –The purpose of the military is to protect the nation from external threat. We have the FBI and many other law enforcement agencies for domestic law enforcement.
  –What does "whole-of-nation" mean? Are we

abolishing state governments? Are we getting ready to implement a military state? Hasn't Federal government always meant national government?

- *Build Unity Within DOD*
  –"To guarantee the DOD remains the greatest joint-fighting force in the world, we will continue to build unity of effort and mission across components, commands, services and theaters. We will ensure meaningful civil-military cooperation, safeguarding the proper balance of civilian and military inputs to our policies and missions. The DOD will demonstrate teamwork at its highest and expect it across every level, because working collaboratively will ensure the greatest success in protecting and defending the nation."
  –This is the full quote and the last bullet point. It is meaningless fluff. More feel good, flower child, kumbaya. Again, what does it mean? It sounds kinda like the teacher monitoring the playground and saying, "OK children, let's play nice now."

What "realizing full potential" means in military:

1. The military has been and will continue to pay for gender surgical procedures, gender dysphoria treatment. This began with Obama, Trump was against it, but the Supreme Court over-ruled him in 2017.[17]

2. "Recognizing that diversity declined significantly as officer grades increased, Congress established the

Military Leadership Diversity Commission (MLDC) in 2009."[18] When Obama had super majorities in Congress, the diversity road to military mediocrity left the station.

Biden Executive Order Update, 37 & Counting.[19]

Table 3. Biden Executive Orders - First Fifty Days in Office (January 20-March 11)

Order	Date	E.O. #	Executive Order Title*	Good for America	Why?
1 to 19	Jan 20-22		See Table 1		
20	25-Jan-21	14004	Enabling All Qualified Americans To Serve Their Country in Uniform	No	Divisive, enforces racial preferences
21	25-Jan-21	14005	Ensuring the Future Is Made in All of America by All of America's Workers	Neutral	Redunant
22	26-Jan-21	14006	Reforming Incarceration System To Eliminate Use of Privately Operated Criminal Detention Facilities	No	Reduces capacity, adds costs, puts criminals on the street
23	27-Jan-21	14007	President's Council of Advisors on Science and Technology	Neutral or No	Depends who the advisors are
24	27-Jan-21	14008	Tackling the Climate Crisis at Home and Abroad	No	There is no Climate Crisis
25	27-Jan-21	14009	Strengthening Medicaid and the Affordable Care Act	No	Revokes improvements made by Trump
26	2-Feb-21	14010	Orderly Processing of Asylum Seekers	No	Reinstitutes Obama 'Catch & Release', will increase illegal aliens, encourage child trafficking
27	2-Feb-21	14011	Establish Task Force on Reunification of Families	No	Sends wrong message to illegals
28	2-Feb-21	14012	Restoring Faith in Our Legal Immigration Systems and Strengthening Integration and Inclusion Efforts for New Americans	No	Invites illegal immigration, increases tax burden on Americans, introduces more crime & illegal drugs
29	4-Feb-21	14013	Rebuilding and Enhancing Programs To Resettle Refugees and Planning for the Impact of Climate Change on Migration	No	You have go to be fucking kidding me!
30	10-Feb-21	14014	Blocking Property Due to the Situation in Burma	Neutral	Does not affect Americans
31	14-Feb-21	14015	Establishment of the White House Office of Faith-Based and Neighborhood Partnerships	No	Adds costs and unnecessary bureaucracy
32	17-Feb-21	14016	Revocation of Executive Order 13801	No	Cancels Trump's Apprenticeship E.O. which enhanced on the job training
33	24-Feb-21	14017	America's Supply Chains	Neutral	Asks for a study, too early to tell
34	24-Feb-21	14018	Revocation of Certain Presidential Actions	No	Cancels 3 positive Trump E.O.'s
35	24-Feb-21	14019	Promoting Access to Voting	No	Implements HR 1 prior to Senate debate. Will legitimize vote fraud
36	8-Mar-21	14020	Establish White House Gender Policy Council	No	See earlier gender idiocy comments
37	10-Mar-21	14021	Guaranteeing an Educational Environment Free From Discrimination on the Basis of Sex, Including Sexual Orientation or Gender Identity	No	See earlier gender idiocy comments

* Some E.O. titles were shortened to fit the chart. Remember: titles do not always accurately reflect E.O. contents.
Source: https://www.federalregister.gov/presidential-documents/executive-orders/joe-biden/2021

Domestic Tranquility Requires Law & Order.

We have law enforcement for Federal Crimes, the FBI. Their leadership is corrupt, as has we have witnessed since 2016. Even President Trump could not fix this... in fact, he was a victim, as were many associated with him (i.e., General Flynn). This is all well documented and in the public domain.

As discussed earlier in this chapter, the specter of domestic military force might soon be taking physical form (i.e., 5,000 National Guard remain on-duty in Washington, D.C.). The statements of the Secretary of Defense are unlike any heard before.

Anarchy and violence, however, is on the rise. The local police have been neutered. They stand by and watch, as stores are looted, cars turned over and burned, and the police themselves are attacked.

Portland, OR. March 11. "Rioters targeted the federal courthouse in Portland, Ore., on Thursday evening in renewed clashes between demonstrators and federal police," reported Zachary Evans of the National Review. As of this writing, that was 14 hours ago. I searched 10 pages deep into Google and found no reporting from the NY Times, Washington Post, Wall Street Journal, CNN, MSNBC, NPR, LA Times, etc. Mr. Evans continues, "Footage showed the rioters attempting to force their way into the courthouse while chanting "f*** the United States!" Later in the evening rioters set a fire outside the courthouse entrance."[20]

Boulder, CO, March 6. "Officers responded to a report of a large party on 10th Street in the University Hill neighborhood between Pennsylvania and College Avenues around 5 p.m. Saturday.

"During that time, a crowd of around 100 people began pelting officers with glass bottles and prompted the activation of the department's SWAT Unit," writes David Mullen of the Denver Gazette. He continues, "By 9 p.m. Saturday, attendees stole a vehicle, damaged eight other vehicles for a total value of $43,500 in damages, stole three street signs, damaged two city vehicles including a BPD armored rescue vehicle and a fire engine, and left two SWAT member teams injured."[21] The police and SWAT team did nothing. Arrested no one on the spot but did arrest one 20-year-old four days later.

Defund the Police. City dwellers, like myself, are beginning to question taking the doggie out after dark. A friend of ours was walking home, after his shift at a nearby restaurant, and was assaulted on the street from behind. He was beaten, kicked, robbed and then left on the sidewalk with two broken ribs. The restaurant is only 8 blocks from our building and the walk is through a mostly residential area.

Thankfully, his incident does not appear in the accompanying Table 5 that lists the top 20 U.S. cities for murders. These 20 cities had a 37% increase in homicides in 2020, the year of 'defunding the police.' The data are from the Uniform Crime Report and were reported in mid to late December 2020, except for Houston and Phoenix (which reported Oct. 31, 2020).[22] For some reason, the FBI does not provide recent crime data.

One of the most extraordinary cultural movements that occurred in 2020 was called 'Defund the Police'. This movement provides more evidence of the insanity that resides on the political left.

By August 2020, 10 cities had announced they would consider defunding their police forces. They were: Minneapolis, New York, Chicago, Los Angeles, San Francisco, Philadelphia, Portland OR, Milwaukee, Denver, Oakland and Seattle.[23] Five of them made the Top 20. The other five and their rank for homicides are: Oakland (25), Minneapolis (29), Denver (30), Portland (38), Seattle (39) and San Francisco (43).

George Floyd died on May 25, 2020 in Minneapolis. The autopsy was not released until August 25. It concluded, "The autopsy *revealed no physical evidence suggesting that Mr. Floyd died of asphyxiation*. Mr. Floyd did not exhibit signs of petechiae, damage to his airways or thyroid, brain bleeding, bone injuries, or internal bruising."[24] The blood chemistry analysis reported in the official autopsy concluded, "4ANPP - a precursor and metabolite of *fentanyl* present in Mr. Floyd's blood. *Methamphetamine* - 19 ng/ML which he described as "very near the low end" and "a stimulant hard on the heart." Fentanyl - 11. He said, "that's pretty high." This level of fentanyl can cause pulmonary edema. Mr. Floyd's lungs were 2-3x their normal weight at autopsy. *This is a fatal level of fentanyl under normal circumstances*."[25]

Table 4. U.S. Top 20 Cities for Homicide in 2020

Rank	City	2020	2019	Trend	New Deaths	Party
1	Chicago[x]	748	481	56%	267	D
2	Philadelphia[x]	469	346	36%	123	D
3	New York[x]	437	314	29%	123	D
4	Los Angeles[x]	343	257	33%	86	D
5	Detroit	327	274	19%	53	D
6	Baltimore	321	333	-4%	0	D
7	Houston	321	225	43%	96	D
8	Memphis	290	191	52%	99	D
9	St Louis	261	194	35%	67	D
10	Dallas	245	199	23%	46	D
11	Indianapolis	214	153	40%	61	D
12	Washington	197	165	19%	32	D
13	New Orleans	194	120	62%	74	D
14	Milwaukee[x]	191	98	95%	93	D
15	Cleveland	175	121	45%	54	D
16	Phoenix	175	110	59%	65	D
17	Kansas City	174	151	15%	23	D
18	Louisville	173	90	92%	83	D
19	Atlanta	150	95	58%	55	D
20	Jacksonville	141	131	8%	10	R
		5,546	4,048	37%	1,510	

Source: Uniform Crime Report Data [22]
[x] Defund Police proclamation

Ten years ago, the officer indicted for Floyd's murder would be exonerated. But now, black lives matter only when a black person dies at the hands of the police. They don't matter in Chicago or Baltimore where black-on-black crime is okay. The murders, riots, property damage and businesses destroyed in the name of George Floyd cannot be erased. No one knows officer David Dorn, who was murdered June 2, 2020, while helping a friend protect his property BLM/Antifa thugs. Officer Dorn was black. The left used Mr. Floyd's death as an excuse promote police brutality and start the 'Defund the Police' movement.

If you listen to or read the mainstream media, however, you may conclude otherwise. Wikipedia titles its George Floyd page, "The Killing of George Floyd."[26] The progressive leftists are running down the street yelling 'Remember O.J. Simpson!"

Kamala Harris was asked what she thought of the 'Defund the Police' issue when appearing on the television show *The View*, her response was,

"I think that a big part of this conversation really is about reimagining how we do public safety in America which I support which is this: we have confused the idea that to achieve safety, you put more cops on the street instead of understanding to achieve safe and healthy communities. That's how I think about this. You know, in many cities in America, over one-third of their city budget goes to the police. So, we have to have this conversation, what are we doing? What about the money going to social services? What about the money going to helping people with job training? What about the mental health issues that communities are being plagued with for which we're putting no resources?"[26]

Why is this happening? Why are murders and crime up dramatically across the country? Check Figure 5 again and look at the column titled Party. See a pattern?

A Dose of Perspective:

Murders in 2020, Top Cities only
- *5,546 Top 20 cities (1,510 more than 2019)*
- *9,726 Top 50 Cities (1,970 more than 2019)*
            Uniform Crime Report Data

Covid-19 Deaths in the U.S. (as of March 3, 2021)
- *Age 0 to 29: 1,972*
- *Age 0 to 39: 7,170*
            CDC – National Center Health Statistics

Abolish ICE. The mission of U.S. Immigration and Customs Enforcement (ICE) is to "strengthen border security and prevent the illegal movement of people, goods, and funds into, within, and out of the United States."[27] Elaine Godfrey, wrote in the Atlantic in July 2018, "While it began as little more than a hashtag on the fringe left, "Abolish ice" has unfurled, almost overnight, into a small movement. A growing number of Democratic candidates and lawmakers have come to view U.S. Immigration and Customs Enforcement as representative of all that's wrong with the Trump administration's immigration practices, but it's not at all clear that every politician embracing the slogan is on the same page—or what the alternative to ice might be."[28]

In October 2020, Tom Homan, former Director for ICE wrote for the on-line news agency The Hill, "For almost three years we have all heard the battle cries from the left to Abolish ICE. Certain members of Congress have used terms like racist, Nazis and Gestapo for ICE officers. Such terms have been voiced – or implied – by Rep. Alexandria Ocasio-Cortez (D-NY), Rep. Ilhan Omar (D-Minn.), Ayanna Pressley (D-Mass.), and Rashida Tlaib (D-Mich.). Same things were said by Rep. Yvette Clark (D-N.Y.) and Debbie Wasserman-Schultz (D-Fla.). I could cite more names, but it is pointless because their opinions are meaningless."[29]

The Boston Herald editorial staff wrote on December 31, 2020, "Biden himself has not called for the agency's abolition, but he has vowed to reverse many of Trump's immigration policies. And Vice President-elect Kamala Harris, while also not asserting that ICE should be abolished, had this to say about the agency: "I think there's no question that we've got to critically re-examine ICE and its role and the way that it is being administered and the work it is doing," she told MSNBC. "And we need to probably think about starting from scratch." *Harris has also compared the agency to the Ku Klux Klan.*"[30] The conclude with the statement, "Catching criminal fugitives, staving off threats to public safety, arresting drug and weapons smugglers and confiscating kilos of fentanyl – these are the things that ICE does. If progressives get their way in undermining and diluting ICE operations, they will throw up serious roadblocks to any efforts to "build back better.""[31]

The consequences for illegal entry into Canada are deportation and loss of the opportunity to apply for citizenship.[32] Canadian immigration lawyer Peter Edelmann told NPR in 2016 he sees a difference between Canadian and U.S. enforcement and punishment. "There does seem to be more acceptance of people living undocumented in some of the cities in the United States. He says he's surprised to hear how people can go for decades in the U.S. without legal status. He says he rarely sees cases of people who go that long without legal status in Canada, but he doesn't think it's just because people are more likely to get caught."[33]

Update Mexico: March 10, 2021. "Detentions on the U.S border have surged since Biden took office on Jan. 20. Mexico has urged Washington to help stem the flow by providing development aid to Central America, from where most migrants come, driven by a humanitarian crisis. They see him as the migrant president, and so many feel they're going to reach the United States," Mexican President Andres Manuel Lopez Obrador said of Biden the morning after a virtual meeting with his U.S. counterpart on March 1," writes Dave Graham for Reuters.[34]

Mexican Cartel Charges to cross the Rio Grande:

Mexicans - $2,500
Central Americans - $3,000
Chinese - $5,000
Russian - $9,000
This is for each person, children, elderly etc.

Interview with U.S. Border Patrol in Starr County, Texas Tucker Carlson Show, March 16, 2021

Supreme Failure. The Supreme Court of the United States has now ruled on all the lawsuits filed against states for election fraud and violations. Their ruling was unified against even giving the plaintiffs a hearing. Initially, they said they needed to wait until the election was over so as not to influence the outcome. Then they set initial hearing dates in February and March 2021. Now, each has been dismissed, one by one, without even getting a hearing. The only new justice supporting giving the cases a hearing was Gorsuch. Alito and Thomas strongly argued for the hearings. The rejections were given without comment. They were just rejected out of hand. The third seat of governmental power, the Judiciary, abandoned America.

Halftime is over. What we have covered in this chapter is just the tip of the iceberg. Our southern border has become a nightmare in just 50 days and gets worse by the day. Women are wearing the pants in the military. Congressional Democrats are trying to pass legislation that will add trillions more to our national debt. They are also pressuring Senators Manchin and Senema to support abolishing the filibuster, which would ensure roaring inflation and economic collapse in 2023 or before. Our situation is so bad, I have considered taking this book to print now instead of waiting another 50 days. This halftime update will close with a graphic updating the national status on Covid-19 mask mandates, school and business openings.

Covid Rules Business and Schools

By April 1st, school openings have improved:

Florida and Iowa are the only states that are 100% back to in-person learning, while those above 70% fully open are: Texas, Alabama, Georgia, Arkansas, Kansas, Nebraska, Ohio and Missouri.[35] Dr. Robert Redfield, former CDC Director, said in a July 2020 interview, "the greater risk to the nation is to keep these schools closed."[36] Teacher unions and Democrat Governors chose to ignore CDC advise.

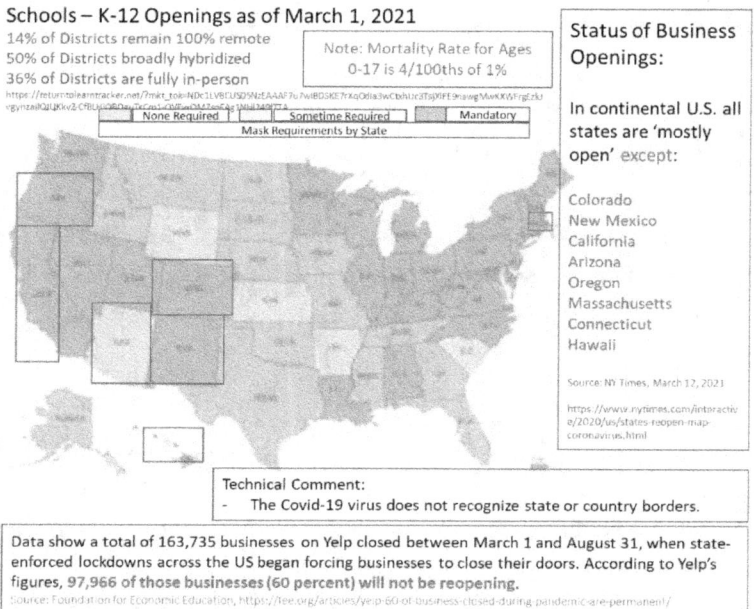

Figure 17. School & Business Openings

Redfield made it clear that, "We're seeing, sadly, far *greater suicides now* than we are deaths from COVID. We're seeing *far greater deaths from drug overdose* that are above excess that we had as background than we are seeing the deaths from COVID."[37]

Covid mortality for the young is almost zero. The flu kills more kids. It has now been established that transmission from kids to adults is low, yet with just 7 weeks of school left, only Florida and Iowa have all kids back in school. (Note: With no negative repercussions.)

Chapter 9
The Canine Idiom

The smallest or least important part of something in control of the larger or more important elements; a reversal of typical roles or dynamics of power.
When the 'tail wags the dog.'

March 4, 2021, the day that will go down in fantasy. Yesterday, (for Democrats reading this, that is the day before today, i.e., March 3, 2021) the Capital of the United States shut down and blockaded itself against an attack from Q-Anon. Folks, this is real history, in real time.

Bart Jansen of USA Today quoted acting Chief of the Capital Police, Yogananda Pitman as telling lawmakers, "The USCP (United States Capital Police) is steadfast in ensuring that an incident of this nature will never occur again, especially with the realization that the possibility of a similar incident occurring in the current environment is a very real and present danger."[1] You read that right folks, the police chief's name is 'Yogananda!'

Credible anonymous sources have told me that the scene in Nancy Peopsi's face-lift room was chaotic. No, it was not the janitor, I mean, the 'sanitation officer.' The behind-the-scenes conversation allegedly went like this:

Speaker of the House Nancy Pelosi: "Q-Anon is coming! Q-Anon is coming!" The speaker frantically raised her arms and knocked out one of her assistants. Witnesses say it was a 'double whammy!'

Chief Yogananda: "We are ready, your Speakerness. We have our Q-Anon glow in the dark badges and have set Q-Anon sensors all over the city."

Pelosi: "I need some expensive ice cream, quick!" Everyone stepped back to give the Speaker more room.

Senate Majority Leader Chuck Schumer: "Chief Yogananda, did you say, "A Real and Present Danger? I saw that movie, it was good."

Pelosi: "We're talking about Q-Anon you idiot. Where are you from, New York? And, the title of the book was, *Clear* and Present Danger."

Chief Yogananda: "I'll have the force watch the movie, your Speakerness, maybe our Q-Anon decoder will uncover the plot."

Pelosi's personal chef: "Here's the Q-Anon Loops you ordered for breakfast, your Speakerness.

Schumer: "Hey, I'll have a bowl with chocolate sprinkles. Chocolate's not a racist term yet, is it Nance? Maybe I should've said, sprinkles of color?"

Pelosi: "I'm surrounded by idiots! We are in the middle of a Covid, Q-Anon crisis! Hey, hands off my Q-Anon Loops."

Schumer: "I never go to battle on an empty stomach, Nance."

Chief Yogananda: "In the 'force' we like Q-Anon donuts. The 'color' coated ones are my favorite. By the way, Your Speakerness, do you have a photographic likeness of a Q-Anon?"

Captain Kirk, to the 'Starship Enterprise': "Scottie, beam me up quick. The Q-Anons are taking over the earth. I'll take Cling-Anons anyday."

Pelosi: "Where's that ice cream, God damn it?"

Fly on the Wall: "The world has been shut down for over a year due to a virus with the mortality rate equivalent to the seasonal flu. Now, the Democrats have shut down Washington, D.C. based on an attack from Q-Anons!"

USA Today reporter Jensen continued, "National Guard troops formed a more visible presence (*Author's question: if you are already visible, how can you be more visible?*) at the U.S. Capitol complex on Thursday, with hundreds of troops unloading from a dozen large tour buses while carting long rifles, helmets and backpacks. On Wednesday, Capitol police released a statement warning of a "possible plot to breach the Capitol by an unidentified militia group." Downtown businesses warned tenants about potential protests."[2]

Our undercover reporter, embedded with the National Guard, allegedly recorded the following confidential, anonymous, unconfirmed, yet expert update:

Trooper #1: "Man, I can't believe they drove us down here in 'Big Bus' tour buses! Talk about embarrassing."

Trooper #2: "Well, at least we got a double-decker."

Trooper #3: "Yea, Pelosi's idea to have 'Hop on, Hop off' painted on the outside was genius. Q-Anon will never see us coming."

Trooper #2: "Dude, 12 Big Bus double-deckers are going to be kinda obvious! You think Q-Anon is not going to notice hundreds of green men with guns getting off 'Hop-on, Hop-off' buses?"

Lt. General Russel Honore: "Listen up you dumb shits. Her Speakerness has assigned me to "lead a team of experts, dubbed Task Force 1-6."[3]

Trooper #1: "One minus six equals minus 5."

Lt. General: "That's right grunt! Her Speakerness majored in math. She wants "the government should create an around-the-clock "quick reaction force" of federal law enforcement officers or members of the National Guard at the U.S. Capitol."[4]

Trooper #3: "President Clinton, what does quick reaction mean."

Bill Clinton: "I did not have sex with that woman."

FBI Director Wray: "Mr. President, that was 25 years ago."

Clinton: 'Yea, but those were the days, Chris 'ol buddy.'

Hillary Clinton: "The whole damn thing was a vast right-wing conspiracy, and I wanted to be President so bad!"

Mike Bloomberg: "Don't feel bad Hil, I spent $2 billion of my own money on the shortest primary campaign in history."

Hillary: "I don't care about you Shortie. It's Me, Me, Me!"

Lt. General: "Look alive everybody, those Chinese tourists are going to take our picture. Put on your official Trump MAGA T-shirts."

Chapter 10
It's Circus Time

*"Just cause you got the monkey off your
back doesn't mean the circus has left town."*
—George Carlin

Personal responsibility is often characterized as a burden. For example, every year, we have to file an income statement with the Internal Revenue Service. It's the law and you risk a heavy penalty if you do not do it. Excluding the rich, who pay someone else to carry their burdens, you have to do it yourself. Thus, it is with a sigh of relief that we say, "I got that monkey off my back," once the task is completed.

Voting is optional, but it's the only time we can personally have say in how our government is run. It is our right as citizens. It is a right, not a burden. There is no penalty if we don't do it. When we vote, we do so with a spirit of trust that our vote will count and those who oversee our elections will honestly carry out their duties. That is their burden, they are required by law to follow the specific procedures created by the legislatures of each state. If they do not, they can be prosecuted. State voting laws have many safeguards built in to protect the integrity of the process. This is done because there are always those who will cheat.

Today, at least half of the country is feeling cheated and rightly so. We entered 2020 as politically and ideologically polarized as we've been since the early 1860's. The 1860 election would test whether we remain a country governed by the people and for the people. The country failed the test, and we had the Civil War.

As I describe in detail in the book *34 Days & Holding: America in the Balance*,[1] many battleground Secretaries of State and Governors used the courts to illegally modify election and voting protocols making fraud and cheating much easier. Republicans sued but the state Supreme Courts in Georgia, Michigan, Pennsylvania, Wisconsin, Nevada and Arizona *dismissed every lawsuit* without public hearings or transparency. The judges allowed the lawsuits to be filed, then *dismissed them out of hand*. They had to get the monkey off their back, so they passed the buck.

This allowed appeals to be filed Federal District courts, which quickly 'got the monkey off their backs' by passing the buck to the U.S. Supreme Court, which *delayed* the hearings until after congressional ratification of the electoral vote on January 6, 2021. Technically, we call this sequence of failures and buck passing a 'cluster f**k.'

"On 'Safe Harbor' Day, December 8, the Attorney General of Texas, Ken Paxton, filed a lawsuit against Georgia, Pennsylvania, Michigan, and Wisconsin claiming pandemic spawned changes to election procedures in those states violated federal law and asks the U.S. Supreme Court to block the states from voting in the Electoral College on December 14. By Thursday, December 10, seventeen other state attorney's general joined in the suit."[2] "Early in the evening, on December 11, the Supreme Court *declined to hear* the Texas lawsuit by a vote of 7-2."[3] Another monkey bites the dust.

With the legal landscape already strewn with monkeys, the U.S. Supreme Court, on January 11, 2021, issued an order that *denied bringing forward the Court's consideration of the lawsuits* challenging election procedures in Pennsylvania and Wisconsin, Michigan, and Georgia.[4] The Court *issued no explanatory statement or details on how each Justice voted*.

"The U.S. Supreme Court on Monday brought a formal end to eight lingering disputes pursued by former President Donald Trump and his allies related to the Nov. 3 presidential election including a Republican challenge to the extension of Pennsylvania's deadline to receive mail-in ballots," wrote Andrew Chung and Lawrence Hurley for Reuters on February 22, 2021. But it was not until March 8 (11 days ago as I write) that the last monkey bit the dust. Alison Durkee of Forbes wrote, "The U.S. Supreme Court denied former President Donald Trump's last outstanding post-election lawsuit in Wisconsin Monday, along with a Georgia lawsuit from pro-Trump attorney Lin Wood, delivering a final blow to the ex-president's legal campaign seeking to overturn the election result as his attorneys argued the case could still be relevant for 2024."[5]

Ms. Durkee also states, "The court's ruling, *issued without comment*, once again strikes down a frequent argument made by Republicans post-election claiming that state officials acted illegally by imposing voting rules instead of deferring to state legislatures. The high court has repeatedly rejected post-election lawsuits *without comment* in recent weeks, including other Trump-led challenges and 'Kraken' lawsuits alleging widespread fraud from attorney Sidney Powell."[6]

Perspective. The Constitution specifically assigns the responsibility for election integrity and process legislation to the state legislatures, without exception. All state legislatures have accepted this responsibility and enacted laws to provide for free and fair elections. No state provides an exception for the Governor, the Secretary of State or the State Attorney General to modify what the elected legislative body has enacted. Yet, in each of these key battleground states, this is precisely what happened. Republicans took the state to court, which in every case dismissed the case or the Judge or Judges ruled to deny. All of this happened before November 3. The blow-by-blow detail is provided in *34 Days & Holding: American in the Balance*.[7]

Proof of numerous types of election fraud had been established before election day. President Trump had warned as early as March that the expansion of mail-in ballots, extensions of voting periods and relaxing of signature verification would create unprecedented opportunities for fraud. He was right. Then, the November 3rd massacre occurred, where election officials in select precincts in multiple states stopped the count, blaming it on vote counting machine 'glitches' and other issues. Poll watchers were denied access, others were instructed to abandon protocols, much of which was captured on video and/or confirmed with hundreds of sworn affidavits. This information served as the basis for the many court challenges to follow, which, as we now know, were *all dismissed without due diligence, transparency, or equal justice under the law*. The Judiciary, from bottom to top, abandoned the people and made a mockery of the word justice.

To say our legal system failed would be mostly incorrect. What was lacking, was honesty and integrity among those few judges who presided over these cases. This includes many state supreme court justices and at least 6 U.S. Supreme Court Justices: Roberts, Sotomayor, Bryer, Kagan, Kavanaugh and Barrett. Of course, certain state Governors and Secretaries of State were corrupt, but an honest judiciary could have addressed their malfeasance and provided corrective action. This did not happen. The people were not represented, and the liars and cheaters got off scot free.

These few judges and justices got the monkey off their back by doing nothing. Their responsibility was not only to hear both sides, but to rule according to law. In these cases, the rule says, 'preponderance of evidence.' Instead, the judges and justice chose to 'turn a blind eye.' They chose to hear no evil and see no evil. The result of their 'looking the other way' is now chaos and tragic comedy. The monkeys didn't go away, they just returned to the backs of the American people, who are now powerless to do anything about it. Its circus time in America and the clowns are in charge.

Who is running the country? President Biden gave a speech yesterday (March 18, 2021) to commemorate the milestone of 100 million COVID-19 vaccine doses. As he read the teleprompter, he said, ""Now when *President Harris* and I took a virtual tour of a vaccination center in Arizona not long ago, one of the nurses on that, on that tour injecting people, giving vaccinations, said that each shot was like administering a dose of hope."[8] I seriously doubt the teleprompter referred to V.P. Harris as 'President.' In December 2020, after taking the vaccine, Biden said, "I took it to instill public confidence in the vaccine. *President-elect Harris* took hers today for the same reason."[9]

Following up on the March 18 President Harris comment, Arab News released video and the following description of what happened when 'President Biden' concluded. "After, what was undoubtedly a moving speech about those who had died since the start of the pandemic, President Joe Biden turned from the press, questions still being asked, and walked towards the door – but Harris beat him to it, racing ahead as if she couldn't leave the room fast enough. All Biden could do was stand back and let her through – no doubt trying to avoid that truly awkward situation when two people try to exit a room at the same time and end up wedged at the shoulders – hardly a scene for a president."[10]

Cristina Laila, reported after President Biden gave his January 26 speech on Covid, "What did we just watch? 78-year-old Joe Biden delivered remarks on the Covid pandemic Tuesday after signing a series of executive orders as he trashed Americans as racist, morally deprived people. A confused Biden mumbled to himself and grappled with his pen as he sat down to sign the orders – then he disappeared without answering questions. Joe Biden reappeared an hour later and struggled to make it through his Covid speech."[11]

So, I ask again. "Who is running the country?" It is clearly not Biden. The 'leader of the free world' will not take questions from a sympathetic press. We are told, he will give one a week from today... that would be March 25th. But we have been told that before. In the meantime, here's what's happening under the 'Big Top.'

Essential Ingredients for a Good Circus

1. Dazzling and Daring Acts
2. Sides Shows
3. Clowns

Dazzling and Daring Acts in the Democrat Circus

What is more dazzling and daring than performing feats no one dreamed possible? Feats that go beyond logic and reason, feats that no sane person would do. Welcome everyone to the Democrat Circus 2021. In the Big Tent on March 20, 2021 (today) the Democrats are showcasing:

Biden Tap Dances on the Rio Grande

'Biden is on his heels amid a migrant surge at Mexico border', reads the headline from the Associated Press. Aamer Madhani and Colleen Long write, "Within weeks of Inauguration Day on Jan. 20, the Biden administration had reversed many of the most maligned Trump-era immigration policies... While the administration was working on immigration legislation to address long-term problems, it didn't have an on-the-ground plan to manage a surge of migrants."[12] They continue, "Since Biden's inauguration, the U.S. has seen a dramatic spike in the number of people encountered by border officials. There were 18,945 family members and 9,297 unaccompanied children encountered in February – an increase of 168% and 63%, respectively, from the month before, according to the Pew Research Center."[13]

The good news that Madhani and Long report is "Biden and others have pushed back on the notion that what's happening now is a "crisis."[14] I feel better knowing that don't you? You can refresh your memory on the obvious border nightmare by reviewing Chapter 4.

Biden on the Trail of Science

'FDA problems under Biden - here's how drug safety, public health issues being compromised' is the headline on Fox News. Dr David Gortler, former Yale University professor of pharmacology and biotechnology, who previously served as an FDA medical officer/analyst and FDA drug, device and vaccine safety expert, writes,

"Thanks to the Donald Trump administration's brilliant endeavor to collaborate with Pfizer and Moderna, and extraordinary efforts of every scientist at Operation Warp Speed, we will soon have the horrible Wuhan, China, pandemic in our rearview mirror. (I find it sad and offensive that Barack Obama glibly dismissed the massive efforts that led to the novel ingenuity behind the COVID vaccine development as "not rocket science.")[15]

"As a scientist, I'm therefore concerned today because along with scores of other political appointees, I was abruptly shown the door the minute Joe Biden was sworn into the White House, even though he didn't - and still doesn't - have an FDA commissioner or senior advisor replace for us. That's hard to believe, but it's true. As a result, the critical and nonpartisan public health projects that we'd been working on under the Trump White House came to an unceremonious, grinding halt. The Biden administration didn't care about our epidemiology and drug safety initiatives - they just wanted us gone. This was profoundly unfortunate and has adversely affected America's public health," continued Dr. Gortler.[16]

Gortler further explained his concern, "Alarmingly, our nation has become dependent on China and India to produce many of our pharmaceuticals over the past decade. Overseas labor is cheap, quality is a mystery, FDA inspections are rare and aggressively unwelcome, and the falsification of quality control data by bad actors is much too easy."[17]

Alarmingly, Dr. Gortler closes his expose by saying, "For over a year, and with assistance of others I'd been laboring on advancing the following tasks – which have been dissolved and are no longer underway thanks to the Biden administration:

- Advancing state-of-the-art human tissue micro-plating research to expedite drug discovery. This technology could also eventually eliminate outdated and cruel animal testing that's currently mandated by the FDA. All Americans love their pets – and animal testing has never been all that enlightening with regard to human drug safety, despite the massive kill rate.

- Clearly labeling pharmacy bottles so that each drug's country of origin is identified, giving consumers transparency and a choice about where their pharmaceuticals come from.

- Returning pharmaceutical production back here to the U.S., so that it can be better monitored for safety and quality control, and we can bring back high-paying jobs for pharmaceutical scientists.

- Implementing outside ethics oversight at the FDA. Accountability must be a cornerstone of public service – and right now, at the FDA, when bad decisions are made, there is no accountability.

- This partial list represents a mere 20% of the FDA initiatives that were ongoing during the Trump administration."[18]

In defense of Biden, it should be noted that he said, "We know what we need to do to beat this virus. *Tell the truth, follow the science, work together.*"[19]

OK, maybe I'm being picky, but we just read a detailed article by one of the lead scientists, telling us Biden cancelled everything that was being done and has left the FDA leaderless. I think it's time to put the clowns in the lion cage.

Biden Winks as Blinken Blinks

'Why did Biden's team seem so unprepared for the hostility of their Chinese counterparts?', read the subtitle of an article in Slate.com. "It's no surprise that the Biden administration's first meeting with Chinese officials went badly. Secretary of State Antony Blinken all but said in advance that it would, calling the session a "one-off," rather than the start of negotiations, and saying he'd use it as an opportunity for an "airing of grievances" about China's bad behavior. It is surprising, though, that the meeting went so badly, and even more surprising that Blinken and National Security Adviser Jake Sullivan, who led the U.S. delegation, seemed surprised that it did," wrote Fred Kaplan.[20] It may be the first time in modern history that the United States began diplomatic relations with a new administration by insulting and listing grievances at the country it invited to the meeting. Embarrassing.

Biden and Putin Sit'in in a Tree – Not!

'Vladimir Putin's Challenge to Joe Biden Has People Questioning Who Would Win Debate', read the Newsweek headline on March 18. "Putin issued the challenge after Biden told ABC News the

Russian president would "pay the price" for allegedly interfering in the 2020 election," wrote Ewan Palmer.[21]

When pressed further by ABC, President Biden decided it would be in America's best interest to call Putin 'a killer', as the ABC questioner put it.[22] Putin then makes Biden and America a laughingstock by challenging him to a live televised discussion.

Big Tent Summary

The two dominant issues that America is facing, and has been facing for over a year, are illegal immigration and Covid-19. Biden has signed 37 Executive Orders and Actions (see pages 45 & 185). Ten (27%) of these orders were Covid-19 oriented and five (13.5%) were illegal immigration oriented. Fifteen orders or 40.5% of his total to date, were focused on the two most important issues. The problem: none of them were good for America. All of them cancelled, negated, or neutered the Trump orders and actions that had both issues well under control. We are not even 60 days into the Biden regime, and we have a colossal train wreck.

> **Train Wreck Definition**: When the lead engine jumps the tracks or derails, it takes the rest of the train with it. When the tracks are fine, the fault is with the engineer

The Side Shows are Fun Too

Side Show #1: Press Secretary Jen Psaki Spins Like a Top

- Dec. 31, 2020 – 'Biden's Incoming Press Secretary: Briefings Won't Be A Platform for Right-Wing Spin', NPR headline.[23]

- Jan. 21, 2021 – 'Jen Psaki Spins Biden's '1 Million Shots Per Day' Pledge as 'Bold Goal' Even After

Reporter Notes U.S. Already Hitting That Mark', Mediaite headline.[24]

- Jan. 21, 2021 - 'Press Secretary Jen Psaki Dodges Abortion Policy Question by Citing President Biden's Catholic Faith', Christian Headlines.com headline.[25]

- Feb. 3, 2021 - 'Unnamed White House correspondent says press secretary probing reporters' questions in advance,' Poynter.org[26]

- Feb. 28, 2021 - WATCH: Jen Psaki's Terrible Spin on the Pork-filled American Rescue Plan', Townhall Video headline.[27]

- March 11, 2021 - 'Jen Psaki Tries To Figure Out How To Spin Migrant Children Issue', Majority Report Video on YouTube.com.[28]

- March 11, 2021 - 'White House Press Behave Like Neutered Hamsters in Letting Jen Psaki Spin the Border Crisis', Townhall headline.[29]

So entertaining, right? For perspective, on January 21st, Jen Psaki, in her first press conference, said, "When the president asked me to serve in this role, we talked about the importance of bringing *truth and transparency* back to the briefing room. There are a number of ways to combat misinformation," she said. "One of them is accurate information and truth and data and sharing information even when it is hard to hear."[30] You go Jen! Absolutely the best side show in the circus.

Side Show #2: Democrats speaking with Diverse tongues.

- Jan. 2, 2021 – "We ask it in the name of the monotheistic god, Brahma, and god known by many names by many different faiths. Amen and awoman." Rep. Emanuel Cleaver (D-Mo.) closes the first session of the 117th Congress.[31]

- Jan. 2, 2021 – "I stand before you as a wife, a mother, a grandmother, a daughter."[32] Nancy Pelosi speaks to Congress to announce the Democrats' move to impeach Trump even though he is no longer President. Nine days earlier, the House passed new rules that ordered the use of gender-neutral words. For example: "the name of the Office of the Whistleblower Ombudsman will be changed to the Office of the Whistleblower Ombuds."[33] I am not making this up.

- Jan. 3, 2021 – "We made this change for the sake of inclusion, not exclusion," House Rules Committee Chairman James McGovern (D-Mass.) as the new 'gender language' House rules were introduced to exclude words that have been common English for over a thousand years.[34]

- Jan. 3, 2021 – McGovern maintained that the motion to recommit "can no longer be used to hijack the legislative process for political gamesmanship." McGovern made this comment prior to introducing rule changes designed to allow the Democrat majority to be able to 'hijack' the process. House Minority leader, Kevin McCarthy (R-Calif.), responded, "The Democrats just destroyed over 100 years of representation in Congress. Nancy Pelosi wants to silence YOUR voice and consolidate what little power she has left,"[35] I guess we are in the 'fácil viene, fácil se va' era of government. (*Author's note: The motion to recommit provides one final opportunity for the House to debate and amend a measure, typically after the engrossment and third reading of the bill, before the Speaker orders the vote on final passage.*[36])

- Feb. 3, 2021 – '*John Kerry flew on private jet to accept climate award: 'Only choice for somebody like me'*, read the Washington Times headline. Kerry, Biden's new 'Climate Czar' took his personal jet that "uses 40 times more carbon-dioxide emissions per passenger than a commercial airplane," to receive a climate award in Iceland![37]

- Feb. 22, 2021 – '"To be honest, I'm not no chemist (sic). This is one of the reasons I ended up being a lawyer, instead of a doctor." Merrick Garland, new Attorney General responded when asked if he would "crack down" on Fentanyl look-alike drugs.[38]

- Feb. 28, 2021 – "What am I doing here?" President Joe Biden while addressing the press at the FEMA vaccination facility in Texas. He was having trouble pronouncing names of state congressional representatives and after stumbling, said, "What am I doing here?"[39]

Side Show Summary

At this point, I am struggling to find the words to succinctly summarize and distil the essence of today's Democratic Party. The side shows we have just visited are only a small sampling of this ethically and morally bankrupt party. The only connective tissue seems to be to the phrase repeated by Democrats *ad nauseum* in 2020, 're-imagine'. They want to re-imagine the greatest country the world has ever known. It harkens back to Obama's 'Hope & Change' baloney. Change what? Re-imagine what? Obama did his 'apology' tour of the world, and it now seems Biden will do his 'bend-over' tour. I think it's time to "send in the clowns... don't bother, they're here."[40]

> **[2022 Update for Perspective**: CNN Political reporters, Jennifer Agiesta and Ariel Edwards-Levy wrote on May 4, 2022, "The US public's view of the nation's economy is the worst it's been in a decade, a new CNN Poll conducted by SSRS finds, with many Americans also saying they feel financial strain in their own lives. That pessimism also reflects on President Joe Biden, whose ratings for handling the economy remain sharply negative. A majority of US adults say his policies have hurt the economy, and 8 in 10 say the government isn't doing enough to combat inflation. Only 23% rate economic conditions as even somewhat good, down from 37% in December and 54% last April. The last time public perception of the economy was this poor in CNN's polling was November 2011, when 18% called economic conditions good."]

As you read on in their article, the most staggering statement reads as follows: "Although economic pessimism is most pronounced within the GOP, it spans party lines. A near universal

94% of Republicans rate current economic conditions in the US as poor, as do 81% of independents and **54% of Democrats**. And across party lines, most Americans say they've heard little or no recent good news on the issue (88% among Republicans, 80% among independents, 61% among Democrats)." (cnn.com/2022/05/04/politics/cnn-poll-economy-biden-approval/index.html)

I devote a completely new chapter (Chapter 13) on Biden's disastrous impact on our economy, social fabric and international relations, but by **all** measures, it is an unmitigated disaster. Most economists, as of early May 2022, are saying we are headed for a recession. So, how do you explain only 54% of Democrats rate economic conditions poorly? What are the other 46% doing? The article concludes by noting that Biden's overall approval "holds steady" at 41%. One partial answer to the question regarding what the 40+% are doing – they are living off the government. Which means they are living off hard-working middle-class Americans.]

Send in the Clowns

This chapter has already reviewed many of the clowns currently running the United States. Here are a few more. We don't have to cast the net far to catch clowns in the Democratic party.

Vice President Kamala Harris. Everyone in the world knows Biden's cognitive decline will eventually require his removal and Harris' ascent. She will be President of the United States before 2024. She dropped out of the Democratic primaries two months before voting and caucuses. She said, "As the campaign has gone on, it has become harder and harder to raise the money we need to compete."[41] She could not raise enough money to stay in the race because Democrat donors concluded the other candidates were better investments. Yet, she will be the next President.

Governor Andrew Cuomo (D. New York). The New York Times podcast called 'The Daily' titled its March 19, 2021 show: 'The Ruthless Rise and Lonely Decline of Andrew Cuomo.'[42] Cuomo's order for Covid-19 infected people to be placed in nursing homes while still infectious resulted in an estimated 15,000 deaths. He could have sent these patients to the hospital ship President Trump sent to New York or to the Javits Center. This is over 30% of the deaths to date in the entire state and almost 50% of the New York City deaths. His senior deputy, Melissa DeRosa, publicly admitted the death total was covered up to hide it from a potential FBI investigation.[43] Now, the FBI, the U.S. Attorney and the New York state Attorney General have active investigations.

Cuomo is also being investigated for sexual harassment accusations from eight *(Update March 30th: a ninth has stepped forward)* women, all of whom have come forward to make public statements. Many high-ranking Democrats have called for his resignation, including Senate Majority Leader Chuck Schumer. Cuomo said he will not resign. Some of the women also reported being harassed, threatened, and bullied by Cuomo staff to keep them quiet. There have also been calls for his impeachment. Amazingly, a recent poll revealed over 50% of New Yorkers did not feel he should resign![44]

We must remember that Hollywood recognized the Governors stellar incompetence and arrogance when the International Academy of Television Arts & Sciences, awarded Cuomo the Clown an Emmy "in recognition of his leadership during the COVID-19 pandemic & his masterful use of TV to inform and calm people around the world. Cuomo *stressed the importance of honesty while facing adversity* when he received his Emmy during a virtual ceremony." Celebrity clowns Robert De Niro, Ben Stiller, Billy Joel, Spike Lee, Rosie Perez and Billy Crystal were effervescent endorsements.[45] Apparently not a one of them lost loved ones due to Cuomo's bold order to infect the nursing homes with fresh virus.

Quote from Cuomo the Clown: "We're not going to make America great again; it was never that great." August 15, 2018 washingtonpost.com/politics/2018/08/15/andrew- cuomo-america-was-never-that-great

Governor Gavin Newsom (D. California). Newsom was elected Governor of California in 2018 with a vote total of 7,721,410. His Republican challenger, John Cox received 4,742,825, giving Newsom a margin of 2,978,585 votes. On March 17, 2021, just over three years after taking office, enough signatures were collected to force a recall election in 2021.[46] The recall effort called "Recall Gavin 2020" that California Secretary of State Alex Padilla approved in June reached 2,117,730 signatures on Wednesday -- its deadline to reach at least 1.5 million for the state to hold a special election that could unseat the Democratic governor.[47]

Newsom subjected Californians to draconian and extreme Covid-19 measures, destroying or severely damaging many small business, restaurants, bars and travel oriented businesses. Yet the virus didn't get the memo. California has over 12,000 more Covid-19 deaths than second place New York (as of March 20, 2021). The homeless situation has been spiraling out of control, crime is increasing. Simply put, California is a disaster.

Since it is essential California remain a Democrat state, the news coverage of the recall was almost zero. "ABC completely ignored the latest developments on both "Good Morning America" and "World News Tonight" on both Wednesday and Thursday. There was similarly no mention on "NBC Nightly News" nor on the "CBS Evening News" during that same time period. NBC spent a total of 24 seconds on Newsom's political woes on Wednesday's broadcast of "Today," noted Joseph Wulfsohn of Fox News.[48]

Clowns in Training. The Democratic party is nothing more than a clown re-education organization, and you have to admire their collective dedication to their calling. The primary objective of a clown, as you know, is to look stupid and say stupid stuff. The Democrats have mastered this skill. Just a few more quick examples:

Responding to the out-of-control crisis at the southern border:

V.P. Kamala Harris responded when asked if she plans to go see it firsthand. The NY Post reported, "Not today," said Harris, who formerly represented border-adjacent California as a senator, before letting out a belly laugh. "But I have before, and I'm sure I will again."[49] Funny stuff. Check out this headline from The Epoch Times today (March 22), 'Children Squeezed Body-to-Body in Illegal Immigrant Facility, Leaked Images Show.'[50] The Democrats, the self-proclaimed champions of the unaccompanied minors, apparently have had their interest wane. To be fair to the rank-and-file Democrats who voted these incompetents into power, don't know about the problem because they watch CNN, MSNBC, NPR, NBC, ABC, CBS or read the NY Times or Washington Post.

Run for the Border: Kamala was appointed by Biden to be the Immigration Czar almost three weeks ago. It seems Kamala has decided getting her vice president mansion remodeled is a bigger priority. As of May 1, 2021, she has not spoken about the growing crisis, much less visited the border, but she is working on 'root' causes.

Rep. Veronica Escobar (D-TX). It is an established fact that several illegal immigrants have tested positive for Covid-19 and yet were ordered by the Biden administration to be released into the country.[51] Texas Governor Greg Abbott (R) said the "Biden administration is effectively "importing" coronavirus into the United States by not adequately securing the southern border."[52] Escobar told MSNBC "that Abbott is engaging in an "old, racist trope" that is "really dangerous."[53] The lie is Escobar's, however. Abbot was just reporting confirmed test data.

Figure 18. An overflow facility in Donna, Texas, in an undated 2021 photo. Note: The shiny silver things on the ground are thermal blankets covering children.
(Photo Courtesy of Democrat Rep. Henry Cuellar's office). theepochtimes.com/terrible-conditions-texas-congressman-releases-photos-of-border-patrol-tent-facility

Homeland Security Secretary Alejandro Mayorkas. On March 1st, Mayorkas said, "the U.S. was not facing a "crisis" at the southern border amid thousands of daily migrant apprehensions, *it's a 'challenge.'*[54] Not quite three weeks later, he told a House committee that the Mexican border situation was "undoubtedly difficult." A day earlier (March 16), he said *he expects more apprehensions along the southwestern border this year than at any time in the past two decades*. When asked by John Katko (R, NY), top Republican on the House Homeland Security Committee, if the situation was a crisis, Mayorkas responded: "I'm not spending any time on the language that we use. I am spending time on operational response on the situation at the border."[55]

Rochelle Walensky, CDC Director, told Stat News there had not been a large exodus of experts from the Atlanta-based agency. "I don't want to say nobody's left, but I really haven't lost much of the greatness that made CDC what it was or what it is."[56] What? Maybe she was nervous? But, later in the interview, she said, "This virus has been humbling. *I'm pretty cautiously optimistic that we know a lot about this virus*, that we know a lot about how we can prevent getting it, what we can do to mitigate. We have a vaccine that's here in really record time. And so, I'm pretty optimistic, except that we have the threat of variants."[57] Oh my God! I would quote more of the interview, but it would destroy any glimmer of confidence you might have remaining in the CDC (*see Author's note in Chapter 3*).

Maj. Gen. Michael McGuire, Chairman of the National Guard Association of the United States. On March 12, 2021 said, "They have completed their mission. They have made us all proud. It's time for local law enforcement to take it from here."[61] He was speaking of the brave troops who were deployed to protect the capital against Q-Anons.

Minneapolis City Council. December 10, 2020. The council cut an additional $7.7 million from the police department. That money will fund mental health crisis teams, train dispatchers to assess mental health calls and have other employees handle theft and property damage reports.[58]

Portland Oregon, City Council. June 2020, the Portland city council cut $16 million from the police department budget. This is the city that set the Guinness book of world records for consecutive days of riots courtesy of the far-left groups Antifa and BLM. On a scale of 1-10 with 10 being astoundingly stupid, the council gets an 11! These people should all be relegated to an 'autonomous zone.' But the tragicomedy gets better, the wimp they elected as mayor, Ted Wheeler, is now asking for 'Refunding' the police $2 million.[59]

I lived in Minneapolis for 15 years and raised my kids there. It used to be a great city. Now, it and Portland have been overrun by imbeciles. There is no other logical conclusion. The mayors and city council members were elected, the people had a choice. One wonders how bad it has to get before the people wake up. But wait, they are already 'woke' so, my mistake.

This list of clowns in the Democratic Party at all levels of government across the country goes on and on and on. The party is no longer the party of John F. Kennedy. Kennedy was a staunch anti-communist, now we have communists exerting outsized influence. Bernie Sanders, A.O.C, and Elizabeth Warren are among three examples. To be fair and balanced, the Republicans have their clowns also, but in a head-to-head comparison, they are paragons of America compared to the Democrats.

The Power Behind the Throne?

We began this chapter by posing the question "Who is in charge in Washington?" Today (March 22nd) Jen Psaki may have given us some insight. A reporter asked Psaki if Obama had visited the White House and how often he and Biden speak. She responded, "President Biden maintains "regular" communication with Barack Obama on a number of issues."[60]

Sadly, the circus will go on. The country is only 60-plus days into this fiasco. The next week or so are likely to be a continuing down the drain spiral of the issues this book has been exposing. Since everyone knows the 'emperor has no clothes', we will now consider what the real drivers of this insanity might be. Hint: Barack Obama may be the mouth, but he is not the head.

> **Author's Changing Perspective on Democrat Voters:** I have spent most of my life living as a political minority in Minneapolis, Chicago and Denver. Thus, most of our friends have been/are Democrats. If politics is avoided,

we always have a good time, agree on most things, etc. I have said many times, "They are good people, but...". These 'good people' are willfully ignorant. I cannot count the times I have encouraged them to compare and contrast reporting on their current news sources and conservative ones. THEY WILL NOT DO IT! You can tell a child to not touch a hot stove, but they might do it once, then they learn. The Democrats keep electing the same charlatans and expect different results. It is mind boggling. They choose to remain ignorant and thus innocent people are harmed. They themselves are harmed. The mule is an appropriate avatar for the party. I can write this without fear because they won't read my books!

Chapter 11
Nine Zeros

"Qu'ils mangent de la brioche"
Marie-Antoinette, ~1789

*"Money, money, money
Must be funny
In the rich man's world"*
Benny Andersson and Björn Ulvaeu
ABBA 1976

The quintessential statement of an arrogant disconnected aristocracy is translated in English, "Let them eat cake." The statement, falsely attributed to Marie-Antoinette, queen of France, probably originated with Jean-Jacques Rousseau, in his autobiography, written before Marie-Antoinette had arrived from Austria.[2]

Money begats power and power begats arrogance. Money, power and arrogance begats elitism. The best example of a modern-day Marie Antoinette is John Kerry. Kerry has been a 'cake-eater' his entire life, thus it was no surprise when he told the 11,000 workers who lost their pipeline jobs due to Biden's Keystone pipeline shutdown, to get jobs making solar panels. "They can make solar panels," Kerry Antoinette said. Later when the new Climate Czar was challenged for taking a private jet to Iceland to receive a Climate Award (for which he did nothing), he said, "If you off-set your carbon, it's the only choice for *somebody like me.*"

(FoxNews Feb. 3, 2021) Elites never mix with non-elites due to hygiene issues, but they have no problem telling us how to live.

According to Forbes, there are 2,095 billionaires in the world today. In round numbers, they are collectively worth $8 trillion.[4] $8,000,000,000,000, the number eight followed by 12 zeros! The United States has 614 billionaires worth $2.9 trillion. Jeff Bezos is number one at $113 billion and Bill Gates is number two at $98 billion (as of this writing).

[**2022 Update**: Divorce of both Bezos and Gates has dethroned them from the leadership of Bezosgateslandia but the metaphor and message of this chapter remain appropriate and the data an accurate snapshot in time. Elon Musk is now the new king.]

> **Author Trivia:** Marie Antoinette does not deserve her villainess reputation. She is known today for a statement she did not make. She is thought of as a self-centered elitist who cared nothing for others. The facts are more interesting:
>
> 1. Were it not for her influence over Louis XVI, France may not have given the fledgling United States the support it needed to gain independence.
>
> 2. At age 14, she was a 'peace pawn' to end war between Austria & France. Imagine a U.S. President giving one of his daughters to one of Putin's sons to keep the peace
>
> 3. She eventually proved herself one of the 'stronger' women behind the throne and exerted significant influence on the affairs of state. Thus, she was hated by many in the French court and the Cardinal.

4. Early on, she was loved by the French people and hated by the French aristocracy who hated Austria.

5. She endured constant slander, court intrigue, & conspiracy that enraged a gullible mob and resulted in her execution.[3]

The most appropriate measure of a person's wealth is their net worth (the value of all their assets minus all their liabilities). Your home is an asset only to the extent of the equity you have in it plus any appreciation in property value. So, for most people, their home is a net liability. This was a major cause of the 2001 subprime loan crisis. People bought homes they could not afford because they were told property values always go up. Bill Gates does not have this worry.

Individual Net Worth in the United States (Feb 2021) [3]

Age Group	Median	Average
< 35	$13,900	$76,300
35-44	$91,300	$436,200
45-54	$168,600	$833,200
55-64	$212,500	$1,175,900
65-74	$266,400	$1,217,700
> 75	$254,800	$977,600

https://www.visualcapitalist.com/visualizing-net-worth-by-age-in-america/

Table 5. Net Worth in the United States Feb. 2021

The net worth of Americans by age group is in Table 5. Jeff Bezos is 57, so his age group has a median net worth of $212,500 and an average net worth of $1,175,900. This demonstrates why averages should not be used to describe the finances of populations, the very rich skew the results to the high side. So, we use the median, the middle number. If we divide the median net worth for those 55-64 into Bezos' net worth, we find that he is 531,765 times richer than more than half of his age group.

The population of the U.S. today is approximately 330,121,581 (that's at 10:28 a.m. mountain time March 6, 2021)[5] There are approximately 26.4 million people in his age group. This is one way to demonstrate the 'wealth gap' or what today is commonly called 'income inequality.' Following are some charts to help visualize the problem.

Gross Domestic Product (GDP) is the economist's preferred measure of the health and vibrancy of a country's economy. It represents the total value of all goods and services produced during a specified time period. If the GDP of a country is growing, it means people are working, making and selling stuff, and providing services; all of which are growing in demand. For there to be demand, consumers must have disposable income (i.e., income left over after they have paid their monthly mortgage, car payment, credit card debt, etc). Our expanding use of buying on credit is growing concern, but let's keep it simple for now. A growing GDP is a good thing. Always.

I will now take a little 'author's license' to help you visualize one of the problems this book is attempting to describe. The country of Bezosgateslandia has a population of 4-5 people and a net worth of $211,000,000,000. 211 with nine zeros trailing behind is $211 billion.

Bezosgateslandia is not listed on the Worldometer list of countries by GDP, but if it were, it would be the 50th largest economy in the world (Figure 17). I admit to taking license by comparing individual net worth to a country's GDP, but believe it is valid in a macro sense.

Another look at the Worldometer, and we learn that there are 190 countries on its list. Bezosgateslandia, has an economy larger and more vibrant than the 140 individual countries below it. Of course, when some of these smaller countries combine economies, they are larger. But, they are countries; Bezosgateslandia is really just two people. Let that sink in.

U.S. Income Distribution. Returning our focus to the United States, we will now look at annual income. Since the residents of

Bezosgateslandia have income swings in a single day that are larger than the GDPs of small countries, I will not attempt to assess their annual incomes. If Jeff Bezos put his entire fortune in a passbook saving account paying 0.5%, he would make $565 million, which would put him well into the top category. So, let's put that in the context of us 'common people.' Biden says 'income inequality' is one of the transformative issues of the day, but is that true?

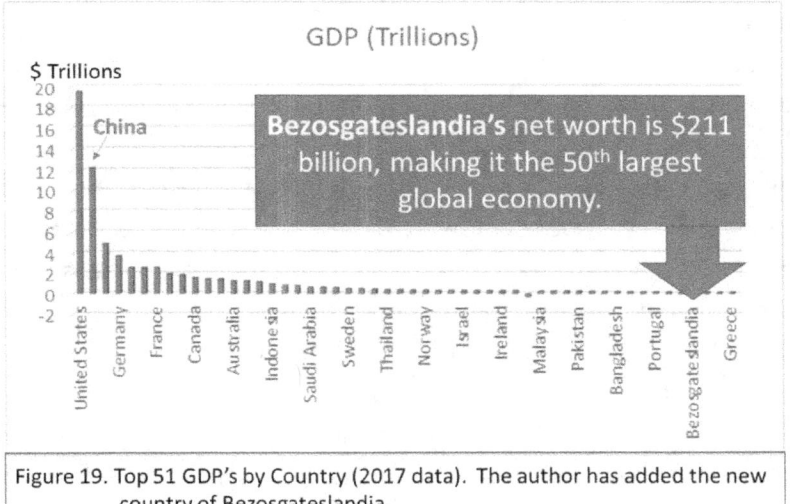

Figure 19. Top 51 GDP's by Country (2017 data). The author has added the new country of Bezosgateslandia.

The other data are from worldometer.com (3/6/21) [6]

Households that earned over $200,000 in 2019 totaled 15.4 million, or about 10% of all American households. A good portion of the members of this group are earning between $200,000 to $249,000 per year.[7] Compare Figures 20 and 21. Figure 20 presents only Census Bureau data, while Figure 21 adjusts the census data with data from the World Inequality Database (WID). The Congressional Research Service (CRS) makes this adjustment to include income from capital gains, which the Census Bureau (CB) excludes. The CRS data allow the CB high income category to be divided into $200,000-$249,000 and $250,000 and above categories. I show both charts so you can see the data in pure and adjusted forms.

The CRS report (Figure 21) shows 6% of the households in 2019 had an income of $250,000 or greater; that equates to 7.7 million households. This includes the billionaires, the $100 millionaire entrepreneurs, business owners, hedge-funders, professional athletes, Hollywood elite, Dr. Anthony Fauci, etc. Of the 7.7 million, 614 are billionaires.

The income level for the bottom half of the country is relatively flat, with the median income at $68,703. Just before we reach this median income, a slow gradual decline begins as income increases. This is normal for a society built on capitalism and free enterprise. Communist economies are the only ones that have no income variation, because the government controls wages. Their leadership, however, becomes wealthy off the back of the people. If then, money means power, both the U.S. and communist countries have the power vested in a few rich people. Is this any different than it has ever been?

In 2010, Emmanuel Saez and Thomas Picketty, published historical data for U.S. income distributions from 1913 to 2010 (Figure 22).[9] Notice how the top line, representing the 90% of wages earners, begins to decline around 1980, while the top 1% begins to increase.

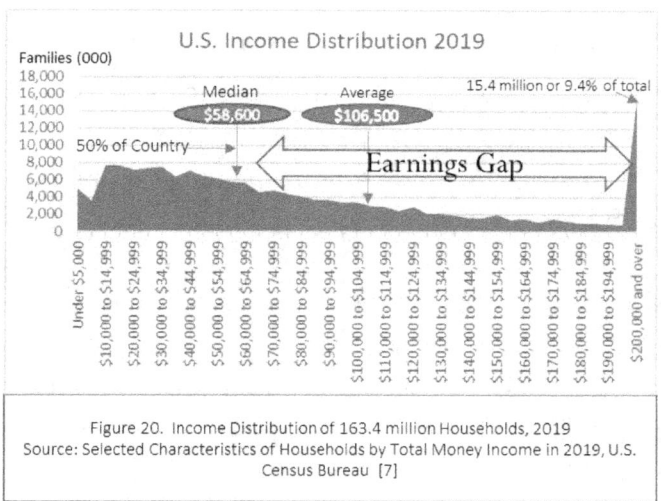

Figure 20. Income Distribution of 163.4 million Households, 2019
Source: Selected Characteristics of Households by Total Money Income in 2019, U.S. Census Bureau [7]

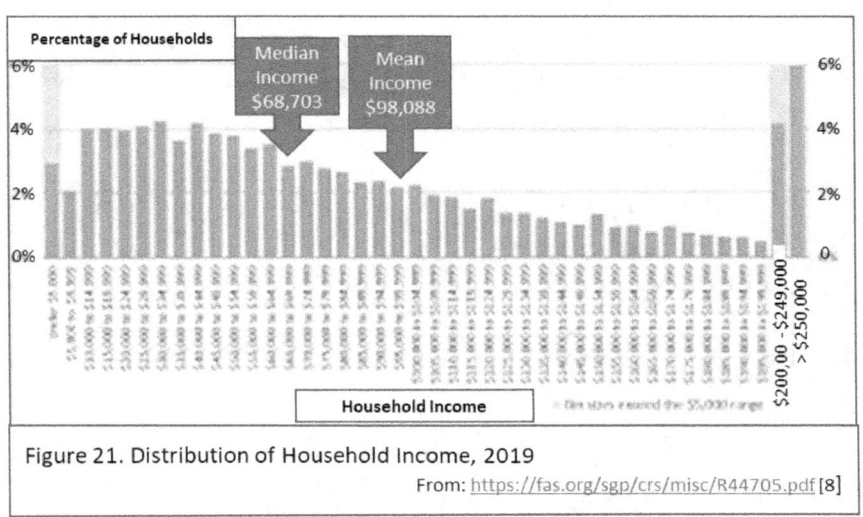

Figure 21. Distribution of Household Income, 2019
From: https://fas.org/sgp/crs/misc/R44705.pdf [8]

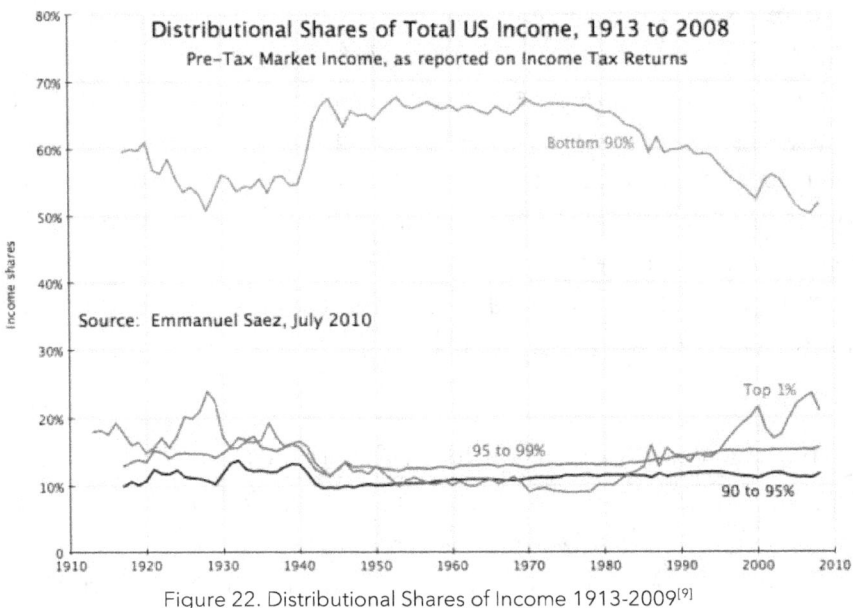

Figure 22. Distributional Shares of Income 1913-2009[9]

This is the beginning of President Reagan's great economic expansion. He did three critical things:

- Decreased personal and corporate income tax rates (i.e., letting people keep more of the money they earned),

- Deregulated business (reduced government intervention) and

- Cut government spending (reducing the size of government).

Presidents George H.W. Bush and Bill Clinton both continued these policies, keeping the expansion going. The Joint Economic Committee Report of 1996 (under the Clinton presidency) concluded:

"The Reagan tax cuts, like similar measures enacted in the 1920s and 1960s, showed that reducing excessive tax rates stimulates growth, reduces tax avoidance, and can increase the amount and share of tax payments generated by the rich. High top tax rates can induce counterproductive behavior and suppress revenues, factors that are usually missed or understated in government static revenue analysis."[10]

Yet, Joe Biden and the Democrats are making 'income inequality' a primary policy focus.

Is Income Inequality a Valid Policy Issue?

Biden's first Executive Order was 13985: *Advancing Racial Equity and Support for Underserved Communities Through the Federal Government* (see page 47). The Democrats mischaracterize data similar to what is presented in Figure 22 to demonstrate 'economic inequality' and justify government intervention. They point to the decline in 'share of income' without clarification that the real incomes for everyone actually went up. The share declines because the pie gets bigger and the 1% is reaping a large share of that increase. But so what. Many of this top group took great risk and worked extremely hard to make their business idea work. Some, maybe most, also had a good dose of luck (i.e., Bill Gates, Sergey Brin, Larry Page and Jeff Zuckerberg). So, should they be penalized or demonized because they had some luck? How absurd.

Democrats know the message of 'it's not fair' and 'stick it to the rich' will always resonate. Their message is a con game. The Reagan-Bush-Clinton expansion was real, and EVERYONE benefitted. Let's get some more historical perspective.

History. Beginning in 1970 and accelerating in 1980s, the bottom 90% of working Americans saw their share of the national income decline by a little over 15% (Figure 22). Democrats point to this fact to make their case for higher taxes as a means to correct income inequality. This misrepresents the data and sets up a 'false equivalence'. As mentioned earlier, everyone benefitted during this expansion. Ask yourself, would you prefer that everyone have the same income or a vibrant, growing economy? If you chose economic equality, then I suggest you move to Russia, China, or Venezuela.

Monica Prasad, professor of sociology at Northwestern University and author, wrote in 2019 for Politico, a progressive on-line news group, "Democrats believe the wealthy have benefited the most from the economic growth of the past several decades, and it's time to ensure that all Americans share in that growth. Some want to reduce inequality for its own sake. Others argue tax revenues are needed for things that most Americans support, including public education, infrastructure, research and development, easing the transition to an automated economy, mitigating climate change, and addressing wage stagnation and the social fraying that it leads to."[11]

She continues, "THE DEMOCRATS OF today should consider what the Democrats of 1980 knew: The top marginal tax rate generates very little income for the federal government. At the time, the 70 percent rate didn't kick in until $212,000, which in today's dollars is over $600,000. Since this was a marginal rate, no one, not even the richest millionaire, paid 70 percent of their entire income in taxes; only the portion of their income above the threshold was taxed at the top rate. Most important, the rich had ways to shift their income to avoid taxes, because the top rate only applied to "unearned income" such as dividends. This meant that whether the goal was to reduce inequality or raise revenue, the top tax rate was not very effective."[12]

OK, so far so good. At this point, I will just caution that the phrase 'the rich' is not defined. Democrats like to target 'the rich' knowing the word triggers emotion. Wealthy divorcees and widows, however, should be careful; they might find themselves in the 'target.'

After four years of the incompetent Jimmy Carter, Americans (including myself) knew they had made a poor choice. Ronald Reagan won the 1980 election in a landslide and hit the ground running. By August 1981, six months after his inauguration, President Reagan signed the Economic Recovery Tax Act of 1981 (ERTA).[13]

The ERTA[14]:

- Cut the highest income tax bracket from 70% to 50%.

- Cut the bottom bracket from 14% to 11%.

- Accelerated depreciation deductions.

- Expanded eligibility for Individual Retirement Accounts (IRAs).

- Reduced the capital-gains tax from 28% to 20%.

- Raised the estate-tax exemption.

Most people are not aware that President Reagan got his B.A. in Economics and was a devotee of Adam Smith and Nobel laureate Friedrich von Hayek. Milton Friedman, also a Nobel laureate and professor of Economics at the University of Chicago, was Reagan's most influential economic advisors. So, when Reagan signed ERTA he knew it would be a shock to the system by having tax revenue decreased in the short term.

The Government bureaucracy was addicted to taxpayer 'revenue' and Reagan was cutting off the flow. The screaming was so loud, that Senate Majority leader Bob Dole scrambled the Republicans to make some minor adjustments.

In 1982, they passed 'The Tax Equity and Fiscal Responsibility Act'. Will Kenton and Janet Berry-Johnson wrote for Investopedia, "Reagan resisted any tax increases for a time, but eventually relented only when he extracted a pledge for even bigger spending cuts as part of the deal. Signing the bill into law, Reagan said he was supporting "a limited loophole-closing tax increase" to raise more than $98 billion over three years in return for spending cuts worth $280 billion during the same period."[14]

Reagan inherited a mess from Carter and delivered a dream to Bush and Clinton. His accomplishment is extraordinary because he did this with Democrat majorities in both houses (Figure 23) and all Americans were winners.

The Federal Reserve did its part through the expansion era by moving interest rates down gradually and then stabilizing them in the Clinton years. The expansion, however, was driven by Reagan's reduction of taxes and regulations and cuts in spending.

In hindsight, it would have been better if Alan Greenspan, Fed chief at the time, had resisted Wall Street's calls for lower interest rates, but he didn't. It set the precedent for a more activist and aggressive Federal Reserve and it gave Wall Street the insatiable thirst for cheap money (Figure 24) and a banker of last resort when they screw up.

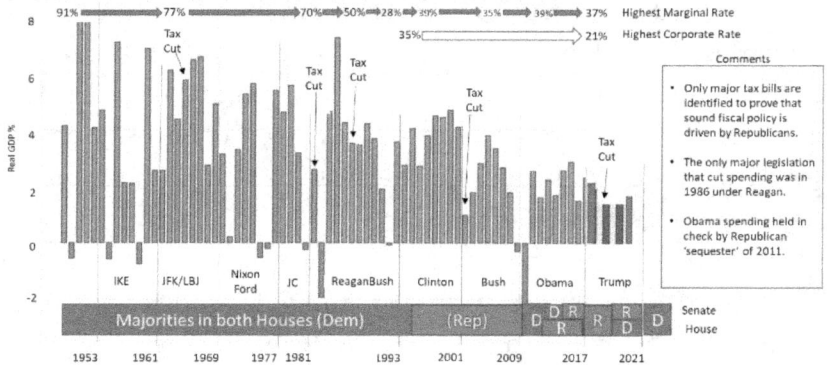

Figure 23. U.S. Gross Domestic Product 1953 – 2020 and Party Dominance
Sources: GDP (Bureau of Economic Analysis)[15]; Party Dominance (U.S. Gov. InfoPlease) [16]

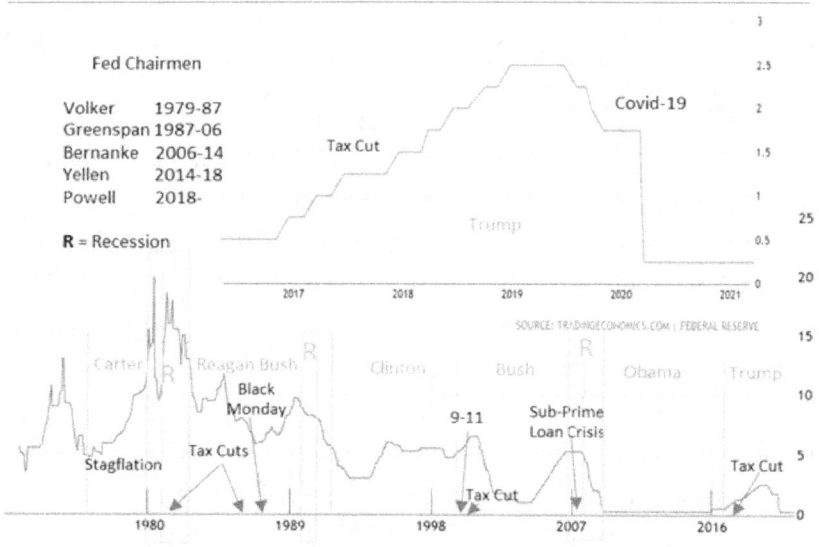

Figure 24. United States Fed Funds Rate 1971-2021
https://tradingeconomics.com/united-states/interest-rate

[17]

From Ben Bernanke to the present, the Federal Reserve has created a house of cards. The activist position the Fed has taken regarding providing easy money and economic stimulus not only weakens the dollar (i.e., America's buying power), it inflates prices and requires the continuance of low rates to keep down the government's interest on its debt (now a trillion dollars per year). President Trump's policies were stimulating the economy, creating jobs and increasing wages. He was also able to hold the Fed accountable. Biden and his administration are pursuing policy that will reverse all of this. He claims income inequality is a problem – it is not. He claims his policies will help 'underserved' (another undefined term) – they will not. It will make things worse. Cheap money benefits the rich not the poor, not the average American and not even the upper middle class. It will further divide the country into have and have nots, the makers and takers.

Prosperity versus Income Inequality

This chapter began with a vignette about how power is derived from money which results in arrogant elitism and a disconnectedness from the common man. We are now witnessing the exhibition of this arrogant elitism and disconnectedness in the Biden administration. They say one thing (i.e., we will help the 'underserved') but they do the opposite (implement policies that do harm to the bottom 75% of America). Examples:

- The offer of broad amnesty to those who have entered the country illegally. This increases the labor force at the bottom of the pyramid, drives down wages, increases the tax burden and will cost many their jobs.

- Stopping the completion of the border wall has significantly enhanced illegal entry, in fact, has invited it.

- Shutting down the Keystone pipeline immediately put 15,000 people out of work. It did not stop the transport of oil, only keeps it from being transported in a safer way (i.e., a pipe versus rail & surface transport). John Kerry arrogantly said these innocent people can find new jobs making solar panels. You cannot get more ignorant or disconnected.

We then took a detailed look at income distribution and allowed the data to prove that income inequality is NOT an issue. It IS make-believe, fantasy, elitist bull***t. The phenomenon of our times is the development of the 'super rich.' To dramatize this category, we created the country of Bezosgateslandia, the 50th largest economy in the world, where all the assets are owned by two people. Then we clarified that a small rich and powerful group has always existed, even in communist countries. Money does bestow power. The 'super-rich' have tremendous personal power and thus constantly face the temptation to use this power and influence inappropriately. Many, maybe most, of the super-rich are good, honest family people. I was fortunate enough to know one of these people pretty well many years ago. He was CEO of the largest privately owned company in the world at the time, Cargill Incorporated. His name was Whitney McMillian. He was completely unpretentious, courteous, engaging, and personable and generous.

People should be measured by their character not by their wealth. Yet the Democrats pit one group against another. They demonize the wealthy as a group but suck up to them behind the scenes.

As with every segment of society, there is a dark side. There are many George Soros types alive and doing damage in the world today. The answer to that is strong representative leadership in government, something of which the left is completely devoid.

The Rise of the Anti-Trump

President Trump's policies and actions were even more effective than Reagan's. He pursued prosperity for all and was delivering on that promise. Now, we have the anti-Trump unravelling the prosperity policies in the name of racial justice and equity. The rule that ALWAYS works best is 'Less is Best' when considering Government Intervention. Democrats ALWAYS reject this rule.

> **Author's Postscript to Chapter 11:**
> The concepts of equity and fairness resonate positively with the average person, but no one can explain what they mean. If they cannot be defined, they cannot be measured. If they cannot be measured, they should not be politicized. Equity or inequity is in the eye of the beholder. When Democrats make 'addressing inequity' a policy issue, they will only create more inequity and division.
>
> There is nothing government does that does not impact the economy. When the economy is impacted by Executive Orders or legislation, every American feels that impact. If the government action creates more government (i.e., bureaucracy and regulation), the impact will be negative. Intervention is the Democrat approach. Every time they intervene, we lose freedoms and life becomes more difficult. More law means less freedom. This is an immutable truth.
>
> Biden & the Democratic party are pursuing interventionist policies. The impact will be negative for the country. There is precedent for everything they are doing or proposing, and it has never worked.
>
> President Biden just said in his press conference today (March 25) that he was hired to solve problems. The 'problems' they are prioritizing, however, are

imagined or manufactured. Racial and/or income inequality is not a societal problem. Climate is not an existential threat. Covid-19 over-reaction has hurt more than it has helped. Government is the problem.

National sovereignty is a serious problem, but they are opening the border. The 1st & 2nd Amendments are in jeopardy and the filibuster rule is being attacked. So far, the Democrat agenda is proving it will Make American Worse Again.

Chapter 12
Beyond Parody

- Jack McDermott: Stop! Who dares to tow the van of the living Christ?

- Driver: The city of New York, Tarzan! $50 for the violation, $75 for the tow and $20 a day for storage.

- Jack McDermott: Father, forgive us for we have sinned! We parked our car in a forbidden zone!"

—From: *The Dream Team* movie, 1989

Forgiveness is a wonderful thing…. for the offender. I thank God for His forgiveness every day, but when the offense was premeditated and intentional, my personal preference is 'you reap what you sow.'

We have now entered the final 30 days of the first 100 days of the anti-Trump; it is, appropriately, April 1st. But who is the fool? Is it the zombie in the Whitehouse, or is it the people who voted for him? I'll let you decide.

Thinking things could not get worse, after the 'halftime' update, was also foolish. We seem to be on the 'cart to hell' painted by Hieronymus Bosch around 1500.[1]

Biden Shows His Love for Spending Taxpayer Money

Trigger alert! This is not an April Fool's joke. President Biden announced, on March 31st, his $2 trillion American Jobs Plan. This is on top of his $1.9 trillion American Rescue Plan that was not needed but passed with no Republican support. He also said in his

Pittsburg speech that another $2 trillion would be proposed for the pending American Families Plan.[2,3] The good news, as of this writing, is that only the 'Rescue Plan' $1.9 trillion bill has been signed into law. The bad news is that there is no longer any doubt that the Democratic Party is hell-bent on destroying the United States. Here are some verbatim quotes from Biden's speech (*all from reference*[3]):

- "And just looking for a little bit of breathing room, just a little bit of light, ordinary Americans, doing extraordinary things, people would break their necks every day for their families and the country they love, a country that in fact which on the day I was elected was in extreme distress with the virus on a deadly rampage that has now killed over 4,500, excuse me, I carry it in my pocket every day, I have the list of exactly how many have died, 547,296 Americans dead from the virus, more than all the people killed in World War One, World War Two, the Vietnam War, 9/11." *Author's comment: It's a good thing he carries it in his pocket, his memory was a little off. Oh, and he forgot to mention Covid-19 was a gift to the world, not just the U.S. from China.*

- "That's why I moved so quickly to pass the American Rescue Plan." (*see chapter 5*)

- "Millions of Americans lost their jobs last year, while the wealthiest 1% of Americans saw their net worth increase by $4 trillion." *(Remember, unemployment remains a problem only in Democrat run states. Review chapter 4 & 11)*

- "It'll grow the economy, make us more competitive around the world, promote our national security interest and put us in a position to win the global competition with China in the upcoming years." *(Author's comment: The exact opposite is what will happen.)*

- "I'll begin with the heart of the plan. It modernizes transportation infrastructure, our roads, our bridges, our airports." "It's about infrastructure." *(Author's comment: Only 29% is for infrastructure.)*

The last bullet point is key because the press is spinning this as an infrastructure bill. No, it's a plan to bankrupt America.

No More Racist Highways & Bridges.

One of the objectives of Biden's 'infrastructure' bill is to eliminate racism from our highway and bridge system. Ian Duncan of the Washington Post writes, "Since she moved back home to Tremé almost a decade ago, Amy Stelly has waged a campaign for the removal of a highway that cuts through her New Orleans neighborhood."[4]

This is the first sentence in Duncan's article titled, *'A woman called for a highway's removal in a Black neighborhood. The White House singled it out in its infrastructure plan.'* Duncan continues, "On Wednesday (March 31st), Stelly's effort gained a considerable boost when the White House named the highway, the Claiborne Expressway, an example of a historic inequity that President Biden's new infrastructure plan would seek to address through billions in new spending."[5] File this under the acronym - ISYN.

The Whitehouse 'Fact Sheet' heading for this proposed appropriation is *'Redress historic inequities and build the future of transportation infrastructure.'* This is so ludicrous and 'in your face,' you have to read the full text to grasp the disdain the Democrats have for American trust.

"The President's plan for transportation is not just ambitious in scale, it is designed with equity in mind and to set up America for the future. Too often, past transportation investments divided communities – like the Claiborne Expressway in New Orleans or I-81 in Syracuse – or it left out the people most in need of affordable transportation options. The President's plan includes $20 billion for a new program that will reconnect neighborhoods cut off by historic investments and ensure new projects increase opportunity, advance racial equity and environmental justice, and promote affordable access. The President's plan will inspire basic research, like advanced pavements that recycle carbon dioxide, and "future proof" investments that will last decades to leave coming generations with a safe, equitable, and sustainable transportation system. And, the President's plan will accelerate transformative investments, from pre-development through construction, turning "shovel worthy" ideas into "shovel ready" projects. This includes $25 billion for a dedicated fund to support ambitious projects that have tangible benefits to the regional or national economy but are too large or complex for existing funding programs."[6]

The Office of Diversity, Equity, and Inclusion.

Antony Blinken, Secretary of State, needs an Office of Diversity, Equity, and Inclusion. Document obtained by Breitbart News say the new office "will provide a framework that transcends historical limitations and promotes boundless possibilities for all individuals regardless of status."[7] Just the thought of 'transcending boundless possibilities' sends chills down my spine. Have you ever walked through one of the hundreds of government office buildings in and around Washington, D.C.? If not, your first impression might be, 'Dude, where are the white people?' So, a little inclusion and diversity along those lines might be good. Anyway, it's only going to cost $2.5 million.

Biden Rewards Illegal Immigrants with Hotel Stays.

"Biden has awarded $86 million contract for hotel rooms near the border to hold around 1,200 migrant family members who cross the U.S.-Mexico border", DHS officials confirmed to Axios.[8] FoxNews (and other outlets) followed the Axios report clarifying that the total is actually $86.9 million for 1,239 beds in hotels.[9]

OK, $86.9 million divided by 182 days (~6 months) equals $477,472 per day. Divide that by 1,239 and we get $385.37 per bed per day. Most hotels have two beds per room, so this makes the room cost $385.37 x 2 = $770.73 per room (or family, if it's one family per room with two beds). I'm sure the American taxpayers will get a thank you note from these people who came into the country illegally.

One More Time with Gusto

Just to refresh the screen for you, we are having the swarm at the southern border because Biden and the Democrats (*see Chapter 4 for details*):

- Rescinded Trump's 'Remain in Mexico' policy and agreement with Mexico.

- Reinstituted Obama's 'Catch and Release' policy (i.e., illegals claim asylum, are granted a court date and then released into the U.S.).

- Terminating completion of the border wall, leaving holes they are literally driving vans through.

Kamala Gets the Call'a

Biden had a brief moment of lucidity when he announced on March 24, that Vice President Kamala Harris would "lead efforts to stem migration across the U.S.-Mexico border" and "Biden said during an immigration meeting at the White House that he had asked Harris to lead the administration's efforts with Mexico and the Northern Triangle – El Salvador, Guatemala and Honduras, countries that will "need help stemming the movement of so many folks, stemming the migration to our southern border," reported NBC News. An administration official said one of the Vice President's objectives is to "addresses the root causes of migration."[10]

Rumor has it that Biden said, as he was going back to the Whitehouse for his nap, 'Got that monkey off my back!' Actually, I made that up. Fact is, that was ten days ago, and no one has heard from the V.P. since. We do know she is yet to actually visit the border.

Senator Ted Cruz (R, TX) did visit the border with several other legislators last week and said, ""True transparency would be to open the Donna facility to press that's at 1,556% capacity when 18 Senators go there Friday,"[11] Cruz tweeted. "Reports about the CBP's Donna facility indicate minors are hungry, have only showered once in 7 days, were forced to sleep on the floor, and haven't seen sunlight in days. Of course, the Biden admin isn't allowing cameras in that facility."[12] Mr. Cruz was able to take photos and video of the human nightmare, even though Biden officials tried to stop him. Biden has issued a gag order for border officials. NBC reported that Border Patrol staff have been told to refer all media requests, even those from local outlets to Customs and Border Protection (CBP) staffers in Washington and to deny all "ride-along" requests. The network attributed the information to officials who asked to remain anonymous."[13]

Author's Thoughts on 'Root Causes'

Before the Democrats burn the country down, I would just like to offer V.P. Harris some ideas on the root causes of illegal immigration and also some solutions.

Possible Causes:

1. Offering jobs with the benefit of not having to pay taxes

2. Providing free education, health care, food, subsidized housing, and other free stuff American citizens pay for.

3. Offering driver's licenses without proof of legal status

4. Offering citizenship to babies born in the U.S.

5. Releasing them after they have broken the law

Solution: STOP doing the above and finish the border wall!

April 2nd Update: The number of migrants apprehended at the U.S.-Mexico border reached the highest monthly total in 15 years, with more than 170,000 crossings recorded in March, according to preliminary Customs and Border Protection (CBP) data.[14]

Evanston, Illinois Votes to Pay Reparations.

'Chicago Suburb Approves $10 Million Reparations Program Funded by Marijuana Tax Revenue,' reads the headline in the Epoch Times on March 23rd. The Evanston city council voted 8-1 establish a reparations process. Eligible black households will receive $25,000 for home repairs or down payments. The plan is to expand the grants to $10 million within 10 years.[15]

In case you are wondering, Evanston is 59.4% white (Non-Hispanic) and 16.2% black. The council claims a 3% tax on marijuana sales will cover the costs. So, in Evanston, the pot smokers will be paying the reparations. I'm sure there is a 'hidden' logic involved.

But, hey, Evanston ain't alone baby. Peter Dixon quoted '1619 Project' leader, Nikole Hannah-Jones in late August 2020, "As Black Lives Matter protests have surged across the United States, *several cities and at least one state have taken significant steps toward offering reparations for slavery and its legacy of systemic racism*, including Evanston, Ill.; Asheville, N.C.; Burlington, Vt.; Providence, R.I.; and California. Discussions about U.S. reparations for Black people have been underway for years, but the momentum "feels different this time."[16] The word 'extortion' comes to mind. BLM has become Jesse Jackson's 'Rainbow Coalition' on crack cocaine. "Give me another hit baby!"

Down with Voting Integrity

The state of Georgia passed legislation on March 25th to improve election integrity. As the liberal Atlanta Journal-Constitution reports, "Absentee voters will be required to submit driver's license numbers or other documentation under a new process for checking their identity, replacing signature matching processes."[17] The gall of these legislators! Requiring proof of identity to vote, how 'Jim Crow' of them.

Reporter Mark Niesse continues. "Over 200,000 Georgia voters lack a driver's license or state ID number, meaning they will need to submit additional proof of their identities."[18] Trump lost by less than 12,000 votes. (For the details on what happened in the Georgia presidential election, read my book *'34 Days & Counting: American in the Balance.'*)

People must show a driver's license, or some other government issued ID that has a photo for a number of things: buying alcoholic beverages, cigarettes, opening a bank account, applying for Food Stamps, applying for Welfare, applying for Medicaid and Social Security, applying for Unemployment, applying for a 'Job' and the list goes on. Buying a gun is on the list too.[18]

The legislature voted along party lines, of course. The Democrats being *against* improving vote integrity. No surprise there, right? *What should not be expected is for* **The Coca-Cola Company, Delta Airlines and Major League Baseball** (MLB) to be against common sense. MLB announced they will not hold the all-star game in Atlanta due to new law. Coke and Delta, both headquartered in Atlanta, have denounced the new law and supported the MLB decision despite estimates that moving the All-Star game will cost the Atlanta community around $100 million. The people hurt by these companies and MLB are mostly minorities. So, what does President Biden have to say about it?

"What I'm worried about is how un-American this whole initiative is," Biden said. "It's sick."[19] Hellooooo, Earth to Biden, is anyone home?

> *President Joe Biden's reaction to Georgia Voting Integrity Law: "What I'm worried about is how un-American this whole initiative is," Biden said. "It's sick."*

Democrats Reconsider Border Wall!

"Department of Homeland Security Secretary Alejandro Mayorkas told department employees he may restart border wall construction to plug what he called "gaps" in the current barrier," wrote Stephan Dinan on April 6, 2021.[20] Mayorkas explained, "The president has communicated quite clearly his decision that the emergency that triggered the devotion of DOD funds to the construction of the border wall is ended. But that leaves room to make decisions as the administration, as part of the administration, in particular areas of the wall that need renovation, particular projects that need to be finished."

Read that last quote a couple of more times and let it sink in. President Trump had the illegal immigration problem under control. The Democrats, the media, 'Big Tech', the U.S. Chamber of Commerce, etc., opposed him at every step, then once in power, reversed all the border security measures in the first week in office.

The Democrats are good at one thing: using mental gymnastics to warp reality while at the same time wringing sympathy out of a pliant, 'soft brained' electorate.

If you are not convinced by now that the United States is rapidly spiraling down the toilet, well, God bless you. Just stop reading now, get you favorite alcoholic beverage or mood-altering substance and enjoy the bonfire.

The Hits Just Don't Stop Coming

The remainder of this chapter will record more 'highlights' from the Biden 'last 100 days' but without comment. The intentions of this President and his administration could not be clearer. The speed at which America's foundations are being attacked may seem sudden, as if out of nowhere, but the process has been underway for many years. In part two, we will consider the origins of this 'conspiracy', how it has permeated every facet of society and where it plans to take us.

Democrats Pursuing 'Hyper-Change'

- Biden issues Six Gun Control Executive Orders. Whitehouse.gov April 7, 2021

- Illegal immigration in March reaches 172,000, a 71% jump. New York Post April 8, 2021

- Biden announces study to explore expanding the Supreme Court, Whitehouse.gov April 9, 2021

- "New York will now offer one-time payments of up to $15,600 to undocumented immigrants who lost work during the pandemic" NYT April 8, 2021

- Seventeen state legislatures—California, Colorado, Connecticut, Florida, Illinois, Kansas, Maryland, Minnesota, Nebraska, New Jersey, New Mexico, New York, Oregon, Texas, Utah, Virginia and Washington—and the District of Columbia—enacted laws to allow in-state tuition benefits for certain unauthorized immigrant students. ncsl.org/research/immigration/tuition-benefits-for-immigrants.aspx

- For the first time, U.S. and Chinese scientists have created embryos that are part human, part monkey, in an effort to find new ways to produce organs for transplants. @NPR

- Progressive lawmakers led Sen. Markey (D-Mass.) & Rep. Ocasio-Cortez (D-N.Y.), formally revived push for a Green New Deal. Politico April 20, 2021

- House votes 216-208 to make D.C. nation's 51st state. Thehill.com April 22, 2021

- Biden promises to reduced CO_2 emissions by 50% at Earth Day Climate Summit. USA Today, April 22, 2021

- The FBI raided the homes of Rudy Guiliani and Victoria Toensing in the early morning of April 28, 2021. Their laptops and phones were confiscated. These were the attorneys that lead the impeachment defense, and the election fraud cases for President Trump. NY Times.

- Tulane University, New Orleans, has hired Hunter Biden to teach a class on 'Fake News. The Federalist, April 28, 2021

- John Kerry, Biden Climate Czar, former Senator and Presidential candidate probably commits treason by divulging top secret information to Iran – Whitehouse has no comment. Townhall, April 29, 2021

- Acting head of the Office of Justice Programs Maureen Henneberg said that prior grant recipients, including cities, counties and states that were recipients of the department's popular $250 million annual grant program for local law enforcement, will no longer be required to cooperate with U.S. Immigration and Customs Enforcement as a condition of their funding. Epoch Times, April 29, 2021

- China is building or planning more than 300 coal plants in places as widely spread as Turkey, Vietnam, Indonesia, Bangladesh, Egypt and the Philippines. NPR, April 29, 2021

- Sky News host Andrew Bolt says the "stupidity" of US President Joe Biden is now a "threat to the West". YouTube April 26, 2021

- "More than 5,300 NYPD uniformed officers retired or put in their papers to leave in 2020 – a 75 percent spike from the year before, department data show." FoxNews April 26

- "Nearly 190 cops left the Louisville Metro Police Department (LMPD) in 2020 and 43 have stepped away from the Kentucky city's agency so far in 2021." FoxNews April 28, 2021

- "Republican South Dakota Gov. Kristi Noem sued the Biden administration on April 30 over their cancellation of Independence Day fireworks at Mount Rushmore this year." Epoch Times, April 30, 2021

- "Houston police discovered a house with more than 90 people packed inside, in what appears to be an alleged human smuggling case, according to authorities on Friday." Epoch Times, April 30, 2021

- "Hong Kong passed a new immigration law on April 28 that gives authorities the power to prevent people from entering and leaving the city, raising concerns that Chinese mainland style "exit bans" will be implemented in the financial hub." Epoch Times, April 30, 2021

- "Mother of 19-Year-Old Fatally Shot in Seattle's 'No Cop Zone' Sues City Over Handling of 'CHOP'" Epoch Times, April 30, 2021

Chapter 13
The Biden Train Wreck – A Damage Assessment of the 1st 16 months

As predicted in the first edition of this book, Biden's first 100 days set the stage for the train wreck that is continuing to unfold. The insane asylum inmates have been in charge for 16 months and this new chapter attempts to provide the damage assessment.

There's nothing like a good crisis

Rahm Emanuel, Obama's former chief of staff, coined one of the most common quotes used to describe the Democrat's style of governing: "Never let crisis go to waste." The corollary to this is of course: if you don't have a crisis, create one. Democrat hair is constantly on fire and their minions are always running around screaming the sky is falling. A recent quote from Obama's former Secretary to the United Nations and now Administrator of USAID, Samantha Powers proves the point. In a May 1, 2022 interview with George Stephanopolous, ABC News, she shilled for Biden's request for an additional $33 billion for Ukraine by saying: "So, never let a crisis go to waste," Samantha Power added as she called on Congress to give Ukraine more taxpayer money." [1]

Democrats like a crisis because it gives them an excuse to expand government, spend taxpayer money and garner more power for themselves and the Washington bureaucracy. They won't spend a dime to secure our southern border, but they are throwing money at Ukraine so fast, it is hard to keep track. In March 2022, Congress approved $13.6 billion for Ukraine war support. The New York Times breaks this funding down into traditional foreign aid ($6.9 billion), military equipment ($3.5 billion) and U.S. military deployment and intelligence ($3 billion).[2] For perspective, President Trump spent approximately $15 billion to build the wall and secure our border with Mexico. Congressional Democrats did not support the funding, but he managed to get most of the wall built through creatively redirecting military budgets.[3] I encourage you to retrieve this Texas Tribune/ProPublica article so you can understand the negative spin applied on this topic by the

Democrats and the left-wing media. The article sells the myth that the wall was a waste of money and bad for America. But, $47 billion for Ukraine is money well spent?! It eventually morphed into $53.6 billion. Biden cancelled the completion of the border wall, and it has cost American lives and tens of billions of taxpayer money. More on this fiasco to come.

This chapter provides brief updates on the Biden administration's blunders at home and abroad. None of this would have happened had President Trump been reelected. None of it. So, here's the Cliff's Notes on Biden and the Democrat's failures since taking office.

Issue 1: The Biden Open Border Policy

The Invasion of America – The Biden Open Border Policy

The Washington Office of Latin America (WOLA) reported in January 2022 that "the agency took migrants into custody 178,840 times last month, probably the tenth-largest monthly total of this century."[4] The data is collected and published monthly by U.S. Customs and Border Protection Agency (CBP). The graphic below shows the trend of apprehensions and encounters since January 2012.

Notice the sharp increase in apprehensions and encounters beginning in the spring of 2020. This was driven by the fear that President Trump would be reelected and that future gaming of the system by appeal for asylum would be terminated. The vast majority of encounters for the remainder of 2020 were single adults, then family units exploded when Biden took office. WOLA explains that 'individual' apprehensions were approximately 135,040 and that the 'encounter' number of 178,840 includes already identified individuals making a second or third attempt. So, if we take the conservative 135,040 times 12, we get over 1.6

million illegals per year. Most of these are single adult males, who have limited skills and do not speak English. In fact, many are gang members, human traffickers, drug smugglers and terrorists. This is not, and never has been, a humanitarian crisis. If single adult male immigration were eliminated, we would not have an immigration crisis. I am not saying the humanitarian aspect does not exist, but where it does, it is due to drug cartels, gangs and corrupt governments. Why should this be put on the backs of hard-working Americans?

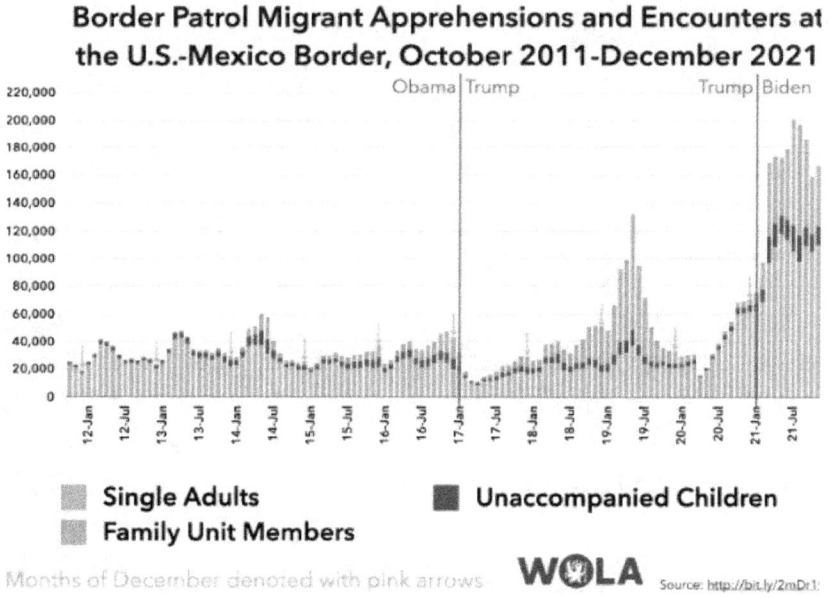

Regardless, how do the 'family units' make their way from Central America to the border? The answer to a certain extent, your tax dollars. Non-governmental organizations played and continue to play a key role in illegal immigration. William La Jeunesse wrote in February 2022, "Getting to the border is half the battle, getting a foothold is another. Playing a vital role in that transition are hundreds of NGOs, or non-governmental organizations receiving at least $137 million in federal grants according to federal budget figures. Grants pay for everything from food, shelter and transportation to legal services that help the migrants traverse Mexico." [5] Yes, you read that right. Biden and his Secretary of Homeland Security Alejandro Mayorkas are using taxpayer money to fund illegal immigration.

La Jenuesse quotes Todd Bensman from the Center for Immigration Studies, "I have been watching the United Nations, UNHCR, distribute cash debit cards to migrants. They're providing food, basic necessities, prescription drugs, etc. They call it movement assistance, which is to say they're providing transportation money so that migrants can continue moving forward." [6] La Jeunesse continues, "Bensman believes the UN and several U.S. NGOs effectively underwrite the migrant pipeline, funneling thousands of individuals without skills or proper papers into U.S. cities using U.S. taxpayer dollars, undermining border security and overwhelming agents with unaccompanied children while cartels import drugs nearby." [7] Notice that the United Nations is a big player in helping people cross into the U.S. illegally. More on that crooked organization, which is mainly funded by the United States taxpayer, in Part 2 of this book.

President Biden and the Democrats are not putting American well-being first. They set the country on a downward spiral and are funding it with American tax dollars. The most urgent and serious initiative they have undertaken is the 'open border' policy. Just look at the numbers in the graphic below provided in the WOLA report.[8]

Illegal immigrants encountered and apprehended for the fourth quarter of 2021 are broken down by country of origin. There were 58,630 from Venezuela, 22,776 from Brazil and 20,476 from Cuba! It is impossible to walk to the U.S. from these countries. The Pan American highway does not connect Panama to South America. These people came to Central America by boat or airplane. As if that is not bad enough, there were 5,391 illegals from Russia and 211 Chinese! Tom Homan, former Director of U.S.

Immigration and Customs Enforcement told Stuart Varney on the business show Varney & Co this morning (May 24, 2022) that it is estimated there have been 700,000 'got-aways' (illegals that escaped being encountered by CBP) since Biden became President. This category of illegals is not families with children, but includes would-be terrorists, gang members and repeat criminals.

CBP Migrant Encounters at the U.S.-Mexico Border, by Country of Origin

October 2021	November 2021	December 2021
Mexico 66,000	Mexico 63,762	Mexico 51,285
Honduras 21,853	Guatemala 20,466	Venezuela 24,819
Guatemala 19,365	Venezuela 20,390	Guatemala 20,966
Venezuela 13,421	Honduras 20,094	Honduras 18,062
El Salvador 9,802	Nicaragua 13,627	Nicaragua 15,298
Nicaragua 9,258	El Salvador 9,663	El Salvador 8,849
Brazil 7,900	Brazil 6,952	Cuba 7,983
Cuba 5,894	Cuba 6,599	Brazil 7,924
Colombia 3,013	Colombia 3,365	Haiti 7,075
Russia 1,577	Russia 1,710	Colombia 4,094
Haiti 910	Haiti 1,022	Russia 2,104
Ecuador 748	India 723	India 1,142
India 706	Ecuador 556	Ecuador 671
Turkey 421	Turkey 536	Turkey 566
Romania 222	Ukraine 227	Romania 376
Ukraine 196	Romania 210	Ukraine 358
China 104	China 100	China 73

VOLA

Source: U.S. Customs and Border Protection

Now, ask yourself why you are hearing this for the first time. Why is this not reported? The answer is because all the megaphones are controlled by the 'Towers of Power'[9] which are run by left-wing progressives.

Is this good for America? Is this good for your children? Democrats seem to think so.

The downside to illegal immigration cannot be adequately quantified in the chapter of a book. It fuels an increase in violent crime, drug use, prostitution, and theft. In general, it threatens the public well-being. It dilutes the personal earnings of American citizens by increasing the costs of health care, public safety and education, while also decreasing the hourly wage potential from low-income workers through increased competition and 'cash' driven (i.e., not reported) income. There is no upside.

As reviewed in Chapter 4, the cost of illegal immigration to the American taxpayer is at least $116 billion per year (in 2018).[10] President Trump's wall cost $15 billion. We have now given Ukraine more than three times that amount with no strings attached nor direct benefits to the American taxpayer received. Each illegal alien costs the taxpayer approximately $8,000 per year, every year. Since Biden's first week in office, more than 2 million illegal immigrants have entered the country (on Day 1 Biden suspended completion of the wall and on Day 2 he suspended the 'Remain in Mexico' policy (which a judge has now reinstated but Mayorkas is not complying with). Two million new illegals equates to an additional $16 billion (for a new lowball total annual cost of $132 billion). This cost estimate is now outdated, low and does not include the costs of crime, drugs, wage deflation etc. It is a nightmare for America but is a foundational platform of the Democratic Party.

Issue 2: Rampant Inflation

Spend More, Get Less – The Economic Platform of the Democratic Party

Inflation will be the number one issue of the 2022 mid-term elections. Everything is much more expensive now than it was at any time during President Trump's administration. For the year 2020 (the final year of Trump's administration), the overall inflation rate was 1.23%. [11] The Bureau of Labor Statistics reported that inflation for the 12-month period ending in March 2022 was up 8.5%. "This was the **largest 12-month advance since December 1981.**" [12] Inflation is a measure of the changing cost for goods over a period of time. So, by the end of March 2022, the average cost of a basket of goods was 8.5% more expensive than it was for the preceding 12-month period.

Paige Terryberry of the John Locke Foundation explained it recently, "The current bout of inflation stems from massive spending: in 2020 and 2021, the government spent the equivalent of 27% of GDP on "Covid relief" and "stimulus," the second-largest fiscal response as a percentage of GDP of any industrialized nation. And this spending was largely paid for by newly created money from the Federal Reserve." [13]

This is an example of how the 'independent' Fed works with the government to finance spending. The Fed 'created' money by buying long-term Treasury bills and other government securities from the Treasure Department. The T-bills are promissory notes the government promises to pay back with interest when they become mature in 10 years. They are essentially a loan. This 'new' money was then used to fund the extraordinary Covid spending. Except, less than 9% of Biden's Covid relief went for Covid (see Chapter 9 for details).

Governments have supplemented their revenue (money in-flows) from taxes, fees and fines with the sale of long-term (usually 10 years) T-bills and other Government Backed Securities (GBS) for a long time. It is normal. Banks, other countries, investment funds and individuals can buy securities from the government.

During the 'quantitative easing' that followed the 2008-2009 recession, the Fed created money (i.e., put more money into the banking system) by purchasing securities on the open market and adding the corresponding funds to the bank reserves of commercial banks. It is intended that banks then lend the money to consumers and businesses.

As Terryberry explained, business and government operate on borrowed money. They are not spending cash on hand to pay wages, buy materials and operate manufacturing. They are paying for these things with money from loans. The loan rate is controlled by the Federal Reserve. The Fed has held this rate at artificially low levels for many years. This has fueled capital investment and risk taking. Thus, manufacturers and government become more and more dependent the reliability of 'cheap' money. This system works as long as demand planning can be based on history and fact-based forecasting. Government intrusion (i.e., excessive and especially, unanticipated spending) screws this up and increases uncertainty. Uncertainty increases perceived risk, which means tighter inventory management (due to risk of not being able to sell), which can put the ability to supply at risk, which increases prices, which stimulates inflation. If there are supply disruptions, like we have had for numerous items, buyers begin to buy in quantity exacerbating the vicious cycle. Government intervention is the problem not the solution. Democrats have never understood this, thus have always been the party of spending and high taxes. The programs of Franklin D. Roosevelt were the cause of the very slow, painful recovery from the depression of the 1930s.

We had rampant inflation under President Jimmy Carter. Carter's incompetence led to the election of Ronald Reagan, who, with Paul Volcker led the U.S. into a long-term recovery by the legislature implementing tax cuts (which reduces the cost of goods and increase discretionary spending for the consumer) and the Federal Reserve increasing interest rates. It took them two years to begin to reap the rewards. Now, after 18 months of Joe Biden, we are looking at a similar scenario. The Fed has begun to increase rates to slow inflation.

Covid Inflation. Two extraordinary root causes of the 2022 inflation spike have been the oppressive Covid-related restrictions on commerce and society (especially in Democrat run states) and irresponsible government spending, including paying people to remain out of the work force.

The initial Covid relief bill (The Coronavirus Aid, Relief, and Economic Security Act, or CARES Act), signed into law by President Trump, was necessary because the government forced the country to lockdown and shutdown. This had never been done before, why was it done this time? It was done because the experts (Anthony Fauci, Barbara Birx, the FDA and CDC) said it was necessary. President Trump had no other option. The continuation of the lockdowns and other draconian restrictions, especially in Democrat run states, completely disrupted every aspect of 'normal' life. Well over 200,000 businesses were unnecessarily shuttered forever, schools were wrongly forced to move to remote learning which isolated children and increased pressure on parents (many of whom lost their jobs or were forced to work from home). We now know, without a doubt, that all of these draconian measures were ineffective. The virus continued to spread. But, since the government did shut down the country, it required that it also provide economic aid to people, critical infrastructure and businesses. The CARES Act approved $2.2 trillion in aid in the form of direct one-time payments to citizens ($300 billion), unemployment benefits ($260 billion), the Paycheck Protection Plan – forgivable loans to businesses ($350 billion), low interest loans to businesses ($500 billion) and state aid ($340 billion). [14]

The lockdowns did not stop viral spread, but they did cause serious problems for manufacturers. Government intrusion and overreach created unanticipated demand for products related to working from home, learning from home, shopping online, getting entertainment at home, etc. It also stimulated hoarding of some consumer goods (i.e., toilet paper). Most consumer goods retailers manage their inventories in a 'just-in-time' fashion, based on historical records of purchases. The government generated fear created a 'feeding frenzy' for several months. Many were afraid to go to retail stores and online buying skyrocketed. This created huge supply issues because the online providers used different warehouse and delivery systems than the retailers. The retailers took it in the chin due to Fauci fear mongering.

Democrat run state governments made the situation much worse by throwing logic and sound science out the window. Restaurants and bars were closed but liquor and 'pot' stores remained open. When restaurants were allowed to reopen, it was with limited tables. We were required to wear a mask when entering and waiting to be seated but could take them off once at our table. The wait staff, however, were required to wear a mask at all times. Then bars could open but had to close early. Signs were put up in city parks encouraging masks and social distancing, even though sunlight kills the virus in seconds. All of this idiocy was done in the name of 'science'. There was no 'science' then, and is none now, to support any of these measures. Yet, the media held Fauci up as a savior and Trump as a villain. The general state of fear created by the government made it easy to control people. I, and many others, made posts on social media trying to provide honest guidance (i.e., no need to wear masks outdoors) only to get banned from the platform for 'disinformation'. It was Orwellian. We would see people driving alone in their cars and wearing a mask. Even today, many people still wear the mask. Fear is a marketer's strongest tool and mankind's greatest motivator. Fear motivated many people to not get vaccinated, because some people died from the vaccinations. It is interesting that federal, state and local governments report the number of cases on a daily basis for Covid, but do not track the flu in the same fashion. Nor does the CDC et.al., track and report the number of people who have died from vaccination complications?

The fear that was and is justified, however, is what is the big government bureaucracy going to do next to makes life more difficult. Today's inflation is one way we are paying for government-induced supply problems and price increases.

Where did the Relief Money go? The U.S. government has spent a lot of money and much of it was unnecessary. Trump's 'relief' package was $2.2 trillion and was necessary because the government forced the lockdowns and restrictions. The Biden administration passed an additional $1.9 trillion for a total of $4.1 trillion. The Committee for a Responsible Federal Budget says $5.93 has been appropriated and $5.18 trillion spent or committed. [15] Thankfully, Omicron was so weak that the symptoms were predominantly 'cold-like' for most people and the Fauci B.S. power had run its course. Chapter 9 reviewed the allocation of the Biden's $1.9 trillion, with less than 9% being used for COVID related issues. But the total allocation was $5.93 trillion, leaving a difference of $1.8 trillion! Where did this $1.8 trillion go?

In a letter to President Biden, Kevin Brady, House Ways & Means Committee Republican Leader, wrote, "American taxpayers deserve an honest and detailed accounting of where the $6 trillion (*author's note: he rounded the $5.93*) in COVID-19 relief passed by Congress has been spent and how much remains. Your Administration has misused taxpayer dollars to spend on items unrelated to COVID-19 and repurposed funds for the southern border crisis of your own creation. The American people deserve transparency and answers to these important questions from their government before being asked to further foot the bill for another attempt by your White House to spend hundreds of billions or even trillions more in the name of 'combatting COVID-19." [16]

A few key points made by Mr. Brady were:

- "The $2 trillion in funding in the Biden Administration's so-called COVID "rescue" bill allocated **less than 9 percent to combatting the virus**, with the remaining 91 percent spending hundreds of billions of dollars to bail out state governments, and build bike trails, new high school weight rooms, apartment buildings, and golf courses.

- The Biden Administration diverted $850 million meant to support the nation's COVID-19 testing capabilities to address the fallout from the Administration's self-induced border crisis – including housing those that illegally crossed the southern border in the wake of Administration policies that weakened border security and encouraged illegal immigration.

- Hundreds of millions of dollars have been diverted from re-stockpiling the Strategic National Stockpile in order to deal with President Biden's border crisis, further undermining America's public health preparedness.

- The almost half a trillion dollars in funds remaining from the $2 trillion in so-called "COVID-relief" enacted in March 2021 should be first used to boost mitigation efforts before asking American taxpayers for more money.

- The Biden Administration has ignored multiple requests for more transparency and accountability on spending from Ranking Members of the House Budget Committee, House Energy & Commerce Committee, House Oversight and Reform Committee, and House Homeland Security Committee." [17]

So, we have had trillions of spending approved by Congress for Covid-19 only to see the Democrats misdirect the funds. For one thing, this is a fraud on the American people and for another, this extraordinary amount of money being pumped into the country by the government dilutes the value of the dollar and therefore is inflationary.

Does the media report this fraud? No. Will there be an investigation? Only by Republican committees who have no power or authority. The Department of Justice (office of the Attorney General and FBI) will do nothing. Would there have been an investigation if Donald Trump did this? Of course.

Overall inflation versus core inflation. The 8+% inflation rate today includes the commodity sectors of energy and food. Since these two sectors frequently are more volatile than other goods, economists usually focus more closely on 'core' inflation (energy and food are stripped out). The San Francisco office of the Federal Reserve wrote in 2004, "The question of the correct way to measure inflation is an important one. Price stability over time, along with "maximum" sustainable economic output and employment, are the Federal Reserve's primary goals in making monetary policy. The maintenance of price stability—avoiding high inflation rates or deflation over time—is important because fluctuating prices distort the economy's price signals and can result in the misallocation of resources. The Federal Reserve carefully reviews and analyzes the available inflation measures to monitor how well it is achieving its price stability goal. One common way economists use inflation data is by looking at "core inflation," which is generally defined as a chosen measure of inflation (e.g., the Consumer Price Index or CPI, the Personal Consumption Expenditures Price Index or PCEPI, or the Gross Domestic Product Deflator) that excludes the more volatile categories of food and energy prices." [18]

This is not to suggest that the overall measure is not used nor important. Society and business cannot function without fossil fuel or food. The cost of goods for all manufacturing includes an energy component. The 'pain at the pump' today, May 11, 2022, is very real. The national average price for regular gasoline one year ago was $2.985 per gallon; today it is $4.404. This $1.42/gallon increase is an over 40% increase in one year. [19] Gasoline was not expensive until Biden became President, but prices were rising due to increasing demand as the country began to return to a post-Covid normal. The government forced Covid shutdown was a knee jerk reaction. Suddenly, people were not driving to work nor taking trips nor flying on airplanes. Oil companies were carrying inventories as per normal and suddenly saw demand fall dramatically. So, they scaled back production and began to carefully sell off inventories. Since they could not, and cannot, predict government interference in normal market dynamics, they remained cautious as restrictions were relaxed. Demand began to increase but production was lagging causing prices to go up. So, price inflation for crude oil, labor, etc. were partially due to the dramatic and unpredicted drop in demand due to the COVID shutdown, followed by a depletion of inventory and then a rapid return to normal demand. Trump carries no blame for this. Oil and gas prices were rising during the last months of Trump's term. But the slope of increase has steepened due to Biden's war on fossil fuel. Of course, were it not for the Fauci medical mafia that forced and extended the shutdowns who knows where we would be today. But Fauci et.al. had the full support of Biden and the Democrats. There were many within the medical establishment that tried to sound the alarm that Fauci and gang we're misleading the people. These people were threatened, attacked, fired, cancelled, etc. This is the dangerous game of subterfuge the Democrats and globalists around the world were and are playing.

The huge supply chain issues were inflationary and caused by the Covid restrictions at Democrat run ports in California and unions leveraging the fear factor to get wage increases and cause labor shortages. It took forever to unload the ships and move the containers. Other key ports around the world suffered similar issues. These supply chain problems did not really become problematic until Biden became President. They played a significant role in reducing product supply, which drove finished goods prices higher.

The Russian invasion of Ukraine is also to blame for increasing crude oil costs. Russia is second only to the United States in crude oil production, closely followed by Saudi Arabia. The United States does not buy a lot of oil from Russia (10% of total exports in 2021) but the European Union does. Over the last 40 years. Europe has made itself dependent on Russia for its energy. In 2021, European Union member countries accounted for 29% of Russia crude oil exports and 16% of its refined products. So, cutting off Russia as a supply source invariably will increase the price of crude.

President Biden issued an Executive Order on March 8, 2022, banning oil purchases from Russia.[20] The ban was effective immediately but did give buyers 45 days to wind down existing contracts (a good thing), but the 45 days have now expired. We will go into more detail on Ukraine later, but it is another example of the game of shadows being played by the Democrats and globalists. First a little more on energy inflation.

When Biden took office, he quickly shut down the completion of the Keystone pipeline that would have carried oil from Canada. Pipelines are the most efficient way to transport crude oil and natural gas. They do not harm the environment, in fact, there is more environmental risk when crude oil is hauled over roads or rail. Ask yourself how it is good for Americans to force inefficient, costly and more dangerous modes of transport for crude oil. Biden also immediately stopped exploration on all Federal lands. Why? How is this good for America to restrict energy raw materials and thereby increase costs?

The American Petroleum Institute writes, "U.S. crude oil production decreased due to a combination of factors – work force shortages, supply chain issues, financial and energy policies – and has been unable to increase in response to higher prices, as it has done in the past. Seemingly long-term policies can affect investment today. Restrictive energy polices -- including undermining pipeline infrastructure, an indefinite moratorium on leasing on federal lands, proposed higher taxes and a clean energy plan to eliminate natural gas in power generation - have not helped to stimulate investment, drilling and production needed to meet demand." [21]

Government energy policy is critical to a fully functioning society and national security. It is a critical political issue we will deal with in more detail later in this chapter. It goes hand in hand with the lie of climate alarmism... another example of Democrat fearmongering.

So, let's close the section on inflation with a perspective from the International Monetary Fund (the IMF is affiliated with the United Nations and has globalist mission) and a review of the actual current inflation of the key durable goods and consumable goods categories. First, the IMF.

Ceyda Oner of the IMF writes, "To the extent that households' nominal income, which they receive in current money, does not increase as much as prices, they are worse off, because they can afford to purchase less. In other words, their purchasing power or real—inflation-adjusted—income falls. Real income is a proxy for the standard of living. When real incomes are rising, so is the standard of living, and vice versa." [22] Pretty obvious but every action from the Biden administration is reducing the purchasing power of all Americans.

Personal wages have increased across the board in the United States, as businesses have had to entice workers to return and, in many cases, give up Democrat created incentives to stay home. But inflation has risen faster and the 'standard of living' for most Americans has decreased since Biden became President. The March 2022 Consumer Price Index Report reveals that the increase in price for fuel oil and other fuels rose 51.7%, gasoline rose 48%, transportation rose 22.6%, energy services (electricity) rose 11.1%, food and beverages rose 8.6%, computers and associated rose 7.6%, apparel rose 6.8%, housing rose 6.4%, recreation rose 4.8%, rent rose 4.4%, medical care rose 2.9% and education rose 2.5%. [23] Without exception, the cost of everything is higher than it was when Biden took office.

The bottom line... run-away inflation is a Democrat (including the Federal Reserve) policy-caused problem that is going to be with us for a while. Period. Need more proof? Just consider: the Democrats are still pushing their 'Build Back Better' program. The Committee for a Responsible Federal Budget estimate the BBB program will cost $5 trillion! [24] The Dems also want to pass a bill that forgives student loans for college students. This would cost American taxpayers $321 billion and essentially set up a situation where college becomes a government benefit and thus an on-going cost. This would become trillions in entitlement spending. On June 2, 2022, Biden's Education Department announced it is forgiving $5.8 billion in student loans for students who took classes from the defunct Corinthian College. To be fair, the Corinthian story is extraordinary since it was accused of misleading students and loan agencies about student prospects for employment. It declared bankruptcy in 2015.

Democrat spending programs, if allowed to continue unabated, will ensure inflation will be here to stay and sink the ship once known as America under a sea of debt for years to come.

These first two issues are killing the country. But we have lots of other issues that the Democrats are fumbling (... is their fumbling intentional – wait for Part 2). So, what is Issue #3? What is the third most important issue facing the country today? Mitch McConnel, ranking Republican in the House of Representatives said at a Tuesday, May 10 press conference, that Ukraine was the most important problem facing the world today. "I think we all agree the most important thing going on in the world right now is the war in Ukraine," McConnel said. [24] Well, I disagree. In fact, America disagrees.

A Quinnipiac poll released on March 30, 2022, found inflation to be the number one concern, followed by Ukraine and then immigration. [25] The choices people were given in this poll were: Russia/Ukraine, Covid-19, Inflation, Unemployment, Climate Change, Health Care, Racial Inequality, Immigration, Election Law, the Supreme Court and Crime.

The results of the poll jibe with reality. Inflation is the number one short term problem we face today. Illegal immigration is the number one long term problem. Since the Russian invasion of Ukraine is dominating the news and near the top of most people's minds, I will address Ukraine next.

Issue 3: Russian Invasion of Ukraine

The first edition of this book predicted the war in Ukraine. Here is what I wrote in the Postscript, May 2021, "Of less short-term global consequence is a Russian escalation of the war with Ukraine. Russia has been moving more troops and armory to the Ukrainian border. Ukraine is not a NATO member and Putin knows Europe and the U.S. will do nothing other than posture."

If I, a private citizen who follows the daily news and work out of my apartment can see the war coming, why couldn't the Biden administration? Why couldn't the NATO members? I think they did see it coming but thought Ukraine would just roll over. No one anticipated the amazing defense Ukraine has managed.

This eastern European tragedy did not have to happen. Had Trump won reelection, it would not have happened. Had Europe and NATO done the right thing decades ago, it would have been impossible. But they did not, and here we are. Consider my blog post from March 13, 2022,

"Say 'Russia' out loud near Biden or any European leader and they shiver in fear (except the leaders of Ukraine, Finland and probably Hungary). Putin carries a big mouth but a little stick. Yet, he is a master poker player. Putin annexed Crimea in 2014 and the west responded with words. He knew NATO would not respond. At the same time, he sanctioned the 'separatists' (Russian military in civilian clothes) insurgency in the Donbas. Obama sent Ukraine blankets & happy meals.

If the leaders of NATO (26 European countries, the US, Canada, Iceland & Turkey) had any balls, they would have admitted Ukraine to NATO 16 years ago when President George W. Bush suggested it. But they didn't, supposedly because it would upset Putin. Of course, it would upset him, but who cares. He was weak back then. With Ukraine as a NATO member, Europe would be much safer because the only buffer country would be Belarus. Having an insecure buffer (Ukraine) only allowed for an incursion that would not be defended (which started in 2014). If Ukraine had been admitted, Europe's energy supplies would be totally secure, and they would have a partner on their border who is not afraid to fight and who offers control & security over the pipelines running through it to Europe. Ukraine is also the breadbasket of the European continent. It was a frigg'in no brainer. So, forget the stupid 'experts' who say one of the causes of this war was 'mentioning' Ukraine as a possible NATO partner…, a comment that is stupid on its face.

Russia's economy is 49th in global rank, slightly smaller than Slovakia's (47th), half that of Denmark's (13th) and 1/3 of Ireland's (3rd). Russia's economy vanishes if you remove fossil fuels. Weak leadership in Europe and the United States has 'allowed' this war and is responsible not only for the deaths of thousands in Ukraine but also a more unstable world." [26]

I wrote that on March 13th, exactly two months ago. Now, the war is 3 months and counting, over 46,000 have died and Ukraine is holding its own in most of the country as Russia has been forced to revise its strategy to focus only on the Donbas region in the southeast. The leadership of Ukrainian President Volodymyr Zelenskyy has been the key. He, rightfully, can now be compared to Winston Churchill as a leader who rallied his people in the face of overwhelming odds. Biden offered to extract Zelenskyy and his family in late February, but Zelenskyy famously replied, ""The fight is here; I need ammunition, not a ride." [27]

The war continues at this writing due to the strength of Ukrainian people, President Zelenskyy's leadership and military assistance from Western countries, mainly the United States. Congress passed a bill to provide $13.6 billion in aid to Ukraine on March 10, 2022. [28] Russia began its invasion on February 24, 2022.

Reluctant Support. Ukraine has been asking for military aid from the west since the 2014 invasion of Crimea. Obama sent blankets. President Trump sent military aid to Ukraine during his administration, but Biden resisted sending anything in 2021, even though it was clear Russia was building troops and preparing to invade. Consider Biden's January 20, 2022, comments: "I think what you're going to see is that Russia will be held accountable if it invades. And it depends on what it does. It's one thing if it's a minor incursion and then we end up having a fight about what to do and not do."[29]

President Zelenskyy tweeted a response to Biden: "We want to remind the great powers that there are no minor incursions and small nations. Just as there are no minor casualties and little grief from the loss of loved ones. I say this as the President of a great power" UA 7:29 AM Jan 20, 2022[30] If only we had a 'Zelenskyy' in the White House.

The White House tried to spin Biden's comment, but the damage was done. Russia now had a clear signal from the U.S. that no other country would come to the rescue of Ukraine. Biden's same day follow-up spin statement was, "If any – any – assembled Russian units move across the Ukrainian border, that is an invasion," Biden said, adding that it would result in a "severe and coordinated economic response" that he has discussed with allies. "Let there be no doubt at all that if [Russian President Vladimir] Putin makes this choice, Russia will pay a heavy price."[31] I'm sure Putin and his generals were having a good laugh. One month later, they invaded.

The invasion of Ukraine would not have happened if Trump were President. So, why did it happen? I mentioned earlier that it is my opinion that the NATO members were OK with a Russian take-over because they believed it would be quick and would secure their Russian oil and gas supply, while satisfying Putin's lust for getting Ukraine under his control. The desire of the Ukrainian people to live free and be able to chart their own destiny was of no consequence to the globalist leaders of the West. The United Nations, the world's 'peace keeping' entity was nowhere to be found in the lead up to the invasion or the sham peace talks in the early weeks. But the stubborn Ukrainians fought back and upset the globalist apple cart.

Political Expediency – A Day Late and a Dollar Long

On May 10, 2022, the U.S. House of Representatives passed a bill giving another $40 billion in aid to the Ukraine war support. The vote was 368-57. The 57 were all Republicans. [32] Thanks to Senator Rand Paul, (R-KY), the Senate vote was delayed but ultimately passed.[33] Senator Paul insisted that language be inserted to ensure an Inspector General will be assigned to track the money to make sure it goes where intended. The real purpose of this bill is that Democrats need to show they support the Ukrainians because the 2022 mid-term elections are now in the primary stage. Where were they before Russia invaded? Biden was OK with a minor incursion. Where are the European countries who are the geographic neighbors of Ukraine? This entire thing is a farse.

Consider:

- The United States had already given $13.6 billion to Ukraine and on May 21st approved another $40 billion for a total of **$53.6 billion**. On May 13, 2022, the European Union announced it is increasing its support to Ukraine to €2 **($2.082 billion)**.[34] So, Congress (all Democrats and a hand full of globalist Republicans) think American taxpayers should provide at least 25 times more funding than Europe even though the war is in their back yard. It makes no sense.

- Since Biden has become President, there have been over 3 million illegal attempts to enter the United States. "Border Patrol set an all-time record for apprehensions there in FY 2021, and since the beginning of February 2021 (Biden's first full month in office), CBP has encountered nearly 2.5 million aliens who have entered illegally or without proper documents at the U.S.-Mexico line. Of those nearly 2.5 million aliens, about 1.356 million have been expelled under Title 42. That still leaves more than 1.124 million who have been processed under the Immigration and Nationality Act (INA) since February 2021," writes Andrew Arthur of the Center of Immigration Studies. [94] The Biden admin has processed 1.12 million illegals and then releasing them into the country. When April-May numbers are added with the almost 1 million got-aways, we have at least 2 million new illegals in the country since Biden became President. At a cost of $8,000 per year, that represents an on-going annual cost of $16 billion. Trump's border wall lacked only a few miles of gaps to reach completion, yet Biden cancelled it. The materials for the wall were already at the work sites and paid for. Biden cancelled Trump's 'Remain in Mexico' order that was significantly retarding illegal entry (months later, a judge ordered it be reinstated, which has been resisted by the Homeland Security Secretary Mayorkas). Biden also terminated the Asylum Cooperative Agreement with Guatemala, Honduras and El Salvador. [35]

- One year ago, April 2021, there had already been more illegal fentanyl seized by Customs and Border Patrol than the full year 2020. "As of April, 6,494 pounds of fentanyl were seized by authorities at the border, compared to 4,776 pounds in all of 2020. Fentanyl is an incredibly potent opioid that is 50-100 times stronger than morphine, according to Dr. Darien Sutton, an emergency medicine physician based in Los Angeles and ABC News contributor. People don't realize how dangerous it is," he said. [36] The question is how much successfully escaped Border Patrol scrutiny and is now in the country?

- "New provisional data released by the federal government estimates that nearly 108,000 people died from drug overdoses from January to December 2021. "That's about a 15% increase from the number of deaths in 2020," says Farida Ahmad, a research scientist with the Center for Disease Control and Prevention's National Center for Health Statistics." [37] It is also twice the number that have died in Ukraine.

- "The $1.5 trillion omnibus spending bill President Joe Biden signed this week – the first since he took office – has **the biggest hike in domestic spending**

in four years. But not all programs are equal. Climate-change boondoggles get billions while border-security funding is slashed by nearly a half-billion — even as illegal crossings continue to spike." [38] This report came out on March 17, 2022.

Connecting the Dots: We began this list of critical issues with the Biden open border policy (the most important long-term and costly issue for America), then moved to inflation (the most important short-term and costly issue for America) and have now discussed Ukraine. Yet, notice, we ended with a comment on the Biden open border policy (or lack thereof). The people of Ukraine want individual freedom. They want the chance to determine their own destiny. Russia is trying to deny them that God given right, and Europe and the United States were happy to look the other way while Russia invaded. It is sickening. So far, over 46,000 people have died in a war that could have easily been prevented. The polls indicate the average American is sympathetic and would like to see America and Europe stop the war, without making it worse. Elections are 5 months away, so the Democrats and many Republicans are sending tens of billions of American taxpayer dollars to Ukraine. But the Biden administration has cut the budget for Customs and Border Patrol. Biden has not even traveled to the border much less acknowledged the gravity of the problem. Over two million new people in the country hiding in the shadows and costing taxpayers over $16 billion per year. This is on top of the $116 billion we have already been paying. 108,000 Americans died from drug overdoses in 2021. These drugs come in via the porous southern border. Biden cut the budget of the agency in charge of securing this border. The money Congress and the President are sending to Ukraine is borrowed. The more debt the country takes on, the more the dollar is devalued, which is an inflationary component. Biden's new omnibus spending bill adds $46 billion in new spending, a 7% increase [39] and a major root cause of inflation.

That Americans identify Ukraine as the number 2 issue today is testament to the effectiveness of the left-wing media. Ukraine should not even be in the top 10. The best thing America can do for Ukraine is kick the damn Europeans in the ass and get them to take care of their own neighborhood. The U.S. has approved $53.6 billion to Ukraine, while the EU just approved aid up to $2 billion. Immigration was the number 3 issue overall in the March Quinnipiac poll, but when you break it down by Republicans, the issues were inflation, immigration, and Ukraine. The Democrats ranked Ukraine as the number 1 issue, followed by inflation and then election laws! What? Independents ranked inflation first, followed by Ukraine with immigration and climate change tied for third. Really amazing. The poll also asked: "what they think is most responsible for the recent rise in gas prices". [40] Before we review the results, remember that the price of a commodity is dictated by supply, demand, and competition. So, if gasoline is in short supply or the industry anticipates a supply issue, the price will increase. The average price of gasoline in President Trump's last month, December 2020, was $2.28/gallon. Fifteen months into Biden's presidency, gas is $4.21/gallon. Almost doubled. The Biden administration and left-wing media are saying the war in Ukraine is the cause, but gasoline prices began rising as soon as Biden became President. In February 2021 the price was $2.59, in April 2021 it was $2.95, by August 2021 it was $3.26 (a dollar more than December 2020), in November 2021 the price had increased to $3.49 and in February 2022 it was $3.61. [41] These increases were all pre-Ukraine. When it was clear Ukraine would be an on-going issue, prices took a big jump to $4.21 by April. So, how did the people answer the polling question?

Eighty-two percent of Republicans said the primary cause was Biden's economic policies. The data I just provided confirm this is the correct answer. Democrats, however blamed the Ukraine war (41%) and oil companies charging more (41%). Independents placed Biden's policies at 39%, Ukraine at 25% and oil companies charging more at 23%.

These results tell us that Democrat and many Independent voters are getting their information from CNN, MSNBC, CBS, NBC, ABC, National Public Radio (NPR), the New York Times, Washington Post of some other left-wing propaganda outlet. These 'news' agencies are willfully lying. The Democrats also trust Democratic Party leadership. The media and the Dem leadership know the truth. The second part of this book explains why they don't tell it. So, those who identify as Democrats in America are living in an imaginary world. The scary thing about this is that 41% of the country identifies as Democrat. Independents are people (like myself) that became disenchanted with party affiliation or have always been non-joiners. Their response to the gasoline question bears this out.

America is a country of the people and by the people. Yet today we have over 40% of the people living in an alternative universe. This is why America is dying. Too many citizens are no longer engaged. Too many citizens are dependent on government handouts, while the working classes are too busy, too distracted, too dumb, fat and happy for their own good. This is major issue #4.

Issue 4: Too Many Americans are Uninformed or are Believing the Lies

If we are a country of the people and by the people, the responsibility for our problems must ultimately be laid at the feet of the people. It is true that much of the news media have become propaganda purveyors of the left. It is also true that the academic, sports, and entertainment towers of power are run by the left and work hard to stigmatize the news outlets that do honest reporting: Fox News, The Epoch Times, The New York Post, The Washington Examiner and many strong web-based news agencies: Town Hall,

Breitbart news, The Daily Caller, etc. They call these outlets 'conservative and far-right'. If you are a follower of one of the 'left-wing' outlets, I encourage you to check out the study on media bias conducted by Harvard University's Shorenstein Center back in 2017. Its conclusions support what I just wrote 100%.[42]

Disinformation. Biden's Department of Homeland Security announced the creation of a 'Disinformation Governance Board' during a budget hearing with a subcommittee of House Appropriations. At the meeting, everyone learned the 'Board' had already been operating for two months but it now needed funding. Of course, the problem is defining 'disinformation'. Biden appointed far-left loon Nina Jankowicz as director. She is on record claiming the reporting on Hunter Biden's laptop was disinformation. Of course, there is now no debate that the laptop exists and contained a lot of incriminating material on Hunter and others. Like it does to a virus, the light of day killed this Orwellian idea.

Disinformation is the game plan of the Democratic Party. Trump's Russia collusion was a complete fabrication paid for by the Democratic National Committee and Hillary Clinton. This fiasco cost taxpayers at least $35 million. This is now all established fact but, back then it was the media and the Democrat's lead topic for 2 plus years. They lied about Justice Kavanaugh, they lied about General Flynn, they lied about Donald Trump, they lie about climate change, they lie about illegal immigration, they lie about Russia, they are quiet on China, they lie about crime, and on and on. When will the people who identify as Democrats wake up?

As we move closer to the mid-terms, the Democratic Party is worried. They have been in power for 16 months and have turned the country into a disaster area. Our 4th most important issue is the fact that too many Americans are uninformed or believing the lies of the left. These people will cast their vote in November.

So, in addition to a porous southern border and inflation, what are the other important issues voters must consider. The answers to this question constitute the remainder of this important chapter.

The Other Important Issues

Law and Order. One of the primary functions of the federal and state governments is to provide for the domestic tranquility and individual safety. Biden and the Democrats are doing a horseshit job.

Time Magazine had a feature article on the increase of crime in America in January 2022. The writers open the article with a Philadelphia story and then say, "Philadelphia is not alone. At least ten other major cities lost historic numbers of residents to murder last year. Nationally, police data suggests homicides rose seven percent in 2021. And while many Americans know that 2020 was a particularly bloody year—with homicides surging 29 percent, with 77 percent of them involving firearms—few realize that gun violence has been rising across this country since 2014. Fatal shootings have increased by roughly 80 percent in the largest U.S. cities since then." [43] The writers begin well, with a tragic story and then some facts, but quickly morph into the politically correct blah, blah, blah on guns and big government solutions. At least they got the facts right.

Who runs the big cities? Democrats! Who claims sanctuary city status? Democrat mayors! Who wanted to defund the police departments? Democrat run cities! Who blames the police when a gangbanger gets shot resisting arrest? Democrats! What does the 2nd Amendment say? American citizens have the right to bear arms. What is the Democrat solution to gun crime? Confiscate the guns! When they confiscate the guns, who will still have guns? The gangs and other criminals! This is not rocket science!

Commit the Crime, You Do the Time – Not! Most crime falls under state law versus Federal law. The laws in each state were enacted to give law enforcement the tools it needed to get the law breakers off the street and paying for their crime. Very simple. But, in most of our large cities today, the law breakers are paying no penalty. The law is not being enforced. The police catch the bad guys, then the prosecutor lets them go with a slap on the hand.

Remember, it is a law of nature that people will do what they get rewarded to do. But it is the corollary to this law that applies to establishing a safe and tranquil society: people will not do the things they get punished for doing. If the criminal is not appropriately punished for his crime, the result will be more crime.

> *If the criminal is not appropriately punished for his crime, the result will be more crime.*

Everyone knows this. The Democrat prosecutors who are letting the criminals off and releasing them back into society know this. The Daily Signal reported in April 2022, "Crime is on the rise in Los Angeles, and the soft-on-criminals policies of District Attorney George Gascon are a major cause, Sheriff Alex Villanueva says. When Gascon took office in December 2020 as one of the successful candidates around the country supported by liberal financier George Soros, he issued a list of crimes that the Los Angeles County District Attorney's Office no longer would prosecute." [44] Gascon looked at the laws and decided he would no longer prosecute violators. These laws were passed by legislative bodies to protect the people and businesses, but Gascon invited more crime by announcing that people committing these crimes would no longer be punished. So, the people of Los Angeles got more crime.

The Heritage Foundation called out the most egregious of the big city prosecutors, "The most prominent rogue prosecutors are

George Gascon in Los Angeles, Chesa Boudin in San Francisco, Kim Foxx in Chicago, Larry Krasner in Philadelphia, Marilyn Mosby in Baltimore, Kimberly Gardner in St. Louis, and Rachael Rollins in Boston." [45] The only logical conclusion is that crime is increasing because the people elected to enforce the law and protect people and businesses are refusing to do their jobs. Why is there no outrage in these cities? Why are we not seeing city councils and state governors hold these prosecutors accountable? Why are the people still electing the Democrats who have failed them for decades?

Equity, Inclusion & Diversity: Creating a world of favoritism & bias.
The mantra of the Democratic party for the last several years has been diversity, equity, and inclusion. They are inclusive unless you are white and male. Then you are a 'bigoted white-supremist of privilege'. In addition to hating white people, they also abhor diversity of thought, which is, by the way, the only kind of diversity that can offer value to a society. If you are white, then you better be gay, or racially fluid (i.e., you are white, black and brown, it just depends on your mood). If you are transgender, you move to the head of the class (even though less than half of one percent of people are transgender). They exclude all who disagree and treat them harshly (i.e., without equity). They establish quotas for every superficial thing that can divide people. Forcing a superficial diversity on society is the most divisive thing that can be done. It weakens the whole because it will inherently exclude people who are more qualified, skilled, and talented. It guarantees mediocrity and failure. It disincentivizes achievement. It destroys normal social discourse. In the Democratic party there is only one way to look at a problem and it is theirs. They are the most egregiously biased, divisive, non-inclusive, hypocritical people on the planet. Where did all this begin? How did we get here? Answer: Modern academia and the embracing of Marxist ideology.

Academia is the seed bed for the diversity, inclusion and equity (D.I.E.) ideas that are dividing America today. Forty years ago, we heard little turmoil about gender dysphoria, systems of privilege, unconscious bias, white supremacy, etc. The roots of these problems started at Cornel University in 1969 with the first 'women's studies course. [46] This Wikipedia citation lays out the evolution of this trip through the tulips as follows:

"Women's studies is an academic field that draws on feminist and interdisciplinary methods to place women's lives and experiences at the center of study, while examining social and cultural constructs of gender; systems of privilege and oppression; and the relationships between power and gender as they intersect with other identities and social locations such as race, sexual orientation, socio-economic class, and disability. **Popular concepts that are related to the field of women's studies include feminist theory, standpoint theory, intersectionality, multiculturalism, transnational feminism, social justice, affect studies, agency, bio-politics, materialism, and embodiment**. Research practices and methodologies associated with women's studies include ethnography, autoethnography, focus groups, surveys, community-based research, discourse analysis, and reading practices associated with critical theory, post-structuralism, and queer theory. The field researches and critiques different societal norms of gender, race, class, sexuality, and other social inequalities. Women's studies is related to the fields of gender studies, feminist studies, and sexuality studies, and more broadly related to the fields of cultural studies, ethnic studies, and African-American studies." [47]

As you can see by the text I emboldened, women's studies has become big business. A citation in this Wikipedia article that was written in 2015 states there are over 700 institutions in the U.S. and around the world that offer course work and degrees in this field.

So, it started with a bunch of hippies in the late 1960's. Now, over 50 years later, they have turned the world upside down.

Here are some examples of how ridiculous this movement has become, with special emphasis on gender insanity.

- Try to become a tenured professor at any college or university today if you are a conservative. The faculty today is uniformly progressive. The Washington Times reported in 2016, "A new study confirms what even the most casual observer of higher education has long known — that conservative professors are vastly outnumbered by liberal ones — but it also shows that the problem is getting worse. Published in Econ Journal Watch last month, the study looks at faculty voter registration at 40 leading universities and finds that, out of 7,243 professors, Democrats outnumber Republicans 3,623 to 314, or by a ratio of 11 1/2 to 1." [48]

- This data proves that the education provided in institutes of higher learning today will be uniformly progressive. Diversity of thought no longer exists on the university campus.

- Michele Obama introduced the non-word 'womxn' as a replacement for women or woman in an early May Instagram post. This caused Piers Morgan to say, "What makes this particularly absurd is that Ms. Obama's post was supposed to be supporting women's rights. Instead, she's trampled on them by pandering to a tiny minority of people who get upset when they hear a word that's been used for centuries to describe people who aren't men." [49]

- As the new congress convened in January 2021, House Speaker Nancy Pelosi and the Democrat majority "permanently establishing an Office of Diversity and Inclusion and other diversity measures, the proposed package would "honor all gender identities by changing pronouns and familial relationships in the House rules to be gender neutral." Previously, Congress operated under a binary rule that "words importing one gender include the other as well." [50]

- The Disney company decided to alienate at least half of its customer base by going completely 'Woke' in May 2021. The New York Post headline in early May read: "Disney goes woke with new anti-racist agenda for employees". Dana Kennedy writes, "Disney is pushing critical race theory on employees through a new plan called "Reimagine Tomorrow," urging workers to recognize their "white privilege," in a battery of training modules on topics such as "systemic racism" and "white fragility," according to internal documents obtained by City-Journal's Christopher Rufo. Staffers are told to reject "equality" for "equity" and must "reflect" on America's "racist infrastructure" and "think carefully about whether or not [their] wealth" is derived from racism, according to the documents. In one anti-racism training course, called "Allyship for Race Consciousness," workers are taught that the US has a "long history of systemic racism and transphobia" and told they must "take ownership of educating yourself about structural anti-black racism. Staffers should "not rely on your black colleagues to educate you," which is "emotionally taxing," the docs reportedly instruct, Disney recommends its staffers hit the books, suggesting one essay that encourages parents to commit to "raising race-consciousness in children" and which teaches that "even babies discriminate" against members of other races." [51]

- One year later, April 2022, Gerard Baker of the Wall Street Journal asked, "Is opposition to parents' rights really the hill for a children's entertainment company to die on?" [52] In his opinion piece, Mr. Baker makes a complete mockery of the Disney Company's extreme commitment to 'wokism'. "It's easy to mock, but when a company whose products have entertained, enlivened, and enriched the lives of billions of children and their parents decides it must take a stand against the Parental Rights in Education Bill, what does it expect? By joining in the campaign to distort the objective of Florida's new law, defame the people behind it, and deprive parents of the right to determine whether their children as young as 5 should be taught about sexual orientation or gender identity in the classroom, Disney executives invite something much worse than ridicule. They risk placing themselves on the side of a small minority of unrepresentative ideologues who are trying to remake the relationship between children, their parents and their teachers." [53]

- The idiots at Disney have dropped using the terms 'boys' and 'girls' at their parks. The reporting staff at Fox News 13 found, "the company is taking out all of its "gendered greetings" in their theme parks' recorded messages to promote a more welcoming environment for guests who do not identify with traditional gender roles." [54] Walt Disney must be spinning in his grave.

- The teacher's unions and leadership of public schools have become overtly aggressive in promoting and indoctrinating children on gender identity and racial orientation. This has stimulated legislative moves in several states to enact laws protecting parent's rights and children's innocence from extreme leftist wokism. Author Stephanie Lundquist-Arora wrote in April 2022, "It is unclear why public education has become obsessed with our children's gender identity and sexual orientation, even at obscenely young ages. What is the end game here?" [55] Yes, what is the end game?

- My daughter and her family were visiting a couple of weeks ago. My youngest grandchild (6 years old) was sitting next to me and said, "Papa did you know men can marry men and women can marry women." He is in kindergarten and completely innocent.

Here is what Harvard Business School advises to ensure an "INCLUSIVE AND EQUITABLE INTERVIEW PROCESSES". I highlight only the first two of six points they make, because the last four are more commonsensical.

1. "Craft inclusive job descriptions that welcome in candidates: To create a welcoming and inclusive

environment in the early stages of your hiring process, it is critical to use inclusive language that invites candidates in. Educate team members who are writing job descriptions about removing gendered language, jargon, and idioms that can make potential candidates feel excluded.

2. Educate interviewers on the benefits of diverse teams to counter "just like me" bias: One way to counter the interviewer's reliance on the "soft stuff" is to build awareness of why workplace diversity (including, but not limited to, race, socioeconomic status, gender, and sexual orientation) benefits an organization. Furthermore, be proactive in attracting a diverse applicant pool. Use filters within the HBS resume database to identify students involved in various student clubs including the African American Student Union, Armed Forces Alumni Association, Asian American Business Association, Black Investment Club, Latino Student Organization, PRIDE, Women in Investing Club, and the Women's Student Association to invite students to apply." [56]

Every business school in the world today offers degrees in Human Resource Management (HR). The universal adoption of HR and its elevation to senior executive status is the biggest mistake business has made in 70 years. Why? This is the area occupied by the touchy-feely hippies and LSD-fried psychologists of the late 60s. It has thus become the office of political correctness. Since they are busy doing very little, they look to academia for ideas like teaching employees to identify 'unconscious bias'. They are so smart, they can tell you when you are biased and don't even know it! The experts at Harvard explain it like this, "Unconscious or implicit bias is the mental processes that cause us to act in ways that reinforce stereotypes even when in our conscious mind we would deem that behavior counter to our value system. Closely related to unconscious bias is affinity bias in which people tend to gravitate towards others who look, act, and think as they do." [57] So, when we get together with friends (i.e., people we like to be around because we think alike) we are actually demonstrating 'affinity' bias. Harvard makes clear that these people are not really our friends because they are causing us to act in ways that reinforce stereotypes while our conscious minds are taking a nap! I admit that when I am unconscious (i.e., asleep) I do have biases. But, Democrats are unconscious all the time hence they vote for idiots like Joe Biden and feel good about themselves. You tell me who has the bigger problem.

Headline: 'Shit Hits the Fan in Wisconsin - Student Calls Other Student by Wrong Pronoun'. Actually, the headline read, "Kiel, Wisconsin school district charges kids for using wrong pronouns" [58] The story opens by saying, "A Wisconsin school district has filed sexual harassment complaints against three middle schoolers for calling a classmate by a wrong pronoun. The school district in Kiel, a city of 3,600 residents, has charged the three eighth-graders at the Kiel Middle School with sexual harassment after an incident in April in which the students refused to use "they" to refer to a classmate who had switched pronouns a month before the alleged incident." [59] I don't know about you, but even though murders, robbers and thieves are being released by District Attorneys, this pronoun crime is serious shit! Those damn eighth-graders need to do time!

Examples of idiocy from the world of diversity, inclusion and equity unfortunately have no end. This is the world young people are growing up in and that parents are having to navigate. It is supported by the Democratic Party, and it is ruining the lives of normal people. Children are subjected to gender indoctrination beginning in kindergarten. In this age of innocence, some make decisions (which are supported by Democrats) to enter into gender altering hormone therapy without their parent's knowledge. Not surprising, suicide among young people is rising and frustration among parents is through the roof.

Education Tyranny. The previous issue of diversity, inclusion and equity (D.I.E.) has permeated every facet of society today but does the most damage in primary and secondary education. Chapter 14 deals with how the education establishment has totally abandoned it mission of teaching and transferring basic life skills to children and young people. The teacher's unions were complicit in the extension of on-line learning well beyond the time needed to for a Covid safe environment. This cheated thousands of students out of a year of learning (I use the term loosely) and social time with their peers. Suicide among kids skyrocketed. That a Wisconsin school would bring harassment charges against 13-year-old kids for using a non-preferred pronoun speaks volumes. The teacher's unions collaborated with the Biden FBI to label parents as terrorists if they vigorously complained at school board meetings. Mark Moore of the New York Post wrote, "House Republicans say they have evidence from FBI whistleblowers that the bureau used anti-terrorism tools to investigate parents who were critical of school boards' COVID-19 policies despite assurances from Attorney General Merrick Garland to lawmakers that such probes would not be conducted." [60] Here are a few more examples:

- Princeton University implements racial preference policies, a white tenured professor objects and is labeled racist and facing dismissal. [61] This is typical of the 'Equity' agenda at colleges and universities. Hopefully, this vagabond will be replaced with a black, transgender person with several preferred pronouns. Equity means special treatment for 'minority groups' as they define them at the time. If the person is 'non-white', then they get extra. Were they born male yet claim to be female, wonderful, they get special treatment. But there is a catch; if they espouse conservative ideas (like Caitlin Jenner), then their 'equity' privileges are not only withdrawn, but they are also isolated, attacked and cancelled. A perfect case study is the action Princeton University took against tenured professor Joshua Katz in September 2021. He objected in writing to the university's policy of showing financial favoritism to 'faculty of color'. They were given "course relief and summer salary" and an extra semester of sabbatical." These big perks essentially meant they were paid but did not have to work. Pretty nice deal. So, Katz wrote an open letter in the university newspaper. Even though he has worked there for 25 years, they are now seeking his dismissal, his former colleagues have written a letter to the President requesting his dismissal and he has become a persona non grata on campus.

Princeton President Christoper Eisgruber wrote, "'While free speech permits students and faculty to make arguments that are bold, provocative, or even offensive, we all have an obligation to exercise that right responsibly." In other words, you can say anything you like as long as it conforms with leftist views and dogma. As is always the case, the Democrat's actions never align with their words. They are hypocrites.

Two professors risked their careers to support Katz. They wrote, "The Diversity, Equity and Inclusion office of Princeton University has a message for incoming students: It wants them to participate in "tearing down" the very institution they have worked so hard to attend. And to drive this message home, the office is more than happy to tear down those who dissent from its official orthodoxy." [62]

- Professor Jonathan Turley, one of the most respected constitutional legal scholars in the country, also reviews another case of university coercion against a tenured professor, Professor of Accounting, Gordon Klein. Klein's crime was **refusing to exempt black students** from his final exam. UCLA sided with the students and pursued his dismissal. Turley reports, "Thousands signed a petition that declares Klein must be fired for his "extremely insensitive, dismissive, and woefully racist response" and "blatant lack of empathy and unwillingness to accommodate his students." [63] UCLA put Klein on leave, conducted an investigation and cleared him of all charges, but he was later denied a pay raise. He is suing them for damages from the loss of earnings from outside consulting.

- The Dean of the UCLA business school, Antonio Bernardo, wrote an open letter to the school regarding the Klein case. His comments expose the justification the progressive left always uses to support their coercive actions to shut down free speech; "Providing a safe, respectful and equitable environment in which students can effectively learn is fundamental to UCLA's mission. We share common principles across the university of integrity, excellence, accountability, respect and service. Conduct that demonstrates a disregard for our core principles, including an abuse of power, is not acceptable." [64]

    If a person's speech or actions run afoul of the progressive, politically correct dogma, then that person is endangering those around them. And woe to you if you react to their coercion. The left can violently threaten you, have you fired, and ruin your life simply for disagreeing with them. And they will do it in the name of 'Equity'.

The Destruction of Energy Security - Using Fake Climate Alarmism.
The climate alarmism that is spread by the Democrats, Academia, and the United Nations is the biggest lie ever told to mankind.... and the easiest to disprove. Slowly rising CO_2 does not threaten life, it enhances it. NASA satellite photos quickly prove the earth has gotten greener over the last 70 years. CO_2 is plant food from the atmosphere. Plants grow faster and are healthier in higher CO_2 environments. This is why commercial greenhouses pump in CO_2. This is why the earth is now greener. This is one of the reasons agricultural productivity (increased crop yield/unit of ground)

continues to increase. This means more food. When farm productivity increases, the cost of production decreases making food at the grocery less expensive. Climate alarmists think all of this is bad.

CO_2 has increased from approximately 280 ppm to 410 ppm since 1950, while global population grew by 5.369 billion over the same period. A 46% increase in CO_2 and a 215% increase in people, most of which are in China and India (two of the worst polluters). Population in 1950 was 2.5 billion and is now 7.869 billion. So, with all these extra CO_2 exhalers on the planet, it should be no surprise that atmospheric CO_2 increased. One giant exhale for humankind equals one very small increase in atmospheric $CO2$. Does this mean we should worry? No, but someone please tell Bill Gates. Bill and his neo-Malthusian (i.e., believe earth is approaching its capacity to carry and support humanity) followers are using this global warming scam to exert global control over all human activity. They are not our friends.

Consider the quality of life virtually everywhere in the world due to the growth in manufacturing and personal mobility. I was born in 1950, so have seen and experienced how life in the United States has gotten exponentially better due to fossil fuel and technology. If you would like to know what life would be like without reliable electricity to heat your home, read Chapter 7 of this book again. The over reliance on wind power in north Texas resulted in the deaths of 23 people and untold agricultural destruction. This will happen more frequently if the neo-Malthusian environmentalists and globalists get there way.

The alarmists (Sierra Club, World Wildlife Fund, Nature Conservancy, Rainforest Action Network, Natural Resource Defense Council, Union of Concerned Scientists, Greenpeace, Earth Justice, 350.org, Environmental Defense Fund, Audubon Association, etc.) claim the sky is falling due to CO_2 increase but the truth is the exact opposite. With increased CO_2, the surface of the earth has more plant cover. Via photosynthesis, plants emit oxygen. See how long you last without oxygen.

We began this section with the title 'The Destruction of Energy' because this is the goal of the climate alarmists. Joe Biden promised to eliminate fracking, which unlocks most of the natural gas used to generate electricity. Barack Obama and Hillary Clinton promised to shut down coal-fired electricity generation. In 2010, half of U.S. electricity came from coal-fired plants. A report by the U.S. Energy Information Administration says, "Most new electric power generators built between 1950 and 1990 were coal-fired. Seventy-three percent of coal-fired electric generators existing at the end of 2010 were at least 30 years old. Nearly half of U.S. electric power generation comes from coal." [65] In 2021, coal supplied 21.8% of U.S. electricity.[66] We went from 50% to 21.8% in eleven years! These Obama-caused decreases in reliable coal-powered electricity has put energy reliability in jeopardy. In 1950 the United States exported 29 short tons of coal, while in 2020 we exported 81 million short tons, almost a three-fold increase. [67] We are still mining coal; it is just being used for power generation in other countries. The environmental alarmists lobby to shut down coal and other fossil fuels in the United States and western Europe while China and India build new coal fired power plants and import our coal. *Coal continues to supply 40% of the world's electricity production, while the addition of natural gas and oil account for 39%.*

When Donald Trump was President, the United States was energy independent. The government was funding research and development for fossil fuel alternatives and also for cleaner production of fossil fuels. With a literal flip-of-the-switch, Biden has changed this. Biden shut down the Keystone pipeline which reduced oil imports from Canada. He banned exploration on Federal lands, which was over-ruled by a federal judge, whose over-rule was then ignored or slow walked by the Department of Interior. Biden Executive Orders have placed moratoriums on new leases on federal lands, off-shore areas and the Alaska artic national wildlife refuge. Plain and simple, Biden has declared war on fossil fuels. For an exhaustive list of Biden's actions to destroy our energy infrastructure, please refer to: barr.house.gov/_cache/files/1/7/17ec008b-f7ea-49e6-b614-ea9b4dd12d6f/16871653E745FF6D04D065F4E6DE8623.a-promise-kept-biden-s-war-on-energy-final-002-.pdf.

The Wall Street Journal quoted a quote from an oil executive, "Biden is signaling that his environmental goals trump energy security and consumer prices," and "that's not lost on public companies or the banks they rely on." [68]

Silvio Marcacci wrote a love letter to the demise of fossil fuel in the March 2022 edition of Forbes that oozes climate alarmist bullshit, but also contains nuggets of fact. The facts he shares with glee will reduce the United States to third world status. Brown outs and black outs will become the norm and the Democrats living in the northern blue states will all be trying to move to Florida and Texas to keep warm.

The following quotes from this Forbes article forecast doom for America. "For context, coal's share of U.S. electricity generation has plummeted from 50% a decade ago to less than 20% today." [69] But, the really bad news is in the following quotes.

"Plant closure announcements have resumed their march to zero, with the U.S. Energy Information Administration (EIA) reporting 12.6 GW of coal capacity will close in 2022, representing 85% of all electric generation capacity retirements this year." "Coal's outlook is even more grim over the next several years. S&P Global Market Intelligence reports utilities will close 51 GW of coal power between 2022 and 2027, followed by a "record plunge" in 2028 with more than 23 GW scheduled closures. Federal rules to keep coal ash and toxic metals out of drinking water will take effect that year – regardless of Supreme Court decisions on the U.S. Environmental Protection Agency's authority to regulate greenhouse gas emissions – and many utilities are not investing in compliance upgrades for plants that keep losing money." [70]

He quotes key energy supply executives: "Paul Chodak, executive vice president of generation at American Electric Power, told S&P the necessary investments to keep plants online and comply with regulations "was not justified" compared to forecast market prices and alternatives like renewable energy. Other utilities seem to agree with him. Duke Energy, the country's second-largest utility, recently announced it will close its 11 coal-fired power plants by 2035 – 13 years earlier than previously expected. Duke says it will replace that generation capacity by more than doubling its renewable energy portfolio to 24 GW by 2030. Georgia Power, one of America's most coal-reliant utilities, similarly announced that it would close all 14 of its coal plants no later than 2035 and double its renewable energy generation with up to 6 GW of solar and wind." [71]

Chodlak said, "...the investments required to comply with regulations 'was not justified'....". These utilities are independent businesses and must turn a profit. They are not philanthropic enterprises and are not government owned and run (which would be socialism in its purest form). The economic problem coal-fired and nuclear energy plants face is caused by government intrusion. The regulatory requirements placed on these plants is enormous and requires regular infusions of capital to upgrade and maintain the plants, but also to feed the bureaucracy's demand for analysis, assessments, monitoring, reporting, and fighting lawsuits. Intrusive government is the problem.

The Sierra Club is one of the leading radical non-profits that lobby the government and lie to their supporters about the threats from climate change. Sierra Club is proud of their record in helping destroy America's energy infrastructure. There website tracks the number of coal-fired plants they have helped shut down ("356 dirty power plants retired: 174 to go") [72] Even if their American funders and supporters knew the truth it would not matter because the multi-millionaire/billionaire class (i.e., a list of these useful idiots can be found by searching on 'Hollywood environmentalists') provide most of their operating funds.

The good news is that the target dates for most of these closures do not begin until 2028, giving Americans time to wake up and put adults back in the White House and Congress. But there is bad news. Jason Hayes, the Director of environmental policy at the Mackinac Center for Public Policy writes, "Whatever hopes people might have had for saving Michigan's Palisades Nuclear Generating station, it's too late. On May 20, the plant shut down, taking with it 6.5% of the state's electricity and 15% of the state's clean energy. This leaves Michiganders with less reliable electricity and higher prices." [73] This sounds like Germany. Why would they allow this plant to be shut down, especially without a reliable replacement? The answer: the power company cannot afford the extraordinary costs of regulatory compliance while the government sets quotas and subsidies for wind and solar.

The chart below shows the growth of nuclear power in China since 1993. In the U.S., the newest reactor to enter service is Tennessee's Watts Bar Unit 2, which began operation in June 2016. No new nuclear power generation in the United States for 38 years! Even though CO_2 is not an issue, nuclear has no CO_2 emission and it is reliable 24/7! Now look at the chart showing China's growth in nuclear again. We are closing nuclear plants and the explanation given is cheap natural gas. OK, natural gas has been a lower cost raw material for many years (present day excluded) but coal, natural gas, nuclear and hydro are all *reliable, 24/7 power generators*. Wind and solar are totally dependent on the weather. Is this sinking in? *Shouldn't the government be concerned about energy security and thus keep all reliable options viable?* They are subsidizing sources that are intermittent and unreliable and shuttering the reliable sources. The power companies are not government agencies; their investors expect a return on their investment. So, why aren't they investing? Because the Democrats continue to throw up economic and regulatory disincentives, while favoring wind and solar. In April 2022, the Biden administration increased the royalty rates for new oil and gas exploration leases by 50%. These were the first royalty increases since the 1920s. So, Biden calls a halt to exploration for fossil fuel on federal lands, the gulf and Alaska, stops the completion of the Keystone pipeline and oil and gasoline prices start to climb. Then the unnecessary war in Ukraine puts a stopper in oil from Russia. What does Biden do? He goes to Saudi Arabia and Venezuela for oil while stifling oil production in the U.S. That is the logic of the Democratic Party. At some point, the question must be asked of Biden and the Democrats how their policies and actions are in the best interest of American taxpayers.

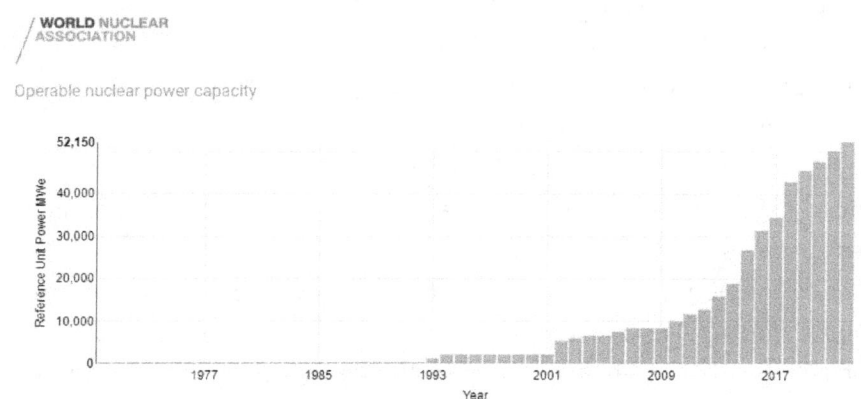

Growth in Nuclear Power Generation in China (from world-nuclear.org/information-library/country-profiles/countries-a-f/china-nuclear-power.aspx)

The Towers of Power sing in unison the 'down with fossil fuel' tune. Every weather report blames every kind of extreme weather event on climate change. Hurricanes, tornadoes, droughts in the west, below normal snow fall, above normal snow fall, wildfires, and the list goes on. All are said to be evidence of impending climate doom. Every National Geographic show or nature show of any kind invokes climate change as the boogie man. It is all a colossal lie. They make the claims without any data to support them. They try to prove wildfires are increasing due to climate change but won't allow you to use data earlier than 1983. Guess they believe the people collecting the data prior to 1983 were idiots. So, it is true, if you exclude the data before 1983 going back 100 years, wildfires are increasing. But even with that as the starting point, it does not correlate with temperature or any other number they might try to hang a hook on. Remember, the earth has only warmed 1.5°F since 1870.

Oh, but the seas are rising faster they shout! No, they aren't. Since 1870, the seas have risen about 2mm/year (as measured by tide gauges). Children understand that when you take ice out of the freezer, it is going to melt. So, it should not be surprising that land ice has melted and slowly caused sea levels to rise as we came out of the Little Ice Age. Most people would expect melt water to be slow since temperatures over the period have only risen a whopping 1.5°F.

They claim a coal-fired or gas-fired electricity plant can be replaced by wind or solar. This is a bald-faced lie. Wind and solar only generate electricity when the wind is blowing, or the sun is shining. This is why people died in north Texas. The nihilist progressives reply, "We will store wind and solar energy in batteries!" And I say, "Oh really?" It is true that large scale utility batteries can and do store electricity generated by wind and solar. An example is the 2017 installed Tesla 100 MW/ 129 MWh Li-ion battery storage project at Hornsdale Wind Farm in Australia. Timothy Lee of Ars Technica writes, "In the long run, massive battery facilities will be needed to shift intermittent solar and wind power in time. But a lot of battery installations today don't have enough capacity to do much of this. Tesla's South Australia battery, for example, *only had enough capacity to supply power for a little over an hour at its full 100 MW power level.*" [74] Suffice it to say, long term and reliable electricity storage in mega-batteries for cities remains a pipe dream. The key component, lithium, is being used in much of today's electronic technology and its supplies, like coal and petroleum are not infinite. We have much more fossil fuel reserves than lithium reserves. Lithium batteries can explode, they last 10 to 20 years and are very difficult to recycle. Plus, in the case of utility scale lithium batteries, the technology is far from reaching a level of reliability that is remotely close to that of fossil fuel energy plants. Yet, the progressive Democrats, environmentalists and globalists try to convince the trusting public that the technology is proven and reliable. Not even close!

Then there is the issue of raw material availability and supply. A conventional car requires copper and manganese whereas an electric car requires copper, lithium, nickel, manganese, cobalt and graphite. A natural gas power generation plant requires only copper. A coal-fired plant requires copper, nickel and small amounts of chromium and cobalt. Solar photovoltaic cells require copper and a lot of 'rare' earth minerals (hence most photovoltaic cells are made in China, the source of the rare earth minerals). Wind requires a lot of copper, zinc, a lot of manganese, plus nickel, chromium, and molybdenum.

The International Energy Agency wrote in 2021, "A typical electric car requires six times the mineral inputs of a conventional car and an onshore wind plant requires nine times more mineral resources than a gas-fired plant of the same capacity."[95]

They provided more detail later in their report, "The types of mineral resources used vary by technology. Lithium, nickel, cobalt, manganese and graphite are crucial to battery performance, longevity and energy density. Rare earth elements are essential for permanent magnets that are vital for wind turbines and EV motors. Electricity networks need a huge amount of copper and aluminum, with copper being a cornerstone for all electricity-related technologies. The shift to a clean energy system is set to drive a huge increase in the requirements for these minerals, meaning that the energy sector is emerging as a major force in mineral markets. Until the mid-2010s, for most minerals, the energy sector represented a small part of total demand. However, as energy transitions gather pace, clean energy technologies are becoming the fastest-growing segment of demand. In a scenario that meets the Paris Agreement goals (as in the IEA Sustainable Development Scenario [SDS]), their share of total demand rises significantly over the next two decades to over 40% for copper and rare earth elements, 60-70% for nickel and cobalt, and almost 90% for lithium. EVs and battery storage have already displaced consumer electronics to become the largest consumer of lithium and are set to take over from stainless steel as the largest end user of nickel by 2040." [96]

This IEA 2021 report is well worth the read if you are interested in a much broader and in-depth status report than this book can provide. They do call out the serious concern about the world's current dependence on China and other unstable governments for the supply of these critical minerals. They do not address the irony that the NGOs (i.e., Sierra Club) and Democrats who cheer for renewables are against mineral exploration and mining in the United States, Canada and Europe.

Electricity is needed to keep us warm in winter and cool in summer. Intermittent sources (wind and solar) are of little value during peak demand periods. There must be a base load of reliable electricity generated from fossil fuels or hydro. Just think about the last winter storm. It blew in with a vengeance and wind turbines were not operating because they cannot withstand wind speeds in excess of 25 mph. [75] As was the case in Texas, they also freeze up if not properly equipped and maintained. These storms always have dense clouds that block the sun and snow blankets the panels. This is exactly the time you need the energy. Once the clouds have cleared and the snow melted, the threat of severe cold has passed. The same is true for hot summers. Brown outs and rolling black outs are the result of demand exceeding the ability to supply. It is impossible to just 'crank-up energy from solar or wind. People can and do crank-up their air conditioners when they get home from work or on the weekends, and reliable fossil fuel or hydro plants crank-up with them. Wind and solar cannot.

It should be clear by now that reliance on wind and solar is a house of cards. Do you want to risk your life in a house of cards?

As a last gasp, the proponents of renewables say confidently, "But, wind and sunlight are free." Yes, the same can be said about water and fossil fuel. They are all there for the taking. Each option requires significant upfront capital to acquire and transform the raw material into electricity. Fossil and hydro do not require storage units (batteries) because the power is generated by rate of burn or flow. These sources can be controlled (i.e., dialed up or down). They are thus reliable under all circumstances. **The key question is what value should be placed on reliability?** The only stake I have in the question is I want to be warm in the winter and cool in the summer and would like to have those comforts at a reasonable and honest price. If solar and wind are the best path to achieve those goals, then prove it and I will be on board. Having said that, I know the premise upon which the public is sold the idea of the need for renewables is bullshit. Climate change is not an existential threat. Thus, I am inclined to distrust the renewable proponents.

I have reviewed many cost comparisons by conservative and liberal organizations and concluded that the perfect cost comparison model has not yet been developed. The pro-renewable organizations try to add 'social' costs that are all bogus. If a cost is not measurable, then it should not be counted. The renewables never account for the cost of transmission lines. Most of the renewable generation is far from population centers, thus must be transmitted great distances. The greater the distance to consumption, the greater the line loss. Reliable plants are required to make room for renewable energy because it must be transmitted and used as it is produced. So, when there is a nice breeze at the turbine site, the gas-fired plant must dial-down to make room for the wind energy, otherwise it is lost. When a fossil fuel plant has to dial down, its cost per unit on that day goes up to due to decreased output. If the renewable energy cannot be transmitted when produced, it is a complete loss, which is a financial loss for that turbine farm. Thus, the wind farms and solar farms live and die based on the governments demand that reliable fossil or hydro plants make room for the renewable energy. Government intrusion is the primary reason there is little investment in new fossil, hydro and nuclear energy production. The bottom line is honest cost comparisons are almost impossible.

We know Germany shut down its carbon free nuclear plants to 'look' green and outsource natural gas from Russia. We also know Germans are paying a lot more for electricity today than 10 years ago. In the end the two components that are important are the cost to the consumer and the value of reliability. No matter where you look today, renewables lose this comparison big time.

Experience thus far demonstrates that an over-sized commitment to renewable energy will increase the consumer price and reduce reliability… a lose-lose for the consumer.

But, the believers shout, 'the experts say'. Remember the axiom, 'People do what they are rewarded to do'. These experts are paid by entities with agendas and if they don't do as they are told, they are fired. The entire electric vehicle industry depends on the success of this lie. There have been and are whistleblowers, but they quickly disappear. Why is that? Because the media destroys them. Their former employer pays them off and forces non-disclosure agreements to silence them. The government, who is in on the scam, will not protect them. So, when someone says that 98% of scientists believe climate change is a threat, this is a lie. There has never been a survey of the scientific community on this question. But, if there was one, the coercive pressure is so threatening, few would honestly answer.

The lie of climate alarmism is found in the data and in common sense explanations like I have just provided. Surveys indicate that most people get this... climate alarmism is more Democrat B.S., just piled higher and deeper.

International Embarrassment: The Biden Foreign Policy Debacle

Since Joe Biden can't even read a teleprompter without making a gaff or forgetting why he is reading it, the thought of him meeting with leaders of other major countries, especially China is terrifying. I think his Chief of Staff is also terrified by this thought, so they are keeping 'Sleepy Joe' in the White House. But this has not prevented his administration from screwing up everything they touch.

The Afghanistan withdrawal. The Time Magazine headline of August 15, 2021, read, "Joe Biden's Botched Withdrawal Plunges Afghanistan into Chaos". Reporters W.J. Hennigan and Kimberly Dozier wrote, "In early July, President Joe Biden informed the American people of the coming drawdown of U.S. forces from Afghanistan after a 20-year occupation. The evacuation would be "secure and orderly," he said, with little chance of a Taliban takeover. "The likelihood there's going to be the Taliban overrunning everything and owning the whole country is highly unlikely," he said. Little more than a month later, Biden has been proven wrong on all counts." [76]

The United States went to war in Afghanistan on October 7, 2001, in response to the September 11, 2001, terrorist attacks. The Taliban were quickly routed by the Americans and the hunt for bin Laden was on. Over the 20-year period, approximately 2,300 troops were killed and over 20,000 wounded. The last 13 American troops to die were due to Biden's moronic decision to perform a spontaneous withdrawal. No planning, no warning, no contingency plans, or what-if scenarios. It was quintessential Joe Biden.

Not only were the Taliban back in complete control of the country, Biden abandoned **thousands** of American citizens. The blog I published on August 17, 2021, sums up the disaster: "The United States left Afghanistan's Bagram Airfield after nearly 20 years by shutting off the electricity and slipping away in the night without notifying the base's new Afghan commander…". "Afghan soldiers who wandered throughout the base that had once seen as many as 100,000 US troops were deeply critical of how the US left Bagram. "In one night, they lost all the goodwill of 20 years by leaving the way they did, in the night, without telling the Afghan soldiers who were outside patrolling the area," said Afghan soldier Naematullah, who asked that only his one name be used." That was July 2, 2021.

Today is August 17, 2021, and the Taliban has taken over Afghanistan, including Bagram Airfield the largest U.S./NATO base in the country. The President of Afghanistan has fled the country. Over 10,000 Americans remain trapped, as well as the patriotic Afghans who served as interpreters, civilian support, and military. They were asleep when the Biden Administration abandoned them.

This is the new progressive America, and it makes me sick. I am not proud to be an American today. Obama went to a Las Vegas fundraiser when the Libyan consulate was overrun resulting in the murder of his ambassador and 3 others. They have been lying about Benghazi ever since. Now, with over 10,000 Americans trapped in Kabul, Biden is holed up at Camp David and incommunicado." [77]

Six months later, in February 2022, the Senate Foreign Relations Committee published a report on Biden's debacle titled, '*Left Behind: A Brief Assessment of the Biden Administration's Strategic Failures during the Afghanistan Evacuation*'. [78] All of the following quotes are directly from this report.

"On April 14, 2021, President Biden announced the full withdrawal of U.S. forces from Afghanistan by September 11, which provided ***150 days to plan*** for and execute the withdrawal."

"While Afghanistan was stable in April, President Biden's interagency ***should have*** begun the planning process for a mass evacuation if it became necessary."

"During the withdrawal, many senior leaders in Washington ***failed to recognize*** or adapt to worsening conditions on the ground. [Author's comment: As soon as Biden made his withdrawal announcement, the Taliban began aggressively moving on Afghan cities]."

"State ***should have*** stepped up its accounting of U.S. citizens and improved the process for Special Immigrant Visa (SIV) applicants and others who assisted the United States."

"With the Taliban hunting down those who had assisted the United States, State ***should have*** planned to relocate a sizable amount of these people."

"The United States ***abandoned Bagram Air Base*** on July 4, ***without even telling the Afghan base commander***. In the process, the administration abandoned a facility that *could have been critical to a better evacuation*. At the same time, *cutting support to the Afghan National Security Forces eliminated their ability to properly defend the country and set the conditions for the rapid fall of Kabul.*"

"The interagency *failed* to keep DoD and State in sync with each other. As the manager of the interagency process, the National Security Council (NSC) had a responsibility to coordinate the withdrawal of all U.S. personnel and the safe operations of anyone who would be left behind."

"Having wasted 115 days, the NSC did not conduct its first senior meeting to discuss the withdrawal until August 14 at 3:30pm, just hours before Kabul fell, when evacuations became life or death for Americans, Afghans, and U.S. military personnel."

The summary of conclusions from the DC meeting on August 14 included actions which *should have been taken months in advance*, including but not limited to: reaching out to third countries to serve as transit points, alerting locally employed U.S. embassy staff about relocation, and standing up a communication/manifest team for flights out of Kabul. *It is inexcusable that the DC met at such a late date.*""

"The remaining two weeks were *defined by chaos*, and impromptu efforts to manage that chaos by U.S. personnel on the ground. U.S. commitments to help NATO allies evacuate their personnel were tested, and *the credibility of the United States was at stake.*"

There is so much damning evidence of Biden and Democrat incompetence in this report, it boggles the mind. I encourage you to read the entire report. But here are some of the critical take-aways:

- 9,000 Americans are still trapped in Afghanistan as of February 2022

- upwards of 80,000 Afghan translators, undercover intel & staff were abandoned

- the largest military base in the country was abandoned

- billions of dollars of sophisticated military equipment was left behind, including 40 Black Hawk helicopters and ScanEagle Drones, 2,000 armored vehicles, 600,000 infantry weapons and other equipment like night vision goggles (all now in Taliban possession).

- the trust of our Allies was seriously damaged

- the good will of freedom loving Afghans was totally destroyed

A leader with integrity would have: 1. Gotten the Americans and Afghan loyalists out first (Biden put their lives in the hands of the Taliban). 2. Extract or destroy the strategic military equipment (this is not rocket science) and 3. Extract the military. But, then Joe Biden is not a leader, much less a good one.

Maybe the saddest part of this Afghanistan debacle is that few Americans know how bad it was and still is because the media does not report it. The Senate minority report was issued only two months ago (March 2022).

Iran Nuclear Proliferation. Joe Biden is letting Russia negotiate with Iran on their efforts to achieve nuclear warhead capabilities. Yes, while Russia is trying to take over the country of Ukraine, the Biden administration is trusting the Russians to act as a proxy for the United States with the Iran negotiations. Michael Goodwin of the New York Post writes, "Russia is acting as a go-between for the United States in nuclear talks with Iran. When I first read that, I thought it couldn't possibly be true. With Russia then massing troops on the Ukraine border, I assumed that even the Biden White House couldn't be foolish enough to trust Vladimir Putin to do anything in good faith or certainly anything in America's interest. Unfortunately, the story was true, and even more alarming, Russia continues to direct the nuclear talks with America's approval while its army simultaneously turns Ukraine's cities into rubble, mercilessly killing civilians and creating the largest refugee crisis since World War II." [79]

Globalizing U.S. Tax Policy. Janet Yellen, Biden's Secretary of the Treasury is lobbying Congress to have the United States join 130 other countries in a global corporate tax agreement. This is absurd and will hurt U.S. competitiveness and reduce domestic tax revenues. President Trump was successful at getting Congress to adjust corporate taxes from a tiered rate that went as high as 39% to a flat 21%. This move keeps companies from moving to tax haven countries and attracts companies to move to the U.S. Yellen's idea is a convoluted global mess that will drop to 15%. There is no reason to do this. There is no analysis that demonstrates this will be good for America. The Tax Foundation says, "The U.S. could lose tax revenue because of this approach. However, U.S. Treasury Secretary Yellen has previously written that she believes Amount A would be roughly revenue neutral for the U.S. For this to be true, the U.S. would need to collect significant revenue from foreign companies or from U.S. companies that sell to U.S. customers from foreign offices." [80] It is unlikely Congress will ratify this agreement.

Chinese Hegemony. China's long game is to dominate the world. They are well into the implementation of their Belt and Road

Initiative that will increase access to markets and give China the dominant hand in those markets. China can implement such plan because it is a communist country. The Chinese people are nothing more than pawns to be used, sacrificed and discarded. We will go into more depth on China in Chapter 15, but the 'weakling in the White House' is America's greatest real and present danger.

Will International Law be allowed to Supersede American Law?
America has been the world's model for the 'Rule of Law', but that is now threatened by a pending United Nations proposal to give the World Health Organization global authority during pandemics. I suggested in this book's first edition that we should not be surprised if a new virus appears on the scene during the months leading up to the mid-term elections.

Enter the Monkeypox. After giving an update on the incidence of monkeypox around the world, Joshua Philipps of The Epoch Times writes, "The timing of all of this is important. It gives the WHO a chance to show its worth, since it's in the process of trying to get new and expansive powers—under the banner of governing global health emergencies." [81]

"The United Nations is considering various amendments to the WHO at its 75th World Health Assembly in Geneva, that could give its director-general, Tedros Adhanom Ghebreyesus, the unilateral authority to declare a public health emergency with far-reaching powers over the laws of sovereign nations. Not only would this give Tedros the ability to declare a public health emergency in any nation he wants—using whatever evidence he wants—but it would also allow him to dictate policies that the target country should adopt to respond to the U.N.'s declared emergency. If a country refuses, a proposed amendment could give the WHO the ability to sanction that country. If you're wondering whether giving such powers to a U.N. agency that couldn't demonstrate its independence from the Chinese Communist Party (CCP) could fly in the face of U.S. law, it seems that President Joe Biden has the answer. Not only is the Biden administration allowing this shift in power to the WHO, but it's also helping advance it." [82]

Philipps continues, "The United States proposed amendments to the WHO in January, which will be considered at the U.N. meeting in Geneva, The Epoch Times reports. These included an amendment that would allow the WHO to make public declarations on a health crisis *without needing to consult with the target country*, and *without needing to get verification from local officials*. The Biden administration's proposals would also give $2.47 billion in funding to the Centers for Disease Control and Prevention (CDC) for things including "enhancements to domestic sentinel surveillance programs," "investments in global genomic surveillance approaches," and other systems." [83]

Philipps smartly ponders where this abrogation of American sovereignty could lead, "Whether or not monkeypox poses a large threat to public health, it presents a serious threat to public freedom. The virus could act as a Trojan horse, carrying inside it all the justifications to grant the WHO a dictator's dream of global power, and give the CDC a system of surveillance beyond anything Orwell could have conceived." [84]

This is a nightmare. It is hard to imagine that anyone with a logical mind could conclude this is a good idea.

Recapping the Issues. The only issue in this update chapter that is new, is Ukraine, but it was predicted. There are many issues threatening America today and all of them have been made worse by Joe Biden and the Democrats. In fact, the issue of climate alarmism is a fabrication out of whole cloth. But it is an existential threat to mankind's freedom worldwide. If those who love freedom and want their grandchildren to prosper in the future, then each American loyalist must be able to win the debate. This is why I wrote *34 Days & Holding: America in the Balance* and this book. If we don't stand for the truth, we will surely fall. If you are one of the millions who don't like confrontation, I understand. Maybe you are a Christian and find solace in the beatitude 'the meek shall inherit the earth' or 'turn the other cheek'. I would just ask you, if that is the right behavior in these times, then why did Jesus overthrow the tables of the money changers. Why did Paul go to the city centers to debate, knowing he would encounter resistance and possibly physical harm? The answer: it was the right thing to do and offered hope to those who were being misled. So, I encourage you to be ready to answer those who are perpetrating the lies with sound reasoned answers. Let's review:

1. Biden's Open Border Policy - Three million undocumented and illegal immigrants are now somewhere in the United States thanks to Joe Biden. Each illegal costs the America taxpayer $8,000 year after year. This number considers the taxes some of them pay. So, in 2022, an additional cost of $16 billion will come out of taxpayer pockets. This is on top of the $116 billion we have been paying. Not factored into this cost are the lives lost due to illegal drugs (108,000 fentanyl deaths in 2021 alone). The increasing insurance costs due to theft, vandalism, etc. is not factored in. It doesn't consider the lives destroyed by prostitution, kidnapping, and drugs. There is NO metric that argues it is good for America to have an open southern border. So, why are the Democrats in favor of it?

2. Inflation and the Economy. Inflation is an insidious tax on everyone, but especially those in the lower income brackets (the very people the Democrats claim to represent). It is a multifaceted issue with many fathers. The Federal Reserve policies of quantitative easing (putting more money into the system) deflates the value of the dollar. A weaker dollar means it takes more of them to buy stuff and pay the bills. Thus, it is inflationary because a basket of goods, rent, etc. takes more dollars now than it did a year ago. When the Fed buys bonds from the Treasury, it is loaning that money to the government at interest. The government then spends the money on all kinds of things, many of which are unnecessary. This wasteful spending is a hallmark of the Democrat party. They claimed to need $1.9 trillion for additional Covid relief but spent less than 9% on Covid stuff. This extravagant spending of borrowed money is inflationary because it creates government created demand spikes for goods. This causes shortages and production ramp-ups which require price increases. The cause of inflation today is Joe Biden, the democrats, and the left-leaning Federal Reserve. At best, they are all Keynesians who believe government spending stimulates the economy, at worst, they are socialists who believe in the purest form that the government should own the banks, manufacturing, etc. Europe has embraced for decades a democratic socialism which has relegated them to an impotent collection of elitists.

3. Ukraine. Ukraine is a European issue and not an existential threat to America. But the democrats (in this case, many Republicans are also democrats) have made it an American issue. Congress has approved giving Ukraine over $50 billion. This is money down a sink hole. There is zero return on investment, yet taxpayer money is now taking wing for Ukraine. When thinking about Ukraine, we must also think about what that money could have done if used for Americans. The extremely serious problem of illegal immigration would be eliminated. We would have a wall and enough border patrol agents and technology to completely secure the border and deport the 25-30 million illegals in the country today. Both actions would reduce government spending by about $150 billion a year. That's a return on investment. We would have money to do important infrastructure projects. But the democrats in Washington don't think like this. The military industrial complex might throw a hissy fit but most Americans probably wouldn't mind.

4. Law & Order. The election year 2020 saw over 400 riots around the country but when Biden was declared winner, they disappeared. The non-murder of George Floyd, the rise of Black Lives Matters and ANTIFA were not the cause of these riots. The jury who found the officers guilty of second-degree murder were themselves being threatened. BLM and ANTIFA are the brown shirts of the Democratic Party. Their services are paid by George Soros and his ilk.

It was the mayors and city councils of Democrat run cities that called for defunding the police. They claim sanctuary city status and then when crime increases and things go to shit, they say they need more money. NO! The people need to stop electing these clowns and put people in leadership that actually care about the people they serve.

These cities and the country are now reaping the whirlwind. The police in some of our major cities have lost confidence in district attorney's office, the mayor and city councils. They are haunted by the fear of being sacrificed to the mob that is screaming racial justice. As a result, safety and tranquility is vanishing. Taking a walk after dark in some cities is no longer safe. My wife and I used to live next to the Botanical Gardens and Chessman Park in Denver, but we left due to increasing crime, the nomadic presence of drug addicts and homeless camps, marches in the park by people chanting left wing slogans, nihilist graffiti on everything and a Democrat major who didn't care. Today (May 25, 2022), the 'weakling in the White House' signed an executive order targeting the police and making their jobs even more difficult. This upside-down crap has got to end.

5. Diversity, Inclusion and Equity (D.I.E.) Dogma. The majority of Americans are friendly hard-working people who resent having religious dogma shoved in their face day in and day out. They just want to live their lives, raise their families and try to build a nest egg for retirement. They want their kids to get an education and have a successful and fruitful life. In other words, they are like most people around the world. These things are not political.

But the Democrats have now morphed into the Big Brother party and want to dictate every facet of life. They want critical race theory taught in high schools. They insist that men who want to compete in women's sports be allowed to do so. They zone neighborhoods to force-fit low-income housing. Harvard University's definition of diversity and inclusion does not include those of Asian descent.

D.I.E. is the most destructive force in America today. It is destroying the social and cultural norms that America was built on. It is ripping our social fabric to shreds. Resist and you are called a racist. Resist at a school board meeting and you may be branded a domestic terrorist by the FBI. Speak out against it at a city council meeting and you may be taken away in handcuffs.

6. The Religion of Climate Change. Angela Merkle, former Chancellor of Germany shut down the German nuclear power grid making the people of Germany totally dependent on other countries for its energy raw material. This allowed her to claim Germany was a global leader in clean energy. This dubious honor has cost the German people dearly. Electricity prices in Germany have more than double since 2011, yet "Almost 60 percent of the EU's energy needs were met by net imports in 2020. Germany's energy import dependency was still higher at 63.7 percent – a slight decrease compared to the previous year's 67 percent," reports Julian Wittengel of Clean Energy Wire.[85] Merkle assured her people that Vladimir Putin would be a reliable supplier of natural gas and oil for their long-term energy needs. But on April 27, 2022, Russia cut off gas supply to Bulgaria and Poland and on May 20, 2022, it added Finland. [85, 86]

A strong argument can be made that were it not for Europe's conversion to the religion of climate change, the invasion of Ukraine would never have happened. Instead of seeking energy security and independence, Europe chose energy dependence from Russia. The stupidity of European leadership is mindboggling.

There is no scientific support for climate alarmism. None. Since temperature records have been regularly recorded, earth's average temperature has risen approximately 1.5°F. At least half of this rise occurred before 1950. Carbon dioxide is not the boogie man. In fact, it is essential for life. The planet is greener because atmospheric CO_2 has increased to a healthy 410 ppm (410 ppm is 4/100ths of 1 percent). Plants fill the lower troposphere with oxygen, without which mankind would cease to exist. The Little Ice Age ended approximately 1870 and we have been slowly warming since, with intermittent periods of cooling. In fact, we went through a cooling period from 1945 to 1979 but you cannot find this trend anymore if you search NASA, NOAA, GSIS, or any other entity that is controlled by the government or gets it funding from the government because they wrote an algorithm to adjust the historic temperature record. Remember the Climate-Gate scandal of 2009 that proved Joe Biden's climate-guy Michael Mann was leading an effort to modify the data to provide a smoother and more steadily upward warming curve. So, the 'historic' data you now find on NOAA's website is 'adjusted' data.

The climate alarmists have no problem admitting to this travesty either. Zeke Hausfather at Berkley Earth published a pretty good article in 2015 (the year the adjustments were enacted) that shows the original data (NOAA Raw vs adjusted (NOAA). [87]

Berkley Earth supports the prevailing climate change ideology, but they do avoid the hysteria. Mr. Hausfather said, "The actual adjustments that NOAA does to the record have a relatively small impact on temperatures in recent years, though small changes can have outsized impacts when calculating short-term trends. The larger impacts of NOAA adjustments by far are in the early part of the record, where they raise temperatures compared to the unadjusted series. Contrary to what most folks assume, the net effect of adjustments is to reduce, not increase, the amount of warming that we've experienced over the past century."

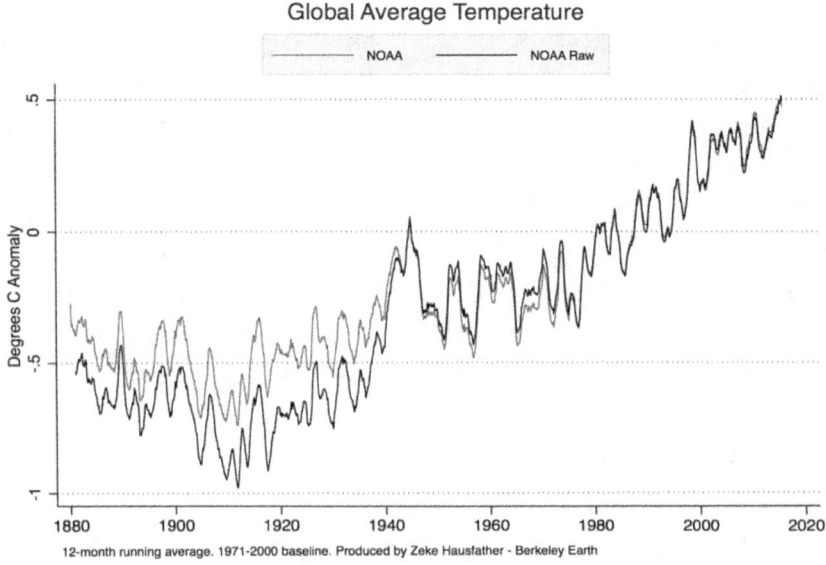

Figure 28. Average Global Temperatures before and after data adjustments. [87]

He continues, "The fact that independent groups like Berkeley Earth find results nearly identical to NOAA should help put to rest any lingering concerns that some nefarious scheme has been hatched among scientists to cook the proverbial book. Rather, temperature data is complex and inhomogeneous, coming from multiple different sources and instruments over the past 250 years. Some adjustments are needed when switching from buckets to ship engine intake valves to buoys, as each will read temperatures a bit differently. The overall effect of these adjustments is small on a global level, however, and they have relatively little bearing on our understanding of modern warming." [88]

First of all, the data represented is not actual temperature data; it is the average of thousands of stations and then subtracted from the average of the preceding 30 years. Thus, the data is called temperature or degree anomaly or departures from the long term (usually 30 years) average. Virtually all temperature reporting agencies use this technique of reporting anomalies, so nothing nefarious about it. The objective is to identify trend. He tells his readers there was no "nefarious scheme" but in fact there was. The objective of the adjustments was to flatten and smooth the curve to show a steadier increase in warming. The adjustments did this by significantly warming the temperatures of the early 1900s. Why would they want to do this? Because the original data show a very rapid increase in average temperature from 1917 to 1944, before atmospheric CO_2 began increasing. The adjusted data better correlates with the slow rise in CO_2, giving them a stronger argument that if CO_2 continues to rise, temperatures will move in synch. So, if the data do not fit your theory, adjust the data. The very rapid warming of 1917-1944 and then cooling (which they now deny happened) from 1945 to 1979 destroys their CO_2 causation theory.

Since I have just used their own article and data to destroy their message, the believers might say, "So what?" Temperatures continued to warm, so big deal. Well, it is a big deal. I began this section reviewing the devastating economic and geopolitical results activist climate policy has caused for Germany, Ukraine and Europe. Imagine how exponentially worse life will be worldwide if the religion of global warming grows unabated. The answer to the arrogant "So what?" question is millions of people will die from excessive cold or heat (gets rid of the oldest and poorest first). The quality of life for all except the elite and the governing masters will be flattened. It will be 1984 in living color. Energy and food are the two most important currencies of life and climate alarmist policy will put them both in control of the utopian globalists. If you get out line, you go to the back of the line.

The average price of gasoline today (May 22, 2022) is $4.71/gallon. As I have demonstrated, this is due to Biden and Democrat policy. The cost of electricity to heat homes, workplaces, etc. will continue to climb and become less reliable as coal-fired power plants are shuttered, fracking for natural gas is banned, and nuclear power plants are not built nor maintained due to government forced environmental regulations. The great push to 2035 and 2050 Net Zero that is being promoted by the Democrats, academia, government bureaucracy (NOAA), and the media will destroy our energy independence, energy raw material supply and electrical production and transportation grid.

The Democrats want to re-imagine America and the World Economic Forum, and its many followers want to re-imagine global society. So, take a moment to imagine the world they are creating by destroying our energy infrastructure. You wake up late on Monday morning because there was a black out (i.e., no electricity). You get dressed in the dark, have a cold breakfast (but don't open the frig because your food will degrade faster). You tell the kids to have a good day at school and leave for work in your car. You didn't get the message that school was suspended due to the black out, so now your kids are on their own at home. At work, it quickly becomes apparent that all of life is at a standstill. With no electricity, no one can do their work. Now imagine this is one of the coldest days of winter. Only those with gasoline or diesel generators have power. The lithium-ion batteries have already been spent. Hospitals have gone mostly dark. The weather service, the news reporting entities, city services are all in the dark. You try to call them, but the line is busy because thousands of others are calling them. But no one is getting through because there is no one there. They are home with their kids praying the clouds will part or the wind will blow. Hopefully there is no snow on the panels and the propellers are not frozen. You have no weather forecast because it takes electricity to power the radar and doppler weather systems. So, you call your husband but his line seems dead. You don't know that he forgot to charge his phone, but you look at your phone charge and see it is half spent. What do you do? You debate if you should sit it out and hope for the best or pile in the car and drive south? But the lines at the gas station give you second thoughts. They can still pump gas as long as they have diesel generators. If they don't have backup generators, then the pumps won't work when the electricity goes out. Without fossil fuel (diesel and gas) delivery trucks will and diesel power trains will grind to a halt. Of course, in a black out electricity is not being delivered, so electric cars will not be able to charge up either. Food shelves will empty in a matter of days.

Climate change is not an existential threat to mankind, but Climate alarmism is.

This extreme scenario is entirely possible if the Democrat's Green New Deal is enacted. The United States has had 9 major black outs since 1965. Most of them only lasted a few hours because the utility companies were able to get power back online. Virtually all the power was being generated by fossil fuels or hydro yet shit still happened. The Northeast black out of 2003 affected 45 million people in 8 states. It was caused by a software glitch. "Most essential services remained operational in most areas, while others failed. Phone services were strained due to the overload in calls. Detroit lost water pressure and was under a water boiling advisory for 4 days after power was restored. Cleveland and New York saw sewage water spill into waterways, forcing many beach closures." [89]

When there are much fewer or no fossil fuels plants to baseload a steady supply of electricity the devastation will be a hundred-fold worse and the time to recovery impossible to predict. The bottom-line folks is that we cannot live without fossil fuel. The Democrats are mortgaging your children's future based on an impossible dream.

7. Indoctrination Replaces Education. This train was the first to leave the station, thus I review it last. We will go into much more depth on this issue in the next chapter but suffice it to say that the vast majority of teachers at all levels of our system of 'education' are products of university indoctrination. The hard sciences of mathematics physics and chemistry remain fairly strong. It is hard to spin a racial angle for mathematics, physics and chemistry, but biology is under full assault. History was the first to go. Howard Zinn's book *'A People's History of United States'* was published in 1980 and has a circulation greater than 2 million copies. Zinn, an avowed communist, cleverly positioned his book as being written from the 'people's' perspective. In the process, the one thing that was lost was perspective. Put Zinn's book in the hands of progressive teachers and the impressionable and trusting students don't have a chance. In the end, they are ashamed of America.

Today, is much worse than the days of Zinn (may he rot in hell). Now we have teacher's unions that put the student last and the activist teachers first. They lobbied the Centers for Disease Control to sustain remote learning and the wearing of masks even though the threat of Covid-19 to young people was close to zero and science had proven masks were no help. The flu is just as dangerous to the very young as Covid. This anti-student and anti-parent action isolated the students, and an entire year of learning was lost. This had nothing to do with science, it had everything to do with power. Like all communist societies in history, the state controls the children. Their parents must be obedient. By the way, suicides deaths among the young far exceeded deaths from Covid (read my book: *34 Days & Holding: America in the Balance*).

During the forced remote learning, parents began to learn about the crap that was being taught to their kids. Critical race theory was one of them. Wikipedia's lead sentence on this topic reads: "Critical race theory (CRT) is a cross-disciplinary intellectual and social movement of civil-rights scholars and activists who seek to examine the intersection of race, society, and law in the United States and to challenge mainstream American liberal approaches to racial justice." [90] Let me repeat the last phrase: *to challenge mainstream American liberal approaches to racial justice*. Let that sink in. The crackpots who created and teach this anarchist crap believe the Declaration of Independence, the Constitution, the Bill of Rights and the rule of law just don't cut it anymore. I say anyone who wants to sign up for this should move to Russia, China or Venezuela. Can I get an Amen?

But the anarchist CRT is not enough for the teacher's unions. They are now pushing 'gender-fluidity' to 6-year-olds. I know this from personal experience, and I am pissed. When they start talking about adult topics to innocent children, that is a bridge too far. It is time to stand up and fight back. I will talk about how to fight back at the end of the book.

Well, of course, these charlatans are also indoctrinating on climate change, diversity, inclusion, equity, white-privilege, and minority entitlement. In other words, they are not teaching at all.

8. The Confluence of D.I.E., the Religion of Climate Change and Business. When issues exist as stand-alone topics they can be more easily dealt with. The rise of Black Lives Matter was built on the emotion of the lies about the death of George Floyd. CNN, MSNBC, NPR etc. fueled the fire and many gullible people jumped on the band wagon. These 'fake' news organizations never spoke of the death of David Dorn, the retired 77-year-old police captain who died at the hands of BLM types when helping a friend protect his business from rioters. But BLM has now been exposed as a Marxist organization that bilked its supporters for millions while enriching its leaders. BLM is now passé.

The greater danger to society is when Marxist/utopian ideas (i.e., Democratic Party) coalesce into a 'norm' or societal expectation. When this point is reached, the average person becomes a 'useful idiot', to borrow the term from Yuri Bezmenov (see Chapter 14). People begin to just follow along because it is the easy road. Individuals stop thinking and group think takes over.

The United States has arrived at this point. Academia and the left-stream media have been preaching the doctrine for 40 years. When I worked for Cargill in the late 1980s through the 1990s, the pressure on business to accept the climate alarmism B.S. had already begun. The seeds of D.I.E. were sown by the acceptance of radical feminism. The academic and media Towers of Power were the preachers of the new religion. Archer Daniels Midland (ADM) was successful at lobbying the government to support ethanol from corn based on the premise that it was good for the environment. We now know that corn ethanol has a large carbon footprint, makes gasoline less efficient and increases the price of corn. Expect the same kind of results from solar and wind. Republican strength in Congress held off U.S. commitment to Climatism, until Obama's last days in office, when he committed the U.S. to the Paris Accords. All the while, the promotion of the emotional and divisive issues of diversity, inclusion and equity grew unchallenged. Jesse Jackson's Rainbow Coalition laid the foundation for corporate coercion. The message they delivered behind closed doors was support our racial initiatives or we will boycott you and slander your corporate brand. A former colleague told me his story of running headlong into this racial favoritism at Frito Lay (now owned by Pepsi). One day he was called into a manager meeting and told that the company was embarking on new promotion and hiring policies that would advantage women and minorities (i.e., non-Caucasians). The message to him was in essence that his career was over because he had the wrong gender and skin color. This was 20 years ago! If you have been in the corporate world for at least 10-15 years, you can identify. Preferential hiring and promotional policies gave us an Academy and media that is now 95% Democrat. These people exerted their educational bias on students and forced the opening of new social science departments based on race and gender. The discipline of Human Relations was elevated to senior status and business began to slowly adopt the egalitarian world view the Marxists have long sought. "In 2019, 181 CEOs announced a commitment to lead their companies for the benefit of all stakeholders rather than just their shareholders. Stakeholders consist of customers, employees, suppliers, communities and of course shareholders", wrote David Nevins of The Fulcrum. [91] In other words, people who have a financial stake in the company (shareholders) are now only one voice the governing board must consider. There will now be non-financial 'stakeholders' that are given a seat at the table also. These non-financial 'stakeholders' can and will come to the board with D.I.E. and Climatism demands. Nevins adds, "The concept that each individual company can serve its own corporate purpose, but also share a fundamental commitment to all society, is becoming more important to consumers as well and perhaps one reason boardrooms across the country are changing corporate policies and investments." [92] It sounds good, like most statements of America and apple pie from the Democrats. But it is not good. It is words on paper that are very loosey goosey. What does a 'fundamental commitment to all society' mean? Well, for banks today it means they should no longer loan money for fossil fuel exploration. It means promoting and prioritizing employees based on their gender and skin color. It could mean prioritizing hiring those who immigrated illegally over native-born citizens. It could mean the eventual collapse of capitalism and free enterprise in America.

This coalescence is now virtually complete. America's most acclaimed banking CEO announced today that he is not 'Woke'. [93] If Jamie Dimon has to make such a claim, you know that the conversion of corporate America to a quasi-socialistic governing philosophy is complete.

By now you are asking why this all is happening. How is this possible? Read on.

Prelude to Part 2

As this book moves into the analysis of 'what does this all mean and why is this happening', I thought it appropriate to provide a brief prelude for this second edition. As with the original text of Part 1 of this book, the original text of Part 2 is unchanged. Where appropriate, new material has been added and is identified in the text as new material. The references that support the new material are cited within the text, so the reference number of the original text could remain unchanged.

What I have given you in Part 1 is just the tip of the iceberg. The walls of our constitutional republican representative form of Democracy are crumbling around us so fast, that this book cannot go to print without my editor asking me if I want to update or add to the latest Democrat-induced tragedy. Internationally, the Ukraine war is being intentionally prolonged by the Europeans and Americans 'slow-walking' military aid to Ukraine. This pro-Russian coalition is bargaining for the annexation of the Donbas to Russia, leaving Ukraine in a no-win position. I predict this will happen by October 2022. The ill-conceived sanctions against Russian oil have only driven global oil prices higher, giving cheap oil to China and India while adding fire to the flame of inflation world-wide. To add insult to injury, the U.S. is standing by while El Salvador allows Russian troops to train in Central America. Colombia has just elected a former FARC guerilla as its President.

On the home front, the Supreme Court reversed the decades old ruling known as Roe vs Wade by a vote of 6-3. A still yet unnamed clerk illegally leaked the preliminary opinion back in May and the Democrats immediately set up camp in front of several conservative Justice's homes (an act in clear violation of Federal law: *18 U.S. Code § 1503 - Influencing or injuring officer or juror generally*.) Even though against the law, President Biden said he supported their demonstrations and our chief law enforcement officer, Merrick Garland remained out to lunch. On June 8, a 26-year-old Californian named Nicholas Roske, was arrested near the home of Justice Kavanaugh armed with a gun, knife and pepper spray. He admitted he was there to assassinate Justice Kavanaugh because he believed he would vote to overturn Roe vs Wade. In tragic irony, as he handed over his gun, he said he also feared Kavanaugh would vote to loosen gun laws.

Official Democrat reaction to the June 24, 2022, ruling as reported by Reuters June 25th:

President Biden: "Today the Supreme Court of the United States expressly took away a constitutional right from the American people that it had already recognized. This is a sad day for the country in my view."

Nancy Pelosi: "This cruel ruling is outrageous and heart-wrenching. But make no mistake: the rights of women and all Americans are on the ballot this November."

World Health Organization: "I am very disappointed, because women's rights must be protected. And I would have expected America to protect such rights."

President Obama: "Today, the Supreme Court not only reversed nearly 50 years of precedent, it relegated the most intensely personal decision someone can make to the whims of politicians and ideologues -attacking the essential freedoms of millions of Americans."

Hillary Clinton: "Most Americans believe the decision to have a child is one of the most sacred decisions there is, and that such decisions should remain between patients and their doctors. Today's Supreme Court opinion will live in infamy as a step backward for women's rights and human rights."

Justin Trudeau (President of Canada): "The news coming out of the United States is horrific. My heart goes out to the millions of American women who are now set to lose their legal right to an abortion ... No government, politician, or man should tell a woman what she can and cannot do with her body."

Emanuel Macron (President of France): "Abortion is a fundamental right for all women. We must protect it. I would like to express my solidarity with all those women whose freedoms have today been compromised by the U.S. Supreme Court."

The Brown Shirts of the Democratic Party (i.e., ANTIFA and BLM): The slogan "if abortions aren't safe neither are you" was spray painted on a Christian pregnancy center in Longmont, CO shortly before the building was torched.

Just as 2020 was the summer of Democrat violence and destruction (400+ riots, at least 23 deaths and millions in property damage across the country), the summer of 2022 is just getting started.

Quick Roe vs Wade Facts: The SCOTUS ruling did not outlaw abortion, it just removed it as a Federal Court ruling. The Constitution says nothing about abortion and thus the initial 1973 ruling should never have happened. Abortion is still legal in many states while many others allow it for a wide range of circumstances. So, why all the Democrat hyperbole? It's an election year and the Democrats, as this book has proven, have only a track record of destruction. Before I close this prelude to Part 2, I leave you with an abortion thought question:

"What is the difference between a 6-month-old fetus and a 6-month-old baby? Pro-abortion advocates are happy to kill one but not the other."

There is no difference, they are both human.

We are in a shit storm of unprecedented proportions. If Trump were President, I doubt any of the nightmares reviewed in this book would have become reality. President Trump was the 'wall' that was protecting America. The powers behind Biden and the Democratic Party are now in control and Part Two of this book explains who they are and where they want to take us.

PART 2

IMAGINING THE FUTURE

Chapter 14
Re-Imagining America

"The urge to save humanity is almost always only a false-face for the urge to rule it. Power is what all messiahs really seek: not the chance to serve."
—H. L. Mencken, *Minority Report*, 1956

The first hundred days will be in the books in 35 days. Obama's promise was to fundamentally change America. He failed, thank God. America recognized his kind of 'change' was not in their best interest, so they elected a leader to fix things. President Trump got the country back on the right track, but, as explained in the book *34 Days & Holding: America in the Balance*[2], a funny thing happened on the way to the 2020 election.

Now we have Joe Biden, who, in 65 days, has done more damage to the country than Obama did in eight years. Those who have eyes to see and ears to hear, know, by Biden's actions, that his interest is not America first. We are now on the road to 're-imagining America.'

The Yuri Bezmenov Prophesy

Thirty-five years ago (1985), a KGB agent who defected to the U.S. in 1970, gave a prophetic interview regarding the fate of America. Yuri Bezmenov told the interviewer that by 1985 that the strategic process of subtly implanting communist ideology had been "basically completed." His exact words were, "Marxism/Leninism ideology is being pumped into the soft head of at least three generations of American students, without being challenged or counter-balanced by the basic values of Americanism and American patriotism."[3] He called this phase of the Soviet 4-step strategy 'demoralization.'

The historical context of Bezmenov's interview is ironic. Ronald Reagan was in the 4th year of his first term and his economic policies were beginning to show positive effects. The U.S. was still in the 'cold war' with the Soviet Union. From 1982 to 1985, the Soviet Union went through four leadership changes, with Mikhail Gorbachev taking over in March of 1985. Reagan and conservatism were ascendant. The Vietnam War was becoming a distant memory. China, under its new leader Deng Xiaoping, was opening to trade with Western countries and a reluctant embrace of controlled capitalism. Mao died in 1976 but, his Great Leap Forward and Cultural Revolution reduced China's population by 40 to 60 million people. So, the 'West' was flourishing while the communists were quietly and patiently seeding America and Western Europe with the divisive and undefinable ideologies of 'equality', 'racism' (which includes 'white supremacy'), 'inclusion' and 'collectivism (which promotes the 'common good' as defined by the elitist Democrats, over the rights of the individual). This began in the 1950's. Bezmenov's interview was in 1985. He believed phase one was complete.

Education in America – 1985

Educational historian and author, Diane Ravitch, of Teacher's College of Columbia University, wrote a critical assessment of American education in the New York Times. Dr. Ravitch began her article by quoting Aldous Huxley's *'Brave New World',* "the regime successfully waged a "campaign against the Past" by banning the teaching of history, closing museums, and destroying historical monuments.[4] Huxley's book was published in 1932.

It is the responsibility of parents to 'train up a child in the way he should go' says Proverbs 22:6. Children learn in three ways; from what they are taught at home, what they are taught at school and personal experience, the school of hard knocks. In 1950, only 35% of the labor force was women, twenty-five years later it was 55% (1985).[5] Many of us were 'latch-key' kids. When we got home from school, our parents were still working. So, quality time with the kids became more difficult as both parents worked. The schools became more and more important. Yet, Dr. Ravitch noted that by 1985 our education system was abandoning honest history.

She wrote, "During the past generation, the amount of time devoted to historical studies in American public schools has steadily decreased. About 25 years ago, most public high-school youths studied one year of world history and one of American history, but today, most study only one year of ours. In contrast, the state schools of many other Western nations require the subject to be studied almost every year."[6]

The socialist/communist Howard Zinn, professor of history at Boston University, published his *A People's History of the United States* in 1980. This book kick started the teaching that America was built on racism, white supremacy, class warfare, social injustice, etc. Bezmenov said American schools were not teaching "basic values of Americanism and American patriotism." He said most of the Soviet's work would be "done by Americans to Americans thanks to lack of moral standards."[7] Zinn's book became a prime example.

Now, in 2021, the teaching of American history, World history, Government, is so warped by socialist, Marxist and post-modern thinking, it is no wonder the fake news media has such an easy time influencing the younger generations. They have no grounding in the moral and ethical values upon the country was built.

I encourage you to listen to the Bezmenov YouTube video. He succinctly describes the nature of the 4 stages: demoralization, destabilization, crisis, and normalization. He said about 85% of the Soviet anti-America program was ideological subversion.[8] They used the "useful idiots' of the 1960's who became college teachers and university professors to serve as the conduit of Marxism to American youth. These people and their converts expanded their presence in universities, then moved into government and private industry, thus slowly spreading the seeds of division and anarchy. I saw this happening first-hand as a university professor in the early 1980's. It was allowed under the name of 'tolerance', 'open dialogue,' and 'freedom of expression.'

Even though President Reagan was able to disrupt and delay many aspects of the Soviet plan, America finds itself today in, what Bezmenov may consider, the 3rd stage: Crisis. The economy has been destabilized, foreign relations are frayed and uncertain and our commitment to a common defense has been weakened. Society, itself has become irreparably fractured. In this weakened state, a crisis is introduced.

A significant portion of the country has become 'demoralized', which means disenchanted and disillusioned with what I would call Americanism. They have bought the Marxist lies without even knowing it and as Bezmenov explained, "exposure to true information does not matter anymore. A person who was 'demoralized' is unable to assess true information, the facts tell nothing to him."[9]

I ran a little social experiment in our local community where I posted verifiable facts regarding Covid-19 survival rates, the damage shutdowns have done and the psychological damage done to children kept from attending school. I avoided making it overtly political, just posted charts, tables of summarized data and succinct quotes from recognized leaders. The longest any post lasted was just over 24 hours. Someone would always take them down. Even though anecdotal, it is evidence that ideological conversion is complete, and the believers (many of our neighbors) are now actively engaged in purging truth and promoting

Newspeak. This is no different from the Cultural Revolution in China.

Teachers Unions 2020 Embrace Marxism

The National Education Association (NEA) is the largest teacher's union in the United States. Tim Walker, in July of 2020, recapped the final speech of NEA President Lily Eskelsen García on the association's website. The NEA has 3.5 million members, who teach our young people. He quotes Garcia, "We are educators and public servants, we are unionists. We are activists. We're patriots.... we are called on to act. So, what will you do? What will you do for your colleagues; your students; the families you love; the communities where you live? What will you do *as we face the most dangerous threat to our democracy that we've ever faced*?"[10]

What was that again? The most dangerous threat to our democracy... what is she talking about? Ms. Garcia continues:

"Throughout U.S. history, people in power have worked the system to make sure their power stayed intact. *Opportunity for others has always been deemed a threat to their bottom line*. This destructive mindset is personified today by the Koch family and other billionaires who have aggressively sought to exploit the working class, tilt tax codes to their favor, destroy the environment ... and support manifestly unfit individuals to higher political office. *They have corrupted our cherished word: freedom*. And they have chosen their champion: Donald Trump." She said, *"Keep America Great" and "Make America Great ... Again, "were" a sick joke, an insult to reality."*[11] OK, right, now we get it.

Eskelsen García was the voice of the NEA. I enumerated the long list of President Trump's most important accomplishments in the book *34 Days & Holding*.[12] The abbreviated list took five single spaced pages. So, Eskelsen Garcia is nothing more than a partisan hack, but let's hear her out. How was the Trump administration threatening our democracy?

"The theme of the 2020 RA is *'Our Democracy; Our Responsibility; Our Time.'* It will take the collective power of NEA members and their allies to deliver a resounding victory for our students at the polls in November, Eskelsen García said in her speech today. But it is also up to educators to leverage electoral success to bring about desperately needed change - *namely uprooting the inequality* that, to the detriment of millions of students, has become entrenched in every ZIP code across the nation," wrote Walker.[13] The NEA President also said, "But what some folks who know that haven't figured out that this wasn't by accident. Exclusion was intentional.... Inequality is by design."[14]

This is a great example of one of Bezmenov's 'useful idiots.'

The American Federation of Teachers website posts their mission in the title of the 'About Us' page:

> *REIMAGINING OUR SOCIETY*
> *AND REWRITING THE RULES TO*
> *ENABLE OPPORTUNITY AND*
> *JUSTICE FOR ALL.*[15]

There are 1.7 million members in the AFT, a part of the AFL-CIO. Nowhere in their 'manifesto' do they say their purpose is to teach or educate. Nowhere! It is un-frigging believable.

Randi Weingarten, President of the AFT and former President of the United Federation of Teachers (UFT), a New York state union with 183,000 members, issued a 2019 press release supporting the impeachment of President Trump, saying:

> "Donald Trump has undermined the rule of law, threatened our national security, and held in contempt the very institutions on which our republic was built, most notably in his use of presidential power to pressure a foreign government to investigate a potential

political opponent. He must be held accountable. No one is above the law.

"As educators, we have worked to defend democracy—in our classrooms and our communities—despite the president's near-constant assault. We are grateful that House leadership will offer the powers of congressional oversight to this fight against presidential corruption and that they will launch a full and transparent inquiry into President Trump's betrayal of American democracy and crimes against the country he swore to protect.

"There is ample precedent and established rule for the House to follow in pursuing the impeachment process. Our nation's foundation—three coequal branches of government that check and balance each other—must transcend politics. Truth and transparency are the strongest disinfectant of all."[16]

President Trump underwent intense scrutiny by the Mueller special counsel investigation and then late in 2019 was impeached based on anonymous false charges. Weintarten and Eskelen Garcia must have received high grades in their Marxist training.

No Infringement Intended. At the bottom of the page on the AFT website is the statement, "Photographs and illustrations, as well as text, cannot be used without permission from the AFT."[17] It seems incongruent to issue a 'press release' and then say it cannot be duplicated or copied without permission. I will leave the question to the Ministry of Truth. Anyway, the following is a paraphrase of the key points in their 2020 Resolution. Written in legal format, they have four 'whereas' statement and 'resolved' statements, the second of which has 15 bullet points. I'm sure the comrades in China and Russia were pleased.

Before proceeding, however, I quote the qualifying statement at the bottom of the website page, accessed March 28, 2021: "Please note that a newer resolution, or portion of a resolution, may have superseded an earlier resolution on the same subject. As a result, with the exception of resolutions adopted at our most recent AFT convention, resolutions do not necessarily reflect current AFT policies."[18]

WHEREAS statement overview:

1. The U.S. has issues, among which are: Covid-19, a weakened economy with higher unemployment, systemic racism, and "a president who has made these crises worse by his actions and conduct, including his willingness to reject the norms of our democracy and the rule of law"

2. "It falls on us in this moment to **reimagine** our society and rewrite the rules" to achieve opportunity and justice for all people

3. COVID-19 has "exacerbated the economic and health disparities and pain long felt by Americans, particularly communities of color, and has brought a new unprecedented urgency to address the imbalance in our economy and society and the decay of our democracy"

4. "Black Americans continue to struggle for full protection under the law and to be recognized as full human beings deserving of basic human rights."

RESOLVED Statement Overview:

1. The AFT firmly believes the foundation of a vibrant and well-functioning democracy and society is a people secured by the freedom to live, safely and securely, and the opportunity to attain a better life. Freedom and opportunity are enabled through good jobs with a living wage and a union, a great public education, adequate healthcare and justice for all. *The AFT will do everything in our power* to meet this moment and restore hope that another future is possible through the work of our members, through collective action, and at the ballot box.

2. "AFT's efforts to *reimagine* a more just and vibrant society and democracy are guided by the following essential principles":

    - "All Americans should have access to a well-paying job ... and real retirement security."

    - "All workers must have the right to collectively bargain..."

    - "Access to high-quality healthcare is a basic human right". Must deliver cradle to grave, high-quality care

    - "All Americans should have the right to affordable, safe and adequate housing";

- "A 21st-century infrastructure investment to maintain not just our roads and bridges but to ensure safe water, public health needs, clean energy, and broadband as an essential public utility."

- "A fair tax system that ensures the rich and big corporations pay their fair share to provide for the common good and fund schools and essential community services."

- "All Americans should have access to a basic safety net, including universal childcare; easier access to unemployment insurance; paid leave; equal pay for equal work; increased Social Security benefits…"

- "Our federal government should never again be unprepared to confront health and safety threats to the American people. Our nation must have a public health infrastructure capable of keeping Americans safe and responding to global health pandemics and other threats…"

- "Safely reopening public schools and colleges **in a way that does not simply seek to go back to life as it was before the pandemic but to fully fulfill public education's promise as the center of democracy** and cornerstone in our community where every child can succeed and where there is joy in learning."

- "Helping all children thrive requires a focus on whole child supports and services. This includes children's social emotional and academic development; rich and inclusive curriculum; and powerful instruction in safe and healthy neighborhood schools; professional learning and collaboration time for teachers as well as appropriate pay; ensuring educators have the freedom to teach; assessment that informs instruction rather than standardized testing that narrows it; and real voice and engagement of parents and the community."

- "Cancellation of all student debt."

- "High-quality, free public higher education for every student that is equitable, accessible and safe; faculty and support staff should be well-supported, paid a living wage, have academic freedom and a right to form a union."

- "Green New Deal that simultaneously addresses the harms of climate change and economic inequality as urgent and severe and that must be addressed together."

- "Ending systemic racism in America…"

- "The restoration of our essential democratic rights made possible through securing the right to vote for all."[19]

We have just reviewed the ideology of the two largest teacher unions in the United States. They are saying these things in the open, hiding nothing; yet parents are too busy and too trusting to take the time to check them out. We are now more than 35 years after the Bezemenov interview and Ravitch NY Times article. These teacher unions exert their influence on K-12 education. Train up a child in the way they should go the Proverb says. These are the people who are 'training' American's children.

> **Author's solution:** Progressives see racism in everything they disagree with. They are the racists. The solution to racial problems (which are real), is:
>
> *"Red, white and blue will bring together black, white and brown."*
>
> We need to focus on what unites us, not what divides us.

Higher Indoctrination

The President of the University of Maryland and two senior colleagues wrote in October 2020,

"The knee on the neck of George Floyd (**Author's comment:** the coroner's report had revealed by this time that Floyd had injected a lethal amount of Fentanyl) aggravated an American psyche (**Author's comment:** No, it activated Antifa, BLM and the left-wing press) already frayed by the pandemic and stay-at-home orders. Protesters from diverse backgrounds marched in the streets across the nation demanding change. (**Author's comment:** demonstrably false again!) Channeling the growing public and private support for meaningful change (**Author's comment:** he mentions change and now meaningful change – sounds like Obama) into action requires Americans, in every sector, to engage in difficult conversations, and to be honest about our problems and deliberate in developing solutions. We in higher education are no exception.

We in this field have an obligation to engage in this work, because we have become more central than ever to our students' American dreams. We hold out to our students the promises of an enriched life and social mobility, and yet we often fall short in providing these to all who arrive on our campuses."

In his 2019 book, the UC Berkeley professor David Kirp called out higher education, naming our poor six-year graduation rate of 60 percent for full-time freshmen at bachelor's degree–granting institutions "the college dropout scandal." And if 60 percent is a "scandal," what do we call the rate for Black students, which is 40 percent? **It would be simplistic—and wrong—to conclude that our students of color are failing. Instead, we must admit that higher education is failing them.**[20]

I have to call a time-out. You probably need to go get a new bottle of scotch and pop a couple of marijuana gummy bears.

Dr. Freeman and associates continue, "Our institution, the University of Maryland at Baltimore County, has made enormous progress on the crisis in student success. In the 1980s, UMBC had a six-year graduation rate for all freshmen of just more than 30 percent, and for Black freshmen, the rate was 10 percentage points lower. Through a range of interventions, (**Author's comment:** my B.S. meter is bouncing off the max! We know what the real innovations were.) we have increased our six-year graduation rate to 70 percent overall, not including the 10 percent who transfer and graduate elsewhere. Moreover, we have no Black-white graduation gap."[21]

"Our faculty and staff serve as mentors, role models, and teachers. (**Author's comment:** sorry folks, but I was a university prof and must say, this guy should do stand-up comedy.) Many institutions have been successful in hiring highly committed minority staff (**Author's comment:** Just curious, why did he add the word 'committed'?) who care deeply about students, but we need to do more to diversify our staff. Meanwhile, the irony is not lost on us (**Author's comment:** I really wonder if this PhD university president knows what the word irony means?) that although some critics of academia attack our culture as being too progressive, we must admit that we in higher education have had only limited success in hiring and promoting Black and Latino faculty. Nationally, at present, non-Hispanic white faculty comprise more than 75 percent of the professoriate, while they are just 60 percent of the population—by 2044, non-Hispanic white people will make up less than 50 percent of the population.[22]

So, basically, the esteemed Dr. Hrabowski, President of the University of Maryland, is saying the key to offering a better education at his university, and by extension, throughout all colleges and universities, is to have, by proportion, fewer 'white non-Hispanic' professors. There are just too many white guys. One of Hrabowski's (who is black) co-authors is a white guy and the other is a white female.

Suggesting a professor's skin color, ethnicity and sexual orientation influence their ability to do the three R's (reading, writing & arithmetic) and be a good educator is patently absurd. In fact, it is racist. Yet this is how progressives and Democrats define diversity, inclusion, and equity. I guess the science is settled. Let's look at the results of this enlightened progressive initiative.

American Students vs the World

The most recent Programme for International Student Assessment (PISA) was 2018. The key finding regarding the performance of 15-year-old students in language proficiency, math and science was "Students in the United States performed above the OECD average in reading (505 score points) and science (502), and below the OECD average in mathematics (478). Their scores were similar to those of students in Australia, Germany, New Zealand, Sweden and the United Kingdom in at least two of these three subjects. The trend lines of United States' mean performance in reading since 2000, mathematics since 2003 and science since 2006 are stable, with no significant improvement or decline."[23] The trend line performance for each subject area from test inception to 2018 is presented in Figure 25.[24] The changes since inception reflect no statistically significant improvement or decline although science proficiency is trending upward, math proficiency downward and reading is unchanged.

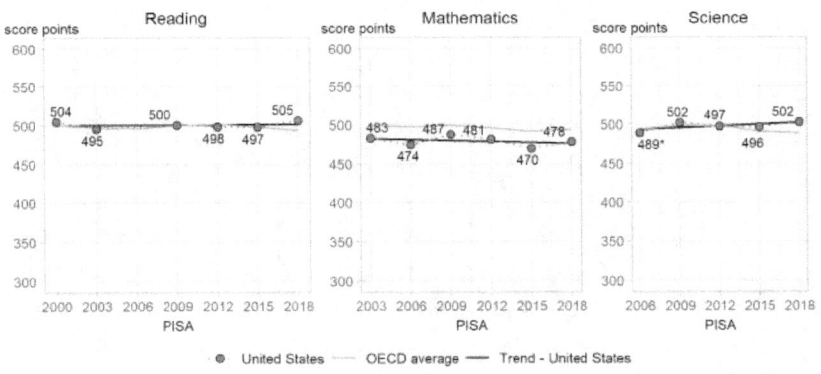

Figure 25. U.S. Student Performance in PISA.[24]

The takeaway is student performance among 15-year-olds is static, it is not changing.

Pew Research summarized the National Assessment of Educational Progress (NAEP) results from 1990 to 2015 (Figure 26). The trends for 4th and 8th graders were steadily improving until 2009 and then plateaued. The significant improvements were at least a doubling of students in the 'proficient' category and a reduction in the 'below average' students by half or more. Why didn't these results show up in the PISA assessments?

After years of growth, math proficiency of U.S. students dips

% at each achievement level of the National Assessment of Educational Progress (NAEP)

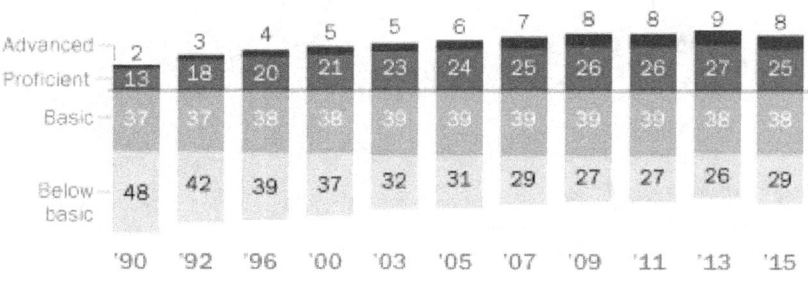

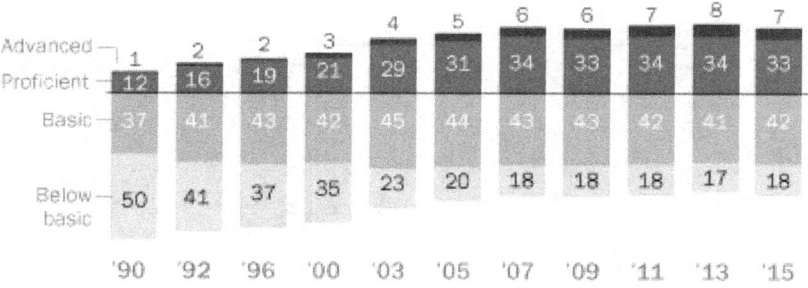

Source: NAEP Data Explorer, National Center for Education Statistics
PEW RESEARCH CENTER

Figure 26. U.S. Math Proficiency NAEP 1990-2015

The NAEP is run by the U.S. Department of Education, these results span the Clinton, Bush & most of Obama's terms. Results flatlined when Obama took over. Then there is the question of why didn't the improvements in the Clinton and Bush years transfer to improvements in PISA? PISA did not begin until 2000, but regardless, PISA shows only slight improvement in science, a decline in math and no change in reading.

The problem, in my opinion, is the growing emphasis on making sure everyone passes and feels good. The President of the University of Maryland told us they have trouble finding qualified professorial candidates among 'people of color.' Yet, these demographics are being awarded PhD's and are graduating high school and college at increasing rates. As this book recounted when reviewing the status of our military, Secretary of Defense Austin said we need to adjust the qualifying criteria so more 'people of color' can make the grade. If you remember, Obama did the same thing to increase racial diversity among air traffic controllers.[25]

The ideology of 'equity' in all its forms is now in hyperdrive and will have tragic effects. As Bezemenov and other communists have openly explained, the way to conquer America is from within, with one primary focus: **the education system**. First, higher education to produce a force of 'enlightened' teachers to populate the K-12 realm. This task was completed decades ago. Now, after 65 years of patient persistence and insidious indoctrination, this process is complete. All the 'Towers of Power' I discussed in *34 Days & Holding: America in the Balance*, are dominated by the ideological left. Wokeness has taken over and the only one who is literally not 'awake' is Joe Biden.

Structural Change

The idea or suggestion that the greatest country in the world needs to be 're-imagined' is extremely dangerous. The Democrats know this. Thus, the terminology and language is always changing to keep the average American in a state of confusion. Enter the term, structural change.

Investopedia defines structural change in an industry or market as a dramatic shift in function, usually brought on by major economic developments.[26] What can cause it? "Structural change is often sparked by technological innovation, new economic developments, global shifts in the pools of capital and labor, changes in resource availability, changes in supply and demand of resources, and changes in the political landscape." [27]

Technology is an example of a 'causative' event that is born from the freedom of ideas, a meritocratic economy and limited government intrusion. The invention of the laptop, the internet and the cellular phone are examples that are healthy. Most of the other causative events listed by Investopedia are politically driven and not healthy. It is these areas the Democrats have in mind when they talk about 'structural change.'

Democrat playbook to permanently 're-structure' America. The website Fivethirtyeight.com published an article on February 26, 2021, that clearly articulated the diabolical and anti-American thinking that exists today in the Democratic party. To avoid any charge of misrepresentation, I will provide verbatim quotes from this article. It begins with the following statement:

"Facing a Republican Party with a growing anti-democratic contingent, Democrats are debating what to do – to bolster their party and, in the view of some in the party, American democracy itself. At the heart of the discussion is how much structural reform do the nation's governmental and electoral systems need."[28]

Perry Bacon, writer for fivethirtyeight, quickly identifies himself and his article as far-left propaganda by immediately impugning the Republican party with easily disproven B.S. (i.e., 'a growing anti-democratic contingent'). It is classic doublespeak and Saul Alinsky style spin. But, his animas toward Republicans is not what is important. I am neither a Republican nor Democrat. I am an American and have no tolerance for spin nor bullshit regardless of where it comes from. I used to be a Republican, but John Boehner cured me of that.

Bacon openly reviews the debate currently going on within the Democratic party. He continues:

"It's often implicit, rather than explicit, as the people doing the debating are trying to persuade – but not annoy – a small group of people in the party who will ultimately decide the Democrats' posture on these issues: President *Biden and a handful of senators*. However Democrats decide to proceed will have huge implications for the party and potentially the country. So let's start by breaking down what I think are the three main camps in this debate and their visions:"[29]

Camp No. 1:
"We are in a Democratic and democratic emergency."

"Key figures: Former Attorney General Eric Holder, Rep. Mondaire Jones of New York, Sen. Jeff Merkley of Oregon, author and Democratic activist Heather McGhee, and former top Obama adviser and "Pod Save America" host Dan Pfeiffer as well as the progressive groups Demand Justice and Indivisible."

"Ideas: Persuade Justice Stephen Breyer to retire as soon as possible and quickly confirm his replacement; get rid of the filibuster; with the filibuster out of the way, pass structural reform legislation, such as an updated Voting Rights Act, a raft of electoral reforms (H.R. 1), statehood for Washington, D.C., and an expansion of the Supreme Court by adding four new justices, as well as creating additional judgeships at the lower court levels."

"The people in this camp don't agree on everything, but they foresee a nightmarish (and fairly plausible) scenario for Democrats, and they're proposing a series of steps to avoid that calamity. Here's the Democratic nightmare: Biden and congressional Democrats pass a few major bills over the next two years but leave the filibuster in place, preventing the passage of major reforms to America's electoral system. A federal judiciary stacked with Trump appointees strikes down all or parts of many of the laws the

Democrats do pass as well as many of Biden's executive actions, leaving Democrats few permanent policy victories and driving down the president's approval ratings."

"Meanwhile, Republicans use their control of most state legislatures to draw state legislative and U.S. House district lines in ways that are even more favorable to the GOP than the current ones and enact laws that make it harder for liberal-leaning voting blocs to cast ballots. Combine gerrymandering, voting limitations, lackluster poll numbers for Biden and the historic trend of voters rejecting the party of the incumbent president in a midterm election, and it results in the Republicans winning control of the House and the Senate and making even more gains at the state legislative level in November 2022."

Camp No. 2:
"Maybe there's an emergency, maybe not; either way, just do popular stuff."

"Key figures: Former Georgia Democratic gubernatorial nominee Stacey Abrams, Rep. James Clyburn, former President Barack Obama, Sen. Bernie Sanders and the liberal group Data for Progress.

Ideas: Get rid of the filibuster to pass popular legislation such as a new Voting Rights Act (H.R. 1), expanded background checks on gun purchases and an increased minimum wage.

But they are pushing for some democratic reforms — in particular, getting rid of the filibuster. I included a number of major Black politicians in this camp because they tend to focus on getting rid of the filibuster as a means of passing laws that protect voting rights. From this camp's point of view, an updated Voting Rights Act is a moral imperative, regardless of its electoral impact, and the filibuster must go if it stands in the way. When Obama referred to the filibuster as a "Jim Crow relic" in his speech last year at Rep. John Lewis's funeral, he shifted the discourse in the Democratic

Party on the filibuster, in my view, by casting it as a barrier to racial justice, a powerful message in an increasingly "woke" party."

Camp No. 3:
"We can and should work with Republicans."

"Key figures: Sens. Dianne Feinstein of California, Joe Manchin of West Virginia and Kyrsten Sinema of Arizona.

Ideas: Keep the filibuster in place and get more legislation passed on a bipartisan basis."

"Democrats would need every Democratic senator on board to get rid of the filibuster, so these members are super-important. And over the last few months, Manchin and Sinema have said they are strongly opposed to getting rid of the filibuster. Longtime senators like Feinstein have hinted in the past that they are wary of such a move too."

"Part of this opposition to getting rid of the filibuster reflects ideological differences – Manchin in particular is more conservative than most (if not all) congressional Democrats. So, he probably isn't dying to get rid of the filibuster to vote for a $15 federal minimum wage, for example, because it's not clear he favors that idea anyway."

"But this bloc also disagrees with the this-is-an-emergency camp about the state of American politics right now. Feinstein is fairly liberal on policy issues. But she, like Manchin and Sinema, has suggested she wants to work in a Senate that is not hyper partisan and seems to believe that is possible. In the view of people in this camp, the Republican Party is not completely dominated by an anti-democratic wing that won't work with Democrats. So, members in this camp view getting rid of the filibuster and other more aggressive moves as not only unnecessary but potentially really bad – making the Senate and Washington overall even more gridlocked and polarized than they already are."

"The people in this group generally aren't as alarmist as the this-is-an-emergency camp. They aren't arguing that American democracy and the Democratic Party are at risk. And thus, this group generally isn't pushing the most aggressive reform ideas, such as adding justices to the Supreme Court."[30]

Consider the following questions:
1. What is motivating the destructive actions of today's Democratic party?

- **Answer:** Power. There is no logical Constitutional foundation for their words, dialogue, actions or policies. Their focus is power and whatever it takes to get it. But power for whom and to what end?

2. What is completely missing from the three options reviewed in the article just summarized?

- **Answer:** A concern for what is best for America. No where do we find them articulating the specifics on a societal, government or economical problem that is based in facts. They play the race card every time on everything and they claim science is on their side with respect to Covid-19 and climate alarmism. None of it is true. All if it is easily disproven.

The New World Order

Henry A. Kissinger, renowned political scholar and 56th Secretary of State of the United States will be 98 years old on May 27, 2021. His leadership brought China into the global community in 1976 while Mao was still Chairman. President Richard M. Nixon is reported to have worried that his administration may have "released a "Frankenstein."[31] Today, on Kissinger's personal website, the first quote about him is from Xi Jinping, President of China and Chairman of the CCP. It reads,

"Dr. Kissinger wrote in his book, World Order, and I quote, that 'each generation will be judged by whether the greatest, most consequential issues of the human condition have been faced...' Let us work together to bring about an even better future for China-US relations."[32]

Kissinger wrote for the Wall Street Journal in April 2020 voicing his opinions on how the world should respond to the Covid-19 pandemic. Patrick Buchanan highlights some of Kissinger's views that call into question where exactly the former Secretary of State's loyalties reside:

- "Kissinger declared that it is now an imperative that the world's leaders, even as they deal with the raging pandemic, begin to make the "transition to the post-coronavirus order." "Failure to do so could set the world on fire."[33]

- "Yet, the ingredients Kissinger considers essential for establishing that new world order appear, like ventilators, to be in short supply. "Sustaining public trust," asserts Kissinger, "is crucial ... to international peace and stability."[34]

- "But how do we trust again our adversary China, after its criminal cover-up of the menace and magnitude of the virus unleashed in Wuhan? How do we trust again this regime that was, until recently, blaming the coronavirus on U.S. Army troops visiting Wuhan?"[35]

- "We must "struggle to heal the wounds to the world economy," said Kissinger. Yet, the crisis has revealed that a prominent feature of this global economy is that China controls the production of medicines essential to keeping Americans alive. Do we want to continue that dependency?"[36]

- "The founding legend of modern government," writes Kissinger, "is a walled city ... strong enough to protect the people from an external enemy. ... This pandemic has produced ... a revival of the walled city in an age where prosperity depends on global trade and movement of people."

- "Kissinger calls the concept of the walled city an "anachronism," a "legend." But is the idea of the nation-state, whose principal duty is the defense of the health, safety and security of the unique people who created it, the "legend"? Or is the real legend, the myth, the idea of some New World Order of countries traveling and trading happily with one another in a federation of the world?"[37]

President Trump was literally the 'wall' protecting America, and the world, from being swept away by the Orwellian tide. Now the global process of re-imagining begins.

Chapter 15
Re-Imagining the World

"Imagine there's no countries
It isn't hard to do
Nothing to kill or die for
And no religion too
Imagine all the people living life in peace,

You may say I'm a dreamer
But I'm not the only one
I hope someday you'll join us
And the world will be as one"
'Imagine' by John Lennon 1971
Imagine lyrics © Downtown Music Publishing

Fifty years ago, John Lennon was imagining a world without borders. Henry Kissinger became the 56th Secretary of State in 1973 and exactly one year ago, published a Wall Street Journal opinion piece saying "The U.S. must protect its citizens from disease while starting the *urgent* work of planning for a *new epoch*."[1] It seems Lennon's vision has come full circle.

The Great Reset

The World Economic Forum (WEF) initiates 'The Great Reset Initiative':

"There is an *urgent* need for global stakeholders to cooperate in simultaneously managing the direct consequences of the COVID-19 crisis. To improve the state of the world, the World

Economic Forum is starting The Great Reset initiative," states their headline on the referenced wef.com webpage.[2]

This is a very curious statement. Who are the 'global stakeholders?' I didn't get a call or email from them and you didn't either. Yet, there is 'an urgent need' for them 'to cooperate' and 'simultaneously manage' the 'direct' consequences of the pandemic.

No Urgency. First of all, the mortality rate of Covid-19 is approximately 0.2%.[3] There is no 'urgency' nor emergency. The world, and especially Americans, have been lied to for months. Former CDC Director Robert Redfield said in an interview, with the Buck Institute in July 2020, that they knew the mortality rate for school age kids was 0.1%, 8 months ago. He said influenza up to ten times more dangerous for kids.[4]

Direct Consequences. The most direct consequences of the virus are almost 3 million deaths (as of April 7, 2021). That's obviously not what they are speaking of. Every other 'consequence' was 'directly' caused by government intervention. Societal lockdowns, school closings, cancelling all forms of social gathering (sports, performing arts, museums etc.).

Simultaneously manage. The WEF is calling on unidentified 'stakeholders' to 'cooperate' in the global management of unidentified 'direct consequences.' Ask yourself this question: Can you manage something that has already happened? Of course not, it's in the past. Whoever wrote and approved this absurd statement is obviously living in a bubble disconnected from the real world. Only those in the bubble know what it means.

Improve the state of the world. This is the end game... a new utopia. This was the end game of Marx, Lenin, Stalin, Mao, Castro, etc. It is 'class warfare' and the appeal to the 'soviet', the 'proletariat', the 'working class', the 'underserved' to use Biden's term. The problem then and now, is 'they' or the 'supreme soviet' or the 'politburo' or the 'United Nations' will decide what is needed to 'improve' the world. They are not going to ask us. Big Brother is coming.

Connecting the Dots

It's time to reflect upon the events of the past five years. As you look back, what was the one event that was the most improbable? Of all the 'surprises', or maybe even 'black swans', which was the most unlikely? I will give you the answer but let's first do another thought exercise. What do you call it when you have several black swans in rapid sequence? Are you willing to bet you can flip a coin and have it turn up heads 10 times in a row? You probably said "No" because the odds are 1 in 1,024. Dr. Redfield said in his July 2020 interview that the Covid-19 mortality rate for school age kids was 0.1%. That's 1 in 1,000,000; yet the schools were closed for months and many remain closed. Answer this: Would you bet that the roulette ball (American wheel) would land on 15 six times in a row? No, you would not, but it is known to have happened once. The odds were 1 in over 3 billion. These are examples of highly improbable outcomes in 'controlled' environments. In the extraordinarily complex 'real' world we live in, having multiple rapid sequence black swans is mathematically incalculable. Thus, we intuitively begin to consider Occam's Razor (The simplest explanation is usually the correct one.) The simplest explanation for a sequence of 'coincidences' is they were not coincidences. They were planned and orchestrated. When the person across the table continues to win with four of a kind, you quickly conclude he has been cheating.

So, let's take a shot at hypothetical explanations for the World Economic Forum statement.

Urgency. On April 6-8, 2021, the World Economic Forum held a meeting in Japan heralded as the 'Global Technology Governance Summit.'[5] *(Author's note: I am writing these lines on April 7th)* This global meeting was announced on December 5, 2020, only four months ago.[42] I have attended several global conferences in my life, and all of them are announced 2-3 years in advance. There seems to have been some urgency at the WEF. December 5th was a Saturday, three days prior to the deadline for states to certify their election results, which technically compels Congress to accept the results. It was a virtual certainty that Joe Biden would be the next U.S. President.

Direct Consequences. As detailed in my book *34 Days & Holding: America in the Balance*, Trump would have been reelected were it not for the timely occurrence of the pandemic. Thus, Joe Biden and the Georgia senate races are a 'direct consequence' of the virus.

Coordinated Management. The WEF summit is taking place in Tokyo as I write these lines. Consider, never in U.S. history has a President so aggressively turned-out Executive Orders. Thus far, it has created a humanitarian crisis on our southern border and begun to drive energy costs higher. Neither would be issues if Trump had won. Many Democratic state governors continue to keep their states at least partially shutdown, even though Republican states have totally opened with no repercussions. The Democrats have passed a $1.9 trillion stimulus that *was not needed*. They are planning $4 trillion more in spending. All with zero Republican support. This will weaken the dollar, effectively reduce wages, reduce buying power and will necessitate a tax increase, which Biden has already announced. Increasing corporate taxes will make the U.S. less competitive and discourage capital investment, which will reduce job growth. The dominoes will keep falling because of Democrat 'coordinated management.' Any thinking person would conclude these are destructive actions and policies. Yet, the Democrats are all in.

Global orchestration takes more time, hence the Tokyo meeting. A large cargo vessel was recently cleared from blocking the Suez Canal. The first time this has ever happened. Is it a 'stretch' to wonder if Covid-19 was planned? It single handedly removed the only barrier to the globalist agenda, President Trump. It also proved an effective mechanism, in the hands of 'coordinated management,' to shut down the world. Is it a 'stretch' to wonder if the Suez Canal event was a test to assess the impact of cutting off a strategic logistical passageway? All of the above is history. Covid happened with impeccable timing. Biden won Georgia, Arizona, and Wisconsin by a total of 43,809 votes. If Trump had carried these states, it would have been an electoral tie at 269 electoral votes. Biden won Nevada by 33,596 votes. *(Read my book 34 Days & Holding: America in the Balance for the details on how the election went down.)* All these 'coincidences' happened in a 12-month period. It is not hypothetical nor opinion.

As described in the beginning of Chapter 13, the long-term Russian strategy to supplant the United States was to subvert from within and create multiple simultaneous emergencies or crises that will overwhelm our capability and capacity. But China has now surpassed Russia in global hegemony.

Nixon's fear is now reality *(see page 252)*. Jin Canrong, a professor and associate dean of the School of International Studies at Beijing's Renmin University of China, explained China's plan in a July 2016 speech, "we first need to create the conditions to make it easier for the United States to make mistakes. Second, we should make it as busy as possible [dealing with problems], to the extent that it will feel depressed and want to give up. Third, we should become intertwined with the United States, so that it can't attack us."[6]

He described four strategic areas of influence:

- Interfere in U.S. elections
- Control the U.S. market via Chinese investments
- Create enemies for the U.S.
- Create international problems.[7]

Here are a few direct quotes from his speech provided in the Epoch Times article:[8]

> "Normally, the difference of votes between two candidates is 10,000 or less. If China has thousands of votes on hand, China will be the boss of the candidates."

> "The best scenario is China can buy the United States and change the U.S. House of Representatives into the second Standing Committee of the National People's Congress,"

> "The U.S. market is open—more open than the Japanese and European ones."

> "If the United States has four enemies, it will totally lose its direction."

> "Terrorism is definitely an enemy of the United States. Russia looks like another one. ... Definitely, the United States treats us [China] as a competitor. ... It's not enough."

> "He cited the Afghanistan and Iraq wars, which he described as "completely not strategically valuable" endeavors that cost the United States "$6 trillion and

10,000 soldiers' lives." The result was that the United States "wasted 10 years" without being aware of China's development and "let China grow big,"

"Another possible tactic would be to sell the CCP's holdings of U.S. Treasury bonds to precipitate a debt crisis, he said. According to the U.S. Treasury, China currently holds nearly $1.1 trillion in U.S. Treasury securities."

"China's industry has a large output, but lacks certain technology," Jin said. "In the past 30 years, we bought technology, 46 percent of which were from Germany. But the United States has the best technology, but it doesn't sell to us. "Americans think that Chinese hackers steal a lot of their things. This may very well be true."

"Jin said key technology for China's J-20 fighter jet and DF-41 intercontinental ballistic missile was stolen from the United States."

'Managed' Crises on the Horizon. So, what crises might be in store that requires WEF 'coordinated management?' Maybe the agenda of their early April 2021, impromptu conference contains the answers.

Global Technology Governance Summit Agenda

The inaugural gathering of the GTGS, that ended April 8th, specified four broad topical areas:[9]

- **"Industry Transformation**: No industry has been untouched by the global response to COVID-19. *The world can no longer operate as it has*, and as such markets will have to respond to its new and evolving needs. To survive, every business in the world will have to become a technology company."

- **"Government Transformation**: The *transformation of government will be front-and-center* in the area of digital infrastructure as technology services become an essential public utility comparable to electricity, water, or roadways."

- **"Global Technology Governance**: The extent to which the benefits of technology are maximized, and the risks mitigated depends on the quality of governance protocols – policies, norms, standards, and incentives that shape the development and deployment of technologies."

- **"Frontier Technologies**: Embracing frontier technologies will be essential across all sectors. Technologies such as 3D printing can revolutionize supply chains, enabling mass customization and offering new pathways to increase the circularity of products. or halt environmental damage caused by climate change."

A review of this four-part agenda quickly reveals the globalist's objective is nothing less than world rule – A New World Order. They say, *"The world can no longer operate as it has."* Of course, it can. But they don't want it to. Even Henry Kissinger has signed on. They say: *"transformation of government will be front-and-center."* Yes, if you are going to take over the world, you would need government transformation. Is this why the Democrats are trying to relax voting laws, expand the Supreme Court, open the southern border, abandon law and order and add Puerto Rico and

Washington, D.C. as states? In other words, you need government to relinquish control to a single global authority. Sounds like Big Brother to me. The third and fourth items are redundant and canards. Their goal is a one world government. So, we know where the WEF is coming from. What else is going on globally, behind the scenes?

4th Industrial Revolution. The Centre for the Fourth Industrial Revolution UAE (C4IR UAE) is a collaboration between the Dubai Future Foundation and the *World Economic Forum* and is the first affiliate centre in the world open since April 2019. The Centre in the UAE serves as a global public-private platform for the collaborative development of technology governance and policy protocols."[10]

Mike Bloomberg and Global Cities.org. Global Cities, Inc. has extensive experience using technology to forge connections among students and educators that promote learning, including through our signature program, Global Scholars.[11]

McKinsey & World Economic Forum. At the Annual Meeting of the World Economic Forum, we engage with business executives, experts, and policymakers to help make ***Change that Matters** (sound familiar?)*. In 2021, there are two events in place of the usual annual meeting. The Davos Agenda, a virtual event in January convened global leaders under the theme of "A crucial year to rebuild trust."[12] The McKinsey website is very insightful. The eight themes[13] that dominated the Davos Agenda in February were (Author's comments in italics follow each point):

    1. Stakeholder capitalism: Shifting toward inclusive growth.
       (*Business is, and always has been, a for profit enterprise. Publicly held companies - they sell stock*

that is traded on exchanges - have always been measured by their ability to provide a return on 'share'-holder investment. The buying of stock is nothing more than loaning the company money. Money can be invested in many different ways and most people want to maximize their return on investment. The concept in the 'stake'-holder structure dilutes the company's focus on its prime objective in the name of touchy-feely socialism. They are called 'B' corporations and allocate board positions to people who ironically have 'no' stake in the company (i.e., community representatives and the like). The B-companies also formally commit to measuring themselves on metrics that have nothing to do with making products or profits. It is the 'new' politically correct 'Kosher' stamp of approval and will be used to hold companies to socialistic demands. It is now a legal business restructuring and will dilute profits and returns to 'share-holders.')

2. The race to net zero: A dominant narrative for government and business alike.
   (*The term used to describe a goal of balancing CO_2 emissions stable - i.e., no 'net' gain in atmospheric CO_2. It is a plan to take from 'rich' countries - mainly the U.S. - and give to poorer countries. It is climate alarmism baloney I have debunked earlier.*)

3. An opportunity for equality: Why governments and organizations must build back better.
   (*The U.S. has offered the best opportunity for equality in the world for many decades, that's why everyone want to move here - i.e., for the*

opportunity. 'Build back better' means post Covid-19, as if the virus caused some structural damage to regional governments. Covid-19 supposedly 'escaped' from a bio-level 4 virology lab in Wuhan, China just in time to be used to shut the U.S. down and give the Democrats leverage to relax voting rules. President Trump engineered an economic recovery that would have been complete were it not for Democrat state governors who kept their states shut down. Now the United Nations, the World Economic Forum, McKinsey etc., want to help the U.S. 'build back better!')

4. Digital regulation and responsibility: Europe speaks out on the need for a legal framework for social platforms.
   (*This refers to control of the internet. Most people now get their information 'on-line.' Many people bank on-line, buy and sell on-line, get entertainment on-line, etc. If a 'global' control structure is accepted by enough major countries, the rest of the dominoes will quickly fall. America could face a choice between isolation or acquiescence. Individual freedom and freedom of speech and expression will be sacrificed.*)

5. Collaboration and the circular economy: Why open markets and supply chains are crucial to global success. "We're in a critical situation with a recession worldwide, and poorer countries are suffering more," said Peter Altmaier, Germany's federal minister for Economic Affairs and Energy. "We need to rely more on open markets and multilateralism." Carlos Brito, CEO of

Anheuser-Busch InBev, spoke about how connected his business is to sustainability: "If we don't use resources in a circular way and in an efficient way, there'll be no planet left."

(*Neither the United States, Europe nor the world is in a recession, but it seems the German Minister of the Economy thinks it is. The only reason global economies have slacked over the past years is the China Wuhan virus induced lockdowns. Government leaders have been sacrificing their own people and economies to give the globalists an economic talking point. As for the CEO of Anheuser-Busch InBev, I will just say, I will never drink another Budweiser, Corona or Stella.*)

6. Multilateralism: The need for global standards to support collaboration. "This is the hour of multilateralism," said Angela Merkel, chancellor of Germany. "If we want to have multilateral agreements, common standards have to be put down with regards to conditions of work and the environment." "We have to be very fast at finding new answers to digitalization," Merkel added. "We need to address global monopolies but going it alone won't suffice to address them."

(*Why is now the 'hour' and why do we have to be 'very fast?' Because the U.S. has a Dodo Bird for a President and will be weak until the Republicans regain Congress in the 2022 elections.*)

7. The ongoing impact of AI and digital: How innovation and technology will affect the global workforce. Vilas Dhar, president of the Patrick J. McGovern Foundation, said that artificial

intelligence (AI) holds the promise of making organizations 40 percent more efficient by 2035. The end goal "is to create an artificial-intelligence-enabled society," said Dhar, with AI being used to create genuine equality.
(*Artificial intelligence takes many forms, many of which eliminate jobs, invade personal privacy and significantly restrict individual freedom. A strong case could be made that the current occupant of the White House is a form of AI. The 'Alexa you installed in your home may soon be telling you what to do or be telling someone else what you're doing. Big Brother is already watching... or is it Big Sister?*)

8. Equality of women: Gender parity at the heart of the recovery. The pandemic has created a "double-double shift" of at least 20 hours per week of additional work for women at home and is potentially exacerbating existing gender gaps.
(Feminists should be outraged that they rank number 8 on the globalist list of priorities. But notice how this priority was supposedly - conveniently - exacerbated by the pandemic. Interesting.)

The above is just an appetizer of the smorgasbord of progressive, utopian lunacy on display globally. I could quote similar tropes from the Club of Rome, the Catholic Church, the Organization for Economic Cooperation and Development (OECD),

What is driving this global insanity?

The Quest for Utopia

It is common today to hear someone make a statement that something in life is dystopian, implying that if that something had not happened or did not exist, we would have utopia. Since Adam and Eve ate of the forbidden fruit, there has been no utopia. There were just two people back then! If you were to ask the next 10 people you meet to describe utopia, there would be some commonality, but there would also be significant disagreement. This is the problem.

The quest for utopia, however, never dies and today we are in the latter stages of the greatest quest for utopia the world has ever seen. We are told we need to pursue the path of 'sustainability' to achieve a better world and even to 'preserve' the world. The problem is no one can define what sustainability means. Sustainability is nothing more than a linguistic bucket to collect and convey other meaningless sound-good buzz words, such as: diversity, inclusiveness, equity, fairness, tolerance, racism, social justice, environmental justice, toxic-masculinity, white-supremacy, self-identification, and the common good.

It is almost impossible to read on-line news or information sites today without running into many of these buzz words. They are invoked by everyone from high school teachers to the President of the United States. You would be hard pressed today to find a global company or large customer-facing company that does not moral preen in their advertising, press releases and websites. With increasing frequency, companies try to gain positive differentiation from competitors by touting their politically correct merit badges. It's called 'virtue signaling.' Virtually all of the world's power bases (i.e., sectors of society that have influence and lead thought and culture) have fully embraced these meaningless slogans, including most Christian denominations. Pope Francis is the first pope in history to openly support gay unions. Regardless of how one 'feels' about this issue, it is inarguably one of the greatest philosophical backflips in Catholicism.

The casting aside of cultural and traditional norms in favor of fuzzy slogans is accelerating and dangerous. Why? Because to invoke the terms as ideas to be discussed is one thing, but to embrace them without debate and make them rules to be enforced is another. Mao had his Red Guard in the mid-1960s; youth informing on parents, neighbors informing on neighbors. His Great Leap Forward and Cultural Revolution resulted in the deaths of over 40 million Chinese. He was pursuing his idea of utopia.

Communism of all forms (Marx, Lenin, Mao, Xi) has been perpetuated by the quest for utopia, which always has at its foundation the nebulous concept of equality. Equality for me but not for thee. Without exception, the results have been disastrous because it requires the subjugation of the individual to the state. Individual rights (including the right of property) and freedoms are the acid that dissolve the bonds of communism, thus must not be tolerated. Liberté, égalité, fraternité (liberty, equality & fraternity) was the outcry, the result was the Reign of Terror.

The quest for utopia, however, does not always start with overt revolutions that overthrow the standing governments. Hugo Chavez was elected. Vladimir Putin was elected. Woodrow Wilson envisioned a League of Nations which invoked a much more subtle nod to the common good and minor compromises of individual state rights and sovereignty.

Vladimir Lenin rallied the people against the Czar on the promise of withdrawing from WWI (they were on the Allied side), the Bolsheviks took power in 1917 and the world had its first communist government. The League of Nations (LON) was created in 1919 at the very end of WWI. Its mission was to foster world peace, which is on everyone's Utopia list, including mine. Twenty years later, the LON mission died as Hitler and Stalin agreed to divvy-up north European countries and start WWII.

Since history is doomed to repeat itself, 50 countries got together in 1945, the end of WWII, and created the United Nations. They were going to do it right this time. The 'History' page on the UN website (un.org) has the following statement: "Now, more than 75 years later, the United Nations is still working to maintain international peace and security, give humanitarian assistance to those in need, protect human rights, and uphold international law."[14]

The primary purpose of the LON and subsequently the UN was world peace. As I write these lines (April 13, 2021) the UN website says that remains their primary mission and has been for the last 75 years. So, how have they done? Do you think the United Nations is an asset for global peace? Is it delivering a good return on the $57 billion they consume every year?

The Axis powers (Nazis & friends) surrendered in Europe May 8, 1945, the Japanese surrendered August 15, 1945 and the U.N. charter was official on October 24, 1945. From May 1945 to January 1, 1950 there were 36 shooting conflicts or wars somewhere in the world.[15] Among these were the first Indochina War, the first Arab Israeli War and the beginning of the conflict in Korea. The sad fact is, there has never been one year, since the United Nations was formed, in which the world has not had war. Not one year!

Many of these conflicts, were fighting communist or radical Islamic insurgencies. The Korean War 1950-1953, the Cuba Revolution 1953-59, the Vietnam War 1955-75, the Chinese crushing of Tibet 1959, the Congo Crisis 1960-65, the Six-Day War (2nd Arab Israeli War) 1967, the Khmer Rouge Cambodian War 1967-1975, Warsaw Pact invasion of Czechoslovakia 1968, Yom Kippur (3rd Arab Israeli War) 1973, Third Indochina War 1975-91, Lebanese Civil War 1975-90, Cambodian-Vietnamese War 1975-89, Uganda-Tanzania War 1978-79, Iranian Revolution 1979, Soviet-Afghan War 1979-89, Iran-Iraq War 1980-88, the Lebanon War 1982-85, the Gulf War 1900-91, Croatian & Bosnian Wars

1991-95, Iraqi Kurdish Civil War 1994-97, Eritrean-Ethiopian War 1998-2000, War on Terror which began September 11, 2001, War in Afghanistan 2001-present, Iraq War 2003-11, Gaza War 2008-09, Syrian Civil War 2011-present, Iraqi Civil War 2014-17, Russo-Ukrainian War 2014-present, Iraq-Syrian ISIS insurgency 2017-present.[16, 17, 18] I only listed wars that might have some name recognition, there are many, many more.

Bottom line: *The United Nations is worse than worthless*; they are part of the problem. They could not have a worse record at keeping or negotiating peace. They have grown from 50 to 193 countries yet have accomplished nothing. Not only do they accomplish nothing; they require more money every year to do it!

We just reviewed a list of continuous global wars and conflicts. In 1945, there was only one power in the world that had nuclear weapon capability, the United States. The Soviet Union soon joined the club, and 'mutual assured destruction' became the by-phrase of the cold war period. Today, China, France, the United Kingdom, Pakistan, India, Israel, North Korea and Iran have nuclear weapon capabilities. The International Atomic Energy Association (IAEA) was created in 1957 as an independent agency under the United Nations umbrella. This impotent organization sat by as nuclear weapon capabilities proliferated. They are a joke.

When a company has an operating division or an initiative that is not making money, they shut it down. When a sports team keeps losing games, the coach is fired, or a new game plan is developed. With an unprecedented and consistent track record of failure, one must wonder why the United Nations still exists.

Ronald Reagan and Donald Trump are the only U.S. Presidents to withdraw some funding from the UN for a period of time. U.S. Representative Ron Paul (R, TX) introduced the *American Sovereignty Restoration Act* in 2007 that would affect U.S. withdrawal from the UN, but Congress would not support it. Only 56 honest, uncompromised congressmen out of 435 voted for the measure.[19] That only a minority of elected officials would stand for

U.S. sovereignty and against waste and fraud was a huge yellow flag 14 years ago. This lopsided vote was against the American people and their children. The warning was sounded, and after eight years of Obamarama, Trump was elected. The people decided the 'change' Obama offered was not for the good. Mr. Trump's election forced the Democrats to show their true colors. Instead of red, white and blue, they were white and blue, the colors of the United Nations.

The U.N. reported in 2020 that it had 114,119 employees and a budget of $57 billion for fiscal year 2019. Remember, the U.S. provides almost 20% of the total funding. Fifty-seven billion dollars for an organization that has consistently failed to accomplish its mission: keeping the peace and providing short term humanitarian assistance. What gives?

We are told the world just has too many problems and no single government has the resources or resolve. A transnational organization is needed. It sounds good but 75 years of failure is a lot of failure. It's time we stop the empty words, discard the appeals to emotion, and tell them to shove the guilt where the sun doesn't shine. But, instead of 'just saying No,' the Democrats, Angela Merkle, Henry Kissinger and Bill Gates are saying 'time is short', the situation is 'urgent' and we 'must act now.' If we don't act 'together' we then share in the responsibility for the tragic outcome we are told will happen. The globalists say, "get that monkey off your back' and give it to the United Nations – all they need are a few tens of billions. My God, what might happen if we cut off funding to the United Nations!

The United Nations, like all organizations and people, will do whatever it takes to survive, even if it means saying there are problems that are not real. They realized long ago that their survival depends on a steady flow of urgent problems. Re-read the McKinsey-WEF list of the eight key issues they say need addressing. Of the eight themes they identified as globally crucial: 1. Stakeholder capitalism, 2. Climate change, 3. Equality of opportunity 4. Digital regulation, 5. Economic collaboration, 6. Multilateralism, 7. Artificial intelligence 8. Equality for Women. The only two issues on this list that are real are digital regulation and artificial intelligence. The other six are fabricated.

Consider the words of Secretary Generals of the United Nations Ban Ki Moon, 2007-16, Kofi Anan, 1997-2006, and the first Secretary General, Dag Hammarskjöld:

> *"Multiple crises – food, fuel, financial, flu – are hitting at once. Climate change looms larger every day.* Each illustrates a 21st-century truth: we share one planet, one home. As people, as nations, as a species, we sink or swim together. The United Nations is doing its utmost to respond – to address the big issues, to look at the big picture." - Ban Ki-Moon October 2009.

> "In the 21st Century I believe the mission of the United Nations will be defined by a new, more profound awareness of the sanctity and dignity of every human life, regardless of race or religion. *This will require us to look beyond the framework of States, and beneath the surface of nations or communities."* - Kofi Annan, December 2001.

> "I have no doubt that 40 years from now we shall be engaged in the same pursuit. How could we expect otherwise? World organization is still a new adventure in human history." - Dag Hammarskjöld, 20 May 1956.[20] *(italics are mine)*

After 75 years, Hammarskjöld's prophecy is debunked. It is no longer the same pursuit. Peace remains a goal this organization has never achieved. Everything else is 'head cheese', it's made from the scraps and waste and is impossible to swallow. In other words, it is worse than baloney. Their new slogan is 'Peace, dignity and equality on a healthy planet.' We know we will not get peace, so we are paying $57 billion a year for dignity, equality and chasing after windmills. What is going on?

Wolf in Sheep's Clothing

The UN claims to do five things:
"Due to the powers vested in its Charter and its unique international character, the United Nations can take action on the issues confronting humanity in the 21st century, including:

- Maintain international peace and security
- Protect human rights
- Deliver humanitarian aid
- Promote sustainable development
- Uphold international law"[21]

Maintaining Peace & Security: A review of the UN record on maintaining peace (synopsis provided earlier) has demonstrated UN impotence. As I write these lines, Russia is building troops on Ukraine's border and China flies daily sorties into Taiwan airspace.

Protecting Human Rights: A quick review of the genocide that has occurred across Africa for decades immediately dispels this myth. China continues to commit genocide against the Uighurs in the Xinjiang region of northwest China.[22]

Delivering Humanitarian Aid: They do legitimately provide humanitarian aid, while enriching dictators and non-governmental organizations (NGOs). The World Health Organization (WHO), charged with providing medical aid and global health monitoring provided cover for China in the early days of Covid-19.

Sustainable development is a complete canard centered on fictious global warming and climate alarmism.

The claim that the UN 'upholds international law' is more absurd than the claim that it 'maintains peace.' No nation should relinquish its sovereignty to a global political body. The absurdity of this claim is evidenced by a case filed by Palestine against the United States for relocating the embassy from Tel Aviv to Jerusalem. Palestine is not even a member of the United Nations.

Silent Spring to Sustainability

Rachel Carson's *'Silent Spring',* published in 1962, awakened society to the importance of effectively managing natural resources and proactively protecting the environment. In 1968, Paul and Anne Ehrlich published *The Population Bomb*, a neo-Malthusian work that prophesied famine due to over-population by the 1970s and 1980s. These two books laid the foundation for what today is called 'the sustainability movement.'

The cultural and societal upheaval of the mid-1960s was well underway by the time the first Earth Day was held April 22, 1970.[23] Eight months later, President Richard M. Nixon, signed the law that created the Environmental Protection Agency (EPA). The Club of Rome followed up on the Ehrlich book and published the first computer modeled population and resource forecast titled *The Limits to Growth* in 1972. Also in 1972, the United Nations convened the Conference on the Human Environment in Stockholm.[24]

Most of the initiatives in these formative years were focused on 'real' environmental problems (air pollution, water pollution, wild-life and wild-lands preservation) and have been largely successful. The world is a healthier place due to these initiatives, but the actions were taken by individual countries not the United Nations. The rich irony of the environmental movement history is that the 1970's were a period of pronounced global cooling. The 'climate' scientists of those days were warning of a 'new ice age.'[25, 26] Twenty years later they were warning of 'global warming.' It sounds like the 'three bears,' "I'm too cold", I'm too hot." But the United Nations is never 'just right.'

Sustainability to the 2030 Agenda

Twenty years after the initial UN environmental conference, the first United Nations Earth Summit was held in Rio de Janeiro, launching the climate alarmism, post neo-Malthusian era. Did the little global cold snap muck things up? Yes. Just as they were building their case for sending the armies of the world to the north Pole with blow dryers, it started warming again. Back to the drawing board. The UN sanctioned a study in 1984 called the Brundtland Commission. It spawned a book in 1987 titled *Our Common Future* which laid the groundwork for the June 1992 Earth Summit in Rio and coined the term 'sustainability'.[27]

Making the most of the Rio boondoggle, the UN also adopted the Rio Declaration[28] and Agenda 21.[29] The Rio Declaration on Environment and Development is a 5-page list of 27 principles which are further articulated in the 351-page Agenda 21 document. The documents are giant 'word salads' that can be condensed into: 'People and countries should respect each other and the world we live in.'

The 2030 Agenda for Sustainable Development was initially published in 2015. It consists of 17 goals, some of which derive from Agenda 21 but many of which are new. Among the new goals are:

- Ensure inclusive and equitable quality education and promote lifelong learning opportunities for all

- Achieve gender equality and empower all women and girls

- Ensure access to affordable, reliable, sustainable and modern energy for all

- Promote sustained, inclusive and sustainable economic growth, full and productive employment and decent work for all

- Build resilient infrastructure, promote inclusive and sustainable industrialization and foster innovation

- Reduce inequality within and among countries

- Make cities and human settlements inclusive, safe, resilient, and sustainable

- Ensure sustainable consumption and production patterns[30]

Notice that each of these items are almost verbatim from the Biden platform. They are still going to eliminate poverty, hunger, and war while insisting that long term weather patterns abide by UN mandates. One wonders if the UN General Assembly sings 'Camelot' before every meeting?

> *"It's true! It's true! The crown has made it clear.*
> *The climate must be perfect all the year.*
> *A law was made a distant moon ago here:*
> *July and August cannot be too hot.*
> *And there's a legal limit to the snow here*
> *In Camelot."*
>
> © 2021 AllMusicals.com

Sounds Good to Me

The globalists and progressives are like used car salesmen. They will tell you anything to get you to buy. They know the 'right' words to say, but if you don't ask questions or know the right questions, you end up with a 'lemon' you can't get rid of. They lied, they got our money, and we got the shaft. We have all learned this the hard way and with respect to physical purchases have become more careful.

Buying an idea, however; is a different deal. The repercussions from purchasing a faulty product are quickly realized and we can often take it back or get a refund. Someone who gives money to the Sierra Club may 'feel' good about it and never realize the Club prioritizes small fish over a dam that would provide fresh water for millions of people. Getting stuck with a defective product is usually not life threatening, getting stuck with bad ideas and policies often times is.

- The people of Venezuela thought Hugo Chavez was going to help them.

- Americans trusted Barack Obama when he said we could keep our plan and our doctor and that health care costs would go down.

- The people of Germany trusted Angela Merkel when she shut down their nuclear power grid.

- The World Health Organization was trusted but provided cover for China until Covid-19 had spread around the world.

- The people of the United States trusted Dr. Fauci.

- The people of Texas trusted the Electric Reliability Council of Texas.

The highway of good intentions is littered with tragedy. The ones who sold the ideas moved on; the ones who trusted them paid the price. Mankind never learns. We let our guard down. We unconsciously decide the risk of 'buying' a bad idea is minimal. And, after all, it sounds good and we're busy. We inherently want to 'believe' in people, so we keep giving them a chance. This book has reviewed the plight of most of America's major cities. Things don't change for the better because the people keep electing the same charlatans. When casting our vote, deciding to support humanitarian issues, environmental issues, donate money, sign petitions, etc, our tendency is a default to feeling and subjectivity. They tug at our heart strings, give us a guilt trip, and we give in. Few take the time to ask questions, 'look under the hood', think, and demand evidence of results.

Money Talks

The Vice President of Bezosgateslandia, Bill Gates, is a major funder of the WHO. He condemned President Trump for withholding funding (which Biden has now reinstated). The philanthropy of Gates is renown. The positive outcomes of his philanthropy are impossible to quantify. But billionaires are also human. Gates is the world's most active billionaire promoter of climate alarmism. Why? It has no scientific foundation.

The scientific community will not challenge him because he is a major source of funding. He is one of the high priests. Here are two quotations from Gates that were made in an interview with the Massachusetts Institute of Technology Review[31] regarding a book Gates published on climate change in 2020:

Q: How do you feel about our chances of making real political progress, particularly in in the US, in the moment we find ourselves in?
A: I am optimistic. Biden being elected is a good thing.

Q: Do you think plant-based and lab-grown meats could be the full solution to the protein problem globally, even in poor nations?
A: I do think all rich countries should move to 100% synthetic beef."

What? Much of the contents of this book could serve as state's evidence in a case to prove Joe Biden is killing America. Gates, however, said Biden's election was a good thing. Then a few minutes later, he categorically says rich countries should stop eating beef! Gates 'believes' ruminant animals are a threat to humanity because their burps contain methane.

To relieve any doubt of his transition to Lalaland, Gates is now providing funding for "the development of sun-dimming technology."[32] There have been evil masterminds in James Bond and Mission Impossible movies with similar altruistic motives. This is Dr. Jekyll and Mr. Hyde stuff.

If money is power, then Bill Gates is one of the most powerful people in the world. Jeff Bezos is THE most powerful person in the world. Together, they OWN the 50th largest country in the world (Chapter 11). [**Update 2022**: Divorce after the publishing of the 1st Edition demoted both Bezos and Gates but does not diminish the point I have made regarding the extremely wealthy]

Facebook and Twitter (run by billionaires Mark Zuckerberg and Jack Dorsey) trampled on the free speech of Americans, including the President of the United States without penalty. Dorsey shut down the URL and Twitter account of the New York Post, the nation's 4th largest newspaper. Jeff Bezos owns the Washington

Post. Microsoft owns LinkedIn. Google search results are controlled by algorithms that intentionally inject progressive bias. Try to do anything today without interacting with Google.

There is no escaping the ultimate weakness of human nature, we want it our way. Billionaires are humans too. If Bill Gates says we should not eat beef and then buys up all the ranch land, what are we going to do?

If Zuckerberg and Dorsey want to cancel your voice, there is no way to stop them. [**Update 2022**: Elon Musk is an unexpected White Knight that may positively impact free speech on social media.]

This is why the Founders established a constitutional republic with checks and balances. The system has worked as long as a majority of the people support self-determination, the rule of law, personal responsibility, accountability, integrity, and honesty. When you look around today, these virtues are in short supply.

The Semblance of Power

Maybe now you are beginning to understand why the teacher unions, the media, academia, the Biden administration, the World Economic Forum, and even the United Nations are all singing from the same song sheet. They all have the semblance of power but are not the source of the power.

There has never been a time when those in power were not willing to accept money for favors. What is new is the convergence of extreme wealth, unprecedented global connectivity, and powerful technology in the hands of a few.

In Summary

The United Nations has great marketing. The Democratic party has great marketing. They know the three great motivators are fear, sympathy, and guilt. There must always be a sense of urgency, crisis, and impending doom. They are masters of class warfare, identity politics and victimhood. The only reason they are successful is because the Orwellian Ministries of Truth (the media, government bureaucracy and academia) are complicit.

Behind the scenes, there is a plethora of utopian visioned organizations. Partially government funded organizations (PGO) such as the World Bank, World Trade Organization and the Organization for Economic Cooperation and Development (OECD); non-governmental organizations (NGO) such as the Council on Foreign Relations, the Club of Rome, the Trilateral Commission, the World Economic Forum and many others and private foundations (Bill & Melinda Gates Foundation, Ford Foundation, the Rockefeller Foundation and many more). They are all globalist in orientation and utopian in character, meaning their solution for human survival is centered in global government and the belief that man can rule over man peacefully. Peacefully is the operative word, hence the drive for gun control (an unarmed people cannot protect themselves).

It all sounds so preposterous, just another conspiracy theory. Yet, it is neither a conspiracy nor a theory. Oxford defines the verb conspire: "to secretly plan with other people to do something illegal or harmful."[33] There is nothing secret about what the UN is doing. A theory is "an opinion or idea that someone believes is true but that is not proved", Oxford definition option 3.[34]

All good lies have a nugget of truth. Of course, we want to be responsible stewards of our planet so life can continue to flourish. Thus 'sustainability' must be good, right? It sounds good. The problem is the UN, the progressives, and all who espouse the doctrine of sustainability will tell you what it means and what is required to achieve it. If the goal posts seem to keep moving or the definition changing, keep your mouth shut or they will shut it for you.

Chapter 16
Antidisestablishmentarianism

"Die Religion… ist das Opium des Volkes,"
Religion is the opium of the people.[1]
—Karl Marx, 1843

"Congress shall make no law respecting an establishment of religion or prohibiting the free exercise thereof; or abridging the freedom of speech, or of the press; or the right of the people peaceably to assemble, and to petition the Government for a redress of grievances." 1st Amendment to the Constitution of the United States.[2]

When speaking of religious freedom, it is common to hear some say, 'Freedom of religion is a first amendment right'. A more attentive reading of the amendment, however, reveals three things with respect to religious freedom:

- The people are protected from having government established religion forced on them.

- The people are free to independently exercise religion.

- The word 'religion' is not defined but the common use of the word at the time meant a system of belief in a higher being. Thus, an atheist was 'not' religious.

In the United States today, atheism is considered a 'belief' system that denies the existence of a supreme being and is thus protected by the 1st amendment.

"The Supreme Court has said that a religion, for purposes of the First Amendment, is distinct from a "way of life," even if that way of life is inspired by philosophical beliefs or other secular concerns. See Wisconsin v. Yoder, 406 U.S. 205, 215-16, 92 S.Ct. 1526, 32 L.Ed.2d 15 (1972). A religion need not be based on a belief in the existence of a supreme being (or beings, for polytheistic faiths), see Torcaso v. Watkins, 367 U.S. 488, 495 & n. 11, 81 S.Ct. 1680, 6 L.Ed.2d 982 (1961); Malnak v. Yogi, 592 F.2d 197, 200-15 (3d Cir.1979) (Adams, J., concurring); Theriault v. Silber, 547 F.2d 1279, 1281 (5th Cir.1977) (per curiam), nor must it be a mainstream faith, see Thomas v. Review Bd., 450 U.S. 707, 714, 101 S.Ct. 1425, 67 L.Ed.2d 624 (1981); Lindell v. McCallum, 352 F.3d 1107, 1110 (7th Cir.2003)."[3]

To summarize, the Supreme Court of the United States, over the course of at least 4 cases from 1961 to 2005, says that religion is:

- A "way of life," even if that way of life is inspired by philosophical beliefs or other secular concerns.

- Need not be based on a belief in the existence of a supreme being (or beings, for polytheistic faiths).

- Nor must it be a mainstream faith.

A lot has changed since the first Puritans arrived. Freedom from state religious systems and the freedom to worship as one chooses were founding principles of the country and the primary reasons the puritans came to America.

Can We have a Word?

"It depends on what the meaning of the word 'is' is," responded President Bill Clinton to a grand jury question in 1998.[4]

Our ability to communicate is rapidly eroding and the lexical compromise is always demanded by the progressives. Orwell recounted a comment from Syme, a 'Newspeak' expert (as opposed to 'Old speak), "It's a beautiful thing, the destruction of words."[5]

When progressivism is losing the argument, they just demand a revision of reality. Consider the willingness of Merriam-Webster to amend the definition of 'racism' to accommodate a 22-year-old University of Missouri student. "It's not just disliking someone because of their race," Mitchum wrote in a Facebook post. "This current fight we are in is evidence of that, lives are at stake because of the systems of oppression that go hand-in-hand with racism."[6] So, Merriam-Webster amended the definition to include the word 'systemic'. Please stop reading for a minute and send an email to Merriam-Webster suggesting a definition refinement and see what happens. In fact, I think I'll do it myself. They opened the flood gates, so let's give it to 'em.

Back to religion. As of this writing, Merriam-Webster defines 'religion' as follows:

1: the service and worship of God or the supernatural or commitment or devotion to religious faith or observance

2: a personal set or institutionalized system of religious attitudes, beliefs, and practices

3: scrupulous conformity (*archaic*)

> 4: a cause, principle, or system of beliefs held to with ardor and faith[7]

Since they weakly rely on the root word religious to define 'religion'; here is how they define 'religious': "relating to or manifesting faithful devotion to an acknowledged ultimate reality or deity."[8] I go through this painful exercise to make two points:

- Dictionaries, like almost everything else in society, have been compromised by politics and the need to stay 'in tune with the times'. If we have to keep checking the dictionary every three months, then we are in trouble.

- Common sense is no longer common, thus, we must appeal to the courts.

Antidisestablishmentarianism

When a country has an official government-endorsed religion, it is referred to as an 'established' religion. The people of the country are not required by the state to actively participate in the religion (except taxes help support it), however, those who do, may receive some privileges. Conversely, those who do not participate may be significantly disadvantaged and even persecuted. This is why the 1st Amendment in the U.S. Constitution is called the 'establishment' clause.

Forty-three of the world's 199 countries have an 'established' religion, 27 of which are Muslim. Islam accounts for approximately 25% of the world population, second only to Christianity (31%). Over half of the Christians are Catholics (~16% of world population). The most globally centric are the Catholics, with a single person at their head. Islam is currently the fastest growing.[9,10,11]

The Church of England is the established religion in England. The 1st Amendment of the U.S Constitution forbids the establishment of religion, hence the separation of church and state. The movement to separate the church or an official religion from the state is called disestablishment. The fight against it is called antidisestablishmentarianism. Of course, this etymological review is all in the context of religion having the singular meaning of devotion to a system that acknowledges God or gods. But the U.S. Supreme Court says that is only one acceptable definition.

Since the concept is convoluted, it may help the reader, to whom this subject is new, to remember that two grammatical negatives results in the positive. Thus, to be against disestablishment is simply to be for establishment. Understanding this issue is critical in our time, as I will now explain.

No Atheists in Foxholes

Since the beginning of recorded history man has had an innate belief in a higher creator being. It was not until the Enlightenment that the concept of God was openly challenged. But people would not let go of God so easily, after all He was their opiate.

Marx's idea was to get rid of God and replace Him with a benevolent supreme soviet to oversee the collective. He did not question the innate need for people to have something to 'believe' in, he was just going to replace it. So, there really are no 'non-believers'. Everyone puts their faith in something and if it is not God (gods) then it must be in man himself. There is no other option.

What's Behind Door #2?

If not God, then man. If man, then what? The answer, Big Brother. After acknowledging the "Laws of Nature and of Nature's God", Thomas Jefferson wrote, "We hold these truths to be self-evident, that all men are created equal, that they are endowed by their Creator with certain unalienable Rights, that among these are Life, Liberty and the pursuit of Happiness. That to secure these rights, Governments are instituted among Men, deriving their just powers from the consent of the governed...".[12]

Jefferson and the signers clearly state that people establish government to ensure that all people have the opportunity to live free and pursue their dreams. This was theirs and is our 'Declaration of Independence'. Independence from what? Answer: a tyrannical, autocratic, dictatorial government.

The United States, and the World, has been held hostage over a year by a tyrannical government. The response to Covid-19 is unprecedented in human history. As I have proven in great detail in the book *34 Days & Holding: America in the Balance* and again in this book, there was and is no scientific foundation to the government's restriction on our freedom. Due to this extreme government overreach, people have taken their own lives, families have lost businesses they spent their lives developing. These businesses employed others and provided for their lives, liberty, and pursuit of happiness. Tens of millions of children have lost an entire year of education and socialization. Tens of millions of Jews, Christians and Muslims have been denied the right to gather for community worship. Millions of people have been denied the opportunity to speak freely by the social media titans Facebook and Twitter. The U.S. Congress does nothing because the Democrats are in lockstep and also have a few Republicans. This has been tyranny. This is tyranny. How does it continue? Answer: its complicated, but it involves religious adherence and faith.

"We Believe"

There is an insanely stupid sign that you see in front yards today that says: "We believe: Black Lives Matter. No Human is Illegal. Love is Love. Women's Rights are Human Rights. Science is Real. Water is Life. Injustice Anywhere is a Threat to Justice Everywhere." This sign is produced by signsforjustice.org. Not one of these slogans is wrong but what is implied is wrong. Of course, black lives matter. No one disagrees. But, when someone is persecuted for saying all lives matter, then there is something really wrong.

This, my friends, is religion. It is a statement of faith. These faithful proudly put the sign in their yard to proclaim their faith. Like most religions, this one requires faith. To state something is real without verifiable evidence is a statement of faith. I have not seen God, but I believe that He is. The people with the signs are the evangelists. Most people keep their faith to themselves, until it is challenged or offended.

To be a Democrat requires blind faith. The data shows that masks did not slow down viral spread, yet the government required them, and many people would scream at you if you were not wearing one. They 'believe' those who have told them masks are necessary. People who enter the US illegally are not 'illegal' according to the Democrats. The faith requires that border security and national sovereignty be surrendered to appease the bleeding hearts. Because the globe stopped warming in 1999, the 'clergy' christened the crisis anew. It shall now be called 'climate change'. Forget the fact that climate has always changed. Forget the fact that when the Founders signed the Declaration of Independence the world was in the middle of the Little Ice Age. Forget the fact that CO_2 is required for life to exist. Without CO_2, life is not 'sustainable'. But Joe Biden announced a new goal of reducing US CO_2 emission by 50% in 9 years![13]

I took a five mile walk through the city today, as I often do. People are still walking around outside with masks on. There is no virus floating around, the sunlight kills virus in seconds. The Governor has even lifted the mandate, yet they still wear the mask. Why? Answer: fear. They 'believe' it keeps them safe because the clergy said it was so.

I was having dinner alone in a small café after a day of consulting work in Michigan. Somehow the topic of climate change came up with the waitress. I have a PhD in the biological sciences and have studied environmental and climatological science for several years. I gave her a couple of basic facts regarding the scam of climate alarmism. She comfortably responded that she disagreed because in her 'experience' everyone 'believed' it was a real problem. When someone 'believes', facts don't matter. Belief cannot be debated.

I will belabor the point no further.

The clergy knows the truth, but many of them also 'believe' their lies are for the 'greater good'. Everyone in, and associated with, The Clergy' has 'skin in that game.' They are vested in its success because they have a lot to lose if it fails. We learned as children that the only way to avoid punishment for telling a lie, is to keep lying and make sure others 'in the know' do not break ranks. Even though they may not have told the first lie, their silence has made them complicit and accessories to the crime. They also have 'skin in the game'. They have made a Faustian bargain. They have partnered with evil to hide the truth, knowing many innocent people will suffer.

But what about those who support the lie by trusting the liar. The example is the person who yells at you for not wearing a mask. It is the person who calls you a 'denier' if you try to point out the falsity of climate alarmism. It is the person who calls you a racist and bigot when you say, 'All Lives Matter'. The list goes on, but should these 'quasi-innocent' people be culpable for supporting the lie? Is it right to hold them accountable for simply misplacing their trust and for putting their faith in the Clergy?

The point of this book and my historical commentary on the 2020 election (*34 Days & Holding: America in the Balance*) is to sound the warning. I am hoping this book will encourage those who believe that the Truth will keep us free will stand up for the truth. I want them to be ready with a clear answer delivered in a calm voice. Post modernism says truth is relative and each person can have their own truth. This is one of the most perverse lies of our time. The Sage told us long ago that we will know a person by what he does, not what he says. He thus is saying each of us carries the responsibility for discernment and the accountability for choosing wrongly. Those who admire and adulate the emperor for his new clothes, when he is in fact naked, made a choice and will be held accountable. Freedom is not free.

We can debate why the average person 'believes' and wonder why they don't ask more questions, do more study or listen to and consider opposing views, but it is fruitless. Most 'believers' are motivated by peer pressure and the need for social acceptance. Their tendency is understandably to go with the flow. It's easier and 'feels' better to be part of the group. The psychology, however, is not what is important. What is important is knowing that there are many who are ready to hear the truth. The question is who will tell it.

The New Faith

We will now close the circle on the critical role religion is playing in the dismantling of America and of global representative governments.

The Old Faiths. The churches have, to a great extent, already embraced the new faith. Their 'old' faith has grown cold. The most common evidence of the new faith overtaking the old is the ubiquitousness of Black Lives Matter signs. They are hanging on Christian churches of all flavors. Pope Francis is the most politically progressive pope in modern times, supporting gay union, climate alarmism and the abolition of borders. Jews, for some reason, have been picked on and persecuted forever. They could put up a BLM sign and it wouldn't matter. Islam has always favored autocracy. In fact, their long-term goal is theocracy. Since, comparatively, they are the 'new faith on the block' across the western world, they smartly keep their heads down. Thus is the state of traditional religion.

The New Faith. The new faith really isn't that new, it is called Humanism. As mentioned earlier, there are only two choices: God or man. The attractive feature of Humanism is its flexibility with respect to traditional beliefs. Much of the monotheistic world, Catholics, Jews, Muslims, and Protestants, are Humanists (Figure 27). Humanism is a perfect fit to the Supreme Courts definition of religion:

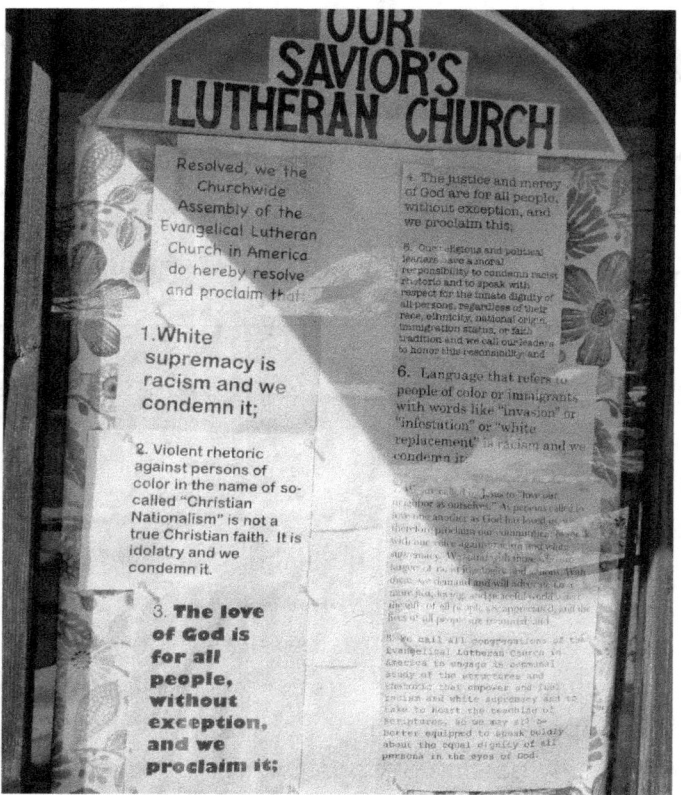

Figure 27: Example of the 'New Faith' diluting the 'Old Faith'.
Photo taken by the author February 26, 2021

- A "way of life," even if that way of life is inspired by philosophical beliefs or other secular concerns.

- Need not be based on a belief in the existence of a supreme being (or beings, for polytheistic faiths).

- Nor must it be a mainstream faith.

There was a time when opposition to the Pope and Catholic doctrine would result in excommunication. No longer. In some Muslim countries the penalty for apostacy is death. Marrying outside the faith remains taboo among the most devout Catholics, Jews and Muslims. I make the statements, not as judgements, but as accurate descriptions. I believe in freedom and have no issues with someone who does not believe as I do… as long as they return the favor.

Humanism does not return the favor. There were Jews who survived Nazi Germany because they were able to hide their ethnicity/religion. Am I suggesting that Nazism was a form of Humanism? Yes. Openly identify as an evangelical Christian today and you will be ridiculed by the Humanists. Openly identify as someone who thinks there should be open debate on the issues of climate alarmism and, at best, you are laughed at and marginalized, at worst you are completely shunned (excommunicated). President Trump sold a lot of MAGA hats during his campaigns, but no one wears them in public.

But, They Mean Well

Human history is littered with pain and suffering caused by the failure of good intentions. Father Paneloux said, "The evil that is in the world almost always comes of ignorance, and good intentions may do as much harm as malevolence if they lack understanding."[14] Another sage said, "The road to hell is paved with good intentions."[15]

At the advice of his medical advisors, President Trump announced a two-week shutdown of all but the most essential segments of society. He is not a scientist, nor a virologist, nor an expert on infectious disease. The world followed suit. The lockdowns, masks, social distancing and self-quarantines did not stop viral spread. The human tragedy caused by government actions based on the advice of Dr. Anthony Fauci and others is incalculable. Much, much worse than the deaths directly caused by the virus. It is probably fair to assume that the initial actions were 'well intended'. The actions were taken by politicians who were and still are 'ignorant' of the science. Fourteen months later there is a national and global movement to 're-imagine' the country and the world. I have proven in this book that this movement did not spontaneously combust. It has been in the works for years.

The Humanist pipers play, and the mice follow. Why do they follow? They 'believe'. Why do they believe? Fear. What is the message preached? We will save you. Who are the preachers? The 'experts.' Who are the Clergy and keepers of the 'word'? Progressive ideologues (Democrats in the US), globalilsts (United Nations, many global corporations, NGO's, environmentalists, feminists, most of the global elites that occupy the Towers of Power described in the book *34 Days & Holding,* and some of the billionaire class).

Do they have good intentions? Does it matter? Are premeditated actions that cause calamity to be forgiven because they were 'well intended'?

We End Where We Began

"Congress shall make no law respecting an establishment of religion or prohibiting the free exercise thereof;"[16] yet this is exactly what they have done. Humanism is the state religion of the

United States. Our taxes fund the religious dogma: climate alarmism, diversity, inclusion, equity, racial bigotry (i.e., black lives matter but white lives do not), extreme feminism, the redefinition of gender and marriage, and open borders. The Towers of Power: Government, Education, News Media, Social Media, Sports and Entertainment preach the new gospel every hour of every day. Innocent school kids are taught the liturgy every day until it becomes reality. The government and the teacher's unions have mandated these teachings without the parent's approval and thus assign themselves preeminence over the parents.

The tenets of the faith are taught rigorously and apostasy severely punished. There are 10 Muslim countries where apostasy is punished by law and in some cases, by penalty of death.[17]

In the United States today, college professors are fired, businesspeople are fired, campus speakers are shut down, businesses are boycotted, scheduled mass gatherings are relocated (i.e., the All Star game of Major League Baseball), juries are threatened and intimidated (the house of a jury member in the George Floyd case was defaced with pig's blood and [**Update 2022**: Leftists protest and demonstrate on the lawns and streets in front of conservative Supreme Court Justices due to an illegal leak of a draft brief regarding abortion]), statues are torn down, public and private buildings are painted with epithets by BLM and Antifa, mayors of major cities paint BLACK LIVES MATTER is giant letters on city streets, and - the list goes on and on.

If this is not religious fervor, I don't know what is. I am old enough to have seen people wearing hooded white gowns and signs identifying different entrances for whites and blacks. To a child, it was confusing, as an adult it is infuriating. That was wrong then and this is wrong now. The followers of this religion say, "Love is Love" and "Let Peace Have a Chance" but those are just words. Their actions clearly and consistently convey the opposite.

Dear friends in America and around the world, I hope this book has helped clarify your understanding of what is happening and that you are motivated to stand firm for individual freedom and the opportunity for all to be able to determine their own life direction and the freedom to pursue their dreams. Violence is not our answer, but as this book has shown, it is often theirs. Cancelling someone is inherently violent. We don't have much time. Read this book and pass it on or encourage others to get a copy.

President Joe Biden, his administration, and the Democrats are dismantling America brick by brick.

Postscript

Carnac holds the sealed envelope with the secret question to his head and pronounces the answer, "The 100 Yard Dash."
Ed McMahon says, "And the question was?"

Carnac opens the envelop and reads: "What happens after you eat a 100-yard prune?"

—Johnny Carson as 'Carnac the Magnificent' from: *The Tonight Show Starring Johnny Carson*, 1966

The 2020 election was the 100-year prune, and we are now nearing the end of the 100-yard dash, or Biden's last first 100 days. Do not be dismayed nor discouraged. We are living in the most exciting time in global history. The "laws of nature and nature's God" have not changed, nor will they. To everything there is a season, but truth, honesty, integrity, compassion and 'real, sacrificial' love are always in season. If God cares for the sparrow, we can rest knowing He cares much more for us.

It's Not the End of the World

This is not mankind's first rodeo, nor will it be his last. The silent majority in America and the world must now stand and be counted. It will not be easy.

This book has recorded most of the significant historical events, decisions, actions and reactions of the Biden administration's first 100 days *and been updated for the first 16 months*. As I have documented in detail, it has been a period of growing darkness.

The long and patient process of upending traditional values, mores and principles has come to a head. The Orwellian prophecies of *1984* and *Animal Farm* seem to be becoming reality. Big Brother is here, and he is watching.

The totalitarian plan articulated by Yuri Bezmenov and professor Canrong is nearing maturity (Chapters 13 & 14). Three or more generations of American youth have now received the liturgy and a new 'Red Guard' could emerge. It is time to be wise as serpents and be ready with calm, fact-based responses. In many cases, we must take the initiative.

Global communism is awake, and the threat of regional military actions could provide the tipping point for the formation of a global alliance or government. The United Nations and World Economic Forum will be ready to appease, in the name of humanity (Humanism).

Here's a short list of likely conflicts and how they could possibly play out:

- China invades Taiwan. China is already posturing for this inevitability. It will be a cake walk and China will rule the South China Sea and the supply routes to the world. China has been building military islands in the South China Sea since 2014. Japan, India, Australia and New Zealand will look to the United States and Europe. Given the weakness of leadership in the U.S. and Europe, the conquest could end very quickly, and we could find ourselves in Kissinger's grand coalition.

- Iran finalizes nuclear missile capability. With Russia providing technical support and China buying their oil, Iran could quickly become the hegemon in the Middle East and leverage this power to neuter Europe and extort Israel and the United States.

- The Wuhan virology lab is still running and could have Covid-22 on the launch

Just one of these catastrophes could be enough to bring Democracy to heel, but two or all three would be overwhelming.

Of less short-term global consequence is a Russian escalation of the war with Ukraine. Russia has been moving more troops and armory to the Ukrainian border. Ukraine is not a NATO member and Putin knows Europe and the U.S. will do nothing other than posture.

North Korea will stand ready to threaten Japan and South Korea, both critical U.S. allies.

Strategically, Russia and North Korea need to move first, most likely summer 2021. Then, as with the Covid-19 timing, China or Iran will move in the winter creating 3 or 4 geographically separated conflicts with only a few months until the U.S. midterm elections. As Russia and China anticipated 65 years ago, the response from the west may well be capitulation. I pray I am wrong.

[**Update 2022**: Sadly, I was not wrong when the above was written in May of 2021. Russia's war against Ukraine is now 100 days old. The Monkeypox (a non-threatening, poorly communicable virus) is making the rounds among gay people and the press is promoting it and stoking fear. The United Nations is promoting provisions that give the World Health Organization the power over established governments. Joe Biden and the Democrats have voiced their support of this initiative. The U.S. has relinquished its seat at the negotiating table for non-proliferation of nuclear weapons in Iran to Russia. Joe Biden told the world he would commit our military to defend Taiwan. So, all the cards I forecasted over a year ago are now in play. The

U.S. mid-term elections are 5 months away. A lot can happen in 5 months.]

Can Anything be Done?

In episode 4, season one of Amazon's *Goliath*, Billy and Patty were taking on the giant legal firm of CoopermanMcBride. The giant had already squashed some people, yet Billy was unwavering. Patty panicked and screamed,

> *"...at the end of the day, they're big and we're little. And they're going to kill us, and I am terrified. I am terrified, do you understand that?"*[1]

Can anything be done? Emphatically Yes! Be like Billy McBride. The truth is more powerful than a sword, so arm yourself with facts not feelings. When in a mixed political group and someone says something that is not based on fact, calmly ask them why they 'think' that. If they say, "Well, Dr. Fauci said so." Then agree with them that he did say so, but that he has flip-flopped his positions on a lot of things. Give them an example (there are many in this book and in *34 Days & Holding*).

Try to remain calm and collected. "A gentle answers turns away wrath, but a harsh word stirs up anger." Proverbs 15:1. It is extremely difficult but proclamations and argument stifle dialogue and generate in-kind responses. Try to lead with questions like: "Why do you think that?" Or "How do you know?" Or "Can you help me understand?" Then gently demonstrate what they are missing. Ask them, "Have you considered?" Or can I follow up with facts. Never say you 'feel', always say 'here is what I know' or here are the facts. If you cannot discipline yourself along these lines, then don't waste your time. Also, don't get discouraged when most people, in one way or another, show no interest. You tried. You may have planted a seed.

So, the first three things to do are **remain calm**, **be engaging but not confrontational**, and **take the time to become knowledgeable**.

Work at getting connected and building your network of like-minded people. Your friends and your self-confidence in the truth, will be your strength. Salt your comments with casual signals that you are not happy about the lockdowns, masks, government overreach, gun control, racial and gender craziness, etc. It is like fishing, with these lures, you will catch people like you.

Stay positive and be encouraging to everyone. Smile. If you don't know the details or facts about something, it is OK to say you 'think' the evidence is counter to what someone said, but you will check and get back to them. Don't let the opportunity pass because you can't remember chapter and verse. They don't know it either. But, saying you don't know or are not sure is better than bullshitting. Remember, this is not about you, it is about the critical issues of our time. Keep the ego and the mouth in check. We can do it.

Write your congressman if you like, but sadly that is usually a waste of time due to our extreme polarization. Very seldom will the elected representative see your note anyway because others screen them. My writing to Diana DeGette about enforcing border control, leaving the 2nd amendment alone or getting rid of the dangerous concept of sanctuary cities would be a waste of time.

If you are a parent, **teach your children**. Know what the schools are teaching. Go to school board and teacher meetings. Speak at city council meetings. Your children are your legacy and the world's future. They are only with you for a short time, and it is primarily the first 12 years that you can have a strong influence. Your busy schedule must be adjusted accordingly.

Never proactively incite or initiate violence. This plays into their hands. Progressives say, "Love is Love" and "Give Peace a Chance", while denying you the right to speak, the right to assemble, the right to bear arms, and so on. If violence comes, walk away if you can. But, if you can't, you have the right to defend life and person. We have the right to protect those we love, the sanctity of our homes, our property, and the innocent.

Freedom lovers must think big picture but take small steps. Rallies are good but we will have the greatest impact by independently engaging people within our immediate circle: family, extended family, friends, colleagues, social groups, etc. When the opportunity arises to speak, take it. It is time to **stop self-censoring. Silence is acquiescence**. If we don't stand, we will surely fall. If we can't speak with 'friends' about sensitive or political issues, then the quality of the friendship should be revisited. True friendship is characterized for mutual respect, brotherly love (*phileo*), generosity, honesty and the knowledge there is reciprocate desire for the others well-being. Going along to get along only demonstrates our fear of rejection. We are humans, rejection sucks. But allowing a falsehood to be put forth without challenge risks others will accept it and thus group think takes over. We all need to **stand up for the truth**. If we don't, who will. Group think is a rapid stream toward the waterfall.

The United States was built on the foundational bricks of "Life, Liberty and the pursuit of Happiness."[2] Our Founders peacefully declared their right to independence from a tyrannical government and we remain free today because they, and the many patriots who followed, believed in the American Dream and were willing to stand together to protect and preserve it.

They declared "these truths to be self-evident,

- That all men are created equal

- they are endowed by their Creator with certain unalienable Rights

- that among these are Life, Liberty and the pursuit of Happiness."[3]

The Declaration also states something that is never considered. Let's read it again: "We hold these truths to be self-evident, that all men are created equal, that they are endowed by their Creator with certain unalienable Rights, *that among these* are Life, Liberty and the pursuit of Happiness."[4] Jefferson is saying there are many 'unalienable' rights and that life, liberty and the pursuit of happiness are the most important. First, it is the 'pursuit' of happiness that is a right not the guarantee of happiness. Secondly, we must consider the other 'unalienable' rights. These rights are the other building blocks of freedom the United States were built upon. They complete the foundation, without which, the nation will crumble.

A reading of the Declaration and the Constitution, which was ratified 12 years later (1788), and the Bill of Rights (ratified 1791) will identify the complete brick by brick foundation. They are:

- Belief that a Supreme God is the source of our unalienable rights. Man nor government has a right to restrict the natural human rights given from God.

- All people are entitled to the 'Laws of Nature and of Nature's God'.

- All people have an inherent right to self-determination – individual freedom.

- A good government will pursue 'laying its foundation on such principles.'

- The supreme purpose for a representative government is to 'ensure domestic Tranquility, provide for the common defense, promote the general Welfare.'

- A representative, constitutionally bound, body must govern at the 'consent of the people.' The Founders warned that this facet of our governmental structure is the weakest link because they realized that power, and the lust for it, carries the inherent seeds of corruption. The Bill of Rights was added 'in order to prevent misconstruction or abuse of its powers.'[5]

- Thus, they established a structure of checks and balances: The Executive, Legislative and Judiciary with the Constitution as the rule book. (Articles I-III)

- They intentionally limited the power and reach of the Federal government and recognized the rights of member states (10th Amendment)

- They made it very difficult to change or amend the Constitution to protect against the subversion of recognized and natural rights. (Article V)

- They specifically identify individual rights of speech, the press, of assembly, of protest, of government responsiveness to problems, of religious belief and practice and of freedom from government established religion. (1st Amendment)

- The Second Amendment protects the right to keep and bear arms.

- "The Fifth Amendment provides several protections for people accused of crimes. It states that serious criminal charges must be started by a grand jury. A person cannot be tried twice for the same offense (double jeopardy) or have property taken away without just compensation. People have the right against self-incrimination and cannot be imprisoned without due process of law (fair procedures and trials.)"[5]

[**Update 2022**: Several who participated in the January 6th break-in of Capital Building are still in jail and have not been charged. ***They have been imprisoned without due process***. Remember, the break-in occurred prior to the arrival of the thousands who listened to the President. Most who illegally entered the building were just following the crowd. It is also known that the FBI had people who instigated the break-in and ANTIFA was there with gas masks on. Two protesters lost their lives at the hands of the Capital and D.C. police: Ashli Babbitt and Rosanne Boyland. Ashli was shot by Lt. Michael Byrd of the Capital Police. It was the only incident of an office pulling their gun. Babbitt was unarmed, yet Lt. Byrd was exonerated. A policeman is serving time in Minnesota for holding his knee on the neck of George Floyd while Floyd was dying from a fentanyl overdose. Rosanne Byrd, stumbled as the protesters were chased out of the Capital building with tear gas and billy-clubs. Rosanne stumbled, was trampled by fleeing protesters and then D.C. Police officer Lila Morris got out her billy-club and beat Rosanne. Some of the protesters tried to help Rosanne and were also beaten with billy-clubs. You can watch this on video. Officer Morris was hailed as a hero at the Super Bowl. [15] The left-wing media slandered both of these freedom loving women and did not honestly report the details of how they died.]

- "The Sixth Amendment provides additional protections to people accused of crimes, such as the right to a speedy and public trial, trial by an impartial jury in criminal cases, and to be informed of criminal charges. Witnesses must face the accused, and the accused is allowed his or her own witnesses and to be represented by a lawyer."[6]

- "The Seventh Amendment extends the right to a jury trial in Federal civil cases."[7]

- "The Tenth Amendment says that the Federal Government only has those powers delegated in the Constitution. If it isn't listed, it belongs to the states or to the people."[8]

- "Neither slavery nor involuntary servitude, except as a punishment for crime whereof the party shall have been duly convicted."[9] 13th Amendment

- "The right of citizens of the United States to vote shall not be denied or abridged by the United States or by any State on account of race, color, or previous condition of servitude."[10] 15th Amendment

- "The right of citizens of the United States to vote shall not be denied or abridged by the United States or by any State on account of sex."[11] 19th Amendment

These are the legally established bricks upon which our free society has been built and that are now being dismantled.

> **Author's Note:** The other amendments not referenced are clarification or improvements upon the founding documents. For example, the 26th Amendment, ratified in 1971, was spawned by the military draft. President Johnson needed more bodies to perpetrate the Vietnam War expansion. It moved the legal voting age from 21 to 18 and was a mistake that should be repealed. Now Nancy Pelosi wants to move it to 16!

Underlying these critical foundational bricks is the bedrock of principle.

The principle of the rule of law, without which anything goes, and chaos prevails, has been violated in grotesque extremes by progressives and Democrats. The principle followed by the Democrats and even liberal Supreme Court Justices is 'everything is relative and must be evaluated in the context of the current time.' Relativism and situational ethics are post-modern deconstructionism. It is building on shifting sand and must be rejected.

Even more basic and foundational are the principles of personal character: honesty, reverence for the truth, acceptance of personal responsibility, honor, honest work and self-sufficiency, compassion, mutual respect, sweat equity, equal opportunity not equality of outcome and "to keep myself physically strong, mentally awake, and morally straight."[12]

Jefferson wrote in 1776, "The history of the present King of Great Britain is a history of repeated injuries and usurpations, all having in direct object the establishment of an absolute Tyranny over these States."[13]

Is our situation today any different? What is freedom worth? The bricks of Freedom are crumbling toward a foundation of sand. Lincoln told us a house divided against itself cannot stand.[14] The Bible says "Everyone who hears these words of mine and doesn't do them will be like a foolish man, who built his house on the sand. The rain came down, the floods came, and the winds blew, and beat on that house; and it fell—and great was its fall." Matthew 7: 24-27.

My friends, we are falling. To continue along the path established over the last 100 days is to travel the road to destruction. If we remain silent, complacent, and resigned, the answer is yes. Never give up, always have hope.

I close with this final, and maybe most important thought, keep things in perspective. The world has always had war and conflict. The world has always had infectious disease and weather catastrophes. The world has always had to contend with despotism. But life will go on. So, try to love all people. Try to be patient with those who lack understanding or have lost perspective. Do what you can and try to make a difference while remembering we are all human, thus our nature is flawed. This is the problem no utopian vision will ever solve. View life as a grand adventure, control what you can and enjoy the ride. We only get one.

References

Part I — The Last 1st 100 Days

Preface: Squirrels in the Attic

[1] Lynch, Amy and Vila, Bob, 'Solved! What to Do About Squirrels in the Attic', bobvila.com, accessed Jan. 24, 2021
bobvila.com/articles/squirrels-in-the-attic

[2] Crosby, P. B., 1979 Quality is Free: The Art of Making Quality Certain. New York, NY: McGraw-Hill Book Company

[3] Shahadi, Jeanne, September 2011, 'National debt: The five-minute primer,' CNN Money, accessed Jan. 24, 2021
money.cnn.com/2011/09/05/news/economy/national_debt_faq

[4] Moore, Stephen, 1993, 'The Growth of Government in America', Foundation for Economic Education, accessed Jan. 24, 2021
fee.org/articles/the-growth-of-government-in-america

[5] Gannis, Scott, June 2020, 'How Bad Is The National Debt?,' seekingalpha.com, accessed Jan. 24, 2021
seekingalpha.com/article/4353472-how-bad-is-national-debt

[6] Ibid 3

[7] Johnston, Roy, January 2021, '34 Days & Holding: American in the Balance,' Publisher: Independently published (January 17, 2021), ISBN-13: 979-8593361660

[8] Gingrich, Newt, January 2019, 'Where's the Investigation into Senator Feinstein's Chinese Spy?', Gingrich360, accessed Feb.8, 2021
gingrich360.com/2019/01/wheres-the-investigation-into-senator-feinsteins-chinese-spy

[9] Ibid 7

[10] Moore, Stephen, 2018, 'Follow the (Climate Change) Money', Heritage Foundation, accessed Jan. 27, 2021
heritage.org/environment/commentary/follow-the-climate-change-money

[11] Staff, 'How Much Money is Spent on Climate Change Research?', accessed Jan. 27, 2021
co2nsensus.com/blog/how-much-money-is-spent-on-climate-change-research

[12] Science Staff, December 2020, 'Massive 2021 U.S. spending bill leaves research advocates hoping for more', Science, accessed Jan. 27, 2021
sciencemag.org/news/2020/12/massive-2021-us-spending-bill-leaves-research-advocates-hoping-more

[13] Ibid

[14] Ibid

[15] Ibid

[16] Davidson, Jordan, January 2021, 'John Brennan: Biden Intelligence Agencies to Investigate Pro-Trump 'Bigots' And 'Libertarians', The Federalist, accessed Jan. 27, 2021
thefederalist.com/2021/01/21/john-brennan-biden-intelligence-agencies-to-investigate-pro-trump-bigots-and-libertarians

[17] Ibid

[18] Ibid

Chapter 1: First Things First

[1] Glasser, Susan B., January 2021, '

[2] Conklin, Audrey, December 2020, 'Bobulinski tells Tucker Carlson that Joe Biden lied about son Hunter's business dealings,' Fox News, accessed Jan 28, 2021
foxnews.com/politics/flashback-bobulinski-tucker-hunter-carlson-biden

[3] Ibid

[4]   Morris, Emma-Jo and Fonrouge, Gabrielle, October 2020, 'Smoking-gun email reveals how Hunter Biden introduced Ukrainian businessman to VP dad,' New York Post, accessed Jan. 28, 2021 nypost.com/2020/10/14/email-reveals-how-hunter-biden-introduced-ukrainian-biz-man-to-dad

[5]   Ibid

[6]   Ibid

[7]   Media Release, 'September 2020, 'Johnson, Grassley Release Report on Conflicts-of-Interest Investigation,' Senate Cmte on HSGAC, accessed Jan. 28, 2021 hsgac.senate.gov/media/majority-media/johnson-grassley-release-report-on-conflicts-of-interest-investigation

[8]   Ibid

[9]   Ibid

[10]   Evans, Zachary, October 2020, 'FBI Investigating Hunter Biden for Money Laundering: Report,' Yahoo News, accessed Jan. 28, 2021 news.yahoo.com/fbi-investigating-hunter-biden-money-222323906.html

[11]   Noah, Timothy, September 1998, 'Bill Clinton and the Meaning of "Is",' Slate, accessed Jan. 28, 2021 slate.com/news-and-politics/1998/09/bill-clinton-and-the-meaning-of-is.html

[12]   ABC News, 'January 1998, 'Bill Clinton in 1998: 'I Did Not Have Sexual Relations With That Woman,' ABC News, accessed Jan. 28, 2021 abcnews.go.com/Politics/video/bill-clinton-responds-monica-lewinsky-affair-allegations

[13]   Politifact Staff, 'Obama: 'If you like your health care plan, you'll be able to keep your health care plan', Politifact, accessed Jan. 28, 2021 politifact.com/obama-like-health-care-keep

[14]   DelReal, Jose A., November 2014, 'Obamacare consultant under fire for 'stupidity of the American voter' comment,' Washington Post, accessed Jan. 28, 2021 washingtonpost.com/news/post-politics/wp/2014/11/11/obamacare-consultant-under-fire-for-stupidity-of-the-american-voter-comment/

[15]   Bresnahan, John and Kim, Seung Min ,June 2012, 'Holder held in contempt,' Politico, accessed Jan. 28, 2021 politico.com/story/2012/06/holder-held-in-contempt-of-congress-077988

[16] Editorial, May 2013, 'Eric Holder's Long History of Lying to Congress,' Investor's Business Daily, accessed Jan. 28, 2021 investors.com/politics/editorials/eric-holder-repeatedly-lied-to-congress

[17] Peralta, Eyder, June 28, 'Holder Found in Contempt of Congress,' NPR, accessed Jan. 28, 2021 npr.org/sections/thetwo-way/2012/06/28/155928783/house-set-for-vote-on-holding-attorney-general-holder-in-contempt

[18] Strong, Jonathan, June 2012, 'In Historic Vote, Attorney General Eric Holder Held in Contempt,' Rollcall, accessed Jan. 28, 2021 rollcall.com/2012/06/28/in-historic-vote-attorney-general-eric-holder-held-in-contempt

[19] Li, Victor, October 2014, 'Eric Holder won't be held in contempt over 'Fast and Furious' documents, rules judge,' American Bar Association Journal, accessed Jan. 28, 2021 abajournal.com/news/article/eric_holder_wont_be_held_in_contempt_over_fast_and_furious_documents_rules

[20] Thiessen, Marc, September 2016, 'Hillary Clinton, who tells dreadful lies,' Washington Post, accessed Jan. 28, 2021 washingtonpost.com/opinions/hillary-clinton-who-tells-dreadful-lies/2016/09/19

[21] Cleveland, Margot, December 2019, 'IG Report Shows Comey Lied To Congress About FBI Investigation Of Trump Campaign,' The Federalist, accessed Jan. 28, 2021 thefederalist.com/2019/12/10/ig-report-shows-comey-lied-to-congress-about-fbi-investigation-of-trump-campaign

[22] von Spakovsky, Hans, April 2018, 'Andrew McCabe Lied. So Will the FBI Apply the Same Rules Against Him That It Applies to All of Us?,' Heritage Foundation, accessed Jan. 28, 2021 heritage.org/crime-and-justice/commentary/andrew-mccabe-lied-so-will-the-fbi-apply-the-same-rules-against-him-it

[23] Editorial Staff, May 2020, 'Disinformation from Schiff, media damaged America,' Boston Herald, accessed Jan. 28, 2021 bostonherald.com/2020/05/17/disinformation-from-schiff-media-damaged-america

[24] Gregory, Paul Roderick, January 2017, 'The Trump Dossier Is Fake -- And Here Are the Reasons Why,' Forbes, accessed Jan. 28, 2021 forbes.com/sites/paulroderickgregory/2017/01/13/the-trump-dossier-is-false-news-and-heres-why

[25] Soave, Robbie, November 2018, 'False Rape Allegations Against Brett Kavanaugh Prove That Due Process Matters,' Reason, accessed Jan. 28, 2021 reason.com/2018/11/05/brett-kavanaugh-due-process-false-rape

[26] Gowdy Kayla, January 2020, 'Kayla Gowdy: Dems' 10 biggest lies in Trump's Senate impeachment trial,' Fox News, accessed Jan. 28, 2021 foxnews.com/opinion/dems-10-biggest-lies-in-trumps-senate-impeachment-trialkayla-gowdy

Chapter 2: Alternative Universe

[1] Serling, Rod, 1960, 'Opening Monologue: The Twilight Zone, season 2,' notable-quotes.com/s/serling_rod.html

[2] Kim, Seung Min, etal., January 2021, 'House Democrats plan to focus impeachment trial on how rioters reacted to Trump's remarks.' Washington Post, accessed Jan. 25, 2021 washingtonpost.com/politics/senate-trump-impeachment/2021/01/25/e747ec76-5f26-11eb-9061-07abcc1f9229_story.html

[3] Trump, Donald J., January 2021, 'Save America Rally Speech,' Rev.com, accessed Jan. 25, 2021 rev.com/blog/transcripts/donald-trump-speech-save-america-rally-transcript-january-6

[4] NBC staff, January 2021, 'Highlights and analysis: Trump commits to 'orderly transition' after mob storms Capitol,' accessed Jan. 26, 2021 nbcnews.com/politics/congress/live-blog/electoral-college-certification-updates

[5] Ruiz, Michael, January 2021, 'BLM activist inside Capitol claims he was 'documenting' riots, once said 'burn it all down,' Fox News, accessed Jan. 26, 2021 foxnews.com/politics/anti-trump-activist-entered-capitol-Wednesday

[6] Agedeppa, Minnie, January 2021, 'Antifa Infiltrated Trump Supporters In Capitol, Evidence Reveals', Christianity Daily, accessed Jan. 26, 2021 christianitydaily.com/articles/10454/20210108/antifa-infiltrated-trump-supporters-in-capitol-tons-of-evidence-reveal.htm

[7] Laila, Cristina, January 2021, 'BREAKING REPORT: Former FBI Agent on the Ground at US Capitol Says at Least One Bus Load of Antifa Thugs Infiltrated Trump Demonstration', Gateway Pundit, accessed Jan 26, 2021 thegatewaypundit.com/2021/01/breaking-report-former-fbi-agent-ground-us-capitol-says-least-one-bus-load-antifa-thugs-infiltrated-trump-demonstration

[8] Ibid 6

[9] Ibid, Preface, reference 7

[10] Myers, Meghann and Altman, Howard, January 2021, 'This is why the National Guard didn't respond to the attack on the Capitol,' Military Times, accessed Jan. 26, 2021 militarytimes.com/news/your-military/2021/01/07/this-is-why-the-national-guard-didnt-respond-to-the-attack-on-the-capitol

[11] Hart, Robert, January 2021, 'Figures Show Stark Difference Between Arrests at D.C. Black Lives Matter Protest and Arrests At Capitol Hill,' Forbes, accessed Jan. 26, 2021 forbes.com/sites/roberthart/2021/01/07/figures-show-stark-difference-between-arrests-at-dc-black-lives-matter-protest-and-arrests-at-capitol-hill/?sh=7688e5775706

[12] Ibid

[13] Ibid

[14] Gearty, Robert, June 2020, 'Deadly unrest: Here are the people who have died amid George Floyd protests across US,' Fox News, accessed Jan. 26, 2021 foxnews.com/us/deadly-unrest-people-have-died-amid-george-floyd-protests-across-us

[15] Moran, Sean, January 2021, 'GOP Stands with Rand Paul Against Donald Trump Impeachment Trial,' Breitbart News, accessed Jan. 26, 2021 breitbart.com/politics/2021/01/26/gop-stands-with-rand-paul-against-donald-trump-impeachment-trial

[16] Ibid

[17] Villarreal, Daniel, January 2021, 'Senator Patrick Leahy Hospitalized Hours After Being Sworn In to Preside Over Impeachment', Newsweek, accessed Jan. 26, 2021 newsweek.com/senator-patrick-leahy-hospitalized-hours-after-being-sworn-preside-over-impeachment-1564697

[18] Zurcher, Anthony, February 2020, 'Democrats 2020: What their key issues are,' BBC, accessed Feb. 9, 2021 bbc.com/news/world-us-canada-46954566

[19] Reklaitis, Victor and Schroeder, Robert, January 2021, 'All of President Biden's key executive orders - in one chart,' MarketWatch, accessed Jan. 28, 2021 marketwatch.com/story/all-of-president-bidens-key-executive-orders-in-one-chart-2021-01-21

[20] Gstalter, Morgan, January 2021, 'Schedule of Biden-Harris Inauguration Day: Timeline of events and how to watch,' The Hill, accessed Jan. 28, 2021

thehill.com/homenews/administration/534962-schedule-of-biden-harris-inauguration-day-timelines-of-events-and-how

[21] Video, January 2021, 'President Joe Biden signs his first executive orders,' YouTube, accessed Jan. 28, 2021 youtube.com/watch?v=NTus5FevWhM

[22] 2021 Joe Biden Executive Orders, Federal Register, accessed Jan. 30, 2021 federalregister.gov/presidential-documents/executive-orders/joe-biden/2021

[23] E.O. 13991, January 2021, 'Protecting the Federal Workforce and Requiring Mask-Wearing,' Federal Register, accessed Jan. 30, 2021 federalregister.gov/documents/2021/01/25/2021-01766/protecting-the-federal-workforce-and-requiring-mask-wearing

[24] LaPook, Jon and Fauci, Anthony, March 8, 2021 'Dr. Anthony Fauci talks with Dr Jon LaPook about Covid-19', 60 Minutes YouTube, accessed Jan. 30, 2021 youtube.com/watch?v=PRa6t_e7dgI

[25] Sharma, Suresh K, etal., July 2020, 'Efficacy of cloth face mask in prevention of novel coronavirus infection transmission: A systematic review and meta-analysis,' Journal of Education Health & Promotion, accessed Jan. 30, 2021 ncbi.nlm.nih.gov/pmc/articles/PMC7497125/

[26] Daoud, A. K., et al. (2021) The Potential for Cloth Masks to Protect Health Care Clinicians From SARS-CoV-2: A Rapid Review. Annals of Family Medicine. doi.org/10.1370/afm.2640.

[27] Rozmajzl, Anthony, December 2020, 'There's Still No Evidence that Either Lockdowns or Masks Are "Game Changers", Mises Wire, accessed Jan. 30, 2021 mises.org/wire/theres-still-no-evidence-either-lockdowns-or-masks-are-game-changers

[28] E.O. 13985, Advancing Racial Equity and Support for Underserved Communities Through the Federal Government,' Federal Register, accessed Jan. 30, 2021 federalregister.gov/documents/2021/01/25/2021-01753/advancing-racial-equity-and-support-for-underserved-communities-through-the-federal-government

[29] Weaver, Matthew, October 2010, 'Angela Merkel: German multiculturalism has 'utterly failed'', The Guardian, accessed Jan. 31, 2021 theguardian.com/world/2010/oct/17/angela-merkel-german-multiculturalism-failed

[30] Bloemraad, Irene and Wright, Matthew, 2014 '"Utter Failure" or Unity out of Diversity? Debating and Evaluating Policies of Multiculturalism,'

International Migration Review, accessed Jan. 31, 2021 sociology.berkeley.edu/sites/default/files/faculty/bloemraad/Bloemraad_Wright_Debating_Multiculturalism_2014.pdf

[31] 'Race and ethnicity in the NBA,' Wikipedia, accessed Jan. 31, 2021 en.wikipedia.org/wiki/Race_and_ethnicity_in_the_NBA/

[32] 'Paris Climate Agreement,' Whitehouse, accessed Jan. 31, 2021 whitehouse.gov/briefing-room/statements-releases/2021/01/20/paris-climate-agreement/

[33] PARIS AGREEMENT, 2015, United Nations, accessed Jan.31, 2021 unfccc.int/sites/default/files/english_paris_agreement.pdf

[34] The Paris Agreement, United Nations, accessed Feb.1, 2021 unfccc.int/process-and-meetings/the-paris-agreement/the-paris-agreement

[35] Ibid

[36] Milman, Oliver, June 2018, 'Ex-Nasa scientist: 30 years on, world is failing 'miserably' to address climate change ,' The Guardian, accessed Feb. 1, 2021 theguardian.com/environment/2018/jun/19/james-hansen-nasa-scientist-climate-change-warning

[37] Spencer, Roy, January 2021, 'Biden to End Fossil Fuel Subsidies: Like the Paris Agreement, it Will Make No Difference,' DrRoySpencer.com, accessed Feb. 1, 2021 drroyspencer.com/2021/01/biden-to-end-fossil-fuel-subsidies-like-the-paris-agreement-it-will-make-no-difference/

[38] Spencer, Roy, 'About Roy Spencer,' Dr.RoySpencer.com, accessed Feb. 1, 2021, drroyspencer.com/about/

[39] Peek, Liz, June 2018, 'China's rising emissions prove Trump right on Paris Agreement,' The Hill, accessed Feb. 1, 2021 thehill.com/opinion/energy-environment/390741-chinas-rising-emissions-prove-trump-right-on-paris-agreement

[40] Ge, Mingpin and Fredriech, Johannes, February 2020, '4 Charts Explain Greenhouse Gas Emissions by Countries and Sectors,' World Resource Institute, accessed Feb. 1, 2021 wri.org/blog/2020/02/greenhouse-gas-emissions-by-country-sector

[41] IEA, January 2021, 'CO_2 Emissions from Fuel Combustion 2020: Highlights,' International Energy Agency, accessed Feb. 1, 2021 webstore.iea.org/co2-emissions-from-fuel-combustion-2020-highlights

[42] Staff, June 2017, 'Reality Check: What do countries spend on climate fund?' BBC, accessed Feb. 1, 2021 bbc.com/news/world-us-canada

[43] Ibid

[44] MacKinnon, Douglas, January 2020, 'Obama should apologize for shameful cash payment to Iran,' The Hill, accessed Feb. 1, 2021 thehill.com/opinion/white-house/477666-obama-should-apologize-for-shameful-cash-payment-to-iran

[45] Goldfarb, Jeffrey and O'Keefe, Ed, June 2014, 'Obama defends decision to trade 5 Guantanamo detainees for Bergdahl,' Washington Post, accessed Feb. 1, 2021 washingtonpost.com/world/national-security/obama-defends-decision-to-trade-5-guantanamo-detainees-for-bergdahl/

[46] Maloney, Suzanne, September 2015, 'Major beneficiaries of the Iran deal: The IRGC and Hezbollah,' Brookings Institute, accessed Feb. 1, 2021 brookings.edu/testimonies/major-beneficiaries-of-the-iran-deal-the-irgc-and-hezbollah/

[47] Ibid Reference 32

[48] Zycher, Benjamin, November 2020, 'The perversities of Biden rejoining the Paris Climate Agreement,' American Enterprise Institute, accessed Feb.1, 2021 aei.org/articles/the-perversities-of-biden-rejoining-the-paris-climate-agreement/

[49] Rapoza, Kenneth, January 2021, 'Climate Czar Kerry Wants Ex-Keystone Workers to Make Solar Panels. That Will Require Importing Less China Solar Panels.,' Forbes, accessed Feb. 1, 2021 forbes.com/sites/kenrapoza/2021/01/31/climate-czar-kerry-wants-ex-oil-workers-to-make-solar-panels-that-will-require-importing-less-china-solar-panels/

[50] Rott, Nathan, January 2021, 'Biden Hits 'Pause' On Oil And Gas Leasing On Public Lands And Waters,' NPR, accessed Feb. 1, 2021 npr.org/sections/president-biden-takes-office/2021/01/27/960941799/biden-to-pause-oil-and-gas-leasing-on-public-lands-and-waters

[51] Ibid Reference 47

[52] Loris, Nicholas, November 2019, 'Staying in Paris Agreement Would Have Cost Families $20K,' Heritage Foundation, accessed Feb. 1, 2021 heritage.org/environment/commentary/staying-paris-agreement-would-have-cost-families-20k

[53] Executive Order 13988, January 2021, 'Preventing and Combating Discrimination on the Basis of Gender Identity or Sexual Orientation,' Federal Register, accessed Feb. 1, 2021 federalregister.gov/documents/2021/01/25/2021-01761/preventing-and-combating-discrimination-on-the-basis-of-gender-identity-or-sexual-orientation

[54] Executive Order 13, January 2021, 'Protecting Public Health and the Environment and Restoring Science to Tackle the Climate Crisis,' Federal Register, accessed Feb. 1, 2021 federalregister.gov/documents/2021/01/25/2021-01765/protecting-public-health-and-the-environment-and-restoring-science-to-tackle-the-climate-crisis

[55] Executive Order 13993, January 2021, 'Revision of Civil Immigration Enforcement Policies and Priorities' Federal Register, accessed Feb.1, 2021 federalregister.gov/documents/2021/01/25/2021-01768/revision-of-civil-immigration-enforcement-policies-and-priorities

[56] Executive Order 13768, January 2017, 'Enhancing Public Safety in the Interior of the United States' Federal Register, accessed Feb. 1, 2021 federalregister.gov/documents/2017/01/30/2017-02102/enhancing-public-safety-in-the-interior-of-the-united-states

[57] Executive Order 13957, October 2020, 'Creating Schedule F in the Excepted Service', Federal Register, accessed Feb 2, 2021 federalregister.gov/documents/2020/10/26/2020-23780/creating-schedule-f-in-the-excepted-service

[58] List of executive actions by Joe Biden', Wikipedia, accessed Feb. 2, 2921 en.wikipedia.org/wiki/List_of_executive_actions_by_Joe_Biden

Chapter 3: Trust Me!

[1] Buckley Jr., William S., Quote re: preferring Boston people to Harvard faculty, brainyquote.com/lists/authors/top-10-william-f-buckley-jr-quotes

[2] Walsh, Susan, January 2021, 'Swearing-in Photo', Vox, accessed Feb. 2, 2021 vox.com/22240601/joe-biden-president-inauguration-day-in-photos

[3] Samenow, Jason, January 2021, 'President Biden sees windiest inauguration since Reagan in 1985', Washington Post, accessed Feb. 2, 2021 washingtonpost.com/weather/2021/01/19/inauguration-weather-forecast-dc/

[4]   Sestito, Maria, January 2021, 'Rep. Raul Ruiz tests positive for COVID-19 ahead of Biden inauguration,' Desert Sun, accessed Feb. 2, 2021 desertsun.com/story/news/2021/01/19/rep-raul-ruiz-tests-positive-covid-19-ahead-biden-inauguration/4221019001/

[5]   Poniewozik, James, January 2021, 'The Inauguration Kept Crowds Out and Tried to Bring America In', NY Times, accessed Feb. 2, 2021 nytimes.com/2021/01/20/arts/television/inauguration-crowd.html

[6]   Cunningham, Paige Winfield, April 2021, 'The Health 202: Sunlight does kill the coronavirus. But not in the way Trump suggested.' Washington Post, accessed Feb. 1, 2021 washingtonpost.com/news/powerpost/paloma/the-health-202/2020/04/27/the-health-202-sunlight-does-kill-the-coronavirus-but-not-in-the-way-trump-suggested/

[7]   Hall, Colby, April 2020, 'Leaked Government Report Shows Sunlight Destroys Coronavirus,' BestLife, accessed Feb. 1, 2021 bestlifeonline.com/new-government-report-shows-sunlight-destroys-coronavirus/

[8]   Does sunlight kill the coronavirus? NACEM, accessed Feb. 2, 2021 nationalacademies.org/based-on-science/covid-sunscreen

[9]   Lytle, David C. and Sagripanti, Jose-Luis, November 2005, 'Predicted Inactivation of Viruses of Relevance to Biodefense by Solar Radiation, Journal of Virology, accessed Feb. 2, 2021 ncbi.nlm.nih.gov/pmc/articles/PMC1280232/

[10]   Sharma, Suresh K., etal., July 2020, 'Efficacy of cloth face mask in prevention of novel coronavirus infection transmission: A systematic review and meta-analysis,' Journal of Education and Health Promotion, accessed Feb. 2, 2021 ncbi.nlm.nih.gov/pmc/articles/PMC7497125/

[11]   Wamsley, Laurel, January 2021, 'What We Know So Far: A Timeline Of Security Response At The Capitol On Jan. 6,' NPR, accessed Feb. 4, 2021 npr.org/2021/01/15/956842958/what-we-know-so-far-a-timeline-of-security-at-the-capitol-on-january-6

[12]   Zantow, Emily, January 2021, 'D.C. National Guard to be deployed during pro-Trump rallies', Washington Times, accessed Feb. 2, 2021 washingtontimes.com/news/2021/jan/4/dc-national-guard-be-deployed-during-pro-trump-ral/

[13]   Ibid 11

[14] Davidson, Jordan, January 2021, 'DC Mayor Told Federal Law Enforcement to Stand Down Day Before Violent US Capitol Riot', The Federalist, accessed Jan. 9, 2021 thefederalist.com/2021/01/06/dc-mayor-told-federal-law-enforcement-to-stand-down-day-before-violent-us-capitol-riot/

[15] Ibid

[16] Ibid

[17] Barr, Luke, January 2021, 'Law enforcement braces for protests as Trump supporters gather in capital', ABC News, accessed Jan. 9, 2021 abcnews.go.com/Politics/law-enforcement-braces-protests-trump-supporters-gather-capital/story?id=75057898

[18] Tur, Katy, January 2021, FBI releases new images of D.C. pipe bomb suspect', MSNBC, accessed Feb. 2, 2021 msnbc.com/katy-tur/watch/fbi-releases-new-images-of-d-c-pipe-bomb-suspect-100241989785

[19] Tan, Shelly, etal., January 2021, 'How one of America's ugliest days unraveled inside and outside the Capitol,' Washington Post, accessed Feb. 3, 2021 washingtonpost.com/nation/interactive/2021/capitol-insurrection-visual-timeline/

[20] Ibid 11

[21] Svab, Peter, January 2021, 'Timeline of Events in DC on Jan. 6,' Epoch Times, accessed Feb. 3, 2021 theepochtimes.com/what-happened-in-dc-on-jan-6-2_3648252.html

[22] Ibid Reference 7, Preface

[23] Gerstein, Josh, January 2021, 'Liberal Utah activist charged with joining Capitol riot', Politico, accessed Feb. 3, 2021 politico.com/news/2021/01/14/liberal-activist-charged-capitol-riot-459553

[24] 'DC Cops Wave Group of Trump Supporters Through Barricade,' Daily Mail, accessed Feb. 3, 2021 dailymail.co.uk/video/news/video-2328024/Video-DC-cops-wave-group-Trump-supporters-Capitol-barricade.html

[25] Gerstein, Julie, January 2021, 'Officers calmly posed for selfies and appeared to open gates for protesters during the madness of the Capitol building insurrection', Business Insider, accessed Feb. 3, 2021 businessinsider.com/capitol-building-officers-posed-for-selfies-helped-protesters-2021-1

[26] Longo, Adam and Boykin, Nick, January 2021, 'Were police complicit in the Capitol riots? Videos show selfies and nonchalant enforcement, but also forceful breach,' WUSA, accessed Feb. 3, 2021 wusa9.com/article/news/local/dc/us-capitol-police-complicit-in-dc-riots-worries-us-congressman/

[27] Robertson, Katie and Hsu, Tiffany, January 2021, '11 Journalists on Covering the Capitol Siege: 'This Could Get Ugly', NY Times, accessed Feb. 3, 2021 nytimes.com/2021/01/09/business/media/journalists-capitol-mob.html

[28] Ibid

[29] Ibid

[30] Ibid

[31] Stocking, Bronson, January 2021, 'Video Shows Trump Supporters Attempting to Stop People from Breaking into the Capitol,' TownHall, accessed Feb. 4, 2021 townhall.com/tipsheet/bronsonstocking/2021/01/07/video-shows-trump-supporters-attempting-to-stop-people-from-breaking-into-the-capitol-n2582785

[32] Ngo, Andy, January 2021, Tweet about Antifa-BLM protests,' Twitter, accessed Feb. 4, 2021 twitter.com/MrAndyNgo/

[33] Baldor, Lolita, March 2021 'More than 1,000 Guard troops now leaving DC; others stay on', AP News, accessed March 31, 2021 apnews.com/article/lloyd-austin-4655374a07a498ff2ac0902de479ac79

Chapter 4: The Urge to Splurge

[1] Editorial Board, January 2021, 'Ease Up on the Executive Actions, Joe,' NY Times, accessed Feb. 5, 2021 nytimes.com/2021/01/27/opinion/biden-executive-orders.html

[2] Still, Ashlyn and Blanco, Adrian, February 2021, 'A visual breakdown of Biden's barrage of executive actions in his first weeks,' Washington Post, accessed Feb. 5, 2021 washingtonpost.com/politics/interactive/2021/biden-executive-orders-breakdown/

[3] Ibid

[4] Ibid

[5] Blankley, Bethany, August 2019, 'Report: Illegal immigration costs taxpayers $116 billion annually; Californians, Texans, Floridians pay the most', The Center Square, accessed Feb. 5, 2021 thecentersquare.com/national/report-illegal-immigration-costs-taxpayers-116-billion-annually-californians-texans-floridians-pay-the-most/

[6] Beitsch, Rebecca, February 2021, 'Supreme Court cancels border wall, asylum policy hearings after Biden shifts,' The Hill, accessed Feb. 5, 2021 thehill.com/policy/national-security/537131-supreme-court-cancels-hearings-on-border-wall-asylum-policy-after

[7] Eustachewich, Lia, February 2021, 'Biden reinstates 'catch and release' policy at the southern border,' The New York Post, accessed Feb. 5, 2021 nypost.com/2021/02/05/biden-reinstates-catch-and-release-policy-at-southern-border/

[8] Elizalde, Elizabeth, February 2021, 'President Biden will raise cap on refugee admissions to 125,000.' The New York Post, accessed Feb. 5, 2021

[9] Tankersley, Jim, etal., February 2021, 'House gives final approval to budget plan including Biden's $1.9 trillion stimulus, fast tracking the process.' New York Times, accessed Feb. 5, 2021 nytimes.com/live/2021/02/05/us/joe-biden-trump-impeachment

[10] Monthly unemployment rate in the United States from December 2019 to December 2020, Statista, accessed Feb. 5, 2021 statista.com/statistics/273909/seasonally-adjusted-monthly-unemployment-rate-in-the-us/

[11] State unemployment rate in the U.S. as of December 2020,' Statista, accessed Feb. 7, 2021 statista.com/statistics/200017/state-unemployment-rate-in-the-us/

[12] Leatherby, Lauren and Harris, Rich, November 2020, 'States That Imposed Few Restrictions Now Have the Worst Outbreaks,' New York Times, accessed Feb. 7, 2021 nytimes.com/interactive/2020/11/18/us/covid-state-restrictions.html

[13] Ibid

[14] Mandavilli, Apoorva, August 2020, 'Your Coronavirus Test Is Positive. Maybe It Shouldn't Be', New York Times, accessed Feb. 7, 2021 nytimes.com/2020/08/29/health/coronavirus-testing.html

[15] Staff, February 2021, 'See Coronavirus Restrictions and Mask Mandates for All 50 States', New York Times, accessed Feb. 7, 2021 nytimes.com/interactive/2020/us/states-reopen-map-coronavirus.html

[16] Sharma, Suresh K., etal., July 2020, 'Efficacy of cloth face mask in prevention of novel coronavirus infection transmission: A systematic review and meta-analysis', Journal of Education and Health Promotion, accessed Feb. 7, 2021 ncbi.nlm.nih.gov/pmc/articles/PMC7497125/

[17] Ibid

[18] Brosseau, Lisa M. and Sietsema, Margaret, April/July 2020, 'COMMENTARY: Masks-for-all for COVID-19 not based on sound data', CIDRAP, accessed Feb. 7, 2021 cidrap.umn.edu/news-perspective/2020/04/commentary-masks-all-covid-19-not-based-sound-data

[19] Ibid

[20] Ibid

[21] Ibid

[22] Ibid

[23] Ibid

[24] Ibid

[25] Ibid

[26] Cuffari, Benedette, 2020 'The Size of SARS-CoV-2 Compared to Other Things', Medical & Life Science News, accessed Feb. 7, 2021 news-medical.net/health/The-Size-of-SARS-CoV-2-Compared-to-Other-Things.aspx

[27] Giles, Christopher, January 2021, 'Trump's wall: How much has been built during his term?, BBC, accessed Feb. 8, 2021 bbc.com/news/world-us-canada-46748492

[28] History of Legal and Illegal Immigration to the United States, Britannica, accessed Feb. 12, 2021 immigration.procon.org/historical-timeline/#2000-present

[29] Personal Responsibility and Work Opportunity Act, Wikipedia, accessed Feb. 12, 2021 en.wikipedia.org/wiki/Personal_Responsibility_and_Work_Opportunity_Act

[30] Ibid 28

[31] Ibid 28

[32] 1996 United States presidential election, Wikipedia, accessed Feb. 12, 2021 en.wikipedia.org/wiki/1996_United_States_presidential_election

[33] Ibid 28

[34] Legal Immigration Family Equity Act, Wikipedia, accessed Feb. 12, 2021 en.wikipedia.org/wiki/Legal_Immigration_Family_Equity_Act

[35] Ibid 27

[36] FACT SHEET: DHS AGREEMENTS WITH GUATEMALA, HONDURAS, AND EL SALVADOR, Dept. Homeland Security, accessed Feb. 9, 2021 dhs.gov/sites/default/files/publications/19_1028_opa_factsheet-northern-central-america-agreements_v2.pdf

[37] Pavlich, Katie, February 2021, 'Biden Guts Policies That Cut Down on Asylum Fraud', TownHall, accessed Feb. 9, 2021 townhall.com/tipsheet/katiepavlich/2021/02/08/biden-guts-policies-to-cut-down-on-asylum-fraud-n2584379

[38] Gonzalez, Daniel, Sep/Dec 2019, 'The 2019 migrant surge is unlike any we've seen before. This is why,' USA Today, accessed Feb. 9, 2021 usatoday.com/in-depth/news/nation/2019/09/23/immigration-issues-migrants-mexico-central-america-caravans-smuggling/2026215001/

[39] Ibid

[40] Ibid

[41] Ibid

[42] Sussis, Matthew, February 2019, 'The History of the Flores Settlement,' Center for Immigration Studies, accessed Feb. 9, 2021 cis.org/Report/History-Flores-Settlement

[43] Case Number: CV 85-4544-RJK(pf), January 1997, 'Jenny Lisette Flores vs Janet Reno, Attorney General of the United States', U.S. Court, Central District California, accessed Feb. 9, 2021 aclu.org/sites/default/files/assets/flores_settlement_final_plus_extension_of_settlement011797.pdf

[44] Ibid 34

[45] Ibid 34

[46] Ibid 34

[47] Ibid 34

[48] Carter, Sara, February 2021, 'Sara Carter: Biden's immigration policy - this is how you embolden human traffickers, drug cartels,' Fox News, accessed Feb. 9, 2021 foxnews.com/opinion/biden-immigration-policy-human-traffickers-drug-cartels-sara-carter

[49] Head, Tim, May 2019, 'Children being bought and sold for sex are the hidden victims of the border crisis', Fox News, accessed Feb. 17, 2021 foxnews.com/opinion/tim-head-border-crisis-children-bought-sold-sex-victims

[50] AP Staff, February 2012, 'Sex-change treatment for kids on the rise', CBS News, accessed Feb. 17, 2021 cbsnews.com/news/sex-change-treatment-for-kids-on-the-rise/

[51] ED Trust, July 2020, 'Parents Overwhelmingly Concerned Their Children Are Falling Behind During School Closures', The Education Trust, accessed Feb. 17, 2021 edtrust.org/parents-overwhelmingly-concerned-their-children-are-falling-behind-during-school-closures/

[52] Waitt, Tammy, January 2019, 'DHS Implements New Migrant Protection Protocols at Southern Border,' American Security Today, accessed Feb. 13, 2021 americansecuritytoday.com/dhs-implements-new-migrant-protection-protocols-at-southern-border-learn-more-multi-video/

[53] Ibid

[54] Ibid

[55] DHS Statement on the Suspension of New Enrollments in the Migrant Protection Protocols Program Dept. Homeland Security, accessed Feb. 15, 2021 dhs.gov/news/2021/01/20/dhs-statement-suspension-new-enrollments-migrant-protection-protocols-program

[56] Morin, Rebecca and Carranza, Rafael, February 2021, 'Biden administration to allow in around 25,000 asylum seekers now waiting in Mexico, USA Today, accessed Feb. 15, 2021 usatoday.com/story/news/politics/2021/02/12/immigration-us-allow-25-000-asylum-seekers-waiting-mexico/6729762002/

[57] Kingsville, TX Unemployment Rate, YCharts, accessed Feb. 15, 2021 ycharts.com/indicators/kingsville_tx_unemployment_rate

[58] FACT SHEET: President Biden Outlines Steps to Reform Our Immigration System by Keeping Families Together, Addressing the Root Causes of Irregular Migration, and Streamlining the Legal Immigration System, White house, accessed Feb. 15, 2021 whitehouse.gov/briefing-room/statements-releases/2021/02/02/fact-sheet-president-biden-outlines-steps-to-reform-our-immigration-system-by-keeping-families-together-addressing-the-root-causes-of-irregular-migration-and-streamlining-the-legal-immigration-syst/

[59] DREAM Act, Wikipedia, accessed Feb. 15, 2021 en.wikipedia.org/wiki/DREAM_Act/

[60] Ibid

[61] Krogstad, Jens Manuel, June 2017, 'Americans broadly support legal status for immigrants brought to the U.S. illegally as children,' Pew Research, accessed Feb. 15, 2021 pewresearch.org/fact-tank/2020/06/17/americans-broadly-support-legal-status-for-immigrants-brought-to-the-u-s-illegally-as-children/

[62] Approximate Active DACA Recipients, September 2017, daca_population_data.pdf, accessed Feb. 15, 2021 uscis.gov/sites/default/files/document/data/daca_population_data.pdf

[63] Approximate Active DACA Recipients, March 2020, daca_population_data.pdf, accessed Feb. 15, 2021 uscis.gov/sites/default/files/document/data/Approximate%20Active%20DACA%20Receipts%20-%20March%2031%2C%202020.pdf

[64] Sessions, Jeff, September 2017, 'Full text: Jeff Sessions on Trump ending DACA program,' Politico, accessed Feb. 15, 2021 politico.com/story/2017/09/05/trump-ending-daca-dreamers-program-sessions-transcript-242326

[65] Lopez, Gustavo and Krogstad, Jens Manuel, September 2017, 'Key facts about unauthorized immigrants enrolled in DACA,' Pew Research, accessed Feb. 15, 2021 pewresearch.org/fact-tank/2017/09/25/key-facts-about-unauthorized-immigrants-enrolled-in-daca/

[66] Deferred Action for Parents of U.S. Citizens and Lawful Permanent Residents (DAPA), Ballotopedia, accessed Feb. 15, 2021

[67] Passel, Jeffrey S. and Cohn, D'vera, June 2019, 'Children of unauthorized immigrants represent rising share of K-12 students', Pew Research, accessed

Feb. 15, 2021 pewresearch.org/fact-tank/2016/11/17/children-of-unauthorized-immigrants-represent-rising-share-of-k-12-students/

[68] Passel, Jeffrey S., et.al., November 2018, 'Number of U.S.-born babies with unauthorized immigrant parents has fallen since 2007', Pew Research, accessed Feb. 15, 2021 pewresearch.org/fact-tank/2018/11/01/the-number-of-u-s-born-babies-with-unauthorized-immigrant-parents-has-fallen-since-2007/

[69] NILC Staff, June 2020, 'Supreme Court Overturns Trump Administration's Termination of DACA', National Immigration Law Center, accessed Feb. 15, 2021 nilc.org/issues/daca/alert-supreme-court-overturns-trump-administrations-termination-of-daca/

[70] Novak, Jake, January 2018, 'Democrats would be crazy to reject Trump's DACA deal', CNBC, accessed Feb. 15, 2021 cnbc.com/2018/01/26/trump-daca-deal-is-a-dream-come-true-for-democrats-commentary.html

[71] Conklin, Audrey, March 2021, 'Migrants wear Biden T-shirts at US-Mexico border, demand clearer policies,' Fox News, accessed March 3, 2021 foxnews.com/world/migrants-biden-shirts-us-mexico-border

[72] Norman, Greg, Jenkins, Griff, March 2021, '108 illegal immigrants released by Border Patrol in Texas test positive for coronavirus, officials say,' Fox News, accessed March 3, 2021. foxnews.com/us/108-migrants-released-border-patrol-texas-positive-coronavirus

[73] Donald Trump's immigration executive order issued January 27, 2017,' Ballotpedia, accessed Feb. 16, 2021 ballotpedia.org/Donald_Trump%27s_immigration_executive_order_issued_January_27,_2017

[74] Blaine, Kyle and Horowitz, Julia, January 2017, 'How the Trump administration chose the 7 countries in the immigration executive order', CNN, accessed Feb. 16, 2021 cnn.com/2017/01/29/politics/how-the-trump-administration-chose-the-7-countries/index.html

[75] FAIR Staff, May 2019, 'The Current State of the Border Fence', Federation for American Immigration Reform, accessed Feb. 16, 2021 fairus.org/sites/default/files/2019-05/Factsheet-The-Current-State-of-the-Border-Fence_1.pdf

[76] DHS Staff, October 2020, 'The Border Wall System is Deployed, Effective, and Disrupting Criminals and Smugglers, Dept. Homeland Security, accessed Feb. 16, 2021 dhs.gov/news/2020/10/29/border-wall-system-deployed-effective-and-disrupting-criminals-and-smugglers

[77] Sands, Geneva and Alvarez, Priscilla, December 2020, 'Biden's desire to stop the border wall could be costly and arduous,' CNN, accessed Feb. 16, 2021 cnn.com/2020/12/05/politics/biden-border-wall/index.html

[78] Ibid

[79] Ibid 70

[80] Katkov, Mark, January 2021, 'Army Secretary Says A 'Non-Scalable' 7-Foot Fence Is Going Up Around U.S. Capitol', NPR, accessed Feb. 21, 2021 npr.org/sections/insurrection-at-the-capitol/2021/01/07/954469642/army-sec-says-a-temporary-fence-is-going-up-around-u-s-capitol

[81] Ibid78

[82] Belmonte, Adriana, January 2021, 'President Trump's wildly expensive border wall policy will leave a lasting legacy,' Yahoo News, accessed Feb. 16, 2021 yahoo.com/lifestyle/president-trumps-border-wall-legacy-225413771.html

[83] DW Staff, January 2021, 'Central American migrants gather for new push towards US', DW News, accessed Feb. 17, 2021 17, 2021 dw.com/en/central-american-migrants-gather-for-new-push-towards-us/av-56254971

Chapter 5: Kumbaya

[1] Biden, Joe, January 2021, 'Inaugural Address by President Joseph R. Biden, Jr.,' Whitehouse, accessed Feb. 21, 2021 whitehouse.gov/briefing-room/speeches-remarks/2021/01/20/inaugural-address-by-president-joseph-r-biden-jr/

[2] Edmondson, Katie, February 2021, 'House Passes Sweeping Gay and Transgender Equality Legislation,' NY Times, accessed Feb. 26, 2021 nytimes.com/2021/02/25/us/politics/house-equality-act-gay-rights.html

[3] Liptak, Adam, June 2020, 'Civil Rights Law Protects Gay and Transgender Workers, Supreme Court Rules,' NY Times, accessed Feb. 26, 2021 nytimes.com/2020/06/15/us/gay-transgender-workers-supreme-court.html

[4] LGBT demographics of the United States, Wikipedia, accessed Feb. 27, 2021 en.wikipedia.org/wiki/LGBT_demographics_of_the_United_States

[5] Siegel, Rachel, February 2021, 'What's in the House's $1.9 trillion coronavirus plan,' Washington Post, accessed Feb. 26, 2021 washingtonpost.com/us-policy/2021/02/26/american-rescue-plan-house-coronavirus-stimulus/

[6] White House, January 2021, 'President Biden Announces American Rescue Plan,' White House, accessed Feb. 27, 2021 whitehouse.gov/briefing-room/legislation/2021/01/20/president-biden-announces-american-rescue-plan/

[7] Federal government responses to the coronavirus (COVID-19) pandemic, 2020-2021,' Ballotpedia, accessed Feb. 27, 2021 ballotpedia.org/Federal_government_responses_to_the_coronavirus_(COVID-19)_pandemic,_2020-2021

[8] Casella, Megan, February 2021, 'The GOP's anti-stimulus rallying cry: What happened to the unspent $1 trillion?' Politico, accessed Feb. 27, 2021 politico.com/news/2021/02/27/gop-coronavirus-stimulus-471815

[9] THE EMPLOYMENT SITUATION - JANUARY 2021 'Bureau of Labor Statistics, accessed Feb. 27, 2021 bls.gov/news.release/pdf/empsit.pdf

[10] McCarthy, Kevin, February 2021, 'The Pelosi Payoff', Twitter, accessed Feb. 27, 2021 twitter.com/GOPLeader/status/

[11] Siegel, Rachel, February 2021, 'What's in the House's $1.9 trillion coronavirus plan,' Washington Post, accessed Feb 28, 2021 washingtonpost.com/us-policy/2021/02/26/american-rescue-plan-house-coronavirus-stimulus/

[12] Drew, Jeff, February 2021, 'House passes $1.9 trillion stimulus bill with a variety of small business relief,' J. of Accountancy, accessed March 3, 2021 journalofaccountancy.com/news/2021/feb/house-passes-stimulus-bill-small-business-relief.html

[13] Cerra, Tom, February 2021, 'Letter to the editor: Too much pork in American Rescue Plan,' Trib Live, accessed March 4, 2021 triblive.com/opinion/letter-to-the-editor-too-much-pork-in-american-rescue-plan/

[14] Psaki, Jen, March 2021, 'Press Briefing by Press Secretary Jen Psaki, March 5, 2021', Whitehouse, accessed March 26, 2021 whitehouse.gov/briefing-room/press-briefings/2021/03/05/press-briefing-by-press-secretary-jen-psaki-march-5-2021/

[15] Sullivan, Dan, March 2021, 'SULLIVAN ANNOUNCES OPPOSITION TO DEMOCRATS COVID "RELIEF" PACKAGE', accessed March 26, 2021 sullivan.senate.gov/newsroom/press-releases/sullivan-announces-opposition-to-democrats-covid-relief-package

[16] Sarbanes, John P., February 2021, 'H.R.1 - For the People Act of 2021', Congress.gov, accessed Feb. 27, 2021 congress.gov/bill/117th-congress/house-bill/1/text

[17] Johnston, Roy, January 2021, '34 Days & Holding: America in the Balance', Amazon.com

Chapter 6: Nothing Like a Good Purge

[1] The Night of the Long Knives, The History Place, accessed Feb. 6, 2021 historyplace.com/worldwar2/triumph/tr-roehm.htm

[2] Eisenhower, Dwight D., May 1954, 'Address at the Columbia University National Bicentennial Dinner, New York City,' The American Presidency Project, accessed Feb. 7, 2021 presidency.ucsb.edu/documents/address-the-columbia-university-national-bicentennial-dinner-new-york-city

[3] Editorial Board, January 2021, 'Opinion: Biden's bold immigration plan would really put America first,' Washington Post, accessed Feb. 11, 2021 washingtonpost.com/opinions/bidens-bold-immigration-plan-would-really-put-america-first/2021/01/21/4efa3f42-5a98-11eb-a976-bad6431e03e2_story.html

[4] Semple, Kirk, January 2021, 'Biden's Promise of Immigration Reform Raises Hopes in Latin America,' New York Times, accessed Feb. 11, 2021 nytimes.com/2021/01/28/world/americas/biden-immigration-reform.html

[5] Entous, Adam, et.al, October 2017, 'Clinton campaign, DNC paid for research that led to Russia dossier,' Washington Post, accessed Feb. 17, 2021 washingtonpost.com/world/national-security/clinton-campaign-dnc-paid-for-research-that-led-to-russia-dossier/2017/10/24/

[6] Solomon, John, October 2018, 'FBI on Russia allegations before surveillance warrant,' The Hill, accessed Feb. 17, 2021 thehill.com/hilltv/rising/409817-russia-collusion-bombshell-dnc-lawyers-met-with-fbi-on-dossier-before

[7] McArdle, Mairead, October 2020, 'DNI Releases CIA Documents on Clinton's 'Plan' to Tie Trump Campaign to Russia,' Yahoo News, accessed Feb. 17, 2020 sports.yahoo.com/dni-releases-cia-documents-hillary-204337457.html

[8] Nelson, Steven, September 2020, 'CIA told Obama of claim Hillary Clinton conjured Trump-Russia scandal: spy chief,' New York Post, accessed Feb.

17, 2020 nypost.com/2020/09/29/cia-told-obama-of-claim-clinton-conjured-trump-russia-scandal-spy-chief/

[9] Jennings, Scott, April 2019, 'Mueller's report looks bad for Obama,' CNN, accessed Feb. 11, 2021 cnn.com/2019/04/19/opinions/mueller-report-obama-jennings/index.html

[10] Finding Lois Lerner in contempt of Congress, Wikipedia, accessed Feb. 11, 2021 en.wikipedia.org/wiki/Finding_Lois_Lerner_in_contempt_of_Congress

[11] Overby, Peter, October 2019, 'IRS Apologizes For Aggressive Scrutiny Of Conservative Groups,' NPR, accessed Feb. 11, 2021

[12] Ibid Preface 7

[13] Zinn, Howard, 1980, 'A People's History of the United States,' Wikipedia, accessed March 1, 2021 en.wikipedia.org/wiki/A_People%27s_History_of_the_United_States

[14] Howard Zinn,' Wikipedia, accessed March 1, 2021, en.wikipedia.org/wiki/Howard_Zinn

[15] Ibid

[16] Billy O'Reilly, Wikipedia, accessed March 1, 2021 en.wikipedia.org/wiki/Bill_O%27Reilly_(political_commentator)

[17] Steel, Emily and Schmidt, Michael S., October 2017, 'Bill O'Reilly Settled New Harassment Claim, Then Fox Renewed His Contract,' New York Times, accessed March 2, 2021 nytimes.com/2017/10/21/business/media/bill-oreilly-sexual-harassment.html

[18] AP Writers, February 2021, "Lou Dobbs Tonight" has been canceled after a decade,' CBS News, accessed March 2, 2021 cbsnews.com/news/lou-dobbs-tonight-canceled-after-a-decade/

[19] Krishnan, Nihal, February 2021, 'House Democrats push TV carriers to stop hosting Fox, OAN, and Newsmax, citing 'misinformation', Washington Examiner, accessed March 2, 2021 washingtonexaminer.com/news/house-democrats-push-tv-carriers-to-stop-hosting-fox-oan-and-newsmax-citing-misinformation

[20] Palpini, Kristin, March 2021, 'Sale Of 6 Dr. Suess Books - Including 'Mulberry Street' - To End Due To Racist Drawings,' Daily Voice, accessed March 3, 2021

dailyvoice.com/massachusetts/worcester/lifestyle/sale-of-6-dr-suess-books-including-mulberry-street-to-end-due-to-racist-drawings/804249/

[21] Phillips, Morgan, October 2020, 'Merriam-Webster changes its definition of 'sexual preference' as Barrett gets called out for using term', Fox News, accessed March 17, 2021 foxnews.com/politics/merriam-webster-changed-definition-sexual-preference-barrett-hearing

[22] Banned & Challenged Books, American Library Association office for Intellectual Freedom, accessed March 3, 2021 ala.org/advocacy/bbooks/frequentlychallengedbooks/top10

[23] Ibid

[24] Trammel, Matt, February 2021, 'Cancel Culture Steals Mr. Potato Head's Manhood', San Angelo Live, accessed March 13, 2021 sanangelolive.com/news/business/2021-02-25/cancel-culture-steals-mr-potato-heads-manhood

[25] Hains, Rebecca, August 2015, 'Target will stop labeling toys for boys or for girls. Good.' Washington Post, accessed March 13, 2021 washingtonpost.com/posteverything/wp/2015/08/13/target-will-stop-selling-toys-for-boys-or-for-girls-good/

[26] Olson, Henry, May 2019, 'Opinion: California wants to teach kindergartners about gender identity. Seriously.' Washington Post, accessed March 13, 2021 washingtonpost.com/opinions/2019/05/13/california-wants-teach-kindergartners-about-gender-identity-seriously/

[27] Patches, Matt, January 2021, 'Disney Plus quietly pulls Peter Pan, Dumbo from Kids profiles over racist stereotypes', Polygon, accessed March 26, 2021 polygon.com/disney-plus/2021/1/27/22252244/disney-plus-removes-peter-pan-dumbo-racist-stereotypes-kids-profiles

[28] Shilling, Rose, October 2020, Here's a recap of companies addressing race on food packaging', Food Engineering Magazine, accessed March 26, 2021 foodengineeringmag.com/articles/99152-heres-a-recap-of-companies-addressing-race-on-food-packaging

[29] Johnson, Kevin, August 2019, 'The final bill for former special counsel Robert Mueller's Russia inquiry: $31. 7 million', USA Today, accessed March 17, 2021 usatoday.com/story/news/politics/2019/08/02/final-price-robert-mueller-investigation-trump-russia-31-7-million/1904722001/

[30] Barton, Tom, November 2020, 'Miller-Meeks' lead shrinks to 6 votes over Hart after full recount in Iowa 2nd District race', Gazette, accessed March 31,

2021 thegazette.com/subject/news/government/rita-hart-mariannette-miller-meeks-recount-senate-20201128

[31] Kainz, Howard, February 2015, 'Firing Professor McAdams: When a Catholic university collides with political correctness,' James G. Martin Center, accessed March 1, 2021 jamesgmartin.center/2015/02/firing-professor-mcadams-when-a-catholic-university-collides-with-political-correctness/

[32] Licea, Melkorka, October 2016, 'Professor who tweeted against PC culture is out at NYU, New York Post, accessed March 1, 2021 nypost.com/2016/10/30/nyu-professor-who-opposed-pc-culture-gets-booted-from-classroom/

[33] Soave, Robby, April 2017, 'PC Hysteria Claims Another Professor, Daily Beast, accessed March 1, 2021 thedailybeast.com/pc-hysteria-claims-another-professor

[34] Flaherty, Colleen, June 2017, 'Old Criticisms, New Threats, Inside Higher Ed, accessed March 18, 2021 insidehighered.com/news/2017/06/26/professors-are-often-political-lightning-rods-now-are-facing-new-threats-over-their

[35] Bret Weinstein, Wikipedia, accessed March 18, 2021 en.wikipedia.org/wiki/Bret_Weinstein

[36] Clark, Chrissy, July 2020, 'Michigan School Fires Popular Teacher for Saying 'Trump Is Our President', Washington Free Beacon, accessed March 18, 2021, freebeacon.com/campus/mi-school-fires-popular-teacher-for-saying-trump-is-our-president/

[37] Prominent Scientist Fired by Gore Says Warming Alarm 'Mistaken'', U.S. Senate Cmte Environment & Public Works, accessed April 10, 2021 epw.senate.gov/public/index.cfm/press-releases-all?ID=5ef55aa3-802a-23ad-4ce4-89c4f49995d2

[38] Haapala, Kenneth, U.S. Government Funding of Climate Change', Capital Research Center, accessed April 10, 2021 climatedollars.org/full-study/us-govt-funding-of-climate-change/

[39] Cost, Ben, March 2021, 'Disney+ prevents kids from watching 'racist' classics including 'Dumbo',' New York Post, accessed March 18, 2021 nypost.com/2021/03/09/disney-forbids-kids-from-watching-racist-classics/

Chapter 7: Don't Mess with Mother Nature

[1] Lewis, C.S, 1943, 'The Abolition of Man',

[2] Ball, Jeffrey, February 2021, 'The Texas Blackout Is the Story of a Disaster Foretold, Texas Monthly, accessed Feb. 21, 2021 texasmonthly.com/politics/texas-blackout-preventable/

[3] Krishnamoorti, Ramann and Hirs, Ed, January 2020, 'Texas Power Generation: Did Coal Get Blown Away By Wind?', Forbes, accessed Feb. 21, 2021 forbes.com/sites/uhenergy/2020/01/13/texas-power-generation--did-coal-get-blown-away-by-wind/?sh=105fbbda2899

[4] Ibid

[5] Ibid

[6] Ibid

[7] Ibid

[8] Ibid

[9] Ibid

[10] Ibid 2

[11] Ibid 2

[12] Ibid 2

[13] Ibid 2

Chapter 8: Halftime Update

[1] Justice, Tristan, March 2021, 'Joe Biden Can't Remember Who His Secretary of Defense Is,' The Federalist, accessed March 9, 2021 thefederalist.com/2021/03/09/joe-biden-cant-remember-who-his-secretary-of-defense-is/

[2] Ibid

[3] Philips, Morgan, March 2021, 'VP Kamala Harris takes another solo call with a world leader,' Fox News, accessed March 9, 2021 foxnews.com/politics/harris-call-norway-prime-minister

[4] Madhani, Aamer, March 2021, 'Biden visits businesses to highlight changes to loan program,' WJHL, accessed March 9, 2021 wjhl.com/news/politics/biden-visits-businesses-to-highlight-changes-to-loan-program/wjhl.com/news/politics/biden-visits-businesses-to-highlight-changes-to-loan-program/

[5] Ibid 3

[6] Darnell, Tim, March 2021, 'Biden under increasing media spotlight for lack of news conferences,' Atlanta Journal-Constitution, accessed March 9, 2021 ajc.com/news/nation-world/biden-under-increasing-media-spotlight-for-lack-of-news-conferences/

[7] Ibid

[8] Van Brugen, Isabel, March 2021, DHS Seeks Volunteers to Assist With 'Overwhelming' Surge at Southern Border, Epoch Times, accessed March 9, 2021 theepochtimes.com/dhs-pleads-for-volunteers-to-assist-with-overwhelming-surge-at-southern-border_3726039.html

[9] Ibid

[10] Ibid

[11] Ibid

[12] DeBonis, Mike, March 2021, 'House Democrats pass sweeping elections bill as GOP legislatures push to restrict voting,' Washington Post, accessed March 10, 2021 washingtonpost.com/politics/house-elections-voting-pelosi-/2021/03/03/e434df58-7c22-11eb-a976-c028a4215c78_story.html

[13] Smith, Allan, March 2021, 'Let the people vote': Biden signs executive order to expand voting access,' NBC News, accessed March 10, 2021 nbcnews.com/politics/joe-biden/biden-signs-executive-action-ordering-agencies-expand-voting-access-n1259906

[14] Phillips, Jack, March 2021, 'House Approves Measures to Expand Firearm Background Checks,' Epoch Times, accessed March 11, 2021 theepochtimes.com/house-passes-gun-control-bill-expanding-background-checks-on-firearm-sales_3729592.html?utm_source=news&utm_medium=email&utm_campaign=breaking-2021-03-11-1

[15] Cronk, Terri Moon, March 2021, 'Austin Outlines His Top Three Priorities on Defense, People, Teamwork,' Dept of Defense Website, accessed March 11, 2021 defense.gov/Explore/News/Article/Article/2526532/austin-outlines-his-top-three-priorities-on-defense-people-teamwork/

[16] Brook, Tom Vanden, February 2019, 'Exclusive: Pentagon spent nearly $8 million to treat 1,500 transgender troops since 2016,' USA Today, accessed March 11, 2021 usatoday.com/story/news/politics/2019/02/27/exclusive-report-shows-8-million-spent-more-than-1-500-transgender-troops-pentagon-dysphoria/2991706002/

[17] DOD Dictionary of Military and Associated Terms, accessed March 12, 2021 jcs.mil/Portals/36/Documents/Doctrine/pubs/dictionary.pdf

[18] December 2018, 'Department of Defense Board on Diversity and Inclusion Report', accessed March 12, 2021 media.defense.gov/2020/Dec/18/2002554852/-1/-1/0/DOD-DIVERSITY-AND-INCLUSION-FINAL-BOARD-REPORT.PDF

[19] 2021 Joe Biden Executive Orders,' Federal Register, accessed March 12, 2021 federalregister.gov/presidential-documents/executive-orders/joe-biden/2021

[20] Evans, Zachary, March 2021, 'Rioters Set Fire to Federal Courthouse in Portland One Day after Fencing Removed', National Review, accessed March 12, 2021 nationalreview.com/news/rioters-set-fire-to-federal-courthouse-in-portland-one-day-after-fencing-removed/

[21] Mullen, David, March 2021, 'Boulder police make first arrest in connection to party turned riot last weekend,' Denver Gazette, accessed March 12, 2021 denvergazette.com/news/courts/boulder-police-make-first-arrest-in-connection-to-party-turned-riot-last-weekend/article_f20c2afe-8204-11eb-84ec-d3ddfe64e34c.html

[22] Uniform Crime Report Data, docs.google.com/spreadsheets/d/1Z9b5mIwztAwmEHJW7Q5DHMjS14-Rs7XIXOt33AI_rDw/edit#gid=1757262194

[23] Levin, Sam, August 2020, 'The movement to defund police has won historic victories across the US. What's next? The Guardian, accessed March 16, 2021 theguardian.com/us-news/2020/aug/15/defund-police-movement-us-victories-what-next

[24] Giordano, Jerry, August 2020, 'New Evidence that Fentanyl Overdose Killed George Floyd,' Ricochet, accessed March 16, 2021

[25] Ibid

[26] Martin, Roland, June 2021, 'Class Is In Session: Sen. Kamala Harris Schools The View's Meghan McCain On 'Defund The Police', RolandMartinShow, accessed March 26, 2020 youtube.com/watch?v=ZXuYThqR7pE

[27] Killing of George Floyd, Wikipedia, accessed March 16, 2021 en.wikipedia.org/wiki/Killing_of_George_Floyd

[28] ICE's Mission, Accessed March 13, 2021 ice.gov/mission

[29] Godfrey, Elaine, July 2018, 'What 'Abolish ICE' Actually Means, The Atlantic, accessed March 13, 2021 theatlantic.com/politics/archive/2018/07/what-abolish-ice-actually-means/564752/

[30] Homan, Tom, October 2020, 'Only the misinformed want to abolish ICE,' The Hill, accessed March 13, 2021 thehill.com/opinion/immigration/519423-only-the-misinformed-want-to-abolish-ice

[31] Editorial Staff, December 2020, 'ICE in Dems' crosshairs as Biden heads to WH', Boston Herald, accessed March 13, 2021 bostonherald.com/2020/12/31/ice-in-dems-crosshairs-as-biden-heads-to-wh/

[32] Ibid

[33] Bergquist, Ella, December 2019, 'Consequences of Crossing Illegally Into Canada,' VisaPlace, accessed March 13, 2021 visaplace.com/blog-immigration-law/consequences-crossing-illegally-canada/

[34] Kaste, Martin, December 2016, 'Police And Illegal Immigration: What Our Neighbors Do,' NPR, accessed March 13, 2021 npr.org/2016/12/21/505538964/police-and-illegal-immigration-what-our-neighbors-do

[35] Change In Instructional Status, Return to Learning, accessed April 7, 2021 returntolearntracker.net/

[36] COVID Webinar Series (TRANSCRIPT): Robert Redfield, MD', Buck Institute, accessed April 7, 2021 buckinstitute.org/covid-webinar-series-transcript-robert-redfield-md/

[37] Ibid

Chapter 9: The Canine Idiom

[1]　Jansen, Bart, March 2021, 'March 4 put Capitol on alert: Nancy Pelosi calls out QAnon conspiracy 'silliness', USA Today, accessed March 4, 2021 usatoday.com/story/news/politics/elections/2021/03/04/u-s-capitol-braces-march-4-security-threat-echoing-jan-6-riot/6918126002/

[2]　Ibid

[3]　Tomlinson, Lucas M. et.al., March 2021, 'Capitol riot task force led by Lt. Gen. Russel Honore recommending 24/7 'quick reaction force', Fox News, accessed March 4, 2021 foxnews.com/politics/capitol-riot-task-force-lt-gen-honore

[4]　Ibid

Chapter 10: Circus Time

[1]　Johnston, Roy, 2021, '34 Days & Holding: America in the Balance', Amazon.com

[2]　Ibid

[3]　Ibid

[4]　Higgins, Tucker, January 2021, 'Supreme Court refuses quick action on last-ditch Trump election lawsuits', Reuters, accessed March 19, 2021 cnbc.com/2021/01/11/supreme-court-refuses-quick-action-on-trump-election-lawsuits.html

[5]　Durkee, Alison, March 2021, 'Supreme Court Kills Last Trump Election Lawsuit,' Forbes, accessed March 19, 2021 forbes.com/sites/alisondurkee/2021/03/08/supreme-court-kills-last-trump-election-lawsuit/?sh=3be61a987637

[6]　Ibid

[7]　Ibid 1

[8]　Nelson, Steven, March 2021, 'Biden calls Kamala 'President Harris' during speech,' NY Post, accessed March 19. 2021 nypost.com/2021/03/18/biden-calls-kamala-president-harris-during-speech/

[9]　Ibid

[10] Staff writer, March 2021, '#PresidentHarris trends after VP commits fat faux-pas at Joe Biden's first press conference,' Arab News, accessed March 19, 2021 arabnews.com/node/1828141/offbeat

[11] Laila, Kristina, January 2021, ''Kiss My Ear' - Joe Biden Jumbles Words During Covid Presser, Calls Out Lawmaker For Refusing to Wear a Face Mask (VIDEO),' Gateway Pundit, accessed March 19, 2021 thegatewaypundit.com/2021/01/kiss-ear-joe-biden-jumbles-words-covid-presser-calls-lawmaker-refusing-wear-face-mask-video/

[12] Madhani, Aamer, and Long, Colleen, March 2021, 'Biden is on his heels amid a migrant surge at Mexico border', AP News, accessed March 20, 2021 apnews.com/article/mexico-immigration-united-states-1efbf1f357a5210d2433b48820b9aa54

[13] Ibid

[14] Ibid

[15] Gortler, David, March 2021, 'Dr. David Gortler: FDA problems under Biden - here's how drug safety, public health issues being compromised', Fox News, accessed March 20, 2021 foxnews.com/opinion/fda-problems-biden-drug-public-health-compromised-dr-david-gortler

[16] Ibid

[17] Ibid

[18] Ibid

[19] Kalter, Lindsay, March 2021, 'Biden: U.S. May Celebrate COVID 'Independence' by July 4', WebMD, accessed March 20, 2021 webmd.com/lung/news/20210311/biden-us-may-celebrate-covid-independence-day-by-july-4

[20] Kaplan, Fred, March 2021, 'A Cold Welcome in Alaska', Slate, accessed March 20, 2021 slate.com/news-and-politics/2021/03/biden-blinken-china-yang-alaska.html

[21] Palmer, Ewan, March 2021, 'Vladimir Putin's Challenge to Joe Biden Has People Questioning Who Would Win Debate', Newsweek, accessed March 20, 2021. newsweek.com/joe-biden-debate-vladimir-putin-killer-1577292

[22] Ibid

[23] Inskeep, Steve, December 2020, 'Biden's Incoming Press Secretary: Briefings Won't Be A Platform for Right-Wing Spin', NPR, accessed March 20, 2021 npr.org/sections/biden-transition-updates/2020/12/31/951452717/bidens-incoming-press-secretary-briefings-wont-be-a-platform-for-right-wing-spin

[24] Richardson, Reed, January 2021, 'Jen Psaki Spins Biden's '1 Million Shots Per Day' Pledge as 'Bold Goal' Even After Reporter Notes U.S. Already Hitting That Mark', Mediaite, accessed March 20, 2021 mediaite.com/news/jen-psaki-spins-bidens-1-million-shots-per-day-pledge-as-bold-goal-even-after-reporter-notes-u-s-already-hitting-that-mark/

[25] Quintanilla, Milton, January 2021, 'Press Secretary Jen Psaki Dodges Abortion Policy Question by Citing President Biden's Catholic Faith', Christian Headlines, accessed March 20, 2021 christianheadlines.com/contributors/milton-quintanilla/press-secretary-jen-psaki-dodges-abortion-policy-question-by-citing-president-bidens-catholic-faith.html

[26] Jones, Tom, February 2021, 'An unnamed White House correspondent says the press secretary is probing reporters' questions in advance', Poynter.org, accessed March 20, 2021 poynter.org/newsletters/2021/is-there-already-an-issue-between-the-white-house-and-the-media/

[27] Baumann, Beth, February 2021, 'WATCH: Jen Psaki's Terrible Spin on the Pork-filled American Rescue Plan', Townhall Video, accessed March 20, 2021 townhall.com/tipsheet/bethbaumann/2021/02/28/watch-jen-psakis-terrible-spin-on-emergency-covid-relief-that-will-be-spent-over-the-next-decade-

[28] Seder, Sam, March 2021, 'Jen Psaki Tries To Figure Out How To Spin Migrant Children Issue', Majority Report Video, accessed March 20, 2021 youtube.com/watch?v=TMWCMhSmxlY

[29] Slager, Brian, March 2021, 'White House Press Behave Like Neutered Hamsters in Letting Jen Psaki Spin the Border Crisis', Townhall, accessed March 20, 2021 townhall.com/columnists/bradslager/2021/03/11/white-house-press-behave-like-neutered-hamsters-in-letting-jen-psaki-spin-the-border-crisis-

[30] Woodward, Alex, January 2021, 'Biden's White House press secretary Jen Psaki commits to transparency in first briefing', The Independent, accessed March 20, 2021 independent.co.uk/news/world/americas/us-politics/jen-psaki-press-conference-today-bide-b1790419.html

[31]   Mastrangelo, Dominick, January 2021, 'Cleaver concludes congressional prayer with 'amen and awoman'', The Hill, accessed March 21, 2021 thehill.com/homenews/532547-cleaver-concludes-congressional-prayer-amen-and-awoman?rl=1

[32]   Dorman, Sam, January 2021, 'Pelosi uses slew of gendered terms despite introducing resolution opposing them', Fox News, accessed March 21, 2021 foxnews.com/politics/pelosi-gendered-terms-rules

[33]   Brufke, Juliegrace and Marcosh, Cristina, January 2021, 'House approves rules package for new Congress', The Hill, accessed March 21, 2021 thehill.com/homenews/house/532548-house-adopts-rules-package-for-new-congress

[34]   Ibid

[35]   Ibid

[36]   Slaughter, Louis M., Rules Chairwoman, 'The Motion to Recommit,' accessed March 21, 2021 archives-democrats-rules.house.gov/archives/recommit_mot

[37]   Richardson, Valerie, February 2021, 'John Kerry flew on private jet to accept climate award: 'Only choice for somebody like me'', Washington Times, accessed March 21, 2021 washingtontimes.com/news/2021/feb/3/john-kerry-flew-private-jet-accept-climate-award

[38]   Lynch, Sarah N. and Chiacu, Doina, February 2021, 'Key quotes from U.S. attorney general nominee Garland on criminal justice policies', Reuters, accessed March 21, 2021 reuters.com/article/us-usa-senate-garland-hearing-quotes/key-quotes-from-u-s-attorney-general-nominee-garland-on-criminal-justice-policies-id

[39]   Joe Biden - "What am I doing here?", YouTube, accessed March 21, 2021 youtube.com/watch?v=VA-2xpqrBwg

[40]   Sondheim, Steven, 1973, 'Send in the Clowns', accessed March 21, 2021, en.wikipedia.org/wiki/Send_In_the_Clowns

[41]   Detrow, Scott, December 2019, 'Kamala Harris Drops Out Of Presidential Race', NPR, accessed March 21, 2021 npr.org/2019/12/03/784443227/kamala-harris-drops-out-of-presidential-race

[42]   Barbaro, Michael with Shane Goldmacher, March 2021, 'The Ruthless Rise and Lonely Decline of Andrew Cuomo', New York Times - The Daily

Podcast, accessed March 21, 2021 nytimes.com/2021/03/19/podcasts/the-daily/andrew-cuomo-sexual-harassement-nursing-homes

[43] Tedisco, James, February 2021, 'Tedisco & Jordan: "Cuomo Lied and New Yorkers Paid and Died"', New York State Senate, accessed March 21, 2021 nysenate.gov/newsroom/press-releases/james-tedisco/tedisco-jordan-cuomo-lied-and-new-yorkers-paid-and-died

[44] Eyewitness News, March 2021, 'Current aide latest woman to allege sexual harassment from Cuomo, NY Times reports', ABC7NY, accessed March 21, 2021 abc7ny.com/andrew-cuomo-sexual-harassment-ronan-farrow-lindsey-boylan/

[45] Campanile, Carl and Golding, Bruce, February 12, 2021, 'Pol calls for Cuomo's Emmy Award to be taken back over nursing home coverup', NY Post, accessed March 22, 2021

[46] 2018 California gubernatorial election, Wikipedia, accessed March 21, 2021 en.wikipedia.org/wiki/2018_California_gubernatorial_election

[47] Conklin, Audrey, March 2021, 'Newsom recall effort organizers say they submitted 2.1 million signatures by deadline', Fox News, accessed March 21, 2021 foxnews.com/politics/newsom-recall-2-1-million-signatures

[48] Wolfsohn, Joseph, March 2021, 'Gavin Newsom recall developments ignored by ABC, get just 24 seconds from NBC', Fox News, accessed March 22, 2021 foxnews.com/media/abc-nbc-cbs-gavin-newsom-recall-california

[49] Fels, Aaron, March 2021, 'VP Harris laughs when asked if she has plans to visit southern border', NY Post, accessed March 22, 2021 nypost.com/2021/03/22/harris-laughs-when-asked-if-she-has-plans-to-visit-border/

[50] Svab, Peter, March 2021, 'Children Squeezed Body-to-Body in Illegal Immigrant Facility, Leaked Images Show, Epoch Times, accessed March 22, 2021 theepochtimes.com/children-squeezed-body-to-body-in-illegal-immigrant-facility-leaked-images-show

[51] Norman, Greg and Jenkins, Griff, March 2021, '108 illegal immigrants released by Border Patrol in Texas test positive for coronavirus, officials say,' Fox News, accessed March 22, 2021 foxnews.com/us/108-migrants-released-border-patrol-texas-positive-coronavirus

[52] Staff, March 2021, 'Biden administration 'importing' coronavirus into Texas by not securing border: Gov. Abbott', Fox News, accessed March 22, 2021 foxnews.com/politics/biden-importing-coronavirus-securing-border-abbott

[53] Hanchett, Ian, March 2021, 'Dem Rep. Escobar: Abbott Saying Migrants Bringing COVID Is 'Racist' and Could Spawn Violence', Breitbart News, accessed March 22, 2021 breitbart.com/clips/2021/03/22/dem-rep-escobar-abbott-saying-migrants-bringing-covid-is-racist-and-could-spawn-violence/

[54] Video, March 2021, 'Mayorkas says there is a 'challenge,' not a crisis at Mexico border', Washington Post, accessed March 22, 2021 washingtonpost.com/video/politics/mayorkas-says-there-is-a-challenge-not-a-crisis-at-mexico-border/2021/03/01/365947b8-08b4-4226-9c7a-ed89cce0a351_video.html

[55] Kanno-Youngs, Zolan, March 2021, 'Mayorkas Says 'Undoubtedly Difficult' Border Problems Are Being Handled', New York Times, accessed March 22, 2021

[56] Braswell, Helen, February 2021, 'CDC director says 'bruises are going to take a long time to heal' at agency', Stat News, accessed March 23, 2021 statnews.com/2021/02/10/cdc-director-says-bruises-are-going-to-take-a-long-time-to-heal-at-agency/

[57] Ibid

[58] Navratil, Liz, December 2020, 'Divided Minneapolis City Council votes to cut $8 million from police budget', Star Tribune, accessed March 26, 2021 startribune.com/divided-minneapolis-council-keeps-mayor-jacob-freys-target-for-a-larger-police-force/

[59] Calicchio, Dom, Marach 2021, 'Portland mayor looks to re-fund police with $2M request as homicides spike - but council support unclear', Fox News, accessed March 26, 2021 foxnews.com/politics/portland-mayor-looks-to-re-fund-police-with-2m-request-as-homicides-spike-but-council-support-unclear

[60] De Lea, Brittany, March 2021, 'Biden regularly consults with Barack Obama on a 'range of issues', Psaki says', Fox News, accessed March 22, 2021 foxnews.com/politics/biden-white-house-communication-barack-obama

[61] Baldor, Lolita, March 2021, 'More than 1,000 Guard troops now leaving DC; others stay on', AP News, accessed March 31, 2021 apnews.com/article/lloyd-austin-4655374a07a498ff2ac0902de479ac79

Chapter 11: Nine Zeros

[1] Temple, James, February 2021, 'Bill Gates: Rich nations should shift entirely to synthetic beef,' MIT Technology, accessed Feb. 19, 2021 technology review.com/2021/02/14/1018296/bill-gates-climate-change-beef-trees-microsoft/

[2] Marie-Antoinette, Wikipedia, accessed March 4, 2021

[3] Ibid

[4] WORLD'S BILLIONAIRES LIST,' Forbes, accessed March 4, 2021 forbes.com/billionaires/

[5] U.S. and World Population Clock,' Census.gov, accessed March 6, 2021 census.gov/popclock/

[6] GDP by Country, Worldometer, accessed March 6, 2021, worldometers.info/gdp/gdp-by-country/

[7] Selected Characteristics of Households by Total Money Income in 2019, U.S. Census Bureau, accessed March 5, 2021 www2.census.gov/programs-urveys/cpss/techdocs/cpsmar20.pdf

[8] CRS, January 2021, 'The U.S. Income Distribution: Trends and Issues,' Congressional Research Service, accessed March 6, 2021 fas.org/sgp/crs/misc/R44705.pdf

[9] Saez, Emmanuel and Picketty, Thomas, 2010, 'The Worsening Distribution of Income: The Top 1% vs. the Other 99%,' AnEconomicSense, accessed March 7, 2021 aneconomicsense.org/2011/12/07/the-worsening-distribution-of-income-the-top-1-vs-the-other-99/

[10] Frenze, Christopher, April 1996, 'The Reagan Tax Cuts: Lessons for Tax Reform, Joint Economic Cmte, accessed March 24, 2021 crab.rutgers.edu/~mchugh/taxes/The%20Reagan%20Tax%20Cuts%20Lessons%20for%20Tax%20Reform.htm

[11] Prasad, Monica, February 2019, 'Actually, it was Democrats who killed the 70 percent tax,' Politico, accessed March 8, 2021 politico.com/agenda/story/2019/02/05/democrats-70-percent-tax-rate-000879/

[12] Ibid

We All Fall Down: The Dissolution of America

[13]   Kagan, Julie and Uradu, Lea D. October 2020, 'Economic Recovery Tax Act of 1981,' Investopedia, accessed, March 8, 2021 (ERTA)investopedia.com/terms/e/economic-recovery-tax-act.

[14]   Kenton, Will and Berry-Johnson, Janet, July 2020, 'Tax Equity and Fiscal Responsibility Act of 1982 (TEFRA)', Investopedia, accessed March 8, 2021 investopedia.com/terms/t/tefra.asp

[15]   Gross Domestic Product, Bureau of Economic Analysis, accessed March 8, 2021 bea.gov/

[16]   Composition of Congress, by Political Party, 1855-2017,' InfoPlease, accessed March 8, 2021 infoplease.com/us/government/legislative-branch/composition-of-congress-by-political-party-1855-2017

[17]   United States Fed Funds Rate1971-2021 Data, accessed March 22, 2021 tradingeconomics.com/united-states/interest-rate

Chapter 12: Beyond Parody

[1]   Triptych of Haywain, Hieronymous Bosch.Org, accessed March 31, 2021 hieronymus-bosch.org/Triptych-Of-Haywain-1-1500-02.html

[2]   FACT SHEET: The American Jobs Plan', Whitehouse, accessed April 1, 2021 whitehouse.gov/briefing-room/statements-releases/2021/03/31/fact-sheet-the-american-jobs-plan/

[3]   Biden, Joe, March 2021, 'Joe Biden Speech on $2 Trillion Infrastructure Plan Transcript March 31', Rev, accessed April 1, 2021 rev.com/blog/transcripts/joe-biden-speech-on-2-trillion-infrastructure-plan-transcript-march-31

[4]   Ibid 2

[5]   Ibid 2

[6]   Duncan, Ian, April 2021, 'A woman called for a highway's removal in a Black neighborhood. The White House singled it out in its infrastructure plan', Washington Post, accessed April 1, 2021 washingtonpost.com/local/trafficandcommuting/highway-removal-infrastructure/

[7]   Wong, Kristina, April 2021, 'State Department to Spend $2.5M to Create Office of Diversity, Equity, and Inclusion', Breitbart.com, accessed April 2,

2021 breitbart.com/politics/2021/03/30/state-department-to-spend-2-5m-to-create-office-of-diversity-equity-and-inclusion/

[8] Kight, Steph, March 2021, 'Scoop: ICE securing hotel rooms to hold growing number of migrant families', Axios, accessed April 2, 2021 axios.com/ice-hotel-rooms-border-migrant-families-7682092b-952c-428e-ae3b-f8b2d4072c0a.html

[9] Kaplan, Talia, March 2021, 'Formerly homeless veteran blasts Biden admin for spending money to house migrants in hotels', Fox News, accessed April 2, 2021 foxnews.com/politics/homeless-veteran-biden-illegal-immigrants-hotels

[10] Eagan, Lauren, et.al., March 2021, 'Biden tasks Harris with 'stemming the migration' on southern border', NBC News, accessed April 3, 2021 nbcnews.com/politics/white-house/biden-taps-harris-lead-coordination-efforts-southern-border-n1261952

[11] Ibid

[12] Ibid

[13] Moore, Thomas, March 2021, 'Border Patrol prevented from talking to media: report', The Hill, accessed April 3, 2021 thehill.com/homenews/media/543608-border-patrol-prevented-from-talking-to-media-report

[14] Castronuovi, Celine, April 2021, 'Number of migrants detained at southern border reaches 15-year high: reports', The Hill, accessed April 3, 2021

[15] Ozimek, Tom, March 2021, 'Chicago Suburb Approves $10 Million Reparations Program Funded by Marijuana Tax Revenue', Epoch Times, accessed April 3, 2021 theepochtimes.com/chicago-suburb-approves-10-million-reparations-program-funded-by-marijuana-tax-revenue_3745460.html

[16] Dixon, Peter, August 2020, 'U.S. cities and states are discussing reparations for Black Americans. Here's what's key,' Washington Post, accessed April 3, 2021 washingtonpost.com/politics/2020/08/24/us-cities-states-are-discussing-reparations-black-americans-heres-whats-key/

[17] Niesse, Mark, March 2021, 'Sweeping changes to Georgia elections signed into law', Atlanta Journal-Constitution, accessed April 3, 2021 ajc.com/politics/bill-changing-georgia-voting-rules-passes-state-house/EY2MATS6SRA77HTOBVEMTJLIT4

We All Fall Down: The Dissolution of America 439

[18] Schow, Ashe, August 2014, '24 things that require a photo ID', Washington Examiner, accessed April 3, 2021 washingtonexaminer.com/24-things-that-require-a-photo-id

[19] Ibid 17

[20] Dinan, Stephan, April 2021, 'EXCLUSIVE: Biden's DHS may restart border wall construction to plug 'gaps'', Washington Times, accessed April 6, 2021 washingtontimes.com/news/2021/apr/5/dhs-may-restart-border-wall-construction-plug-gaps

Chapter 13: The Biden Train Wreck – A Damage Assessment of the 1st 18 months (NEW)

[1] Miami Standard Staff, May 2022, '"Never Let a Crisis Go to Waste" – Samantha Power Celebrates Fertilizer Shortages That will Force Farmers to Transition to "Natural Solutions" (VIDEO)', The Miami Standard, accessed May 8, 2022, miamistandard.news/2022/05/01/never-let-a-crisis-go-to-waste-samantha-power-celebrates-fertilizer-shortages-that-will-force-farmers-to-transition-to-natural-solutions-video

[2] Pallaro, Bianca and Parlapiano, Alicia, May 2022, 'Visualizing the $13.6 Billion in U.S. Spending on Ukraine', The New York Times, accessed May 8, 2022, nytimes.com/interactive/2022/03/18/upshot/ukraine-aid-details.html

[3] Trevizo, Perla and Schwartz, Jeremy, October 2020, 'Records show Trump's border wall is costing taxpayers billions more than initial contracts', Texas Tribune/ProPublica, accessed May 8, 2022, texastribune.org/2020/10/27/border-wall-texas-cost-rising-trump

[4] Isacson, Adam, January 2022, 'Weekly U.S.-Mexico Border Update: December's migration data; DHS Secretary hears complaints; "Critical Incident Teams", WOLA.org, accessed May 8, 2022, wola.org/2022/01/weekly-u-s-mexico-border-update-decembers-migration-data-dhs-secretary-hears-complaints-critical-incident-teams

[5] La Jeunesse, William, February 2022, 'Nonprofits and NGOs assisting migrants who cross the border: humanitarian support or abetting a crime?', Fox News, accessed May 8, 2022, foxnews.com/us/ngos-assisting-migrants-who-cross-border-humanitarian-support-abetting-crime

[6] Ibid

[7]   Ibid

[8]   Ibid 3

[9]   Johnston, Roy, January 2021, '34 Days & Holding: America in the Balance', published by Johnstini Enterprises

[10] Ibib Chapter 4 reference 5

[11] U.S. Inflation Rate 1960-2022, MacroTrends, accessed May 9, 2022, macrotrends.net/countries/USA/united-states/inflation-rate-cpi#:~:text=U.S.%20inflation%20rate%20for%202020,a%200.31%25%20increase%20from%202017.

[12] TED: The Economics Daily, April 2022, Consumer Prices Up 8.5 percent for the year ending March 2022', U.S. Bureau of Economic Statistics, accessed May 9, 2022, bls.gov/opub/ted/2022/consumer-prices-up-8-5-percent-for-year-ended-march-2022.htm#:~:text=The%20Consumer%20Price%20Index%20increased,month%20advance%20since%20December%201981.

[13] Terryberry, Paige, January 2022, 'Government Spending Is the Cause of, Not the Antidote for Record Inflation', John Locke Foundation, accessed May 10, 2022, johnlocke.org/government-spending-is-the-cause-of-not-the-antidote-for-record-inflation

[14] CARES ACT, Wikipedia, en.wikipedia.org/wiki/CARES_Act

[15] Staff, 2022, 'Covid Money Tracker', Committee for a Responsible Federal Budget, accessed May 24, 2022, covidmoneytracker.org

[16] Brady, Kevin, January 2022, 'Letter to President Biden on Covid-19 Spending', House Ways & Means Committee, accessed May 15, 2022, gop-waysandmeans.house.gov/wp-content/uploads/2022/01/Letter-to-President-Biden-on-COVID-19-Spending-1.5.22.pdf

[17] Ibid

[18] Federal Reserve Staff Writers, October 2004, 'What is "core inflation," and why do economists use it instead of overall or general inflation to track changes in the overall price level?' Federal Reserve Bank of San Francisco, accessed May 11, 2022, frbsf.org/education/publications/doctor-econ/2004/october/core-inflation-headline

[19] AAA Staff Writer, May 2022, 'Gas Prices', accessed May 11, 2022, gasprices.aaa.com

[20] White House, March 2022, 'FACT SHEET: United States Bans Imports of Russian Oil, Liquefied Natural Gas, and Coal', White House, accessed May 11, 2022, whitehouse.gov/briefing-room/statements-releases/2022/03/08/fact-sheet-united-states-bans-imports-of-russian-oil-liquefied-natural-gas-and-coal

[21] Foreman, Dean, March 2022, 'Digging into Crude Oil, Gasoline and Natural Gas Prices 3.0', American Petroleum Institute, accessed May 11, 2022, api.org/news-policy-and-issues/blog/2022/03/10/digging-into-crude-oil-gasoline-and-natural-gas-prices-30

[22] Oner, Ceyda, 2022, 'Inflation: Prices on the Rise', International Monetary Fund, accessed May 11, 2022, imf.org/external/pubs/ft/fandd/basics/inflat.htm

[23] Statista Staff, May 2022, '12-month percentage of change in the United States' Consumer Price Index (CPI-U) in March 2022, by expenditure category', Statista, accessed May 12, 2022, statista.com/statistics/216055/annual-percentage-of-change-in-the-us-cpi-u-by-expenditure-category

[24] Meads, Tim, May 2022, 'Mitch McConnell Claims 'We All Agree The Most Important Thing Going On In The World Right Now Is The War In Ukraine', Daily Wire, accessed May 12, 2022, dailywire.com/news/mitch-mcconnell-claims-we-all-agree-the-most-important-thing-going-on-in-the-world-right-now-is-the-war-in-ukraine

[25] Quinnipiac University, March 2022, 'Inflation Tops Russia-Ukraine War As Most Urgent Issue In U.S., Quinnipiac University National Poll Finds; 52% Disapprove Of GOP Senators' Handling Of Ketanji Brown Jackson Hearings', Quinnipiac University Poll, accessed May 15, 2022, poll.qu.edu/poll-release?releaseid=3841

[26] Johnston, Roy, March 2022, 'The Cause of the War in Ukraine', Johnstini.com blog, accessed June 20, 2022, johnstini.com/blog/f/the-cause-of-the-war-in-ukraine

[27] Devore, Chuck, February 2022, 'Ukrainian President Zelenskyy Declines to Evacuate: 'I Need Ammunition, Not A Ride', Federalist, accessed May 13, 2022, thefederalist.com/2022/02/26/ukrainian-president-zelenskyy-declines-to-evacuate-i-need-ammunition-not-a-ride

[28] Snell, Kelsey, March 2022, 'Congress passes $13.6 billion in Ukraine aid along with government funding NPR, accessed May 13, 2022, npr.org/2022/03/09/1085509937/house-advances-13-6-billion-in-ukraine-aid-along-with-government-funding

[29] Khalid, Asma, January 2022, 'How Biden is trying to clean up his comments about Russia and Ukraine', NPR, accessed May 13, 2022, npr.org/2022/01/20/1074466148/biden-russia-ukraine-minor-incursion

[30] Zelensky, Volodymyr, January 2022, 'Response to Biden re: Minor Incursions', Twitter @zelenskyyus

[31] Ibid 26

[32] Schnell, Mychael and Brooks, Emily, May 2022, 'House approves $40B in aid for Ukraine; 57 Republicans vote 'no'', The Hill, accessed May 13, 2022, thehill.com/news/house/3483993-house-approves-40b-in-aid-for-ukraine-57-republicans-vote-no

[33] Carney, Jordain, May 2022, 'Rand Paul objection delays $40 billion Ukraine aid package', The Hill, accessed May 13, 2022, thehill.com/news/senate/3486654-rand-paul-objection-delays-40-billion-ukraine-aid-package

[34] von der Burchard, Hans, May 2022, 'EU to increase military support funding for Ukraine to €2 billion', Politico, accessed May 13, 2022, politico.eu/article/eu-to-increase-military-support-fund-for-ukraine-2-billion

[35] Reuters Staff, February 2021, 'Biden administration suspends Trump asylum deals with El Salvador, Guatemala, Honduras', Reuters, accessed June 20, 2022, reuters.com/article/us-usa-immigration-centralamerica/biden-administration-suspends-trump-asylum-deals-with-el-salvador-guatemala-honduras

[36] Barr, Luke, May 2021, 'More fentanyl seized by CBP so far in 2021 than in all of 2020', ABC News, accessed June 20, 2022, abcnews.go.com/Politics/fentanyl-seized-cbp-2021-2020/story

[37] Chaterjee, Shitu, May 2022, 'Overdose deaths continued to rise in 2021, reaching historic highs', NPR, accessed May 13, 2022, npr.org/sections/health-shots/2022/05/11/1098314220/overdose-deaths-continued-to-rise-in-2021-reaching-historic-highs

[38] Sheffield, March 2022, 'Carrie, Biden cuts border funding as his policies are about to overwhelm it', New York Post, accessed May 13, 2022, nypost.com/2022/03/17/biden-cuts-border-funding-as-his-policies-are-about-to-overwhelm-it

[39] Ibid

[40] Ibid 25

[41] Staff, April 2022, 'Petroleum and other Liquids', US Energy Information Administration, accessed May 16, 2022, eia.gov/dnav/pet/hist/LeafHandler.ashx?n=PET&s=MTTUPUS2&f=A

[42] Patterson, Thomas, May 2017, 'News Coverage of Donald Trump's First 100 Days', Harvard Kennedy School, accessed May 16, 2022, shorensteincenter.org/news-coverage-donald-trumps-first-100-days

[43] Abt, Thomas, et.al., January 2022, 'Violent Crime in the U.S. Is Surging. But We Know What to Do About It', Time Magazine, accessed May 16, 2022, time.com/6138650/violent-crime-us-surging-what-to-do

[44] Allen, Virginia, April 2022, 'LA Sheriff Charges That Criminals Profit by Policies of Soros-Backed District Attorney'. The Daily Signal, accessed May 17, 2022, dailysignal.com/2022/04/14/la-sheriff-charges-that-policies-of-soros-backed-district-attorney-profit-criminals

[45] Smith, Zach, February 2022, ' It's Not Just Rising Crime: Rogue Prosecutors Are a Huge Problem', Heritage Foundation, accessed May 17, 2022, heritage.org/crime-and-justice/commentary/its-not-just-rising-crime-rogue-prosecutors-are-huge-problem

[46] Women's Studies, Wikipedia, accessed May 19, 2022, en.wikipedia.org/wiki/Women%27s_studies#:~:text=The%20first%20accredited%20women's%20studies,in%201969%20at%20Cornell%20University.

[47] Ibid

[48] Bradford, Richardson, October 2016, 'Liberal professors outnumber conservatives 12 to 1: Study', Washington Times, accessed May 18, 2022, washingtontimes.com/news/2016/oct/6/liberal-professors-outnumber-conservatives-12-1

[49] Morgan, Piers, May 2022, "Womxn': Michelle Obama's 'mark of disrespect' to 'vast majority' of women', Sky News, accessed May 18, 2022, skynews.com.au/opinion/piers-morgan/womxn-michelle-obamas-mark-of-disrespect-to-vast-majority-of-women/video/5302aa67003c4cb2171850814c1dd67c

[50] Srikanth, Anagha, January 2021, 'House introduces gender-neutral language in new rules for Congress', The Hill, accessed May 18, 2022, thehill.com/changing-america/respect/diversity-inclusion/532518-house-introduces-gender-neutral-language-in-new

[51] Kennedy, Dana, May 2021, 'Disney goes woke with new anti-racist agenda for employees', New York Post, accessed May 18, 2022, nypost.com/2021/05/08/disney-goes-woke-with-new-anti-racist-agenda-for-employees

[52] Baker, Gerard, April 2022, 'Disney Decides to Go for Woke', The Wall Street Journal, accessed May 18, 2022, wsj.com/articles/disney-woke-florida-dont-say-gay-parents-students-teachers-movies-cartoons-world-lgbtqia-sogie-gender-expression-transgender-crt-critical-race-theory-11649082625

[53] Ibid

[54] Staff Report, March 2022, 'Disney no longer saying 'boys and girls' in recorded park greetings in order to promote gender inclusion', Fox News 13, accessed May 18, 2022, fox13news.com/news/disney-no-longer-saying-boys-and-girls-in-recorded-park-greetings-in-order-to-promote-gender-inclusion

[55] Lundquist-Arora, Stephanie, April 2022, 'Gender Indoctrination in Public Schools Has Gone too Far', Inside Sources, accessed May 18, 2022, insidesources.com/gender-indoctrination-in-public-schools-has-gone-too-far

[56] Carnahan, Becca, August 2021, '6 BEST PRACTICES TO CREATING INCLUSIVE AND EQUITABLE INTERVIEW PROCESSES', Harvard Business School, accessed June 20, 2022, hbs.edu/recruiting/insights-and-advice/blog/post/6-best-practices-to-creating-inclusive-and-equitable-interview-processes

[57] Carnahan, Becca and Moore, Christopher, July 2020, 'Actively Addressing Unconscious Bias in Recruiting', Harvard Business Review, accessed June 20, 2022, hbs.edu/recruiting/insights-and-advice/blog/post/actively-addressing-unconscious-bias-in-recruiting

[58] Vincent, Isabel, May 2022, 'Kiel, Wisconsin school district charges kids for using wrong pronouns', New York Post, accessed May 19, 2022, nypost.com/2022/05/14/kiel-wisconsin-school-charges-kids-for-using-wrong-pronouns

[59] Ibid

[60] Moore, Mark, May 2022, 'Republicans say FBI used anti-terror tools to target outspoken parents', New York Post, accessed May 19, 2022, nypost.com/2022/05/12/fbi-tracked-parents-opposed-to-covid-policies-republicans-say

[61] Turley, Jonathan, September 2021, 'Princeton Facing Possible Legal Action After Labeling Professor Racist for Opposing Race-Based Faculty Perks', Jonathan Turley.org, accessed May 20, 2022, jonathanturley.org/2021/09/

30/princeton-facing-possible-legal-action-after-labeling-professor-racist-for-opposing-race-based-faculty-perks

[62] Ibid

[63] Turley, Jonathan, September 2021, 'UCLA Professor Sues Over Suspension Following Controversy Over Race-Based Grading', Jonathan Turley.org, accessed May 20, 2022, jonathanturley.org/2021/09/29/ucla-professor-sues-over-suspension-following-controversy-over-race-based-grading

[64] Ibid

[65] USEIA Staff, June 2011, 'Most coal-fired electric capacity was built before 1980', U.S. Energy Information Administration, accessed May 21, 2022, eia.gov/todayinenergy/detail.php?id=1990

[66] USEIA Staff, 2022, 'What is U.S. electricity generation by energy source?', U.S. Energy Information Administration, accessed May 21, 2022, eia.gov/tools/faqs/faq.php?id=427&t=3

[67] USEIA Staff, 2022, 'Coal imports and exports', U.S. Energy Information Administration, accessed May 21, 2022, eia.gov/energyexplained/coal/imports-and-exports.php

[68] Editorial Board, March 2022, 'Biden's Fossil-Fuel Blockade', The Wall Street Journal, accessed June 20, 2022, wsj.com/articles/joe-bidens-fossil-fuel-blockade-onshore-drilling-leases-oil-gas-russia-11646409502

[69] Marcacci, Silvio, March 2022, 'So Much For Coal's Rebound - Plant Closures Come Roaring Back. It's Time To Unlock A Just Transition.', Forbes, accessed May 21, 2022, forbes.com/sites/energyinnovation/2022/03/15/so-much-for-coals-rebound-plant-closures-come-roaring-back-smart-policy-must-unlock-a-just-transition/?sh=3a78cf5274e9

[70] Ibid

[71] Ibid

[72] Sierra Club, 2022, 'Climate and Energy', Sierra Club, accessed May 28, 2022, sierraclub.org/climate-and-energy

[73] Hayes, Jason, May 2022, 'Why Electricity Blackouts are Coming to Michigan', Wall Street Journal Volume CCLXXIX No. 124

[74] Lee, Timothy, March 2021, 'Report: Tesla is secretly building a giant 100 MW battery in Texas', Ars Technica, accessed May 29, 2022, arstechnica.com/science/2021/03/report-tesla-is-secretly-building-a-giant-100-mw-battery-in-texas

[75] Clayton, Dillion, October 2021, 'Why Do Wind Turbines Stop? Reasons Explained', Energy Follower, accessed May 21, 2022, energyfollower.com/why-do-wind-turbines-stop

[76] Hennigan, W.J. and Dozier, Kimberly, August 2021, 'Joe Biden's Botched Withdrawal Plunges Afghanistan Into Chaos', Time Magazine, accessed June 20, 2022, time.com/6090523/biden-afghanistan-withdrawal-taliban

[76] Johnston, Roy, August 2021, 'While They Were Sleeping', Johnstini.com, johnstini.com/blog/f/while-they-were-sleeping

[77] Risch, James E., February 2022, 'Left Behind: A Brief Assessment of the Biden Administration's Strategic Failures during the Afghanistan Evacuation', Senate Intelligence Committee, accessed May 23, 2022, foreign.senate.gov/imo/media/doc/Risch%20Afghanistan%20Report%202022.pdf

[78] Goodwin, Michael, March 2022, 'Biden is letting Putin run the Iran nuclear talks', The New York Post, accessed May 23, 2022, nypost.com/2022/03/12/biden-is-letting-putin-run-the-iran-nuclear-talks

[79] Bunn, Daniel and Sean Bray, April 2022, 'What's in the New Global Tax Agreement?', Tax Foundation, accessed May 23, 2022, taxfoundation.org/global-tax-agreement/#:~:text=Additionally%2C%20the%20agreement%20sets%20up,turning%20the%20agreement%20into%20law

[80] Philipp, Joshua, May 2022, 'Monkeypox 'Games' Could Lay Groundwork for WHO Pandemic Response Takeover', The Epoch Times, accessed May 25, 2022, theepochtimes.com/monkeypox-games-could-lay-groundwork-for-who-pandemic-takeover_4484764.html

[81] Ibid

[82] Ibid

[83] Ibid

[84] Wettengel, Julian, March 2022, 'Germany and the EU remain heavily dependent on imported fossil fuels', Clean Energy Wire, accessed May 22,

We All Fall Down: The Dissolution of America 447

2022, cleanenergywire.org/factsheets/germanys-dependence-imported-fossil-fuels

[85] Tsolova, Tsvetelia and Koper, Anna, April 2022, 'Europe decries 'blackmail' as Russia cuts gas to Poland, Bulgaria', Reuters, accessed May 22, 2022, reuters.com/business/energy/gazprom-says-it-halts-gas-supplies-poland-bulgaria-payments-row-2022-04-27

[86] Associated Press Writers, May 2022, 'Russia has cut off its natural gas exports to Finland in a symbolic move', NPR, accessed May 22, 2022, npr.org/2022/05/21/1100547908/russia-ends-natural-gas-exports-to-finland

[87] Hausfather, Zeke, November 2015, 'Nature Not NOAA Ended the Slowdown in Temperatures', Berkley Earth, accessed May 22, 2022, berkeleyearth.org/nature-not-noaa-ended-the-slowdown-in-temperatures

[88] Ibid

[89] Electric Choice writer, '9 of the Worst Power Outages in United States History', Electric Choice, accessed May 22, 2022, electricchoice.com/blog/worst-power-outages-in-united-states-history

[90] Wikipedia writers, 'Critical Race Theory', Wikipedia, accessed May 22, 2022, en.wikipedia.org/wiki/Critical_race_theory

[91] Nevins, David L., May 2021, ''Stakeholder capitalism' is part of a sea change in boardrooms', The Fulcrum, accessed June 2, 2022, thefulcrum.us/big-picture/stakeholder-capitalism

[92] Ibid

[93] Hetzner, Christiaan, June 2022, 'I'm not woke': JPMorgan CEO and 'red-blooded capitalist' Jamie Dimon fires back at criticism of stakeholder capitalism', Fortune Magazine, accessed June 2, 2022, fortune.com/2022/06/02/jpmorgan-jaime-dimon-woke-wall-street-gop-republicans/

[94] Andrew R. Arthur, February 2022, 'Nearly 1.06 Million CBP Encounters at Southwest Border Thus Far in FY 2022', Center for Immigration Studies, accessed June 2, 2022, cis.org/Arthur/Nearly-106-Million-CBP-Encounters-Southwest-Border-Thus-Far-FY-2022

[95] IEA staff, May 2021, 'The Role of Critical Minerals in Clean Energy Transitions', International Energy Agency, accessed June 3, 2022, iea.org/reports/the-role-of-critical-minerals-in-clean-energy-transitions

[96] Ibid

Part II — Imagining the Future

Chapter 14: Re-Imagining America

[1] Temple, James, February 2021, 'Bill Gates: Rich nations should shift entirely to synthetic beef,' MIT Technology, accessed Feb. 19, 2021 technologyreview.com/2021/02/14/1018296/bill-gates-climate-change-beef-trees-microsoft/

[2] Ibid 34 Days

[3] Bezmenov, Yuri, 1985, 'KGB defector Yuri Bezmenov's warning to America', YouTube, accessed March 26, 2021 youtube.com/watch?v=bX3EZCVj2XA

[4] Ravitch, Diane, November 1985, 'DECLINE AND FALL OF TEACHING HISTORY', The New York Times Magazine, accessed March 27, 2021 nytimes.com/1985/11/17/magazine/decline-and-fall-of-teaching-history.html

[5] Labor force participation rate of women 1950 to 2015', Bureau of Labor Statistics, accessed March 27, 2021 bls.gov/spotlight/2017/women-in-the-workforce-before-during-and-after-the-great-recession/pdf/women-in-the-workforce-before-during-and-after-the-great-recession.pdf

[6] Ibid 4

[7] Ibid 2

[8] Ibid

[9] Ibid

[10] Walker, Tim, July 2020, 'NEA President: Educators Will Help Determine Our Democracy's Future', NEA, accessed March 25, 2021 nea.org/advocating-for-change/new-from-nea/nea-president-educators-will-help-determine-our-democracys

[11] Ibid

[12] Ibid 34 Days

[13] Ibid 10

[14] Ibid 10

[15] REIMAGINING OUR SOCIETY AND REWRITING THE RULES TO ENABLE OPPORTUNITY AND JUSTICE FOR ALL', AFT, accessed March 25, 2021 aft.org/resolution/reimagining-our-society-and-rewriting-rules-enable-opportunity-and-justice-all

[16] Weingarten, Randi, September 2019, 'AFT President Randi Weingarten on Formal Impeachment Inquiry', AFT, accessed March 28, 2021 aft.org/press-release/aft-president-randi-weingarten-formal-impeachment-inquiry

[17] Ibid15

[18] Ibid 15

[19] Hrabowski, Freeman, et.al., October 2020, 'Higher Education Should Lead the Efforts to Reverse Structural Racism', The Atlantic, accessed March 29, 2021 theatlantic.com/ideas/archive/2020/10/higher-education-structural-racism/616754/

[20] Hrabowski, Freeman, et.al., October, 2020, 'Higher Education Should Lead the Efforts to Reverse Structural Racism', The Atlantic, accessed March 29, 2021 theatlantic.com/ideas/archive/2020/10/higher-education-structural-racism/616754/

[21] Ibid

[22] Ibid

[23] Staff Report, 2018, 'PISA 2018 results', PISA, accessed March 29, 2021 oecd.org/pisa/publications/PISA2018_CN_USA.pdf

[24] Ibid

[25] Pew Staff, February 2019, 'After years of growth, math proficiency of U.S. students dips', Pew Research, accessed March 29, 2021 pewresearch.org/fact-tank/2017/02/15/u-s-students-internationally-math-science/ft_17-02-14_stem_mathprof-2/

[26] Duke, Selwyn, 2014, 'Danger in the Skies: Obama Dumbed-down Air-traffic Controllers With "Diversity" Rules', The New American, accessed March 29, 2021 thenewamerican.com/danger-in-the-skies-obama-dumbed-down-air-traffic-controllers-with-diversity-rules/

[27] Ganti, Akhilesh and Estevez, Eric, January 2021 'Structural Change', Investopedia, accessed April 3, 2021 investopedia.com/terms/s/structural_change

[28] Ibid

[29] Bacon, Perry, February 2021, 'Democrats Are Split Over How Much the Party And American Democracy Itself Are In Danger', fivethirtyeight.com, accessed April 3, 2021 fivethirtyeight.com/features/democrats-are-split-over-how-much-the-party-and-american-democracy-itself-are-in-danger/

[30] Ibid

[31] Joscelyn, Thomas, April 2020 'Henry Kissinger's Illusory World Order', Foundation for Defense of Democracies, accessed April 5, 2021 fdd.org/analysis/2020/04/08/henry-kissingers-illusory-world-order/

[32] Quotes About Henry Kissinger, accessed April 5, 2021 henryakissinger.com/quotes/

[33] Buchanon, Patrick, April 2020, 'Kissinger calls for a new world order', APP, accessed April 5, 2021 app.com/story/opinion/columnists/2020/04/08/henry-kissinger-calls-new-world-order/2961577001/

[34] Ibid

[35] Ibid

[36] Ibid

[37] Ibid

Chapter 15: Re-Imagining the World

[1] Kissinger, Henry, April 2020, 'The Coronavirus Pandemic Will Forever Alter the World Order', Wall Street Journal, accessed April 15, 2021 wsj.com/articles/the-coronavirus-pandemic-will-forever-alter-the-world-order-11585953005

[2] The Great Reset, WEF.com, accessed April 6, 2021 weforum.org/great-reset

[3] Bhattacharya, Jay, October 2020 A Sensible and Compassionate Anti-COVID Strategy,' Imprimis, accessed April 7, 2021 imprimis.hillsdale.edu/sensible-compassionate-anti-covid-strategy/

[4] Ibid Chapter 8, Ref 36

[5] Global Technology Governance Summit, World Economic Forum, accessed April 7, 2021 weforum.org/events/global-technology-governance-summit-2021/about,

[6] Hao, Nicole and He, Cathy, March 2021 'CCP Adviser Outlines Detailed Plan to Defeat US, Including Manipulating Elections', Epoch Times, accessed April 10, 2021 theepochtimes.com/mkt_app/xi-jinpings-adviser-outlines-plan-for-ccp-to-defeat-us-including-manipulating-elections_3748196.html

[7] Ibid

[8] Ibid

[9] WEF Announces Global Technology Governance Summit and Flagship Report,' Modern Diplomacy, accessed April 7, 2021 moderndiplomacy.eu/2020/12/05/wef-announces-global-technology-governance-summit-and-flagship-report/

[10] Global Platform in AREA 2071, Center for the Fourth Industrial Revolution, accessed April 11, 2021 c4ir.ae/

[11] Global Cities, accessed April 11, 2021 globalcities.org/vision-mission

[12] mckinsey.com/featured-insights/world-economic-forum/davos-agenda/perspectives/headlines-from-the-davos-agenda

[13] Ibid

[14] List of Wars 1945-1989, Wikipedia, accessed April 13, 2021 en.wikipedia.org/wiki/List_of_wars:_1945

[15] Ibid

[16] List of Wars 1990-2002, Wikipedia, accessed April 13, 2021 en.wikipedia.org/wiki/List_of_wars:_1990

[17] List of Wars 2003-present, Wikipedia, accessed April 13, 2021 en.wikipedia.org/wiki/List_of_wars:_2003

[18] Paul, Ron, 2007, 'American Sovereignty Restoration Act', Wikipedia, accessed April 14, 2021 en.wikipedia.org/wiki/American_Sovereignty_Restoration_Act

[19] Secretaries-General, accessed April 14, 2021 archives.un.org/content/secretaries-general

[20] Heller, Tony, Climate Scientists Rewriting the Past', Real Climate Science, accessed April 18, 2021 realclimatescience.com/climate-scientists-rewriting-the-past/

[21] United Nations, 'What We Do', accessed April 18, 2021 un.org

[22] BBC Staff, March 2021, 'Who are the Uighurs and why is China being accused of genocide?', BBC, accessed April 19, 2021 bbc.com/news/world-asia-china-22278037

[23] Yeo, Sophie, April 2020, 'How the largest environmental movement in history was born', BBC, accessed April 21, 2021 bbc.com/future/article/20200420-earth-day-2020-how-an-environmental-movement-was-born

[24] Environmental movement, Wikipedia, accessed April 21, 2021 en.wikipedia.org/wiki/Environmental_movement

[25] Another Ice Age?', Time, accessed April 21, 2021 content.time.com/time/subscriber/article/0,33009,944914,00.html

[26] El-Hai, Jack, April 2017,'In 1975, Newsweek Predicted A New Ice Age. We're Still Living with the Consequences', Longreads, accessed April 21, 2021 longreads.com/2017/04/13/in-1975-newsweek-predicted-a-new-ice-age-were-still-living-with-the-consequences/

[27] Our Common Future, Wikipedia, accessed April 21, 2021 en.wikipedia.org/wiki/Our_Common_Future

[28] Rio Declaration, United Nations , accessed April 21, 2021 un.org/en/development/desa/population/migration/generalassembly/docs/globalcompact/A_CONF.151_26_Vol.I_Declaration.pdf

[29] AGENDA 21, United Nations, accessed April 21, 2021 sustainabledevelopment.un.org/content/documents/Agenda21.pdf, 351 pages

[30] Transforming our world: the 2030 Agenda for Sustainable Development, United Nations, accessed April 21, 2021 sdgs.un.org/2030agenda

[31] Temple, James, February 2021, 'Bill Gates: Rich nations should shift entirely to synthetic beef', MIT Review, accessed May 3, 2021 technologyreview.com/2021/02/14/1018296/bill-gates-climate-change-beef-trees-microsoft

[32] Cohen, Ariel, January 2021, 'A Bill Gates Venture Aims To Spray Dust Into The Atmosphere To Block The Sun. What Could Go Wrong?', Forbes, accessed May 4, 2021 forbes.com/sites/arielcohen/2021/01/11/bill-gates-backed-climate-solution-gains-traction-but-concerns-linger/?sh=4f94b1b5793b

[33] Definition of conspire, Oxford on-line dictionary

[34] Definition of theory, Oxford on-line dictionary

Chapter 16: Antidisestablishmentarianism

[1] Marx, Karl, 1843, 'A Contribution to the Critique of Hegel's Philosophy of Right', Marxists.org, accessed April 22, 2021 marxists.org/archive/marx/works/1843/critique-hpr/intro.htm

[2] Constitution of the United States', accessed April 22, 2021 constitution.congress.gov/constitution/amendment-1/

[3] KAUFMAN v. McCAUGHTRY, FindLaw, accessed April 22, 2021 caselaw.findlaw.com/us-7th-circuit/1467028.html

[4] Slate Staff, September 1998, 'Bill Clinton and the Meaning of "Is"', Slate, accessed April 22, 2021 slate.com/news-and-politics/1998/09/bill-clinton-and-the-meaning-of-is.html

[5] Orwell, George, 1947, '1984'

[6] AP Staff, June 2020, 'Missouri woman prompts Merriam-Webster to redefine 'racism'' ABC News, accessed April 22, 2021 abcnews.go.com/Entertainment/wireStory/missouri-woman-prompts-merriam-webster-redefine-racism

[7] Definition of Religion, Merriam-Webster, accessed March 30, 2021 merriam-webster.com/dictionary/religion

[8] Definition of Theory, Merriam-Webster, accessed March 30, 2021 merriam-webster.com/dictionary/religion

[9] Masci, David, April 2017, 'Key facts about government-favored religion around the world', Pew Research, accessed April 22, 2021 pewresearch.org/fact-tank/2017/10/03/key-facts-about-government-favored-religion-around-the-world/

[10] List of religious populations, Wikipedia, accessed April 22, 2021 en.wikipedia.org/wiki/List_of_religious_populations

[11] Toro, Ross, February 2013, 'The World's Catholic Population', Live Science, accessed April 22, 2021 livescience.com/27244-the-world-s-catholic-population-infographic

[12] Declaration of Independence, National Archives, accessed April 24, 2021 archives.gov/founding-docs/declaration-transcript

[13] FACT SHEET: President Biden Sets 2030 Greenhouse Gas Pollution Reduction Target Aimed at Creating Good-Paying Union Jobs and Securing U.S. Leadership on Clean Energy Technologies', Whitehouse, accessed April 24, 2021 whitehouse.gov/briefing-room/statements-releases/2021/04/22/fact-sheet-president-biden-sets-2030-greenhouse-gas-pollution-reduction-target-aimed-at-creating-good-paying-union-jobs-and-securing-u-s-leadership-on-clean-energy-technologies/

[14] Camus, Albert, 1947, 'The Plague', published by Gallimard (French) and Hamish Hamilton 1948 (English)

[15] Bohn, Henry, 1855, A Hand-book of Proverbs

Postscript

[1] Goliath, 2016, 'It's Donald', Amazon Studios, accessed April 5, 2021 subslikescript.com/series/Goliath-4687880/season-1/episode-4-Its_Donald

[2] The Declaration of Independence, 1776, archives.gov/founding-docs/declaration-transcript

[3] Ibid

[4] Transcription of the 1789 Joint Resolution of Congress Proposing 12 Amendments to the U.S. Constitution, National Archives, accessed April 30, 2021 archives.gov/founding-docs/bill-of-rights-transcript

[5] Declaration of Independence: A Transcription', National Archives, accessed April 30, 2021 archives.gov/founding-docs/declaration-transcript

[6] Ibid

[7] Ibid

[8] Ibid

[9] Ibid

[10] Ibid

[11] Ibid

[12] What are the Scout Oath and Scout Law?,' Scouting, accessed April 30, 2021 scouting.org/about/faq/question10/

[13] Ibid 5

[14] Lincoln, Abraham, 1858, House Divided Speech, AbrahamLincoln.org, accessed April 30, 2021 abrahamlincolnonline.org/lincoln/speeches/house.htm

[15] Downey, Jr., Kevin, January 2021, 'Cop Beats Unconscious, Dying, Female Trump Supporter; Probe Deems It 'Objectively Reasonable'', PJ Media, accessed May 27, 2022, pjmedia.com/news-and-politics/kevindowneyjr/2022/02/10/cop-beats-unconscious-dying-female-trump-supporter-probe-deems-it-objectively-reasonable-n1558188

Acknowledgements

Thanks to Debby for tolerating me for the past 6½ months over which I have written *34 Days & Holding: American in the Balance* and this book. It has been a marathon.

Thanks to Elizabeth Beeton at B10 Mediaworx for invaluable assistance in formatting and layout.

Thanks to friends who have supported me.

Thanks be to God.

About the Author

The author grew up in a little town called Weslaco, 5 miles from the Rio Grande River in south Texas. Graduating from high school in 1968, the only way to avoid going to Vietnam was a college deferment from the draft. His number in the 1969 draft was 63; military service was guaranteed. With 6 credits remaining for completion of the B.S. degree, he was called up, but failed the physical exam due to a back injury and a broken ear drum. He completed a B.S. in Botany, M.S. in Plant Genetics, and a Ph.D. in Plant Science, joining the Agronomy faculty at Oklahoma State University in 1980. In 1984, he was enticed away from the Ivory Tower to work in the agribusiness and food industry. He retired after 32 years, after holding Director and Senior management positions with 4 global companies. He and his wife retired on the same day, May 31, 2016, and moved to Denver to be near grandkids.

The author is fanatical about the pursuit of truth. When it comes to politics, the first question is; "Is it good for America?" He has no political party affiliation but describes himself as an independent compassionate conservative.

www.ingramcontent.com/pod-product-compliance
Lightning Source LLC
Chambersburg PA
CBHW071226070526
44583CB00017B/2072